RETHINKING DEVELOPMENT

Kerala's Development Experience

About the Author

Professor M.A. Oommen, currently Senior Fellow, Institute of Social Sciences, New Delhi is an economist with a rich collection of professional papers and books to his credit. He has taught in the Universities of Kerala, Calicut and Botswana, besides being the Director of the Institute of Management in Government, Thiruvananthapuram.

RETHINKING DEVELOPMENT

Kerala's Development Experience

Volume 1

Editor

M. A. Oommen

INSTITUTE OF SOCIAL SCIENCES

CONCEPT PUBLISHING COMPANY

ISBN 81-7022-764-X (Vol. 1)
ISBN 81-7022-765-8 (Vol. 2)
ISBN 81-7022 766-6 (Set)

First Published 1999

Printed and Published by
Ashok Kumar Mittal
Concept Publishing Company
A/15-16, Commercial Block, Mohan Garden
New Delhi-110059 (India)

Phones: 5648039, 5649024
Fax: 091-(11)-5648053

DEDICATED TO

RASHTRAPATIJI SHRI K. R. NARAYANAN

PROUD SON OF KERALA

PREFACE

KERALA State was formed on 1 November 1956 as part of the States' Reorganisation exercise integrating Malabar from Tamil Nadu with the princely States of Cochin and Travancore. That Kerala has made significant progress in several areas of human attainments is now widely known and well documented. The United Nations and most of its affiliates—the UNESCO, UNICEF, UNDP as well as the World Bank and ILO—have acclaimed the achievements of Kerala and some even held it out as a 'model' for the less developed world to emulate. Kerala's social development was achieved through a long process of social intermediation and public action whose roots go back to pre-Independence times.

Along with high social development, Kerala is beset with several problems like a very high rate of educated unemployment, lack of excellence in education, low level of investment and productivity in productive sectors and social anomie resulting in high suicide rates and the like. Therefore, the oft- repeated questions have been: Is Kerala's development experience a sustainable one? How far is it replicable? And several others. The euphoria over the exceptionally unique achievements on the social development front was increasingly giving way to a feeling of pessimism and even cynicism over the viability of this pattern of development. Given the dismal performance by the productive sectors of the economy and the financial crisis facing the State, scholars have been deeply concerned about the sustainability of Kerala's pattern of development experience. To what extent this was replicable has been, therefore, a moot question.

The International Congress on Kerala Studies organized by the A. K. Gopalan Centre for Research and Studies, Thiruvananthapuram, on 27-29 August 1994, convened by the veteran Marxist thinker and leader E.M.S. Namboodiripad in his capacity as Director, A.K.G. Centre was a loud expression of the growing concern about the threats Kerala society faced. This Congress evoked enormous enthusiasm among scholars working on Kerala; the large number of papers presented on various facets of Kerala's development was an eye-opener. During and after the Congress it was felt that what has been happening in Kerala in the field of Human Development must reach out to a wider audience.

The following year Professor M.A. Oommen and I had the opportunity to participate in the Social Summit held in Copenhagen : both in the NGO Convention prior to the Summit and the Summit itself. In the Summit as well as in the various Prepcom meetings where we participated, the major thrust of discussion was poverty eradication and human development. Kerala's experience came up in several group meetings and presentations and some of our comparative highlights on Kerala were eagerly sought after. While in Copenhagen Professor Oommen and I decided that an International Conference on Kerala's Development Experience should be organized in New Delhi, the national capital with the widest participation possible, including countries like Costa Rica and Sri Lanka. The idea that germinated in the Social Summit 1995 became a reality in 1996 with the International Conference for four days from 8 to 11 December.

The Conference drew upon the wealth of ideas and papers presented in the 1994 Thiruvananthapuram Congress, research done at the Centre for Development Studies, Thiruvananthapuram, and by a vast number of other social science research centres, University departments as well as individual scholars all over the world.

The International Conference on Kerala's Development Experience (ICKDE for short) primarily sought to reappraise the issue of the sustainability of the Kerala Model and to draw lessons for the nation and the wider humanity enveloped by global capitalism. Specifically, the focus was on the following questions:

* What contributed to the evolution and shaping of the 'Kerala Model'?
* What are the major problems faced by the 'Kerala Model' today?
* What is the 'model' that is to be or could be sustained in a dynamic world?

* Why has Kerala, despite its high human development, failed to trigger economic growth?

* Is it correct to club Kerala along with Sri Lanka, Costa Rica and other such countries, which show low-level income and high human development index?

About 150 papers that were presented in the five Symposia and 12 Working Sessions spanning over 70 discussion hours could be considered as part of the search towards answering some of these questions and probably many more. We then thought of producing a book in two volumes on the theme of rethinking development based on Kerala's experience and lessons. The real moment of truth for the editor arose when he had to choose about thirty papers from such a wide assortment of good papers and then be loyal to the title under which they were assembled.

In designing the structure of the Conference as well as in the choice of papers for inclusion in the two volumes we proceeded on the assumption that development relates to a comprehensive social reality, and that a multi-disciplinary approach is required. We thought, even literature, art and culture are relevant to the enquiry. Through this volume we hope to initiate a series of debate as Kerala steps into the new millennium. We hope the people of Kerala and scholars all the world over will rise to the occasion and join the debate.

We received support for the International Conference from various quarters. Eminent persons from Delhi and outside gave their valuable time. Mention may be made of those who worked in the Organising Committee: Prof. K.N. Panikkar, Prof. Omcheri N. N. Pillai, Prof. T. K. Oommen, Prof. Meenakshi Gopinath, Dr. Susan Visvanathan, Mr. V.K. Madhavan Kutty, Mr. Anand, Mr. V. Abdullah, Dr. K. Satchidanandan and Mr. Raman Mahadevan. The Kerala Government through its Ministers Shri T.K. Ramakrishnan, Shri P.J. Joseph and Smt. Susheela Gopalan, and the State Planning Board through Dr. I.S. Gulati, Dr. Thomas Isaac and Shri E.M. Sreedharan rendered good help to make the programme a success. The Netherlands has a very special relation with Kerala. I first broached the idea of the international conference with Mr. Peter

Kuperus, Head, Development Department, the Royal Netherlands Embassy. He enthusiastically supported the project and encouraged us in all possible ways. H.E. Mr. J.H.J. Jeurissen, the Ambassador of the Netherlands, took keen interest. Words are inadequate to express our deep sense of gratitude to the Ambassador and his colleagues for supporting this project.

The United Nations Development Programme (UNDP) was equally enthusiastic about this programme and extended its cooperation. UN Resident Coordinator in India, Mr. Hans C. von Sponeck and his collegues Mr. R. Sudarsan and Mr. Bhaskar Bhattacharji took keen interest at the various stages of the conference. We extend our very special thanks to them.

Perhaps the most memorable event was the address by Shri K.R. Narayanan the then Vice-President of India. While inaugurating the conference in his scholarly, inimitable but intimate tone he echoed with deep insight the concerns of all those interested in the future of the State. We are, indeed, grateful to him for permitting this volume to be dedicated to this great son of Kerala.

I must place on record my appreciation to all the staff members of the Institute. As one person they rose to the occasion and faced the challenge of organising such a big conference. The secretariat was headed by Shri Raman Mahadevan. In his own characteristic style with great insight of Kerala history and society he planned and organised the conference. It was a big achievement. He was ably assisted by Ms. Janki Turaga. Our thanks go to them in no small measure.

Ever since Professor M.A. Oommen joined the Institute of Social Sciences as Senior Fellow, he has been an inspiration for all of us, with his new ideas and scholarly insights. I wish to place on record our heartfelt gratitude to him for his contribution to the success of the conference and for the editing of these volumes.

March 31, 1999

GEORGE MATHEW
Director

CONTENTS

CONTRIBUTORS

N. H. ANTIA a medical doctor (FRCS), is founder Director, The Foundation for Research in Community Health, Mumbai.

BARBARA H. CHASIN is Professor, Department of Anthropolgy, Mont Clair State University, USA.

RICHARD FRANKE is Professor, Department of Anthropology, Mont Clair State University, USA.

RAJAN GURUKKAL is Director, School of Social Sciences, M.G. University, Kottayam

C.T. KURIEN is Professor Emeritus, Madras Institute of Development Studies. Before that he was the Director of the Institute.

M.G.S. NARAYANAN was Member Secretary, Indian Council of Historical Research. He was Professor and Head, Department of History, University of Calicut.

T.K. OOMMEN is Professor, Centre for the study of Social Systems, School of Social Sciences, Jawaharlal Nehru University, New Delhi. He was President Internationaional Sociological Association (1990-94).

M.P. PARAMESWARAN was formerly a Scientist with the Babha Atomic Energy Research Centre, Trombay. Founder of Kerala Sastra Sahitya Parishad, he is currently a social activist.

K. RAMAN PILLAI is retired Professor and Head, Department of Politics, Kerala University.

B. RAJEEVAN is Professor of Malayalam, Government Victoria College, Palakkad.

E.V. RAMAKRISHNAN is Professor, Department of English, South Gujarat University, Surat.

K. SATCHIDANANDAN well known Malayalam poet is currently Secretary, Sahitya Akademi, New Delhi.

K. SARADAMONI is retired Professor of Economics, Indian Statistical Institute, New Delhi.

JOSEPH THARAMANGALAM is Vice Pr sident, Sasthri-Indo-Canadian Institute, New Delhi and Professor, Department of Sociology/ Anthropology, Mount St. Vincent University, Halifax Canada.

MEERA VELAYUDHAN is Coordinator (Gender Studies) Instititue for Environmental and Social Concerns, Bhuj—Kach, Gujarat.

INTRODUCTION

M.A. OOMMEN

"To achieve as much as Kerala has done for a population of its size is no mean record in world history"

—Amartya Sen

No single region on the globe has attracted so much scholarly attention, as did Kerala in recent times. Even international institutions have hailed the experience of this region. By the 1970s, Kerala had already become "an object of fascination for scholars and policy makers concerned with development", the world over (R. Jeffrey (1992): p. xi). No wonder, the literature on Kerala's development has been as profound as it is prolific. The enquiry and debate on Kerala still continue unabated. The papers in the two volumes, chosen out of over 150 presented in the *International Conference on Kerala's Development Experience* (ICKDE) organised by the Institute of Social Sciences on December 8 to 11, 1996 form part of this ongoing debate.

Walled off by the Western Ghats and watered by the Arabian sea, the small strip of land called *Keralam* (this endearing Malayalam term has been Anglicised into Kerala), with only 1.2 per cent of the geographical size of India, but housing a population as large as Canada and almost double of Sri Lanka and ten times that of Costa Rica, has attracted the attention of the world for its achievement in human development comparable to that of the affluent countries. That this has been achieved without conquest or colonialism, foreign aid, or high economic growth, but through a unique confluence of historical factors and forces has surprised both theoreticians as well as policy makers.

Kerala's development experience has been widely referred to as the 'Kerala Model' (a large part of vol. I is devoted to its critique), which is but a *post facto* generalisation of an experience historically evolved but promoted by public action[1] (which *inter alia* includes socio-religious reform movements, a wide and active press, adversarial politics etc.) and sustained by social demands. This 'model' obviously is in sharp contrast to the conventional *ex ante* economic models built on such variables as income, savings, investment, capital-output ratio and the like. Neither an ideal type nor a predictive construct, the Kerala Model is at best only "a specific set of social, political, cultural and economic experiences in a specific trajectory of historical developments" (Michael Tharaken (1997): p. 8). Still dynamic and live, the 'model' continues to be a paradigm meaningful for democracy and people's well being.

The myth that there is no alternative for the 'tadpoles' of the world (underdeveloped/developing countries) except to grow like the 'frogs' (the developed capitalist countries) has been successfully promoted as exemplified in the terms developing, developed and the like, widely used in development discourse today. The ideological hegemony and the move towards homogenisation of the cultures of the world implicit in such a 'tadpole philosophy' of development remains almost unquestioned. Probably, a David is needed to encounter the Goliath. It is in this setting that Kerala's development experience needs renewed examination. A development model in whatever way you would like to characterise it has relevance only to the extent it contributes to improve human wellbeing in a sustainable way. Otherwise, it will be a 'thing of beauty', with joy for none.

In recent history, the IMF, the World Bank and now the World Trade Organisation (WTO) are successfully selling the idea that market mediated allocation of resources is the most rational and efficient organising principle available to humanity for managing a community's resources. They have derived the needed theoretical scaffolding from neoclassical economics. As the World Bank puts it: "Competitive markets are the best way yet found for efficiently organising the production and distribution of goods and services. A consensus is gradually forming in favour of 'market friendly' approach to development" (World Bank, 1991): p.1). With the debacle of the so-called socialist experimentations, expressions like "the end of history" and "the end of ideology" have gained currency. Though in veiled tones, echoing the sentiments underlying "the end of ideology" assertion, *The Economist*, observes: "Left and right, eagerly or reluctantly, bow down before global capitalism" (*The Economist* (1997): p.5). Indeed, this homogenising development paradigm has overshadowed the world although the recent meltdown in East Asia has inflicted a stunning blow to it. To treat development primarily as a flow of goods and services is to confuse objectives with instruments. Besides alienating a substantial section of human beings, this development paradigm simply ignores the rich and varied cultural domain of human existence as well. Moving away from commodities and income to functionings and capabilities as the essence of development, Amartya Sen identifies Kerala as a successful case of human development (see Sen (1992): pp 125-127). It is in this context that the quest for alternative development paradigms assumes added significance.

A high human development experience without a sharp rural-urban divide or obvious gender disparity, an extremely respectable food and nutritional security, a social security system that covers most of the unorganised sector, a female-male ratio consistently well above that of all India average (and even above that of Japan), remarkable fertility decline achieved as a matter of choice, exceptional cultural attainments like greater learning time and wider reading habit (a library in all the villages), collapse of an oppressive caste structure (with not only untouchability, but with non-approachability and unseeability as its dominant character) and imparting self-respect to the 'lower' caste/strata people, abolition of feudal relations of production in the agrarian sector, a multi-religious, multi-cultural population flourishing in symbiotic relationships—these indeed are no small achievements. Kerala has actually overtaken China with considerable rapidity in raising life expectancy, reducing infant mortality, cutting down fertility rate below replacement rate and so on only during the last decade. (Dreze and Sen (1995): p.201), see also Irudaya Rajan and Zachariah, vol. II). Himself a physician and a health economist, one author in volume I estimates that Kerala's health status is achieved at a cost of $ 15 per capita as against $ 4000 per capita in the so-called developed countries (NH Antia, vol.I). All these and more which constitute the 'Kerala Model' have challenged conventional theories and notions in economics (e.g. growth first doctrine and trickle down theory), demography (e.g. fertility decline happens with high per capita income, high degree of urbanisation and industrialisation), classical communism (e.g. communists will not come to power through the ballot box) and in several other disciplines. Kerala's development experience is a reminder to development theorists to take geo-history and political economy into account to make the sub-discipline of development economics empirically relevant.

Regarding the question of replicability, it is presumptuous to assume that the social, economic, cultural and political processes that shaped a sub-national entity like Kerala could be replicated in its entirety in the rest of the country. Yet, we maintain that there is tremendous scope for selective replicability. To say that implementation of land reforms, education without gender disparity, prevention of child labour, taking steps towards preventive health care on a mass scale, building houses for the homeless with a firm goal to provide decent shelter for every household, ensuring a public distribution system involving food grains, sugar, edible oil, kerosene, vegetables, etc. throughout the length and breadth of the State and the like, are not replicable is tantamount to escaping from the national commitment to implementing the Directive Principles of State Policy enshrined in the Indian Constitution.

Kerala's remarkable fertility decline mediated through the women's agency too has extremely important lessons for the rest of India (see Dreze and Sen (1995): p.168). The fact that Malabar, a part of the British ruled Madras Province until 1956 and which was way behind Travancore and Cochin in social sector development, notably with respect to literacy rate, fertility and infant mortality rates, could catch up with the rest of Kerala in a short period clearly suggests that given social demand and political initiatives, several of these attainments can be effectively replicated in the rest of the country.

Kerala has now launched a massive experiment in local democracy and participatory planning far outdistancing the rest of the country (see Harilal and Thomas Isaac, vol.II). As in the case of land reforms, universal education etc., the State government is only attempting to implement the relevant statutes of part IX of the Indian Constitution added by the 73rd and 74th Amendments to the Constitution.

Despite its remarkable and somewhat unique development experience, of late, Kerala is said to be passing through a severe sustainability 'crisis', a term quite often employed to draw attention or to start a debate. By sustainability we mean the ability of the social and economic system to meet the challenges thrown up by the uncertainties of the system and to progress on its own internal capabilities without compromising the needs of the future generation. Many scholars have been alarmist, while some are optimistic given the resilience and dynamism of the people of the State. One scholar who has made a study of the financial problems of the State has concluded that "the Kerala model of development has almost reached the end of its tether" (George KK (1993); see also George (ICKDE-Sovenir)[2].

In 1990, a two-volume Special produced by *Economic and Political Weekly (EPW)* was entitled 'Kerala Economy at the Cross Roads' and was meant to address "the crucial question of the economic performance of Kerala against the background of its achievements in the social sphere" (EPW, nos. 35, 36 and 37, September 1990). Summing up the deliberations of the first International Congress on Kerala Studies held in August 1994, at Thiruvananthapuram (in which 1600 scholars/activists drawn from 23 countries participated), two scholars who worked behind it speak of "the grave crisis that has characterised the State during the past two decades. The spheres of employment and material production have been in the grip of stagnation. All round, there have emerged visible signs of decay, resurgence of casteism and communalism and a virtual political stalemate with the Left failing to effect a decisive breakthrough, degeneration of popular culture and so on.

Even the much acclaimed progress in education and health, looks vulnerable" (Isaac and Tharakan (1995): p.1993). Social thinkers and all those concerned about Kerala's future will be disturbed at these observations which in a way bring home the issue of the sustainability of the 'Kerala Model'. A model that is not sustainable will turn out to be a tragedy. In fact the overarching theme of our Conference was the sustainability of the development experience of Kerala.

The first volume has two components: one, which seeks to situate the 'Kerala Model' in its historical and social context, and the other which is a general critique of the model made by individual scholars. The first eight papers include the chairperson's report on the working session on *Social Structure and Social Change*. This report is added as it contains certain general observations, which we thought could serve as a backdrop to the section that follows. The six papers that follow, written by scholars from different disciplines ranging from anthropology to medicine, critique the Kerala Model in an effort to identify the negative and positive aspects of the experience.

It is not all fashionable in development discourse to examine literature, culture and even history while exploring social reality. Many an economist does not want his/her discipline to be "the happy hunting ground of the charlatan and the knave". The real question is, can any science compromise on its subject matter for the sake of elegance and still call it a science ? The papers in this volume proclaim to the world that the reality of development experience and more so of a highly literate state like Kerala can be understood only from a holistic approach covering literature, culture, history and the like.

Since Kerala has achieved almost total literacy, it has a large reading public (the first three positions in regard to newspaper circulations in India go to Malayalam newspapers). Categories such as region, nation, class, culture, society, and the like are constructed in the popular imagination of the reading public as much through their involvement in the imaginative narratives of fictional works as through their engagement with reality. Malayalam literature and art have influenced as well as have been tremendously influenced by changes and developments in Kerala's society (See Ayyappa Paniker (ICKDE); P. Govinda Pillai, (ICKDE), Satchidanandan, vol.I; E.V. Ramakrishnan, vol.I; B. Rajeevan, vol.I).

Kerala has a geography, ecology, economy, history and even Brahminism distinctly different from the rest of India which explains its present day settlement pattern, rural-urban continuum, cropping pattern (which surprisingly has more similarity with Sri Lanka than with the rest of India), unique credit institutions (chitties and kuries) and so on. Based on a fairly detailed historical analysis of the cultural symbiosis of Kerala, resulting from the presence of heterogeneous groups from across the sea and the cultural synthesis of Aryan and Tamil groups within the land operating silently for many centuries, M.G.S. Narayanan (vol. I) advances an interesting hypothesis that all these have "moulded the Kerala temperament with its openness, adjustability, extreme individualism with defiance of leadership and authority, all these promoting laziness at home and hardworking habits outside. They have played a crucial role in fixing the parameters of development in our times". Undoubtedly, colonialism too has affected the world-view and socio-cultural reconstruction of the Kerala people. But it bore within itself the force to question the truth about themselves (Rajan Gurukkal, vol.I). Various subaltern movements, social and religious movements, left forces and creative writings have changed the character of Kerala's everyday life, impregnated with ritual, custom, code and the like. The dividing practices that concealed exploitation and inequality behind the masks of the natural and the providential came to be visible in their inhuman shapes (see Satchidanandan, vol. I; Rajan Gurukkal, vol. I). The dividing practices that continue to conceal exploitation, inequality and lovelessness behind the masks of consumerism, global capitalism, struggle for political power and the like remain to be made more visible by social thinkers and creative writers of this little land and of the wider world. Indeed, this should continue to be the overarching concern of all those who are worried about the sustainability of Kerala's development experience and making it some thing of an example in the struggle of Homosapiens for a better world.

For any society to stay viable, its economic sustainability is crucial. Economic sustainability in this context has three basic aspects: sustainability of the production base, for the present as well as for the future, financial sustainability of the public sector and meeting the threat posed by globalisation and structural adjustment. Some of the relevant problems are discussed in a few basic papers in the two volumes.

Kerala's land reforms, although the most progressive in the country in altering the relations of production, have not fully given the land to the real tiller of the soil or turned out to be the best way of efficiently organising agricultural production. No wonder, leasing is reappearing (see T.A. Thomas *et al.*, vol.II). Peasantry as a class is disappearing. Farming has become a secondary occupation to the majority of landowners. Terms of trade has turned acutely adverse to agriculture. Wages rates are inordinately high. All these have adverse consequences to agricultural production and productivity. Based on a detailed investigation, M.K. Sukumaran Nair (vol. II) examines the problem of the sustainability of the Kerala Model from the reality of rural labour shortage in an economy of labour surplus. "Lack of appreciation of some of the biophysical and socio-economic features unique to Keralam" and reliance on several national policies also have proved counter-productive (K.N.S. Nair, vol.II). Kerala, which has been uniquely multi cropping, has turned monocultural. No wonder, the slump in rubber prices following globalisation has impacted on Kerala's agricultural economy more sharply than in the past. The failure to build a sustainable industrial base, especially based on local resources, has added poignancy to this situation. Distorted energy planning has turned out to be extremely costly in building a sound industrial base (R.V.G Menon, vol. II). Although Kerala had a respectable industrialisation at the eve of Independence, the public demand culture of Kerala (competitively promoted by nearly 18 political parties) has got distorted so as to stifle the forces of production and technological progress, be they in the large number of public sector enterprises or agro-processing sector in which Kerala had considerable comparative advantage or other fields. Indeed a lot of policy failures too have affected the growth of a strong production base. This needs to be addressed with vision and urgency.

Tharamangalam's paper (vol.I) needs a special mention in this context because he has characterised the 'Kerala Model' as a 'development debacle' and asserts that it bears within itself the seeds of its own destruction. (A summary version of this paper published in the *Bulletin of Concerned Asian Scholars*, vol. 30, no.1 (1998)) generated a wide-ranging debate involving several scholars on Kerala both Indian and foreign). The innumerable arguments and assertions of Tharamangalam and others, who support his theses may be broadly summed up (rather risky exercise) thus. First, the Kerala Model is a "no growth or anti-growth model" judging from the performance of the Kerala economy during the last two decades or so. It has failed to provide employment to its growing unemployed. Therefore, it is unsustainable. Second, every inch of Kerala society is so much charged with partisan politics that it is difficult to pursue collective goals in any meaningful manner. There is a profound cultural crisis. Third, the dialectics of a patronising State that implements reform and welfare and distributes the collective pie to various demand groups, on the one hand, and political mobilisation by organised groups, continuously putting pressure on the State, on the other, has reached its limits today. The Kerala Model has come to a dead end.

Without indulging in polemics a few general comments seem to be in order. One, economic growth is only a necessary condition, but not a sufficient one. It is to be understood only as an instrumental variable. Even strongly cited economic growth 'models' like that of Punjab have failed to provide high literacy, high female-male ratio, high life expectancy and the like to their people. True, the share of Kerala's SDP in India's GNP has declined from 3.4 per cent in 1980-81 to 2.8 per cent in 1990-91. But it has increased although marginally since then (2.92% in 1995-96) to tell the world that there is potential even to take a u-turn as agriculture potential is fully tapped, as energy situation improves, the information technology takes firm root and correct policy initiatives implemented. Has Kerala which produced Schumpeterian entrepreneurs (who lifted the large paddy lands from backwaters and built a mini Holland, and domonstrated financial entrepreneurship of a high order etc (Oommen (1972); Oommen (1976)), completely run out of steam? Of course, getting locked up in luxury buildings and consumer durables, foreign remittances have failed to provide the needed investment. More importantly the growing consumer demand for goods whose value keep rising compared to the value of exportables from the State, a real 'scissors crisis' has been there for quite sometime. The net leakage cannot be filled in by gulf remittances *adinfinitum* which is under serious threat as oil prices have already started a down slide. There is no alternative to purposive policy initiatives and imaginative political actions.

Two, while admitting that public action has got distorted, the best way out has to be sought in relevant public action itself. When Sree Narayana Guru hoisted the 'Ezhava Shiva' and Ayyankali drove his bullock cart through the roads meant only for caste Hindus risking his life, when the communist party fought the feudal relations of production, or when agitations and movements like the Malabar mutiny and the Vaikom Satyagraha took place, we have been witnessing the momentous struggles of a people for freedom from oppressions of various sorts. Although 'mass' agitations have been more frequent than in the past, they are but a ghost of their historical counterparts. Kerala has to realise this sooner than later. The so-called enlightened public remains indifferent to corruption, (poor quality roads, cost and time overruns of irrigation projects and even fiscal crisis could be traced to this to a certain extent). The bureaucratic leviathan reigns strong. While 'participatory freedom' is a great reality in Kerala, 'procedural freedom' and in some important respects 'transactional freedom' have been a casuality.[3] Even enabling freedom suffers as education, health and the like persistently lose quality. When contractors of every hue, including the powerful liquor lobby, are unionised to fight for their rights, public action gets routinely distorted.

Rights have become the preferred mode of practising politics the world over. This has been very much so in Kerala. But sensitivity to the issues of obligation and reciprocity is the best way to make rights a relevant social praxis. The thesis of Jeffrey, Dreze and Sen and several others, that public action has been the locomotive of Kerala's progress still has considerable substance. Even so, salvation lies in reorienting this strategy with vision, commitment and recapturing the zeal of the past. The need to promote the current initiatives towards participatory democracy is stronger now than ever before. A top down approach in party politics and development initiative is not the way to promote democracy and participatory public action. Left politics has to see the writing on the wall and respond creatively[4]. This is a historic opportunity as Kerala enters the new millennium to give it a new sense of direction and hope.

Three, scholars who see in the 'Kerala Model' the seeds of its undoing should know that the paradox of shortage of labour in the field and growing educated unemployment in the State is as much due to the decline in the traditional division of labour as due to a repetitive and purposeless university system. This in a way badly restricts internal freedom. When a modern "low" caste parent asks: "Why not your children climb the trees and plough the muddy field?" is not he/she symbolising development and change? She is probably building her world-view in the image of her former masters. If a million Tamil labour moves into Kerala attracted by the high wage, Kerala labour moves out to Gulf or to the United States due to a different push factor. How can we turn this brain drain and skill drain into an affirmative action and effort towards a new lease of life and work culture is an important question today. Kerala has a diaspora which is resourceful and rich and should have been used for rebuilding the State, something which China has done in a meaningful way (see M.A. Oommen (ICKDE)). It is important that Kerala produces a document and a plan of action for a *sustainable Kerala* sooner than later with the cooperation of scholars, NGOs, Malayalee diaspora, politicians and others.

The Malayalee is visibly ubiquitous in this globe. This in no small measure is due to Kerala's investment in human capital. Paradoxically Kerala has not produced even above average universities, leave alone excellent ones. Excellent medical colleges, institutions of technology, management, or even political thought are conspicuous by their absence. The emerging lesson that quality and dynamic restructuring are as important as quantity especially in regard to vital areas like education, health, transport and democratic institutions can be missed only at Kerala's peril. If Germany, a country that imparts long duration (up to two years) training in skills ranging from haircutting to fence making faces unemployment, how much more so will a State education system that routinely reproduces the Macaulian legacy? For a State that never had any heavy industries or mineral resources to back its growth, failure to build on its comparative advantages could be very costly if not ruinous.

Four, if the workers of Kerala are to be faulted, the elites and intelligentsia have to share a greater part of the blame. When for example, a college teacher (or any other upper/middle class person) finds that an agricultural worker or last grade government employee does not 'behave', it is important to note that they are only trying to imitate their more educated fellowmen.

Five, it has been hypothesised by many, notably by Robin Jeffrey (1992) and Jean Dreze and Amartya Sen (1995) that women's agency and autonomy have been one of the major factors that contributed to Kerala's development model. I think it is extremely relevant here to quote from the *Report of the Working Session on Women and Development* (ICKDE), in which thirteen papers were presented: "An almost united opinion that emerged was that the Kerala Model is surrounded by a whole lot of myths which need to be broken even to understand the present condition of women. The papers highlighted the disturbing trends of the growing insecure environment and violence against women including domestic violence, indications of a dip in the sex ratio in particular in 0-6 age group, the emergence of a clear preference for the male child, widespread incidence of dowry and perhaps, even a sex bias or preference for males in employment. The Kerala development experience had ideologically developed a "public" sphere with new and more aggressive notions of maleness/manhood and this was discussed within the context of the role of the media in creating a new morality... The Session voiced the need to reevaluate the role of public actions informing the Kerala Model"

(ICKDE). Two papers in this volume draws attention to the gender insensitivity symptoms of modern Kerala society (Ammu Joseph, vol.II; see also K. Saradamoni, vol.I). It is equally important to examine the role of ideology in shaping people's perceptions of reality with reference to ideas of femininity (see. B. Rajeevan, vol.I and Meera Velayudhan, vol.I). The observation of Satchidandan that the sizeable women's writings in Kerala "appears more like a wish fulfilment than a reflection of reality" and failed to promote social change is also a fact to be underscored. The need to fight against the phallogocentric social order and freeing Kerala from the grip of culture industry, greed and consumerism and transforming Kerala's every day life pattern is more relevant today than ever before (see Satchidanandan, vol.I, M.P. Parameswaran, vol.I).

Six, the crises in the quality of such services as education, healthcare, social security entitlements, transport system and the like which have traditionally moulded the Kerala Model of development are as much due to financial unsustainability as due to the failure of public action and public policy and can be remedied only through appropriate policy initiatives. (See for e.g. N.V. Varghese (vol.II), Raman Kutty (vol.II), N. H. Antia (vol. I), M.N. Prasad (vol.II), M. H. Suryanarayana (vol. II), (K.R. Nayar (vol. II)). Although Kerala schools have all the objective conditions needed for better learning by students and quality education why Kerala lags behind other less endowed regions is examined by Varghese with profound insight for policy (vol. II). Suryanarayana's well substantiated inference that by both economic and physical access criteria, Kerala is the most food insecure State in India needs serious attention. The empirical study by Gasper showing that the cost of subsidisation is over 99 per cent in medical education throws several policy insights into the questions of financing of health care and higher education in Kerala (see C. Gasper, vol. II).

Kerala has one of the richest biomass, biodiversity and marine resource potential per unit area in this planet. An ecological overkill has already damaged them considerably. The need for a proper environment management with community's cooperation and participation is acute indeed. (see C.P. Geevan, vol. II, K. Sreedharan (ICDKE)). There is also an opposite view that Kerala has a comparative advantage under the new TRIPS regime (See Sandhya Mohan (ICKDE). The present road density of the State, over five times the national average, has reduced Kerala's agricultural land and led to deforestation, destabilisation of hill slopes, soil erosion, interference with natural drainage and so on. The problem is compounded by the poor maintenance of roads and exponential growth of motor vehicles. Kerala has one of the highest incidence of death due to road accidents in India today. Why have the large number of natural ports not relieved the acute cargo and traffic problem of Kerala? (see M.N. Prasad, vol.II).

Indeed, Kerala has to sit back and think on the various challenges and hopes thrown up by its development experience rather than seeing them as explosives waiting to cause havoc. (see Irudaya Rajan *et al,* vol. II). Richard Franke and Barbara Chasin (vol. I) bring together in one place the analytical components of the "crisis" of the 'Kerala Model' based on their extensive research on Kerala, including the study of the transformation of a village spread over two decades. They pose several pertinent issues which are critical to any rethinking on development in general and of the Kerala praxis in particular. After highlighting the threat posed by the structural adjustment regime now underway in India, the two US scholars conclude: "As the brutality of the New World Order imposes itself on nations and cultures unprepared or unable to defend their most vulnerable group, Kerala for all its shortcomings, might become even more of a Model". This, of course, has to be attained by purposive public action with deeper roots in the people rather than party-sponsored salvos.

We may now turn to the question of clubbing Kerala with Sri Lanka and Costa Rica as models of high physical quality of life coexisting with low economic growth. UNDP (1996) has recently widened the list to include countries like Jamaica and Peru. (see also C.T. Kurien, vol.1). It is in this setting that ICKDE organised a symposium in which scholars from Costa Rica, Sri Lanka and Kerala participated. Without entering into any debate on the issues raised, I venture to make the following observations also as part of our effort towards 'rethinking development' in the context of Kerala.

First, Kerala's experience has been so rich, varied, and unique that clubbing it with these countries (except Sri Lanka in certain significant respects) is incorrect. The saga of transformation of a society, mired in oppressive caste rigidity, to one of self dignity and assertiveness (the latter virtue today, allegedly erring on the wrong side is a different issue) has no parallel in human history. That the female life expectancy of Kerala is now heading towards 80 (see Irudaya Rajan, *et al.* vol.II) is no mean achievement. All these have been accomplished, as we have noted at the outset, without regimentation or costly economic growth or foreign aid or following the IMF-World Bank prescriptions.

Second, Kerala is a sub-national entity and not a nation-state. To begin with, it did not have the backing of a sterling balance as was the case in Sri Lanka, or foreign aid as in the case of Costa Rica. Indeed, Kerala which shares a surprising similarity with Sri Lanka in regard to cropping pattern might have added more to India's sterling balance (of course with no benefit to it) than Sri Lanka had accumulated on the eve of its Independence. Also Sri Lanka had the benefit of foreign aid. Costa Rica received "extraordinary support" of foreign aid. "As late as the 1980s, it was still important for the US to maintain a democratic showcase, neighbouring the Sandinista Nicaragua" (Jorge A. Chaves (ICKDE)). The route chosen by Kerala to reach its social development goal is clearly different from that of others in certain significant respects.

Third, although Costa Rica had a Communist Party and a Catholic Church (Sri Lanka too had a Communist Party in its mainstream politics and a coalition government), to lend support to its social welfare measure, it is doubtful whether any of the countries clubbed with Kerala had a history of mass movements that it experienced. Although with tremendous discomfort about the unsustainability factors threatening Kerala (increasing suicide rate, crime rate, alcoholism, visionless politics, fiscal unsustainability, ecological overkill, misdirected savings and aggressive consumerist tendencies, phallogocentricity etc.), I am inclined to assert, along with some of the authors in the two volumes, that, given the sustaining growth of the physical qualities of life like falling death rate, IMR, increase in life expectancy with prospects of unemployment of young to decline perceptibly in the future and readiness to organise and carry out mass actions with strong disposition to debate ideas etc, Kerala still has weapons to build a new model taking account of contemporary challenges. (see also Franke and Chasin vol. I, M.P. Parameswaran, vol. I).

Four, sustainability is the acid test on which the various country experiences are to be judged. And here it has to be understood in a dynamic sense as the growing capability to respond to the various endogenous (particularly the several second generation problems like growing proportion of the aged) and exogenous problems like structural adjustment that confront the people. Costa Rica is in a deep debt trap today with foreign exchange and fiscal crises pushing the economy almost to a breaking point. It does not have the buffer of 'Gulf remittances' of Kerala or even of Sri Lanka. Sri Lanka and Cost Rica, known for their State intervention for decades, took to structural adjustment and paid the high price by damaging their economies and social welfare achievements.

Five, the development base of Kerala is much wider and inclusive than that of Sri Lanka. Any strategy that socially excludes or discriminates is a threat to basic freedom. Kerala stands heads and shoulders above others in this respect, especially when we note that it has a population of 32 million (a little over that of Canada) whereas Sri Lanka's population is less than 18 million and that of Costa Rica 3.3 million.

One important lesson that has to be learned from the experience of Kerala, Costa Rica, and Sri Lanka is that the Western type of growth based on infinite multiplication of wants is unsustainable. Incidentally, there is a need to invent new tools for measuring development and change as some authors have suggested in volume one. If it were necessary to consume as much natural resource-coal, oil, iron, copper, wood etc. as an average American or Japanese citizen did to attain an equivalent life expectation it would not be possible for two thirds of humanity to "progress". A nuclear scientist turned social activist of Kerala who founded several popular movements arguing in this vein in his paper rightly observes: "Welfare depends not only on wealth, but also on equity, justice and wisdom—wisdom in using resources and wealth" (MP Parameswaran, vol.I K. Saradamoni, vol.I). Will this community-in-struggle reorient its development trajectory seeing the warnings and writings on the wall is the critical issue confronting all those who want sustainable development in Kerala. Where does Kerala stand in terms of the five freedoms which mirror development (admirably advanced by Amartya Sen)? Indeed, Kerala like the rest of the world and more meaningfully than any other region is on the threshold of history as the old millennium yields to an expectant new one. To be forewarned is to be forearmed. Despite the large flow of foreign remittances, Kerala has failed to build a sustainable economy, although they enabled the State to hold the fort with remarkable ease. The damaging impact of Gulf money also needs independent investigation. A radical reorientation of its health and education sector is a prime requisite. A viable multi-cropping based agricultural sector coupled with a hightech small industry sector within a decentralised planning framework is not an infeasible project. Evolving a progressive and socially responsible public action process especially in the trade union front is also a crying need. Industrialisation that builds on its comparitive advantages is also equally important Ego-centric, rhetoric oriented politics should yield to by purposive action-based politics. To reflect and act with vision and wisdom is the challenge before the scholars, politicians and people of Kerala. Literature and art must disengage from the micropolitics of everyday and must be challenged by the crying evils of communalism, corruption, crimes, social anomie, gender hegemony, human rights issues and so on as in the past. Right responses could mean a shining place for Kerala in the map of human history and could provide a viable alternative to Euro-centric visions of development.

[I am thankful to T.T. Sree Kumar for his helpful suggestions.]

NOTES

1. Amartya Sen has been formulating on his own and along with J. Dreze, a theory (or hypothesis) of public action (as against market mediated growth only approach) which emphasises participation by the public in the process of social change by building people's capabilities and expanding their choices. The most prominent among those who identified 'public politics' and 'public action as important dimensions of the Kerala Model include Robbin Jeffrey (1992); Dreze and Sen (1989); Dreze and Sen (1995); Ramachandran V K. (1997) in Dreze and Sen (1997).

2. Papers not included in the two volumes, but presented in the Conference and included in the *Abstract* of papers or in the Conference Souvenir are documented in this Introduction by adding ICDKE in brackets to the name of the author with more details given in the References at the end.
3. In his forthcoming book *Development as Freedom*, Amartya Sen has identified five freedoms as important to evaluating development. They are *internal* freedom, *participatory* freedom, *transactional* freedom, *procedural* freedom and *protective* freedom (see Interview with Amartya Sen by V.K. Ramachanrdan in *Frontline* November 6, 1998).
4. The insightful observations of Olle Tonquist (1995) need a fair reexamination on a more comprehensive basis in the present context.

REFERENCES

Chaves A. Jorge (1996), "Costa Rica's Recent Development: The Role of Welfare State and of Favourable External Conditions", ICKDE.

Dreze Jean and Amartya Sen (1989), *Hunger and Public Action* , Oxford and Clarendon Press.

Dreze Jean and Amartya Sen (1995), *India: Economic Development and Social Opportunity*, Oxford University Press.

Dreze Jean and Amartya Sen (1997), *Indian Development: Selected Regional Perspectives*, Oxford University Press.

George, K.K. (1993), *Limits to Kerala Model of Development: An Analysis of Fiscal Crisis and its Implications* Centre for Development Studies, Thiruvananthapuram.

George K.K. (1996), "Wither Kerala Model"? *Souvenir*, ICKDE.

Govinda Pillai P. (1996), "Malayalam Literature and Art and the Changing Social Context" *Abstract*, ICKDE.

Isaac Thomas and M. Tharakan (1995), "Kerala: Towards a New Agenda", *Economic and Political Weekly*, August 5-12.

Oommen M.A. (1972), *Small Industries in Indian Economic Growth: A Case Study of Kerala*, Research Publications, New Delhi.

Oommen M.A. (1976) "Rise and of growth of Banking in Kerala", *Social Scientist*, November.

Oommen M.A. (1996), "Working towards a Sustainable Kerala/India", Presidential Address, ICKDE.

Paniker Ayyappa (1996), "Social Change and Cultural formation in Kerala", *Abstract*, ICKDE.

Ramachandran V.K. (1997), "Kerala's Development Achievements" in Dreze and Sen (1997).

Robin Jeffrey (1992) *Politics, Women and Well being*, Oxford University Press.

Sandhya Mohan (1996), "Biodiversity and Intellectual Property Rights: Opportunities for Kerala", *Abstract*, ICKDE.

Sen Amartya (1992), *Inequality Reexamined*, Clarendon Press, Oxford.

Sreedharan K. (1996), "Environmental Conscience in Kerala: A Historical Perspective", *Abstract*, ICKDE.

Tharakan, Michael K (1997), *History as Development Experience: Desegregated and Deconstructed Analysis of Kerala*, Ph.D. dissertation, M.G. University, Kottayam.

The Economist, September 20, 1997.

Tornquist Olle (1995), *The Next Left?* NIAS Reports no.24, Copenhagen.

World Bank (1991), *World Development Report 1991: The Challenge of Development*, Oxford University Press.

ONE

GODS AND ANCESTORS IN DEVELOPMENT

A Study of Kerala

M.G.S. NARAYANAN

The term '*Development*' is used with a special connotation in Economics to refer to production, market operations and standard of life. They function within a framework produced by natural and human resources interacting upon each other over a period of time, but the influence of the past on the course of Development is not easily quantifiable. Therefore it is often left out.

We assume here that such an influence exists to a considerable extent, and that the major factors involved in the process can be identified and related to trends of Development, although the study necessarily remains impressionistic and subjective. The special features of Kerala's geography—location and resources—have certainly been active behind the *Kerala Model* of Development, and these can be analysed by economists with the help of statistical information. That is not being taken up for discussion here. We discuss in this paper the historical process—the settlement patterns, the evolution of social structure and attitudes arising out of them—in relation to Development as it is being manifested today.

The term *Gods* is used in the title of this paper to represent the sum total of natural forces and resources. The term *Ancestors* is made to stand for all the generations of the past that contributed to the creation of the history of Kerala and thereby shaped the present socio-cultural and national identity of Kerala.

Trade Winds and Cultural Symbiosis

While Kerala forms an integral part of the land mass of India, it is also connected by invisible bonds to the West Asian and

European worlds. This connection was established by means of the so-called Hippalus wind or trade wind, which enabled effortless and risk-free transportation across the Arabian Sea back and forth between the Egyptian-Syrian-Arab-Persian side and the Malabar coast. For merchants the incentive to take advantage of this wind was provided by pepper for which Kerala enjoyed a world monopoly. The discovery of this commodity solved to some extent the problem of winter survival for Europeans until the modern age. Pepper was a necessity for them but the high price made it a luxury in practice. They also found that Kerala was rich in other spices and perfumes.

All this led to hectic activity by the Roman traders (see the observations of Pliny, Ptolemy and the Periplus in this regard) and they made Kerala almost a commercial appendage of the Roman empire. There were loud complaints in the Roman Senate about the drain of gold through the Indian trade—a way of referring to the trade with the Malabar coast of India. It is authenticated by the recent discovery of large hoards of Roman gold coins from Kerala and other parts of South India. From the Kerala side the long-term importance of this one-sided relationship lies in the fact that apart from the deposit of gold coins, it eventually caused the growth of small Jewish and Syrian Christian pockets in the harbour towns and created a continuous flow of commodities and culture.

Though early history is shrouded in legends, it is occasionally illumined by the Tamil Sangam literary references to the *Yavana* ships and their gold, wine and women. Then we have clear statements in the precisely dated copper plates of the 9th and 10th centuries about the Syrian Christian trade settlement in Kollam (Quilon of the British period) under the leadership of Mar Sapir Iso and the Jewish settlement in Kodungallur (Cranganore of the British period, known as Muziris to the Greeks and Muciri or Muyirikkode to the Tamils and Keralites) under the leadership of Joseph Rabban. While the Jewish colony did not grow and spread beyond the suburbs of Kodungallur, and later on got shifted to Cochin, the Christian colony expanded through conversion and prospered, and became responsible for the growth of a parallel culture by the side of the Brahminical culture in Kerala. They seem to have converted several families from the upper caste of Namputiris, and continuing their connection with Syria, remained in the good books of the *Naduvazhi* chiefs of the post-Cera period also.

In the 16th century the Portuguese adventurers tried to enlist the support of this Christian community by a show of strength. But they had only partial success and embarked on a policy of conversion from the lower castes. On the whole the Christian community was active throughout in the field of trade and commerce. Protestant missionaries also came from the West in the modern period. The London Mission Society was active in South Kerala and the Basel Mission Society in North Kerala. Both had the support of the British authorities. They introduced the press culture in Kerala before it was introduced in other parts of India. They became agents of Modernisation through their schools, colleges and technical training institutes. A good number of European trading companies had established their offices in the port towns of Kerala. The Christian Missionaries, often supported by the British Government agents, European planters and European Company officials, came to sponsor and stimulate social reforms to liberate the low castes from feudal bondage. Though their profession of altruism and idealism need not be taken at face value, and the reforms obviously served the self-interest of these groups directly and indirectly, they triggered changes beyond all calculations at that time.

These moves promoted conversion to Christianity and improved the economic, social, political and cultural status of the Christian communities. They also stimulated and strengthened the organisational and reformist activities of low caste groups like the Ezhavar who were ritual outcastes but economically, socially and culturally advanced. Even the lower castes of Pulayar, Cerumar and Parayar were awakened to a new consciousness of rights and possibilities, both those who were converted and those who refused to be converted. Again, the upper castes of Nayars and Namputiris were alerted by the new threat of conversion that eroded the foundations of their social status. Modernisation of the Christians and the lower castes, through education and the new forms of employment forced the upper castes also to take up reforms, education and, organised agitation. Community organisations became the instruments for starting colleges, fighting elections and promoting industrial enterprise. The process of Modernisation through Christianisation and Westernisation that began with the Christian community, spread to other communities by way of appreciation and imitation or fear and competition.

This chain reaction followed the Christian challenge to the caste system, which the Portuguese had started in the 16th century for their own political and economic ends related to Colonialism. The policy of confrontation was continued in different ways by the other foreign Christian outfits that followed them into Kerala. As a result, caste barriers broke down, feudal privileges weakened and cash economy was firmly entrenched. Competition replaced conformity and submissiveness, and the obstacles in the path of Modernisation started melting slowly. Though technical know-how was far behind that of the West, and production was lagging behind due to administrative controls and the negative policies adopted by the new rulers and political movements, large scale migration of the young scientists, technicians and ambitious industrialists from Kerala to other advanced centres created new links with the First World. Kerala society benefited from these links with improved educational and medical facilities, housing, consumer goods, transport and communication. Collaboration with European traders and industrialists led to the transfer of technology in small doses. In this sense historians armed with hindsight cannot view Colonialism and Imperialism as unmixed evils in the way they were depicted by the nationalist, communist and revivalist intellectuals who championed the cause of resistance.

The Christian and other communities that had broken their feudal bonds found it easy in the post-independence period to take to the market economy of the West and prosper through migrations to and contacts with different parts of Europe and America. In other words the Christian community which had religious, cultural and economic links with the West became the model for other communities in replacing matriliny with patriliny, in taking to modern English education and morality, and in moving into the fields of industry, trade and commerce. This Christianisation had a crucial role in facilitating the entry of Kerala into the Development era. The Christian community had its roots in Kollam and Kodungallur, but Kodungallur lost its importance as a harbour town after the big upheaval of land known as *Pudu Veypu* (New Deposit of Land) in 1341 A.D. However, they continued to flourish in and around Kollam, the old headquarters of Venad or Travancore in South Kerala. Therefore, that part of the State had an earlier start and lead in the transformation of society from medieval feudal age to the modern industrial age.

The rule of Marthanda Varma in Travancore in the mid-eighteenth century is generally taken as the landmark indicating this change. The enlightened monarchs of the new centralised state of Travancore were quick to take advantage of their British and European connections in order to lay the foundations of a modern welfare state by patronising English education, industrial projects and the participation of the people in administration. The Christians remained loyal to the rulers, and the social control of the church protected them from the destructive influence of the Communist ideology which mobilised the people against the capitalist type of Development. Thus the Western influence that had started with pepper trade in the period of the Roman empire, and created a permanent base for itself through the establishment of a Christian community of traders, can be identified as an important factor leading to Modernisation and the urge for development in Kerala. This was again strengthened by the associated phenomenon of large-scale migration of Keralities to Europe and America and other parts of the world which had come under Western rule. When compared to other parts of India, this relationship made Kerala society as a whole more open to Western influence.

In a different way also the Arabian sea link played a significant part in differentiating this part of India from others and promoting big changes leading to Development in an unconventional manner. From the 7th century onwards an expanding Islamic empire had emerged in West Asia. Very soon it split over into Europe and got entangled in rivalry and conflict with the European powers. At the same time the Arab Muslim traders had also started knocking at the gates of Kerala. They already had a good share in the sea trade of the peninsula by the middle of the 9th century as attested by the *Kufic* signatures of Muslims found in the list of witnesses attached to the Syrian copper plates. Their power gradually increased and, by the beginning of the 12th century they found an open welcome at the newly opened harbour town of Kozhikode (Calicut of the British period, coming up under the Zamorins who were the erstwhile governors of the Ernad district), and became the chief carriers of the maritime trade in pepper and spices, ivory, sandalwood and timber, in the northern half of Kerala.

This irritated the Christian traders of Europe for whom the prices now shot up as the commodities from South India were being heavily taxed in the hostile territories of West Asia. Their desperate struggle for escape continued for about three centuries, and finally, resulted in Vasco De Gama's discovery of a direct sea route from Western Europe to Kerala. The consequent conflicts with the Muslim leaders are not relevant here except in the sense that the Muslim trading community of North Kerala survived in spite of the fact that they lost their monopoly of the sea trade. What is important for our discussion at the present stage is the fact that this community also was well-integrated with the majority community of the Hindus till the Mysore invasions created a lasting cleavage. They multiplied fast and many from the lower castes were converted during the Mysore period, but on the whole they were excluded from all forms of modernity, and remained poor and illiterate. The establishment of the Christian British power in India caused a further decline in their fortunes. In the first quarter of the present century the domination of the same British power in West Asia led to the liquidation of the *Khilafat*—a fact which made these Muslims turn their face away completely from Modernisation.

However, the advent of the petro-dollar boom in the Gulf area gave these people an unexpected chance to become junior partners in Modernisation. They were employed in large numbers in the Gulf and earned money which could be used as capital, and they also began to appreciate modern education, medicine, travel and many other modern amenities of life. In the course of a generation the Muslim community in Malabar crossed many hurdles and several hundreds became the beneficiaries of the economic development in the Gulf region. Other communities also got a fair share of this prosperity in due course. This is another historical channel provided by the Arabian Sea link through which Modernisation came to Kerala.

There is yet another community in Kerala, which came by sea many centuries ago, not from West Asia but from Sri Lanka— the Ezhavar or the Ezham people, as indicated by their name and their traditions. They included Sanskrit-knowing physicians, fencing masters and toddy tappers, but most probably their Buddhist affiliations prevented them from getting absorbed in the Brahmin-dominated caste society of Kerala. The rich and poor among them remained ritually under-privileged, until the close of the 19th century when a great movement under a great leader used the Hindu philosophy of Vedanta, snatched from the Brahmins, to fight back and claim equality and respect denied to them by caste prejudice. This was not merely the starting point of Ezhava liberation because it produced a chain reaction which shook all the Hindu communities out of complacency. This general commotion loosened the bonds of the feudal society and opened the floodgates of modern education, land reforms and political and administrative changes.

Aryan-Tamil Synthesis: Namputiris and Nayars

We may notice that the socio-economic, religious and cultural links of Kerala with the Roman empire, West Asia, Sri Lanka and Modern Europe display a certain uniform character. They were inspired and contrived by the same forces of nature acting behind the scene and went through the same historical process. Traders attracted by the prospect of securing rare products were guided by the ocean winds. Once they landed in Kerala they received a warm welcome and patronage by one king or chieftain or the other. The natives were generous in accepting and tolerating their exotic creeds and languages because they were at the receiving end of the benefits of sea trade. The foreigners retained the initiative, set up small colonies which prospered and increased in number and influence in due course. They gave this western strip of land on the slopes of the Western Ghats in India a distinctive character among the different regional divisions of the country, and made it an integral part of the dynamic, fast-changing Western world, preparing it in different ways to participate in Modernisation.

Long before the growth of transport and communication as a result of industrial revolution, and the consequent emergence of a world market, the natural network of the trade winds and the natural monopoly products of Kerala had been responsible for worldwide contacts and the establishment of a multi-religious, multi-cultural population in Kerala. Influential groups within this society, like the Christian and the Muslim communities, were socially and culturally attached to the West or West Asia, and found it possible to move in step with the changes there, or at least use the first opportunity to benefit from those changes. Others like the Ezhavar, who were disgruntled with the lower caste status accorded to them, were prepared to take up the role of opposition to caste authority within caste society, when the time was ripe, by putting their Buddhist cultural heritage and accumulated wealth to good practical use.

These friendly contacts and peaceful settlements were encouraged by the attitude of the natives. While profits and revenues from trade certainly played a part in shaping this attitude, it was made easier by the fact that an innovative group of Brahmins who deviated from the orthodox prescription for exclusiveness and married into the native ruling families and warrior families were at the helm of affairs. When they reorganised society according to the *Varna* scheme, some time during the 8th-9th centuries, they were ready to persuade the rulers, who were the sons of Brahmins, to accord the status and role of the *Vaisya* group to the foreign trading communities. In the Cera period itself the foreign merchants were granted aristocratic privileges usually reserved for the members of the first three *Varnas* only. The foreign merchant guilds called Ancuvannam (Jews) and *Manigramam* (Syrian Christians) were treated in the same way as the indigenous merchant guilds called *Ayyavole* and *Nanadesi* were treated elsewhere in India. We may briefly describe this background to complete the picture.

Kerala was also an integral part of the relatively unchanging Hindu world in India. It is necessary to appreciate this fact in order to understand the historical processes that shaped the personality of Kerala. In fact certain natural forces, again related to the monsoon, and the migratory trends of people, had contributed largely to the making of the special character of agrarian society in this region. Heavy rains for much of the year, combined with the presence of numerous West-flowing rivers, led to an abundance of water supply throughout the land. Thus a thick forest cover might have been created in the pre-historic period, and made human habitation difficult and scanty until they had iron tools in the megalithic age. This possibility explains the absence of the relics of Old Stone Age and New Stone Age on a large scale in Kerala except in some parts of the eastern High Ranges. When small agricultural groups began to settle down in Kerala, they found no need to cling together in fortified villages with clusters of houses near the river-banks and lake fronts, as in many other parts of India.

We find relatively small stone-built graveyards and burial urns of the megalithic people scattered all over the hilly tracts and central plains of the State. In other areas the agricultural villages dependent on adequate water supply were few and far between, and that created much conflict and feelings of insecurity among the people. This condition had necessitated collective efforts under the leadership of chieftains for irrigation and self defence. On the other hand the availability of water almost everywhere in Kerala with heavy rains, handy wells and house tanks gave rise to another pattern of settlement. Villages had households with small compounds that were scattered over a wide area. These had open boundaries, without the mud-wall fortifications found elsewhere, though each house and compound usually had its fence to protect cultivation from stray cattle.

The absence of the need for serious collective effort for survival weakened leadership at the political level, discouraged centralisation of power and wealth, and promoted extreme individualism at an early stage of social evolution. The only large state in pre-modern period was the Cera kingdom, which was geographically co-terminous with the present day Kerala State. It was a loose federation of *Naduvazhis* nominally acknowledging the sovereignty of the Ceraman Perumal and supporting him in defensive wars against the other Tamil powers, but free to govern their territories as they liked. There was a Brahmin oligarchy which propped up the Perumal, a member of the old and prestigious Cera dynasty. Most of the Perumals were saintly scholars who remained submissive to the power of Brahmin councillors called *Tali Adhikarikal.* State formation was weak and state military enterprise in the imperial Cola style was out of question.

In the Cera period the quasi-autonomous Brahmin settlements were administered by the *Sabha* under the supervision of *Naduvazhis* who were mostly the sons of Brahmins on account of the *Marumakkattayam* system which promoted *sambandham*, a form of Brahmin-Sudra matrimonial alliance. Even this Cera 'Empire', as it is mistakenly called by some historians who took the royal titles at face value, had only a precarious existence for three centuries, within which the rulers were subordinate to the Colas for more than half a century. Subsequent to the disappearance of the Ceraman Perumal at the beginning of the 12th century, the land of Kerala was governed by dozens of *Naduvazhis* under a feudal system which went by Brahminical codes of morality, precedents and traditions until the British power overpowered and subjugated them without resorting to any massive military enterprise. Commerçe and diplomacy rather than conquest by arms brought about the British company's rule in Kerala. In the absence of a strong State with the political will to concentrate authority and maintain law and order, a self-regulating social system organised in terms of communities prevailed, and they managed their affairs through consensus in caste councils or local bodies nominally subject to the local potentate. This made community organisations more powerful, but more secular and democratic at the same time, and more tolerant of each other since they had to survive through adjustments and accommodation. The principle of cultural symbiosis governed the community relations in Kerala.

The *Naduvazhis* themselves did not have much power or wealth, and their chief source of income was the revenue from sea trade. For this reason most of them had their capitals located near the seashore. The foreign traders from Romans to the Arabs and the British were welcomed in spite of their alien creeds, languages, customs and costumes. The old copper plates make it clear that the Syrian Christians and Jews were treated on par with the native aristocrats and granted the 72 privileges and self-governing rights, and the same treatment was extended to the Arab Muslims when they came. These foreign traders who established small outposts also responded to such gestures with friendship as they depended on the pleasure of their clients for protection and continued assistance. While the foreigners who came as conquerors put the natives on the defensive and led to prolonged conflicts elsewhere in India, Kerala was largely free from such misfortunes in the formative stages of the regional culture. Consciousness of human socio-cultural diversity, toleration towards alien ways of life, and readiness to adapt and adjust became hallmarks of the Kerala character and temperament. This has contributed much towards making their ventures outside the State and the country successful and productive.

Apart from the cultural symbiosis induced by the extraordinary conditions of maritime trade and commerce described above, there was another major historical trend at work in Kerala which contributed to the evolution of the typical Kerala traits in social structure and cultural attitudes. This may be described as the synthesis of Aryan and Tamil cultures. It produced a fusion of ethnicity, religion and culture. The most conspicuous expression of this fusion is found in the institution of *sambandham*—a form of Aryan-non-Aryan matrimonial alliance. It was a one-way traffic which permitted Kerala Brahmin males to cohabit with the non-Brahmin females without taking up the responsibilities of parenthood. It was a demonstration of Brahmin supremacy in a society with a majority of non-Brahmin people. Still it was unique in India and made possible under special circumstances obtaining in this region.

Though we have no detailed information about the beginning of this custom or the associated custom of *Marumakkattayam*, their existence is attested in the Cera period in the corpus of epigraphic evidence. Many factors might be related to this practice. First of all, the Aryan Brahmin movement southwards from the Indo-Gangetic plains over a long period in search of arable land is an established fact of Indian history. The history of the land is the history of land grants after the period of the Mauryan empire. The driving force in this movement was the spirit of adventure on the part of the younger sons of the family. It was convenient for the community to have them go out to seek new land under new patrons because that would help them keep the family property undivided. However, by the time they reached Kerala from South Karnataka along the Westcoast, some time about the 7th or 8th century, they had reached the land's end. Another stream of Brahmin immigrants coming through the Eastcoast had already occupied the Tamil lands on the other side of the Sahya ranges. Therefore these Brahmins of the 32 *grama* settlements were forced to discover other outlets for their younger sons if they were to keep their family property undivided.

Since the local communities were matrilineal, the devise of *sambandham* for the younger sons in the families of the local rulers would have been convenient for both sides. For the Brahmins this practice avoided the problem of the claims of the children of younger sons for the family property, and at the same time gave a chance to get entrenched in power as the fathers of the ruling princes and the husbands of the princesses. For the native chiefs it was an opportunity to have the Brahmin seed in the family, to get fair-skinned progeny conversant with the superior Brahminical culture. As the Brahmins of India had already developed an advanced system of science and technology, especially in the fields of agriculture, astronomy, medicine and political economy, it was generally believed that their presence would bring prosperity and power to the rulers and the people. The Chalukyas in Deccan had already provided such a success story that was an object lesson to the rest of South India.

The unique and innovative process of racial and cultural integration evolved in Kerala through Aryan-Tamil race mixture had far-reaching consequences. It created a Kerala Brahmin model different from the Gangetic model. Though they followed the same philosophy and forms of worship, their socio-political organisation moved closer to that of the non-Brahmins, and they were accepted as leaders and masters without serious resistance by the native population with whom they were largely integrated. The notorious Brahmin exclusiveness which had made the *Agraharas* and *Brahmadeyas* into islands surrounded by a hostile native population, and converted their temples into fortresses in Andhra, Karnataka and Tamil Nadu, was not implemented with the same force in Kerala. The Kerala Brahmins adopted the *Sankara Smriti* which deviated from the other *Smritis* and legitimised 64 *anacaras* or anti-rituals which were taboo in other parts of India. Thus a Namputiris-Nayar elite emerged, and this group supervised agricultural activity and conducted the administration in the principalities of Kerala. This Aryan-Tamil synthesis gave birth to the Malayalam language and the Malayalee culture. It was on this foundation of Aryan-Tamil synthesis that the structure of the cultural symbiosis of different communities took shape in due course. Therefore the Brahmin-non-Brahmin conflict which figured prominently in Tamil Nadu and Karnataka did not materialise in Kerala.

Natural Wealth and Human Resources

The above survey would suggest that an aptitude for innovation, openness and tolerance became part and parcel of the Kerala temperament at an early stage. It would also reveal that Kerala had a dual identity. It was a member of the Arabain Sea Community receiving, absorbing and transforming impulses from Europe and West Asia from early historical times. At the same time it also functioned as a regional unit of the Hindu society and culture with some characteristics common to all India and some special attributes. Like other parts of the sub-continent Kerala too received its quota of Brahmin settlements and temples, developed ruling class which promoted Sanskritic learning and culture and re-organised society according to the *Varna* scheme with regional modifications and Brahmin dominance.

The location of the land at the south end of the peninsula, a long seacoast endowed with natural harbours, the trade winds in the Arabian sea which created an Arabian Sea Community of countries, the heavy rains and fertile soil with abundant water supply throughout the land, the protective walls of the Western Ghats which prevented frequent attacks but kept open the channels of trade and culture contacts, and the absence of extremes in climate provided the natural setting for the growth of society in Kerala. In the early historic period these blessings of nature invited settlers who came by land and sea, but in the long run they were counter-productive. They induced complacency and lethargy. A simple style of life close to nature, a ritual-ridden Namputiris-Nayar elite leadership and an elaborate caste system with a feudal political economy were established in the middle ages. The system resisted change for centuries so that only the advent of European colonialism offered the possibility of radical new intiatives.

However, when such a possibility arose, the population of Kerala which, thanks to the principle of culture symbiosis, included a substantial element of Christian and Muslim groups having active links with the dynamic West, was much quicker than the population of most other parts of India to respond positively. They were able to embark on a course of changes which led them to participate in the process of Development taking place in the West and later on in West Asia. Historically speaking, the process of Westernisation was inaugurated in the Vasco de Gama epoch in Kerala in the 16th century, long before the process began to operate in other parts of India in the 18th and the 19th centuries. The integration of the Tamil community with the Aryan settlers through the process of cultural synthesis produced the Nayar community and promoted Sanskritisation, resulting in the emergence of a Kerala identity, complete with its own language and culture, by about the 15th century of the Christian era. The integration of the Christian and Muslim communities with the Kerala social complex through the process of cultural symbiosis paved the way to Westernisation in the modern age. With all our criticism against Colonialism we have to recognise that the impetus given to Westernisation by the Colonial regime opened the door to Modernisation in India as a whole. In Kerala the process started early and developed quickly as there was an indigenous cultural base.

The advent of the Aryan Brahmin settlers from the northern side along the sea coast, the tradition of matrilineal succession among the native communities, the crucial decision of the Brahmin settlers to effect a compromise in their laws which prescribed exclusiveness, the emergence of the Malayalam language and the Malayalee society and culture from an Aryan-Tamil synthesis, the inability to generate large surplus in wealth or centralised State power, the conspicuous development of community self-government in the absence of State supremacy, and the self-sufficiency and self-reliance of individuals and small groups—these are the chief traits of the agrarian order that was established in Kerala by the end of the first millennium of the Christian era.

Alongside the agrarian order and parallel to it a commercial order was also growing up from the early centuries of the Christian era, when maritime contact was established between Kerala and the Roman empire. The swelling population of Syrian Christians who were welcomed and accorded aristocratic status by the rulers looked upon maritime trade as the chief source of revenue. And the Arab Muslims and modern Europeans who followed in their footsteps later on, introduced new elements which established continuous active links with the West and West Asia. The indirect influence of the new egalitarian faiths created an atmosphere conducive to social reform and this resulted in a peaceful and successful anti-caste movement led by the Ezhava saint Sreenarayana. The liberation from caste hierarchy, the craze for social reforms and modern education promoted by the community organisations, the capitalist form of agriculture arising from the land reforms effected by Communists, the taste of industrial development acquired through migration of skilled and unskilled labour into the developed regions—these are some of the prominent items of the social scenario in Kerala today.

Certain features of the settlement patterns and cultural attitudes of Keralites, arising out of proximity to nature have also to be considered. As the bounty of mother earth gave them enough to eat without too much exertion, and protected them from the ravages of climate, and the ocean mother brought them gifts of gold and ideas of change from the other shore, the inhabitants of the land generally cultivated a slow pace of life and a complacent attitude. There were not many rich and powerful people in Kerala on the same level as in other states of India; and not many starving idiots either. The blessings of nature expressed in plentiful water supply, fertile soil and the absence of extremes of climate created a large middle class in traditional society-upper middle class, midddle middle class and lower middle class respectively. People with a small thatched house and a small compound around it were quite self-sufficient as they could survive happily without buying grains or vegetables and without paying huge taxes. They could manage with a single cloth and a change all round the year, and treat an upper cloth as a luxury article. A large number of people were accustomed to a high quality of life in what would appear like poverty in other countries.

The palaces were as big as the middle-class houses elsewhere, the temples were small, the paddy fields were composed of a few acres on the average, and even the chieftains mostly walked barefoot, and usually ate from plantain leaves. With uneven land, criss-crossed by numerous rivers and rivulets, roads and vehicles were not of much use and big armies and big caravans of merchants were not practicable. Small groups of warriors could be hired by traders and pilgrims for safety in travel. Such groups, known as *Cangatam*, guarded the temple properties. Houses including palaces and temples were thatched neatly and strongly with palm leaves or coconut leaves. Rice gruel or cooked rice with vegetables constituted a sumptuous meal even for the great ones. Coconut water formed the national beverage before tea and coffee were imported in the last century. Bananas and coconuts were the offerings to gods and guests alike. These and a number of edible vegetables were available in all seasons in all compounds. The lower castes enjoyed fish and fowl for eating, and palm toddy for a happy drink at the end of the day. Tapioca imported from South America became the staple food of the poor in the 18th century. With palm leaves and small pointed iron rods as writing instruments, literacy was not beyond the reach of people even in remote villages. Wooden planks for sitting and dry grass mats for sleeping were the only furniture needed in the house, though wooden cots were added to them in rich houses.

Bullocks for ploughing the fields, dogs for hunting in the jungles and a few iron-tipped ploughs and sickles constituted the entire wealth of whole villages. Renowned warriors had a few gold ornaments and iron swords and shields and long clothes twisted around the body, but these were lifelong possessions often passed from generation to generation. The personal wealth of the great Zamorin of Calicut or Taccoli Otenan or Kunjali Marakkar celebrated in folksongs and chronicles, would appear as a prescription for poverty in other societies and other ages. Even rich and famous courtesans known as *Koottaccis*, described as heroines in medieval poems like *Unni Neeli* and *Unniyacci*, walked about with one or two servants and performed their dance in small village shrines. Highways were not many, horses were few, and umbrellas made of palm leaves were the order of the day. Men and women usually went half naked, but starving beggars are not reported anywhere. There were no large kingdoms and strong forts in Kerala, and no great urban centres.

In spite of these 'shortcomings', the people maintained a high standard of cleanliness, and education was fairly widespread with community schools run by the writer subcaste of '*Ezhuttacens*'. Weapon practice was imparted in *Kalaris* which also functioned as rural medical centres. Moreover, the *Ayurveda* physicians, including Ezhavas with a Buddhist legacy, were committed to free service for the people as a hereditary occupation. Herbal medicines were picked up from the compounds as and when the need arose. There was no demand for tailors as the climate did not make a lot of stitching compulsory. Proximity to nature and simplicity of life style created a rough equality among the different castes in spite of the rank inequality of castes in rituals and ceremonies. Only the slave castes of Pulayar, Parayar, Cerumar etc. who were considered outcastes, formed an exception to these rules. The rest of Kerala society irrespective of creed or community or means of livelihood enjoyed a decent standard of life.

It is true that important modern gadgets have changed the style of life completely even in villages. Nevertheless, the average Malayalee has inherited the knack of making the best of life with the minimum of material comforts and amenities. The thirst for knowledge and the firm belief that progress is achieved through education is bequeathed to him by his predecessors who had as their model the Namputiris who led a simple life and often devoted his leisure to the cultivation of arts and literature. The Namputiris or Kerala Brahmin who was the husband of Nayar women and the father of the landlords and warriors, could not keep a great distance from the common folk in spite of his ritual purity and superiority complex. Therefore the higher Brahminical culture percolated to large sections of Kshatriyas, Ambalavasis and Nayars and from them to lesser castes, as it had never happened in other parts of India. We may observe that the typical Malayalee added a love of knowledge and inner respect for culture to his openness of mind and readiness to mix with others, wherever he went and whatever he chose.

There are some negative aspects of this Kerala temperament which are also part of the historical legacy and thus equally relevant in a discussion on Development. The people of Kerala had not experienced the impact of centralisation of power in the State before the British rule. As such all their social instincts are tuned to voluntary individual effort, and the intense hero worship and conformity to collective norms found in Tamil Nadu and Karnataka have not figured very much in politics or social life. On the contrary the tendency to criticise and question authority is prominently displayed. At the extreme level this takes the form of cynicism and destructiveness. It is not easy for Keralites to merge their ego in team spirit and work jointly as part of a movement or organisation. The average Malayalee might exceed in personal courage and come out with shining colours in a crisis or emergency, but history has not offered many examples of constructive projects undertaken by big teams over a long period of time.

For the middle-class Malayalees—they easily form the majority in Kerala—it is difficult to come out of traditional lethargy and complacence because he has been accustomed to a life of ease and comfort with very little expenditure of energy. He comes out only when he is driven to a corner with the threat of suffering and starvation. Though lazy, he may become active and highly enterprising, once taken out of the home surroundings. Outside Kerala and outside India the Malayalee is often praised by experts for hard work and enterprise. This paradox may also be traced back to the traditions of social life nurtured in a green paradise of nature.

The Kerala Model of Development: An Explanation

What seems to have surprised and puzzled the economists who formulated the concept of a Kerala model of Development is the fact that in Kerala where very little industrial growth and capital investment are visible, and where the problems of educated unemployment, strike and sabotage discourage large scale organisation and long term planning, the quality of life is almost as high as in the affluent society of Europe and America, in terms of living conditions, educational facilities, and health care. The prosperity and quality of life achieved by large sections of society in Kerala are not easily explained in terms of the laws of development operating in the West and some regions of Asia and Africa. It is with this problem in mind that we have turned to history for possible clues and highlighted the relevant aspects of regional experience.

Looking back into the past we find that as early as the early centuries of the Christian era, Kerala had been sucked into the commercial network of the Roman empire. As the basic conditions which led to this relationship - the Kerala monopoly of pepper and spices in the ancient world and the convenient trade winds which carried the sailing vessels across the Arabian sea - continued for many centuries, pockets of Christian and Muslim communities were created in Kerala. Thanks to the special character of the polity and society in Kerala, with its water surplus households and compounds constituting a single big chain of undemarcated open villages, and the small size of the principalities waiting for foreign guests to enrich them, these new communities were pampered and sustained and permitted to be fully integrated in the native community life. This was made possible by the leadership of an innovative Brahmin group which created an Aryan-Tamil synthesis and went ahead to promote the principle of cultural symbiosis among the heterogeneous communities who came to settle down in Kerala.

The net result is that Kerala, the tiny, overpopulated, underdeveloped, southern State on the westcoast of the Indian peninsula, is geographically and politically part of India, but economically and culturally very much part of the affluent society of the West and West Asia. The ethnic, religious, linguistic and cultural links binding big chunks of the Kerala population to the First World are very strong, but invisible to a professional economist who is not familiar with the strange history of Kerala and the pattern of distribution of its population throughout the world today. As a result of certain historical trends a disproportionately and unbelievably large part of the earning population is scattered all over the globe. Their impact on Kerala economy and society has to be taken into account in a serious study. The society in Kerala has now become practically an extension of the First World society across oceans and political frontiers. Twentieth century capitalism, with its new series of industrial revolutions, has already made political maps and geographical configurations largely irrelevant or deceptive in the study of economic and sociological trends. The active links which a large section of Kerala population is having with the developed world through immigration and communication, through money transfer and dissemination of knowledge, has now made Kerala, more than many other parts of India, a commercial and industrial appendage of the West and West Asia.

In this context any consideration of the question of development in Kerala economy should ignore the conventional idea of

Kerala as a small insignificant entity on the geographical and political map of India, and discuss it in terms of the distribution of Kerala population, their family connections and the flow of money and consumer goods through legal and illegal transactions. There are a large number of Keralites outside Kerala in the First World countries, in comparison with the number of those within Kerala. Several thousands of Keralite families are divided in space, half of their members living in Kerala and the other half making money outside. A good part of the money earned by Keralites abroad flows regularly into Kerala creating almost a parallel economy. Whether this is wisely invested in Kerala or outside is another problem, outside the scope of the present enquiry, but the fact that a portion of it is distributed in the market and the service sector is important here. It generates economic activity and increases the quality of life. Just as many well-trained Kerala technicians, doctors, engineers, scientists and teachers are working, earning and living in the First World, a good number of Keralites, who are foreign-trained experts, are doing so in Kerala. A good majority of those Keralites who are outside not only send money, but construct houses, invest in projects and shares, and prepare to come back to settle down eventually in Kerala. Therefore any social-scientific study of Kerala, especially an economic study, has to take the non-resident Keralites and resident Keralites together as a single unit for the purpose of the formulation of concepts and principles.

Those non-resident Keralite Indians are part of the Kerala economy and society in practice. The industries and business and all kinds of market operations in which they participate have their impact on Kerala and Keralites. For all practical purposes they are part of the First World and they have made their land, where they have their heart, home and money, affiliated to the First World. The productive concerns in which they work may not be located in Kerala state, but their profits and ideas return to Kerala in spite of the geographical distance. Kerala enjoys the privilege of being part of the affluent world in economic and social terms, with the advantage that it is less crowded and less polluted for the dependants and relatives of the non-resident Keralites. A survey of history helps us to understand the way in which, and the circumstances through which, Kerala has become a junior partner in the development process and the affluence of the First World.

In other words the socio-economic system of Kerala is not merely a matter of recent growth, but the roots of certain trends are found hidden in the remote past. This would sound like a platitude but it needs to be highlighted in view of the obsession with a narrow concept of economic determinism, combined with the conventional notion of discussing issues of Development within geographical and political boundaries. The belief that there is only one path for Development, the path followed by the Western pioneers in this field, has to be discarded, though the paramount influence of the West cannot be ignored. Perhaps it is necessary for us to reiterate in this connection the basic premise of modern social science that economics, history, sociology, anthropology etc. are not separate sciences but only branches of a single large social science. It is only by the combined use of the methods and findings of the different branches that we are able to comprehend the complex phenomenon of Development in a global sense. The variations in the character and course of Development are the contribution of the empirical situation in each region, controlled by natural resource potential and historical experience. The case of Kerala provides a good illustration of this principle. Knowledge of the currents of history may help us to channelise its flow in certain ways, even though the mainstream defies our attempts to divert its course.

Two

EVERYDAY AND THE AVANT-GARDE

The Contexts of Modernism in Malayalam Literature

K. SATCHIDANANDAN

'Everyday'—an inadequate yet useful translation of the French term *la quotidienne*—contributed by Henri Lefebvre to the conceptual vocabulary of Marxist thought—refers to that which repeats itself consistently in daily life, something excluded by most philosophers of the West—from Plato to Hegel—from serious consideration. Henri Lefebvre in philosophy and James Joyce in literature explored this dimension of daily life that Marx in spite of his orientation towards it could not explore, completely preoccupied as he was with the domain of labour and of capital. 'Everyday', Lefebvre says, is a kind of screen that both shows and hides, reveals both what has and has not changed. It is what Hegel called 'The prose of the world' something considered unworthy of study like labour before Marx, or libido before Freud. The 'everyday' is first a modality of extending the capitalist mode of production, that once established, integrates industry, agriculture, the historical city, and the space and produces everyday life; secondly it is also a modality of administering society. The predominance of the repetitive here becomes a way of life, a base of exploitation and domination, a relation with the world and with human being. Repetition marks and suppresses the fear of death, a major reason for the success of the instituting of everyday in the modern world. It dissimulates the tragic; this tragic period hides from itself the tragedy it lives. It satisfies the very needs it produces on the one hand and on the other provokes a malaise, a profound dissatisfaction, an aspiration for something else. Thus the concept is not an object constructed according to certain epistemological rules, nor is it apprehended by a deconstruction of reality. It is *le vecu* (lived experience) elevated to the status of a concept and to language. This is done not to accept it but to change it, for this everyday is modifiable and transformable and its transformation must be an important part of any project for society. Any resolution should change not just the political personnel and institutions but the everyday life colonized by capitalism. Culture too is part of this everyday, at least in our time, for it is not merely a state palimpsest of texts, it is livid and active, 'a sleeping beauty who dozes not on flowers or fragrant grass but on a thin mattress of texts, quotations and musical scores under a vast canopy of books and theses : the coming of the prince awakens her and everything in the forest comes to life along with her' (H. Lefebvre : 'Toward a Leftist Cultural Politics : Remarks Occasioned by the Centenary of Marx's Death' in Carp Nelson and Lawrence Grossberg (ed.) *Marxism and the Interpretation of Culture,* London, 1988).

Such an awakening took place in the history of Kerala's everyday only in the early decades of the twentieth century. Till then Kerala's everyday was impregnated with ritual, custom and code. The body was considered an extension of nature and even social codes of exploitation and dividing practices were identified with the laws of nature. Everything immediately given was considered legitimate, unquestionable, inescapable. Caste, sub-caste, landlordism and royalty were considered ordained by nature, fate or God. The city could hardly be distinguished from the village and the machine, from the tool. The oil-press and the farmer's wheel were close to the carpenter's hammer and the pulley at the well. The 'literary' in the period is dominated by the sacred and the mythical, the popular articulations of everyday life existing as a parallel stream dubbed 'folk' poetry. The poetry of Ezhuthachan, Chereussery, Poonthanam or Unnayi Variyar refuses to deal directly with everyday though the situations and passions expressed in them do have a universal human core. A work like *Jnanappana* can only come from the observation of the ways of the world, and Sita, Yashoda or Damayanti have something prototypical about their states and fates. Kunchan Nampiar is one poet, who, probably inspired by the folk, enlivens his puranic narratives with humorous interpolations of the contemporary everyday. The 'author' was yet to emerge as a category, as literature was seldom recognized as 'literatures' in its present sense; it was ritual, performance and entertainment.

'Literature' and 'the author' emerge as definite categories only with the formation of the public sphere in Kerala that was part of general democratic movement of dissent, reform and awakening. This Renaissance began as a self-criticism of the feudal caste society. The dividing practices that concealed exploitation and inequality behind the masks of the natural and the providential now became visible and came to be identified in their inhuman shapes. The placid surface of the everyday suddenly became turbulent as almost every caste was looking at itself in relation to those above and those below, trying to purge itself of evil customs and practices, to abolish or weaken the sub-caste system and educate itself in modern knowledge and useful crafts. All castes were involved in this upheaval though the main thrust was subaltern as only the truly oppressed led by Sree Narayana Guru or Ayyankali alone were capable of thinking in terms of a casteless society which to the 'upper' castes would mean deprivileging and loss of dominance. Sree Narayana's success lay in his recognition of the relationship between discourse and power, his subtle reversal of the significance of the oppressor's legitimating discourse through a secular reading of their sacred texts and a subversive use of their signs, symbols and images that together transformed Kerala's everyday making visible the till-now invisible mechanisms of division and tyranny. The formation of the Indian National Congress with its total disavowal of colonialism produced the first line of truly secular intellectuals in Kerala from Swadeshabhimani Ramakrishna Pillai and K. Kelappan to K.P. Kesava Menon and Mohammad Abdu Rahman and later the first socialist intellectuals like A.K. Gopalan, Comrade Krishna Pillai, K.P.R. Gopalan and E.M.S. Namboodiripad. This double renaissance ushered in the second modern phase of everyday in Kerala's popular history: bodies were no more bound by the labours, spaces and distances ordained by caste. Everyday was a site of democratic conflicts and resolutions from which came up a public sphere of debate and consensus. Literature was now constituted as a specific category; the authorial institution was built up along with a new critical academy that came up with norms and standards gained especially from the Sanskrit and English classics that came to be widely translated into Malayalam in those days. Together they consolidated 'the aesthetic' as a specific realm of culture that had a mediated relationship with the everyday and transformed literature from the sacral to the secular. The condification of grammar and translations, especially that of Holy Bible, helped the growth of style in prose, original epics and verse narratives that often had an oblique relationship with reality were complemented by novels, short stories and essays that often took off directly from the lived experience of the society. Ulloor's *History of Malayalam Literature,* the poetical works of Vallathol and Kumaran Asan, the novels of C.V. Ramanpillai and O. Chandumenon, organisations like Bhashaposhini Sabha and Sahitya Parishad and journals like *Swadheshabhimani, Kerala Patrika, Kesari, Mangalodayam* and *Bhashaposhini* along with the translations of ancient and modern classics activated the growth of the public sphere helped on by the spread of modern education and printing technology. Literature was released from its ritual use with the undermining of traditional word pictures by the basic ideology of fair exchange.

The anti-feudal struggles led by the Congress Socialists and the Communists added a class dimension to the struggles of the everyday as well as literature. The notion of class as applied to history, politics and culture, in however primary and simplistic a way, helped to re-orient the forces of renaissance towards a resurgence of the marginalised, mobilised for the first time on a non-caste basis, that of class. While it is true that Kerala's Communist Movement later developed links with Pan-Indian and international working class movements, it was in itself an indigenous democratic phenomenon with its roots sunk deep in the social reform and anti-colonial movements of Kerala in the early decades of the century: a fact that explains its resilience and endurance even in the era of the confusion and collapse of international communism. The ideas of class struggle that flourished in the already upturned cultural soil of Kerala also came to influence literature. The relationship between what came to be loosely called the 'Progressive Movement' in literature and the overall process of Kerala's societal movement towards socialism and secular democracy is more one of structural over-determination than of synchrony. The *Jeevat Sahitya* movement launched in 1937 can properly be considered the first avant-garde movement in Malayalam literature, for, like all avant-garde movements, it not only changed the modes of literary expression but tried to re-define the norms and canons of literature ultimately interrogating the institution of literature itself. Its aim was to promote "a literature that changes with the changing life to express reality in novel modes free from the burden of the mystical past and a philosophy that fights reactionary views about religion, society, sexuality, family and war." The organisation considered "everything that provokes a critical revaluation of systems and institutions from the point of view of the common interest of the majority of mankind" to be progressive and "everything that drags man into inertia and lifelessness" as reactionary. By the time the first conference of the Progressive Writers' Association was held after seven years almost every major writer in Kerala—poets like Vallathol, Changampuzha, and G. Sankarakurup, fiction writers like Basheer, Thakazhi, Karoor, S.K. Pottekkat, Kesava Dev and Ponkunnam Varkey and critics like Joseph Mundassery and M.P. Paul besides fellow travellers and communist activists like K. Damodaran, Cherukad, D.M. Pottekkat, M.S. Devadas, Kedamangalam Pappukkutty, Primji and others had been won over by the Movement whose roots, again, lay in the renaissance writers like Kumaran Asan, V.T. Bhattathiripad, K.P.Karuppan and Sree Narayana himself. The Movement captured the everyday in all its energy and diversity: the writers used different idioms even while they shared the same concerns. Whole sections of people sentenced to the culture of silence spoke through these writers many of whom were liberals inspired by Gandhi and Lenin alike. Landless peasants, fishermen, untouchables, the rural poor, impoverished craftsmen, men and women forced into begging and prostitution and urban workers: all these subaltern layers of society found a place in literature for the first time after the age of the folklore. This change of content engendered a stylistic transformation. In poetry it appeared chiefly as a replacement of Sanskrit metres by Dravidian and folk metres and rhythms and a considerable reduction of the Sanskrit element in the vocabulary. In creative prose it meant the introduction of a strong dialectal element borrowed especially from the marginalised classes, castes and minorities and the consequent disavowal of the laboured linguistic sublimity of earlier fictional modes. In short it privileged realism against mysticism in both content and style. Writers like Vailoppilly, Idassery and Uroob who stood mostly outside the movement also could not but respond to the new social and literary ferment. By 1948 the broad consensus-perspective that had held writers of various persuasions together in the Movement gave way to sectarian views of commitment to the partyline. Calls for formal vigour were wrongly condemned by the champions of contentism as decadent formalism and aestheticism that finally led to a split in the Movement. The theoreticians of the Progressive Movement failed to see the relative autonomy of literature as a level of the cultural formation with its own history and its own rules of formal evolution. They equated literature with ideology and considered it a direct expression of the author's personal ideology thus unknowingly subscribing to the idealist theories of expressivity. They underrated the importance of the context, intent and ideology of reading that can make the work appear socially irrelevant or appropriate it for social transformation. Their opponents too lacked self-understanding in so far as they did not recognize the radical potential of their writing. Writers like Vailoppilly, Idassery of Uroob who had a rather tense relationship with the Movement were in fact much more progressive than K.P.G. Kedamangalam or D.M. Pottekkat with their explicit commitment, for, the former revealed more extensively, deeply and innovatively the complex contradictions of the multi-layered society.

Industrial capitalism never made its real debut in Kerala: yet the capitalist value systems, norms and perspectives on life and literature had begun to penetrate Kerala's everyday by this time. The forces of renaissance had weakened, turned conservative and status-quoist, leaving enough space for the values of acquisition, greed and consumerism to influence life. The old life however remained underneath as a subterranean force at times disrupting the rhythms of modern life. At times it evoked nostalgia as in the poetry of P. Kunhiraman Nair, at times it was built into an utopian project for an egalitarian future as in that of Vailoppilly or was caught in its morbidity, incest, decadence, anger and conflict with the modern as in the fiction of M.T. Vasudevan Nair. The obscurantists found a rallying point in their opposition to the first communist movement in the State: they feared the impact of the land-reform movement and of educational reforms. The emergence of the second, modernist, avant-garde in Malayalam literature roughly coincides with this period of middle class discontent resisted alike by progressive as well as feudal forces. By the time the whole of Kerala society was on the path of 'middle classing': the land reform, education and the standardisation of comforts had turned the everyday of the Malayali into the average of the social practice of the middle classes, of course, with a supra-everyday level lived by the upper classes and an infra-everyday level lived by peasants, tribals and others. The middle classes could not identify themselves with either of these classes and found themselves left to float in an uncertain time-world where their identity is problematised and existence is played out through alter-lives constructed in imagination. At the same time, the countryside and the town had become one big semi-urban continuum in Kerala. Modernism—in Malayalam fiction especially—came mostly from the Malayali diaspora in the big Indian cities. Fiction writers like O.V. Vijayan, Kakkanadan, M. Mukundan, V.K.N., M.P. Narayana Pillai, Paul Zachariah and Sethu and poets like Madhavan Ayyappath, M.N. Paloor and Kadammanitta lived in Delhi, Bombay or Madras, away from the social reality of Kerala, a sure basis for their feeling of loss and alienation. Most of them came from the villages and had a past of communist activism or sympathy. The gradual deadening of progressive sensibilities, the revelations about Stalinism and the Zhadanovist dogmatism of Kerala Marxist critics had together estranged them from Marxism that they began to identify with totalitarian tyranny. If communism was a God that failed, it was darkness also at the Congress-noon since the party was as distant from Gandhian ideals as could be. In literature, the Progressive Movement appeared a lost cause: naturalism in fiction and romanticism in poetry were fast losing their charm and usefulness. The paperback revolution had also acquainted these writers with the modernist experiments in Europe in which they found models that would save them from the new aesthetic impasse. E.V. Ramakrishnan in his recent book 'Making it New : Modernism in Malayalam, Marathi and Hindi poetry' has characterised the first phase of modernism—of the late 50s and the 60s—as 'high modernism' as different from the avant-gardist modernism that emerged in the 70s. It would be wrong to consider the early modernists aestheticists and status-quoists since the deep despair, anger and irony in Ayyappa Paniker, N.N. Kakkad, Attoor Ravivarma or Kadammanitta Ramakrishnan came from their scepticism regarding the system. We have to see the modernism in Malayalam as an indigenous literary phenomenon despite certain Western influences which Malayalam literature has always been under. It was unfortunate that it got interpreters like K.P. Appan who were entirely Eurocentric in their approach and mechanically applied Western paradigms and rubrics to the modernist works in Malayalam. E.V. Ramakrishnan also seems to apply Peter Burger's distinction between the aestheticist high-modernists and the radical avant-gardists to the two phases of modernism in Malayalam with little consideration for their specific historical contexts. The difference between the two phases—both of which I consider avant-gardist—it seems to me, lies in the modes and premises of their criticism of society: the first phase attempted a liberal-humanist critique while the second adopted more radical stances. Both questioned the literary institution in different ways. The black humour and irony characteristic of a lot of writing of the sixties are instruments that attempt to subvert not only the social order but the literary order too. They were after forms that would best express the structures of their modern subjectivity. Discontinuity, the foregrounding of the signifier, use of irony and black humour, the employment of various masks, the metophoric as different from metonymic modes of writing, re-visioning of myths and archetypes, surrealism, fantasy and experimental syntax and structuration were strategies employed for this purpose. Strategies and attitudes varied from author to author and from text to text. The self-confident subject of idealistic cognition theory conceives himself as self-present and regards language as the belated embodiment and representation of a content previously present in his own consciousness, but the subject of modernism looks at language as a medium of self-discovery rather than self-expression. Literature here negates ossified linguistic and mental cliches that are the results of instrumental rationality. The asocial in art, as Adorno says, is the definite negation of a definite society. Whereas the novels of Vijayan, Kakkanadan, Mukundan and Sethu and the stories of Zachariah and M.P. Narayana Pillai negate values to the point of anarchy, the poems of Ayyappa Paniker (e.g. 'Mrutyupooja', 'Cartoon poems') or Kadammanitta negate the present order through irony or anger. In another set of works like the non-sense poems of Kunjunni, M. Givindan, N. N. Kakkad and Ayyappa Paniker and the self-reflexive stories of V.K.N Zachariah or V.P. Shivakumar, the very institution of literature is subjected to criticism. Like the works of Dadaists in Europe, they criticise not any school that preceded them but literature itself with its established notions of what it should be. Whereas during the period of realism, the development of art was felt to lie in the growing closeness of representation to the everyday in this phase of self-criticism. The one-sidedness of this construction becomes visible. Realism comes to be understood not as the principle of artistic creation but as the sum of certain period procedures (Peter Berger: *Theory of the Avant-garde*). Habermas's characterisation of art as a sanctuary for the—perhaps merely cerebral—satisfaction of those needs which become quasi-illegal in the material life-process of bourgeois society's needs like the 'mimetic commerce with nature' and 'the happiness of a communicative experience not subject to the imperatives of means-ends rationality and allows as much scope to the imagination as to the spontaneity of behaviour' may well explain the playful element in the modernist Malayalam writing of the first phase.

They were reacting to the "flat, opaque and prosaic nature of our public speech where the practical end of communication spoils the quality of expressive means" (Renato Poggicli, *Avant-Garde and the Kitsch,* 1939). The function of their new, often dark, language was at once therapeutic and cathartic in respect to the degeneration afflicting common language. They were also the first to respond adequately to the complexification of the everyday experience in Kerala's society, react violently to the sexual repression characteristic of the Malayali psyche, and to take up the ontological—rather than metaphysical—anxieties and uncertainties that confront contemporary existence. Modernism in Malayalam grew directly out of our own pre-modern writings (e.g. K. Ayyappa Paniker is impossible without the poets before him from Kunchan Nambiar to Vailoppilly, or O.V. Vijayan without Basheer, and Uroob): its angst was not derivative but was deeply rooted in the perplexities of Kerala's intelligensia confronted with the issues of self-subjectivisation, the crisis of idealism in national life and the repression of desire. The libidinal-political fiction of the sixties are certain stammering attempts to articulate some silenced aspects of Malayali middle class life in the background of their political uncertainty and doubt; their apparent ahistoricity is a call for the historicisation of those deeper aspects of existence suppressed by or unrepresented in the era of progressivism, and their sensuous language that glows with desire is a tool to express the complicity between politics and sex or desire and transcendence. The paradigmatic texts of modernism like-wise reflected the mood of the radical left. A critique of everyday that turned the historical time into reflected time in the circles of home and of fellow-radicals, an expression of middle class intellectuals's sense of guilt and self-ridicule, a direct criticism of upper class institutions and mentalities and a mediated articulation of the torments and dreams of the lower classes, a satirisation of the complacent old Left that seemed to have compromised: such were the orientations of the writing of the seventies that also had built into it a critique of the liberal-humanist modernist avant-garde of the sixties. The paradigmatic avant-garde texts of the seventies like *Allopanishad* (Pattathuvila) *Thookkumarangal Nhangalkku* (*Gallows for Us*, M. Sukumaran), *Bengal* (K.G. Sankara Pillai), *Pani* (*Fever*, K. Satchidanandan), *Samkramanam* (*Transformation*, Attoor Ravivarma) and *Santha* (Kadammanitta) have everyday built into them and transformed into the site of historic struggles. The radicals inspired by the ideas of Third World revolution represented an internal critique of modernism, in an era of the increasing commodification of life and literature, and of the colonisation of the popular unconscious by pulp fiction, commercial cinema, television soaps and advertisements that resolved contradictions among the people and fulfilled their wishes by easy, imaginary means. Everyday was coming increasingly under the grip of the culture industry whose invisible *weltenschauungs*, hyperreal images and stereotypes had penetrated deep into the perceptions of everyday. The popular film and fiction sought to divide the world into a public space dominated by men and a private space reserved for women. Women increasingly became the show-piece and the object of desire. Even employment and the unitary family have only made women's lives more helpless and leisureless. They not only continue to be under-represented in democratic bodies but continue to be assigned roles in public life that are only extensions of their domestic work. This also coincides with the onslaught on environment by various agencies from the timber-mafia to the tourist trade. The neorich culture of opulence without content, the spread of alcoholism that cuts across classes, the rapid increase in sexual, communal and political violence, the high rates of morbidity and suicide also seem to be the symptoms and products of a larger social malaise generated by unemployment, loss of identity, economic uncertainty and social discontent prompted especially by the new disparities created by foreign remittances. A society where class mobility is decided by sheer chance rather than by intelligence, industry or efficiency, is the ideal earth for irrationalism, fantasy and surrealism. The magical and the grotesque that dominate Kerala's literary sensibility today is perhaps an indirect reflection of Kerala's bizzarely comic reality on creative and critical imagination. No wonder Marquez, Borges, Calvino, Kafka and Rushdie find a ready and unsurprised clientele in Kerala.

This complex and contradictory reality of the everyday in contemporary Kerala seems to have made a monolithic avant-garde impossible and inadequate in its literature. The struggle is no more on a single front, but is transversal and multifaceted. While the old 'progressive' avant-garde continues to bring forth new talents, it has lost its monopoly over commitment as radicalism is no more confined to the class front alone. Today's avant-garde appears to have more than one organising principle. The most significant of them is gender. Women's writing in Kerala seems to have come a long way from Lalitambika Antarjanam, K. Saraswati Amma and Rajalakshmi. While Madhavikkutty (Kamala Das) still continues to be the finest exponent of the feminine psyche with its long-borne scars and unfulfilled longings, the new generation fiction writers like Sarah Joseph, Manasi, Ashita, Gracy and Chandramati appear more self-conscious in their effort to fight the 'phallogocentric' social order. So are the later Sugata Kumari, Vijayalakshmi, Savitri Rajeevan, V. M. Girija and others in poetry. They are after a new libidinal economy and a counter language, a 'mother-tongue' that is capable of transcending male rationality. Some of them indulge in revisionist myth-making that attempts a deconstructive reversal of the patriarchal logic of status-quoist myths. Sarah Joseph in short story and Vijayalakshmi in poetry have taken up situations from *Ramayana* and the *Bible* along with popular legends for a feminist re-interpretation. Women's writing in Kerala appears more like a wish-fulfilment than a reflection of reality since the actual state of women at home and in the work-place remains unchanged or has even become worse if one goes by the increasing number of gang-rapes and export of women for flesh-trade while the women's movement continues to be weak and fragmented, and the old canons of life and literature continue unchallenged. Even the aggressive treatment of women as mere objects of desire in some paradigmatic modern novels like *The Legends of Khasak* has not been sufficiently interrogated; this is also true of the actual treatment of women in social life. Still the women writers seem to be the only collective avant-garde in contemporary Malayalam literature while there are many individual writers who have taken radical avant-garde stances. Anand ever questioning history and reality from the victim's gray margin and N.S. Madhavan who reacts intensely to the morbid, the schizoid and the rabidly communalised aspects of outer and inner life are two such writers who continue to interrogate reality and art in innovative modes and metaphors. K.G. Sankara Pillai's anti-colonial stance as that of Attoor Ravivarma in poetry with its ecological and regional political implications is another instance of individual avant-gardism. The post-cognitive and ontological questions about the self and the world, and the confrontation of different worlds that seem central to post-modernism are yet to be taken up seriously by the majority of our writers who seem to stop at the surface of the everyday and not to see its seething insides. However, literature today seems to concern itself more with the micro-politics of everyday than with the macro-politics of the State taking up questions of identity, gender hegemony, eco-fascism and the communalisation of individuals and institutions. In political terms, the axis seems to be shifting from the commitment to a one-dimensional revolution to an anxious concern for all forms of structural oppression and a faith in micro-revolutions waged simultaneously on a hundred fronts. The polyphonic textuality of the new literature is possibly a product of this multi-dimensional engagement with a hydra-headed reality.

THREE

FROM REGION TO NATION AND BEYOND

Allegories of Power in Malayalam Fiction

E.V. RAMAKRISHNAN

Novels, as narratives, contribute towards projecting a shared sense of the community. Apart from representing social reality, novels or fictional narratives in general also exercise social control by projecting symbols and modes of life into the life of the community, particularly in those less easily defined but basic areas such as norms, values, and personal and interpersonal behaviour' (Joan Rockwell, 1974:4). The manner in which fiction intervenes in the ideological sphere of choice related to the problems of daily living makes it an important source material for monitoring social trends. Since Kerala has achieved a high degree of literacy, it has a sizeable reading public for whom the novel remains the most popular and accessible form of literature. Categories such as 'region', 'nation', 'class' and 'culture' are constructed in the popular imagination of the reading public as much through their involvement in the imaginative narratives of fictional works as through their engagement with reality. The present chapter attempts to examine the manner in which the nation-region dialectic operates in Malayalam fiction.

The first significant novel in Malayalam, *Indulekha*, published in 1889, indirectly refers to the political process that informs the social transformation in a premodern society. One of the major themes in *Indulekha* is that of education which implies the acquisition of a new identity that alters the relationship between the individual and social institutions. During this period the nation as a secular modern State is not defined in political terms. The evils of the colonial power structure are not confronted in this phase as the accent is on the benevolent aspects of colonial education and the resultant thrust to social reforms. In fact, the author of *Indulekha* has recorded that the novel was written at the request of some of his acquaintances who were eager to listen to the stories of English novels. This new narrative, thus, articulates a cultural space which is progressive, vaguely nationalist and modern. In the discourse of social reforms that underlines the central conflict between tradition and modernity, the nation as a political entity in the making can be discerned. This is testified by the controversial 18th chapter of the novel which carries a debate on several issues such as atheism, English education and the Indian National Congress. The relevance of this digressive discussion lies in the fact that it integrates into the plot "the vital issues Indian society faced at that time." (K.N. Panikkar, 1995 : 144).

Here it may be recalled that there has been intimate transaction between periodical journalism and the novel. In the late 19th century the appearance of several journals in Malayalam points to the emergence of a new type of subjectivity in the society. Under the editorship of C. Kunhirama Menon, a journal called *Kerala Patrika* was started from Calicut in 1885. *Malayali* was started in 1886 from Trivandrum, under the editorship of C.V. Raman Pillai and *Malayala Manorama* started in 1890 from Kottayam. All these journals contributed towards the deepening self-awareness of the literate middle class which came to be increasingly mobilised both politically and socially. The names of these periodicals call attention to the regional identity of Kerala and its linguistic homogeneity is recognised as an important factor contributing towards its political destiny. The subjectivity which is fostered by regional narratives at this stage is both inclusive and progressive in that it views the larger collectivity of the nation as an extension of the region.

In the first half of this century several popular movements in Kerala energized the social scene. The region and the nation became inextricably intertwined in the twenties as issues such as casteism, the hegemony of the upper castes, the rights of peasants and workers got incorporated into the nationalist struggle for freedom. The nationalist romantic phase in literature has produced memorable works in poetry. The idealistic nature of this phase may be largely responsible for its lesser impact on fiction. But by the thirties this idealistic view integrating the region and the nation came under severe strain. In fact the rise of the progressive movement and the social realist mode coincided with a moment of disenchantment with the nationalist movement. By 1938, landless peasants, teachers and factory workers began to organize themselves locally. Their militant struggles emphasized the primacy of the region over the nation. Progressive literary movement, though inspired by the ideals of the October Revolution and the models of European realism, has used art as a means of mobilizing the less privileged sections of society. The novels written by Thakazhi, Basheer and Pottekkat remind us that inherent in the term 'nation' is 'the natio' which means a local community, domicile, family, conditions of belonging'. Solidarity is always established at the subliminal layer of organic relationships.

A novel like The *Scavenger's Son* published in 1947 charts the slow emergence of political consciousness among the oppressed. Chudalamuthu the main character realizes much later in his life that his acquisitiveness and dreams of upward mobility are self-defeating unless the power structure that generates scavengers changes. Thakazhi writes: "It is not scavengers who create scavengers. Even if a father thinks a child should not become a scavenger, that child might become one" (Thakazhi, 1947: 110). From Chudalamuthu to his son Mohanan, the society has moved a long way. Mohanan tells his friends: "In reality, it is not the individual boss who is the worker's enemy. It is the boss's government" (*ibid*). Mohanan dies a martyr in the cause of a revolutionary dream. What makes *The Scavenger's Son* a moral fable is its emphatic statement about the need for workers or peasants to organize themselves to be heard.

The same theme has been treated in Basheer's novels differently. Both Thakazhi and Basheer seem to be asking the question, 'whose nation is it anyway?' Basheer's *Voices* also published in 1947, is an angry book that articulates the anguish and the violence at the very root of the concept of modern nation. In his extensive journeys through the length and breadth of the country' Basheer had witnessed the turbulence of Indian society. *Voices* is born of the realization that the modern State is a monolithic violent entity that will have no place for the marginalized and the homeless. The disjointed narrative is made up of drifting voices from the world of tramps, criminals and prostitutes. The central voice is that of an ex-soldier afflicted by venereal disease who is haunted by the deprivation of the life he has led. He has no means of relating himself to any idealistic notions of a popular nation-state. The hallucinatory nature of this narrative metaphorically sums up the existential choices that have to be made before the moral conscience of the nation can be reclaimed.

If Basheer and Thakazhi represent the marginalized, disenfranchised voices that are yet to find a place in the scheme of the nascent nation-state, the barrack stories of Kovilan confront the fact of the state in all its post-colonial complexity. The army's fiercely hierarchical world replicates the divisions of our society into the elitist officers and the subaltern sepoys. The speaking voice of the barrack stories is literally that of the subaltern made up of landless peasants and the lower class rural youth educated in vernacular medium. These jawans are firmly rooted in their cultures and feel suffocated in the alienating atmosphere of the colonial structure of the army. The anxieties and struggles that attend ordinary living beings leave them no time to comprehend the larger national contexts in which they fulfil politically defined roles. The nation as a culturally defined ideal is at variance with the post-colonial reality of the ruthless nation-state. A novel such as Kovilan's *Himalayam* demystifies the mythical associations of the snow-clad mountain peaks which turn out to be killing fields for those who worship the mystique of the divine Himavat. What Kovilan's barrack stories demonstrate is the colonial nature of our post-colonial institutions. A jawan is a smouldering volcano held in check by his poverty and the oppressive nature of the hierarchical structure of the army establishment.

The barrack stories by Kovilan written during the fifties mark a stage where the contradictions between the people and the nation are deepening into a crisis. In the fictional works of M.T. Vasudevan Nair, N.P. Muhammad, T. Padmanabhan and Madhavi Kutty, the displaced individual looms large over the narrative. M.T. has been particularly successful in narrativizing the self-formation of the rural youth trapped in the competitive urban world where the value system is alien and ruthless. No writer in Malayalam has explored the depressing world of defeat and despair, its suppressed rage and gnawing self-pity with such psychological precision. M.T. figures in this discussion mainly for his graphic portrayal of the oppressive sense of decay that fills broken homes. The drifting, lonely individual at the heart of his fictional world recognizes no collectivities and has no allegiance to the larger, extended familial bonds. In *Kalam,* Sethu is haunted by the emptiness of his success gained at the cost of betraying all those who loved and trusted him. The central theme of M.T.'s best fiction is the corruption and disruption of domestic space. Since man's social self is primarily constituted in the domestic sphere, this corruption leads to the disintegration of society. In these chronicles of homeless exiles and introvert rebels, the earliest intimations of modernism can be discerned. Their distrust of political action is a pointer towards the failure of organized movements.

In the post-1960 period, the proletarian base of radical political movements gets progressively eroded as the lower ranges of the bureaucracy, petty traders and various groups of highly paid artisans begin to control the decision-making apparatus of these organizations. The stories of Pattathuvila Karunakaran and M. Sukumaran probe this growing gulf between 'the *langue* of the law and the *parole* of the people' (Homi Bhabha, 1990: 2). Themes of betrayal and sacrifice recur in their stories as they feel that the dilution of ideological fervour forced upon popular movements by an acquisitive middle class originates from a deeper attitude of cynicism. In the extended allegories of M. Sukumaran, the role of the State as a repressive apparatus and the victimized state of the marginalised sections is forcefully portrayed. The modernist writers of the 60s and 70s are haunted by the bad faith born of double consciousness—their felt need to transcend and transform the given and their awareness of the erosion of the social solidarity that can activate social change. Writers like O.V. Vijayan, Anand and M. Mukundan have critically dealt with this ideological vacuum.

O.V. Vijayan's novel *The Saga of Dharmapuri* and his stories collected in *After the Hanging and other Stories* track down questions of ideology involved in the day-to-day business of living. Vijayan's grotesque world has a strong sense of the malevolent that pervades our society. In *The Wart* what begins as a mole-like growth on the face of the narrator grows into a defiant and invincible tumour, the size of a coconut and finally becomes a cancerous ulcer with its own independent will. When the wart finally falls off his body, the narrator is reduced to a worm. What the story allegorically shows is how the violent experience of the Emergency had radically altered the optics of relation between the individual and the State. In the post-colonial period the nation has become a massive bureaucratic apparatus that has absolute control of its human resources. The nationalist discourse legitimizes itself by invoking the spectre of chaos and fragmentation. In *Dharmapuranam* Vijayan deconstructs the genteel ironic mode of mimetic fiction to subvert the nationalist discourse based on a patriarchal concept of order and stability. Vijayan's erotic and scatological metaphors point to the violation of the individual's solitude which is the first moral code to be broken when fascist tendencies surface in the State. The life-giving libido degenerates into a massive desecration of the body. This collectivization and consequent brutalisation of the State is the subject of Anand's *How Deserts Originate.* In this novel the novelist remarks that culture basically is accountability but in post-colonial India it has become accounting. Anand suggests that deserts originate in the human minds corrupted by absolute power. The novels of Anand do not identify with any region. In its delocalised narrative and prosaic language devoid of metaphorical flourishes, Anand conveys the centrality of rationality in his treatment of contemporary history.

In his most recent novel *Govardhan's Journeys* Anand records the sordid tales of a variety of characters drawn from history, mythology, literature and real life in search of justice and human dignity. The sagas of their sufferings attest to the built-in violence of our social and political institutions which have become insensitive to the popular aspirations and human values.

In the post-1960 period the relation between the nation and the region has been rendered problematic by several forces of mediation. The first of these is the internalization of metropolitan attitudes and mindset. Novels such as Mukundan's *Delhi* and Anand's *The Crowd* had critically analysed this phenomenon in the 60s and 70s. Though Kerala has no metropolis to speak of metropolitan experience has penetrated the region. The nation-region dialectic cannot ignore the reality of this cultural onslaught. It is not surprising that the region is not central to some of the best fiction written in this period such as O.V. Vijayan's *Pravachakante Mozhi*, Anand's *Marubhoomikal Undakunnathu*, N.S. Madhavan's 'Higuita' or N. Prabhakaran's 'Pigman'.

Another equally important phenomenon is the cultural impact of the Malayali diaspora. The mobility of the Malayali migrant and the steady urbanisation of Kerala society have contributed towards the assimilation of new domains of experience into Malayalam fiction. Zacharia's 'Salam America' and M.T. Vasudevan Nair's 'Sherlock' are set in America though they are two of the best Malayalam stories written in this century. The cultural dynamics of the diaspora is felt in two ways. Firstly, it encourages avant-garde and innovative approach to language. The vibrancy and metaphorical density of the fictional imagination in Mukundan's *Adityanum Radhayum Mattum* and Anand's *Govardhante Yatrakal* demonstrate this element. Both these novels are highly innovative, technically flawless, delocalised narratives where space-time relations are fluid and flexible. Secondly, the awareness of Malayali diaspora influences the manner in which identity is perceived and imagined. There is increasing realization about the plurality of our multiple selves and the need to represent them in complementary terms. 'Regionalism' could be a limiting, negative cultural attribute if it is seen in reductive terms privileging only one of the several dimensions of a person. In a spirited defence of the need to recognize the essential multiplicity of our identities, Anand says:

> For long we have interpreted the human condition in terms of the oppressive apparatus of hierarchical power structure crushing people. But now, the dynamics of power prey upon us not only from above, but also laterally and even from within. It is not a single government, but several governments at work on us. Each one of them robs us of our imagination, drains us of our poetry. They are eager to reduce us to one-dimensional men. To make us only that and nothing but that and turn us against everything else. (Anand, 1994).

In the post-colonial period there is a growing distance between the state and the nation. 'The hierarchical power structure crushing the people' also belongs to the centralised state which homogenizes all people into a uniform and unified culture, obliterating local identities.

In fact, Vijayan's first novel, *Khasakkinte Ithihasam,* maps a sub-culture which is being forcefully brought into the mainstream through formal education. In the novels of Vijayan and Anand there is a growing awareness of the nation-state coming into conflict with nationhood. Nationhood, for them, lies in the shared historical experiences of the region and their cultural specificities which resist the centripetal force of the authoritarian state.

The cumulative impact of metropolitan experience and Malayali diaspora has come to redefine the very concept of the region. In the political domain, regional cultures have become more assertive and vocal but cultural boundaries are becoming increasingly blurred. A short novel such as Zacharia's *Praise the Lord* uses an English title and brings into the ambit of fiction several cultural issues related to the region, the nation and beyond with eloquence and fluency. This speaks of a new subjectivity which is alert, critical and a sensibility that cannot be contained by the provincial and the parochial. The local and the regional contain dimensions which are national as well as metropolitan. The growing assertiveness of women's writing in Malayalam demonstrates how metropolitan theory can inform articulation and critical evaluation of region specific experience. The post-modernist writing in Malayalam will have to cope with the formidable challenge of making sense of a complex social reality where boundaries between constructed categories such as region and nation have become unreal. For the adventurous novelist, the real test of his allegiance to the region consists of the fact that he explores the full potential of the linguistic possibilities of Malayalam.

REFERENCES

Anderson, Bendict (1991), *Imagined Communities: Reflections on the Origin and Spread of Nationalism,* Verso, London.

Anand (1994), *Marubhoomikal Undakunnathu,* 1996. *Govardhante Yatrakal.* Both from D.C. Books, Kottayam.

Aiyappan, A. (1965), *Social Revolution in a Kerala Village,* Asia Publishing House.

Bhabha, Homi K. (1990), *Nation and Narration,* Routledge, New York.

Gellner, Ernest (1986), *Nations and Nationalism,* Select Book Service Syndicate, New Delhi.

Graff, Harvey J. (Ed.), (1981), *Literacy and Social Development in the West : A Reader,* Cambridge University Press.

Hobsbawm, E.J. (1990), *Nations and Nationalism since 1780,* Cambridge University Press.

Kovilan (1980), *A Minus B.* (tr. by N. Kunju), Kerala Sahitya Akademi, Trichur.

Mukundan, M. (1992), *Daivathinte Vikrithikal,* D.C. Books, Kottayam.

Panikkar, K.N. (1995), *Culture, Ideology, Hegemony: Intellectuals and Social Consciousness in Colonial India,* Tulika, New Delhi.

Ramakrishnan, E.V. (1995), *Making it New: Modernism in Malayalam, Marathi and Hindi Poetry,* IIAS, Shimla.

Rao, M.S.A. (1957), *Social Change in Malabar,* Popular Book Depot, Bombay.

Rockwell, Joan (1974), *Fact in Fiction: The Use of Literature,* Routledge & Kegan Paul.

Thakazhi (T. Sivasankara Pillai), (1993), *Scavenger's Son,* tr. by R.E. Asher, Heinemann, London.

Vijayan, O.V. (1988), *The Saga of Dharmapuri,* Penguin, India.

________ (1989), *After the Hanging and Other Stories;* Penguin, India, 1995, *The Legend of Khassack,* Penguin, India.

FOUR

FROM CASTE TO SEX

A Study on Sexuality and the Formation of Modern Subject in Kerala

B. RAJEEVAN

"Is the body of Chandala girl
Barren to the sperm of a Brahmin ?"

I deem this couplet of Mahakavi Kumaran Asan—poet-disciple of Sreenaraya Guru and social reformer—as a key to the object of my analysis, the shift of political technologies at the level of bodies and its effects on the process of social transformation in Kerala. The question raised in this couplet not only places the body as the central component in the operation of power-relations but suggests the possibility of the displacement of the body from one mode of techniques of power-relations to another. Here, it is concerned about the displacement of the body from the grip of the techniques of caste system in Kerala, into a field of discourses and practices of sex whereby the caste bodies transform themselves into sex bodies.

To trace the history of the formation of the present day sexuality in Kerala and to delineate its effects in the making of the modern Malayalee subjectivity, this analysis concentrates on the differences and effects of starkly contrasting disposition of bodies, i.e., the caste-subcaste and the modern social system. This analysis mainly passes through three stages. First, it explains the structure of self through the analysis of the constitution and deployment of bodies and the position of sexuality in life in the erstwhile caste-subcaste system in Kerala. Then it explains how the new differentiations and discourses based on gender replace the techniques of caste-sub caste division and lead to the emergence of a sex body which simultaneously forms itself as a locus of a desiring subject. Finally, it picks up some different strands from the history of the body of Malayalees to deal with some present day problems in their sexuality and subjectivity.

I

Though the erstwhile caste-sub caste system in Kerala had some peculiarities of its own, it was a version of Brahmin-centred Varna-caste system that prevailed elsewhere in India. In such societies, the main concern of the dominant section was to avoid the danger of admixture of blood, and to keep the division of labour based on the dividing practices of the caste system intact. There was no possibility of the emergence of a class of free citizens over slaves as in the case of Greek and Graeco-Roman societies. Not only that this lack of structure of free self in this model is the peculiar trait of the earlier Indian societies, but the conditions in which the life activities of the individuals, even the ones generally considered as the most internal and subjective, were externally determined by customs and codes which meticulously prescribed each and every act of the individual from birth to death, without leaving any space for the free act of the self. As mentioned earlier, this is also applicable to the caste-sub caste village societies in Kerala.

Here, I look at some important modes of techniques which defined and determined the design of the bodies as bodies inscribed with caste, and the spatial deployment of the bodies according to their status in the gradation of the caste system in Kerala. As the observance of untouchability among the castes and castes within-the-castes was relentless, it was highly necessary to distinguish the caste, of the body at the very sight itself. The style of clothing, the shape and position of the tuft of hair and the differing styles and materials of the ornaments functioned as the caste marks of the bodies.

The clothing of Malayalees up to the beginning of the 20th century was not primarily related to the sense of nakedness of the body.[1] As the style of the wearing of clothes with conspicuous differences, of each caste and sub caste, was prescribed by customs, clothing functioned as a sign-system to designate the caste of the body.[2] According to the grades in the system, one would wear a cloth on his/her waist strictly limiting the lower end above the knee-joint or up to the knee-joint or above the ankle or stretching down the ankle. Nobody could transgress this custom as it was equal to the violation of one's caste identity which would cost one one's life.[3]

The shape and position of the tuft of hair of the men and the hairbun of the women in the caste society in Kerala were also considered as an inalienable part of religious and caste identity. *Sankarasmriti*, the basic code for the Kerala Brahmin customs, prescribed in detail the position and nature of the tuft, violation of which according to one's personal fancy would result in his/her being ex-communicated. There were inviolable rules regarding the shape and position of the hairbun of woman, from the upper caste to the lowest ones. While it was the right of the upper caste woman to wear the bun of hair with a slant to the left side of the head, the low caste woman wore it above the right ear. We can assume from the position taken by K. P. Padmanabha Menon, the great liberal historian, with regard to the problem of the cutting of the tuft of hair of Malayalee males, how deeply rooted the sense of identity of the Malayalee Hindus was, to the wearing of the tuft of hair.[4] While he argues rationally for the covering of women's breasts, he stood staunchly against the removal of the Malayalee male's tuft of hair.

The differences in the number and shape of sandalwood pastemarks on the forehead of the Hindu men and women and the fashion, number and the metal of the ornaments of women also could strictly specify the caste or sub-caste of the person who wore them. For example, three crescent-shaped lines, one above the other, with sandalwood paste on the forehead of the womenfolk of the aristocratic Brahmin, distinguished them from their counterparts in the inferior Brahmin groups wearing three straight strokes on their forehead. By wearing bracelets made of brass, the aristocratic Brahmin women set themselves apart from the womenfolk of other inferior Brahmin sub-castes who wore bronze bracelets. This difference was based not only on the metal of the bracelets but also on their number. If the aristocratic Brahmin women wore fifteen brass bracelets on the right hand and fourteen on the left hand, the less aristocratic Brahmin women wore ten bronze bracelets on the right hand and nine on the left hand. This rule was inviolable, since even a slight violation would confuse a caste with a sub-caste which might have very serious consequences.[5] I stop this description here, since such practice constituting caste and sub-caste bodies are innumerable.

Then we come to the dividing practices of the bodies into caste and sub-caste groups. In Kerala, all the castes including the ruling caste were untouchable to the Brahmins. Bodies of all the other castes except that of Brahmins were considered as having an inherent polluting effect; the lower the caste, the greater the pollution.

Because of this, all the castes, including the lowest ones, observed the custom of untouchability. The concept of untouchability was also based not on the direct physical touch of the bodies, but on the polluting effect of the body and the relative purity of the body being polluted. So, the touch of the caste body was a spatial act and sometimes pertaining to speech. The division and distribution of bodies into hierarchically or mutually untouchable groups were designed by the strict stipulations regarding the spatial deployment of the bodies. The distance the bodies of the lower castes had to keep from the upper caste to avoid pollution, was stipulated as follows according to the census report of 1911:[6]

Ezhava, Commala, Pana, Kaniya	24 feet
Araya, Mukkuva, Vala, Vela	32 feet
Kanakkan	48 feet
Pulayan, Ulladan	64 feet
Nayadi, Parayan, Vettuvan	72 feet

Besides these practices, there was also a codal authority. While all the upper castes in India used *Manusmriti* as their code of life, the Kerala Brahmins had *Sankara Smriti* which stipulated that they should follow 64 specific practices which were deviations from the Pan-Indian practices. Like all the other *smritis* of

India, *Sankara Smriti* also meticulously designs every act of Brahmins from their birth to death, without leaving any free space.

The above account which determines the constitution of caste body, would help us reveal the structure and nature of the self in the caste society in Kerala. Here is one more exposition from a different angle regarding the concept of body which may lead us to a better understanding of the self. The analysis of the function of the punitive operations and the objects of punishment in a society may bring to light some crucial clues about the concept of body in it. In the caste society of Kerala following the pan-Indian pattern, the severity of crimes and offences was assessed absolutely according to the grade of the caste in which the offender was born. If anybody of low caste origin violates the forbidden limits of pollution, a Nair who belonged to the community which functions as "the eye", "the hand" and "the order" of the system was supposed to hack him to death at once. Like this, in the case of all other offences, the object of punishment was the very body of the offender. The function of this excessively violent and ritualistic type of punishment was not at all meant to cure or correct the offender.[7] The various types of trials by ordeal practiced in accordance with the caste of the offender make it clear that the offending body was the immediate and direct object of the punitive methods of all the ordeals by fire, water and poison—the ordeal of weighing the body itself before and after the swearing shows that the accused and the body were considered to be one and the same.[8]

I present here all the techniques and procedures of the total determination of the body, from without, only as a device to deduce the internal effects on bodies as thinking, feeling and imagining bodies. As the bodies were under the total grip of techniques of power-relations in the caste-sub caste system and as there was thus no space and time structured for the bodies to act freely, the infolding of the bodies as subjects in the Western model was not possible at all.[9] The studies of Michel Foucault make it clear that the 'techniques of the self' in the Western Christian societies by which the individuals can affect their own bodies, souls and thoughts so as to form and transform themselves, are not only integrated with customs, codes and texts but also with the reflexivity of the self exploring itself, trying to tell the truth of oneself to self and others.[10] If we put it in a progressivist tone, without liberating bodies from the grip of the caste system there was no possibility of the emergence of a self-reflexive subject which can internally relate conducts of the bodies to the codes and texts, in opposition to the external determination of the body and self in the Indian context. The self-reflexive and the self-narratable subjectivity in the Western Christian cultures were deeply associated with sexuality. Hence, in such societies sexuality has become problematised. It is in this problematised sexuality that the individual recognises himself/herself based on his/her individuality as a desiring subject. This was not the course of the events in the history of the subject in the Indian caste societies.

This awareness of the difference of the structure of the self may lead us to an understanding of the nature of subjectivity and sexuality in the caste-sub caste system in Kerala. In the caste-sub caste society of Kerala, the nature of relationships between the male and the female bodies was controlled and channelised for the reproduction of the caste bodies without upsetting the system. The main concerns of the upper castes were purity of the blood which ensures the uncontaminated continuity of the caste, purity of the body and of rituals that confirm the conditions of life—this worldly and other worldly. So, in the caste society, sexuality was subjected to their life and relegated as part and means of their main concerns.

The nature and functions of the major institutions related to the sex-life of upper castes and lower castes amply explain that sexuality was in no way associated with the forms of subjectivity in the caste system of Kerala. The actual marriage ceremony among the Nairs and Ezhava castes, was the tying of the token of wedlock (*Thalikettu Kalyanam*) around the girl's neck, which was performed at a very early age—before the girl attained puberty.[11] By this ceremony, the girls were not being married to any particular person within the caste. It was only a ceremony of initiating the girls into the female fertility. Their actual sexual union with males who are entitled by custom, was not considered as significant to be ceremonial. Especially in the matrilineal joint family, fixing the father of children was not a problem, as they unequivocally belonged to their mother. The only form of marriage in which the male and the female united ceremonially was the Brahmin's sacred marriage by fire. Only the eldest son in the Brahmin joint family was entitled to marry from his own caste. The wife of the Brahmin in this marriage was called by the same word for the ceremony of this marriage—"*Veli*". Actually, she was considered only as an object for ceremonies who had to preserve and propagate the purity of the caste and to participate in the rituals as a part of the male. In this form of man-woman relationship, the main concern is not sex but blood, the fluid form of body which was not sexualised. The chastity trial (*smarthavicharam*) of Brahmin woman was also related to this concern of the purity of blood of Brahmins.[12] The practice of concubinage of the younger brothers of the Brahmin family with the lower caste woman (not below the Nairs) was contained in the matrilineal system where sex had, on the one hand, not become an object of power-relations and on the other, been confined to the secrecy of the procreative couple.

This analysis shows that in the caste-sub caste society of Kerala, sex was not problematised and, in turn, life was not sexualised.

II

If this is the case of the past society of Kerala up to the close of the 19th century, we have to reckon with the emergence of the modern desiring subject as the formation of a new phenomenon. We can observe that the past society of Kerala which was divided and sub-divided into groups of bodies of castes and sub-castes, has transformed itself into a modern society of individual subjectivity through various types of discourses and practices. But the modern subject in Kerala was being installed simultaneously with the appearance of the new sexuality. It was through the process of transforming caste bodies into sex bodies that the modern subject in Kerala came into being.

The Christian missionary activity which gained momentum during the British rule prepared the ground for this breakthrough. It was during this time that Christian values directly confronted the structure of a caste-ridden society in Kerala. A study of the 19th century Malayalam novels, especially *Slayer Slain (Khathaka Vadham)* and the *Victory of Saraswathi (Saraswathee Vijayam)* will bring this fact into light.

The Christian missionary activity brought in a new universal concept of man by introducing a new differentiation of human bodies across the existing caste-sub caste division. This new differentiation was the one that was based on sex difference.* One of the main social activities of the missionaries in Kerala was founding of schools for the backward classes. In these new schools, they divided students into groups of boys and girls, and introduced a new disciplinary concept based on this division over and against the division of the caste-sub caste system. They even started separate schools for boys and girls and thus they turned these schools into model training centres of this division based on sex.

But this new division introduced by the missionaries did not seriously affect the old dividing practices of the caste system as a new subjectivity was yet to emerge. It was Sri Narayana Guru who utilized the male-female differentiation for the generation of a new subject. The Guru took this division based on sex to prove

---

* It may appear odd to say that the division based on sex difference, which is considered to be a difference so elementary and natural, is a new one. If we are critical about our own notions with which we see the world as they are historically constituted, we can also historically analyse what is seemingly so elementary and natural. So, through this method, it will become clear that not only the differentiation of male and female is historically constituted but the differentiation itself has a history. For example, in the Greek anatomy and medical theory, there was a "one sex model" that regarded male as normative and female as the inferior version of the male itself. And we should know that it was not until the 18th century that for various reasons the modern Western notion of opposite sex was constituted. In Kerala, this model was introduced only by the close of the last century.

the identity of human essence the bodies belonging to the same species acting as sexual opposites. Thus, this division enabled him to introduce the new category of Man who has one Caste and one Religion and one God.

The Guru says in 'The Characteristic Traits of Caste' (*Jathi Lakshanam*).[13]

> Those who mate and beget
> Are all in one species
> Those who do not
> Are not of the same species
> And those living with mates
> Also belong to one species.

With Sri Narayana Guru the male-female division began to grow into a differentiation connected with subjectivity. The externally determined division of bodies as caste bodies began to be replaced by the division of bodies propelled by the body itself which became a desiring body or a locus of sexuality. This means that the caste bodies began to be transformed into sex bodies.

The Guru proposed several techniques related to body and self to activate the division based on sex. He founded *ashrams* and *sanyasi* groups. His new concept of *sanyasa* was based on purification of the desiring body by renouncing sexual and sensual pleasures, whereas the old Indian concept of *sanyasa* was considered as a set of techniques of self and body for training them in the practice of renouncement.

In his teachings and directions about the *ashrams*, schools and '*Sabhas*' the Guru's concept of sex segregation was prominent and evident. In 1920 he directed his disciples as follows:

> "Ashrams, school and Sabhas
> Should be set up
> Separately for men and women".

So, the teachings of the Guru can be considered as a historic moment connecting subjectivity with sexuality in the process of the making of the modern man in Kerala.

The emergence of the new literary works since the close of the 19th century is deeply related to these events leading to the formation of a new subject. For example, the famous poem *Duravastha* (Hard Times) of Kumaran Asan can be considered as a victory of sex over caste, sex division over caste division. This poem narrates the story of the coming together of a Brahmin girl and a Pulaya (untouchable) youth, leading them to self-knowledge of their own subjectivity and sexuality and their consequent union in sex. And the other renowned poems of Asan depict the contradiction involved in the self-purification of the desiring body, renouncing sex and its pleasures.

Along with these events, the functions of the new institutions and practices like the new family system and marriage are to be taken into account in the creation of a private sphere in the life of modern Malayalees. At the same time, we have to recognise the so-called public sphere as a field of proliferation of sexualities which ensures the centrality of sex in life and makes it a secret archive of the purifying hermeneutic of the subject.

The major event in this process of differentiation based on the new notion of male and female is the transformation in the concept of the female body in Kerala. As in the case of the general Indian pattern, in Kerala too, female sexuality was not juxtaposed to male sexuality. It is evident from the ambivalent attitude in the pattern in which the female sexuality was constituted—as formidable and lovable, auspicious and impure, violent and tranquil—that the female body was ranked and placed on par with the natural phenomena and beings which human beings have to control and are to be depended upon. Such a conceptualization of gender differentiation was easily workable in the joint family system in Kerala. In all the castes, woman was considered auspicious since she has the gift of fertility. As puberty marks the onset of fertility, all castes celebrated the first menstruation or '*Ritu*'—a Sanskrit word which also means seasons in nature. So, the woman's body in the joint family system in Kerala might have been considered as an object or phenomenon in nature which is to be depended upon, feared, nourished, and utilised. With the introduction of the new conceptualisation of gender based on the male-female opposition, the concept of a woman's body in the joint family system had to undergo radical transformations. That is, the female body, had to transform itself into a sexualised object from a body, the core of which was not a desiring subject.

Though the techniques and practices involved in this transformation are various and complex, I focus myself on the history of woman's breasts in Kerala—which may exemplify the process of sexualisation of the female body.

Till the close of the 19th century, all the Malayalee males and females, from Namputiris to Nayadi, did not cover their body above the waist. Except the Brahmin women who covered their body, that too only when they had to get out of their abode, the whole female folk amongst Hindus in Kerala lived bare-breasted. *Kuppayamiduka*, a phrase in Malayalam which means wearing of a blouse, was used by Hindus as a term for conversion into Islam or Christianity. This clearly indicates how the wearing of dress (or non-wearing of it) was deeply related to the caste and religious customs of Malayalees, than to the sexuality of the nakedness of their bodies.

In Kerala, even in the beginning of this century, it was not the non-covering of female breasts but, on the contrary, the covering of it, which was considered obnoxious and as a violation of customs. In his autobiography C. Kesavan—a leading social reformer and statesman—describes an experience of his mother-in-law, which is very much revealing.[14] In those days, though wearing a blouse was forbidden, she ventured to wear one which she had managed to smuggle into her husband's house. But the consequence was bitter. Viewing the covering of her breasts with a blouse as something outrageous, her mother-in-law began to beat her up mercilessly. Since then, she used to cover her breast with the blouse only in the bedroom, in front of her husband. Note the interesting reversal of the universal concepts and practices relating to nudity and sexuality. Here, while living bare-breasted all day, the wife covers her breast only in the secrecy of her bedroom, to be appreciated by her husband. This event, in which the female breast in Kerala transforms itself into an object of sexuality through a sense of nudity and self-consciousness, clearly illustrates a significant moment in the history of women's body in Kerala.

The famous drama *Ritumathi* (The Pubescent Girl) of M.P. Bhattathirippad deals with the conflicts involved in the problematisation of women's body and its sexuality.[15] A Brahmin girl who had some school education (which was not usual), wants to cover her breasts with a blouse, out of self-consciousness of the nakedness of her breasts and feeling of shame. Her paternal uncle, an orthodox Brahmin who happened to be her guardian, takes a relentless stand against her wish. The conflict leads even to a physical confrontation between the girl and her uncle in which the uncle rips away the blouse from her breasts. On his part he does this out of a deep sense of morality and custom as a responsible Brahmin. But then, the girl was helplessly wriggling in shame and trying to cover her breasts with her arms as if she was sexually assaulted. They are in two different worlds, dramatically opposite and can, in no way, communicate with each other. The uncle represents the old order where women's body was not transformed into an object of new sexuality. The girl acts as a sexually objectified body and as a sexual subject.

The series of struggles in South Travancore from the beginning of the 19th century regarding the right of low caste women to cover their breasts also deserves a detailed analysis disregarding the humanist and progressivist notions in the context of the emergence of the new sense of nudity and the sexualisation of women's breasts and the transformation in the concept of women's body as a major event in the history of sexuality and subjectivation in modern Kerala.

III

Now, I come to the problems of the present day sexuality in Kerala. As we have seen, in the process of sex becoming the truth of subject and subject as the locus of sexuality, the modern society of Kerala transformed itself into a society in which sex has become central. This centrality of sex is of course related to the occurrence of a shift in the political technology of bodies from that of caste to sex. If the caste body was the direct and immediate object of the exercise of power in the caste society in the modern power-relations, sexual subjectivity became the object of its exercise and thus the desiring body of the subject became an indirect target through the proliferation of pleasures. In this state of multiplication of sexualities and forms of sexual subjectivities, the man-woman relationship in Kerala faces some problems which deserve serious concern. I would like to present two of them here: one related to the past and the other, to the future.

Though sexuality had been subjugated to the main concern of life in the society of Kerala, there were inviolable customs and taboos relating to man-woman relationship. It is a mistaken notion prevalent even today that the caste society in Kerala was a permissive one. Almost all the foreign visitors and conquerors including Tipu Sultan saw the sex life in the joint family system in Kerala as a type of prostitution and even promiscuity. They were not able to understand the underlying logic of the morals of the joint family system, of the morals which contained and preserved the tribal taboos and customs. In the joint families in Kerala, sex relation was strictly restricted to those who were entitled to it by custom. And the others who were not entitled, were prohibited not only to mingle, but even to see each other. The architecture of Nair and Namputiri joint family houses very well explains this by its discrete structuring of space planned to prevent mutual sight and touch of males and females. My point is that, contrary to the prevailing notions, there were strict prohibitions and taboos in the disposition of man-woman relationship in the caste society. As we have seen, though the very notion of what constitutes the differentiation of male and female has been subjected to a radical transformation in Kerala in the modern times, some elements of the old prohibitions and taboos have been carried over to the present day: such as the mutual untouchability of the bodies of men and women. Thus, into the new social differentiation based on gender introduced by Christian Missionaries, this old element of prohibition was also being incorporated. In other words, some elements of prohibition of the old, non-sexualised society have been carried over to the present day sexuality where it has become central. The sexualised body carrying the memories of tribal prohibition as a technique of its self-controlling practice in the midst of the present day proliferation of sexuality has become a grotesque sexual object to others and subject to itself. Pertaining to the untouchability of sex bodies in Kerala, Vaikom Muhamed Basheer, the great author, in one of his stories, says that in Kerala, it is really more difficult to walk in the midst of women without touching their bodies, than passing through a thick thorny bush.[16]

The problems relating to the future are the gestures of the emergence of a new subjectivity of women in Kerala defying the modes of objectification of women's body through which they were totally confined to a female sexual subjectivity. Disregarding the female subjectivity, the new women in Kerala began to constitute themselves as a different entity, through practices in self and society on par with men. The emergence of this new subjectivity and its consequences inside and outside homes began to disturb the male-dominating structures of relationships in sex and life. Not only that, this situation engenders violence on the part of males but the habitual acts of males towards female are experienced by the latter as intolerable and violent in the context of the emerging identity of women.

As the increasing practices and discourses of the sexualization of bodies and the technology of manipulation and control of sexual bodies are intricately related to the modes of relations of power, the solution to present day problems demands specific forms of resistance. The specific forms of resistance from the part of women against the male dominating ideological structures, and not against men, may help them to disentangle their bodies from the grip of power to attain their emerging new identity.

REFERENCES

1. K.P.S. Menon, *Atmakatha.*(Malayalam)
2. C. Kesavan, *Jeevitha Samaram.* (Malayalam)
3. Kanippayoor Sankaran Naboodirippadu, *Ente Smaranakal.* (Malayalam)

4. K. Padmanabha. Menon, *Ara Noottandinu Munpu.* (Malayalam)
5. K. Padmanabha Menon, *Ara Noottandinu Munpu.* (Malayalam)
6. K. Padmanabha Menon, *Kochi Rajya Charithram.* (Malayalam)
7. *Sankarasmrithi,* Laghudhara Prakasika.
8. C. Achutha Menon, *Cochin State Manual.*
9. Gilles Deleuze, 1987 *Foucault,* University of Minnesota Press.
10. Michel Foucault, *Care of the Self.*
11. Census Report (1901), Travancore.
12. William Logan (1901), *Malabar Manual.*
13. *Sree Narayana Guruvinte Sampoorna Krithikal*, Mathurbhoomi, (Malayalam).
14. C. Kesavan (1968), *Jeevitha Samaram,* National Bookstall, Kottayam.
15. M.P. Bhattathiripad, *Rithumathi* (Malayalam).
16. *Basheer Sampoornakrithikal*, D.C. Books (Malayalam).

FIVE

REFORM, LAW AND GENDERED IDENTITY

MEERA VELAYUDHAN

I

Since the 1970s, a number of studies have debated issues arising from the idea of the "Kerala Model" which upheld the State's achievements in terms of equity, balanced socio-economic growth, quality of life, female education, societal changes in attitudes to family size and so on. They have linked the question of demographic changes to movements for social justice, to political and economic reforms based on the interests of the poor and to the long period of various kinds of institution building which preceded these changes UN ((1977); Ratcliffe (1978) and Morns *eval* (1982)). Could the Kerala Model be duplicated? The debate continues.

More recently, research and feminist scholarship in particular noted that the impact of colonisation, the changes in land relations, commercialisation of the economy, the growth and spread of formal education provided the basis for the growth of public politics and the emergence of ideas concerning the distribution of wealth and power in Kerala. These developments, it was felt, prepared the ground for significant changes in the position of women in Kerala from 1880s to 1950s (Jeffrey (1993)). A study on the disintegration of matriliny among the Nairs stated that women themselves appeared to have been ignorant of their role and this may have been the reason why women's special rights could be taken away. While admitting that the popular demand and pressure to bring about changes in inheritance laws was broadly motivated by the growing ideas of justice and fairness in society, the study noted that "contradictions emerge in the social process" (Mehra and Saradamoni (1983)). A significant study points to the historical re-ordering of power relations within the Nair matrilineal *tarawad* (joint family) as underlying the changes in kinship and its role in the creation of new identities for women and men and for Nairs as a caste in this century (Arunima (1996)). The limited scholarship that exists today on gender and kinship relations among the low castes, indicates that the impact of colonisation, with its legal systems and reallocation of resources, though profound was not uniform across or within colonised societies. Changing forms of division of labour and wider economic processes constantly redefined the role of women in society. These also signified varying implications for women in terms of support structures and choices (Ganesh and Risseeuw (1993)). An early study on the decline of matriliny and its impact on Ezhavas, a major low caste, stated that women in 1944 enjoyed less freedom of movement than their mothers did (Aiyyappan (1944)). Was monogamy and patriliny, then, a part of a political message and wider political process? (*Hindu*, May 9, 1936 in Jeffrey (1993): 54).

Our study of the social reform movement among the Ezhavas points not only to a contest between different traditions within the movement but also to the development of several spheres of autonomous activity by women. These informed women's social position and roles (Velayudhan (1991)). However, the discourse within the Ezhava social reform movement on matriliny, inheritance, form of marriage and the ensuing campaign for a law of succession and marriage for Ezhavas was predicated upon a distinct construction of gender and cultural codes. These, in a fundamental way, outlined the varied contests within the social reform movement and the construction of a gendered identity. This chapter will focus on the latter aspect.

II

Undoubtedly the most widespread mass movement that Travancore had known, the social reform movement among the Ezhavas, arose in the context of the emergence of new social classes in

Travancore from among the non-dominant castes and communities. The Ezhavas following diversified occupations took advantage of the new opportunities that arose under the impact of colonisation changes in land relations, commercialization and the rise of an educated middle class. Many small scale capitalists and traders emerged among them. A small section acquired superior tenancy rights and landed property. An English educated middle class emerged as also a large working class (Isaac (1983)).

A new social and cultural discourse signified the changing environment. This chapter will consider the discourse around the *Sree Narayana Pariplana Yogam's (SNDP Yogam)* campaign for a law of succession and marriage for the Ezhavas and the Report of the Ezhava Law Committee, 1919 prepared for the Sree Mulam Popular Assembly of Travancore. This issue had been raised at successive sessions of the Sree Mulam Popular Assembly and several memorials had been presented to the Government (Ezhava Law Committee (1919)). In 1916, the Government constituted a committee which included prominent Ezhavas such as the popular poet and SNDP Yogam's leader, Kumaran Asan, M. Govindan and N. Kumaran. The Government called on the representatives of Ezhava organisations, religious leaders, educated middle class, and the government employees as the main witnesses.

Women were viewed as subjects generally incapable of expressing informed or competent opinions. This is evident from the Committee's directive to the Tahsildars to select witnesses for examination including "a few lady witnesses also, provided they were deemed competent to give evidence". Among the 863 witnesses, only 10 were women. "In Kayamkulam centre alone four ladies were examined. All the lady witnesses gave ready and intelligent answers to the questions put to them. They seem to have taken pains to study the questions framed by the Committee and bestowed sufficient thought on them. We may here record our appreciation of the interest, mostly well-informed, evinced by the ladies who subjected themselves to viva voce examination as well as by others who sent written answers", the Committee stated.

The thrust of the campaign by the social reform movement to change the laws of succession and marriage prevailing among

Ezhavas in Travancore had a distinct character. While scholarship is limited, a pioneering study indicates that the Ezhavas, ranked below the Nairs as a polluting caste, were traditionally and mainly share-cropping tenants working in the gardens or rice fields owned by Nairs or Namputiris. Having localised matrilineage, the members of the property group owned the hereditary right of tenure of plots of land and were attached to a Nair landowning family. In the latter half of the 19th century, Ezhava matrilineal *tarawads* began to lose their hereditary rights to fields and crumble owing to the development of extensive cash-crop farming and general absorption into a market economy. Many Ezhavas became short-term share-croppers holding gardens as individuals while a considerable number lost all rights of tenure and became wage labourers. Some went into trade and professions or became landlords in their own right (Schneider and Gough (1962)).

In Travancore, a significant section of the Ezhavas followed *marumakkathayam* system, a section followed the *Makkathayam* or patrilineal system of succession and inheritance, while a third section followed a mixed system or *Misradayam* where a separate or self-acquired property of a man dying intestate was shared between his children and his *tarawad* (Ezhava Law Committee (1919): 5). A High Court statement noted that in southTravancore, Ezhavas had no settled practices and "tended to adopt from time to time what appear to them best and follow spasmodically some of the customs prevalent among the dominant caste in their immediate vicinity" (Special Appeal No 322 of 1089, cited in Regulations and Proclamations of Travancore, vol. V, pp. 775-76, Regulation 111 of 1100). In some areas of Travancore, the Ezhavas following *marumakkathayam* had gradually adopted the *makkathayam* system. This, the Ezhava Law Committee held, had led to a decline in family disputes and litigation. This may have been possible owing to their contacts with neighbouring *makkathayam* areas and the influence of religious organisations.

The attempt of the Ezhava social reform movement was to forge a community identity by uniting all sections of the caste through a common law of inheritance. With a view to initiating this change, Sree Narayana Guru, in a message to the SNDP in 1909, had stated, "Where *marumakkathayam* system is followed in the community, legal provision should be made to give wedded wife and children the right to a portion of the man's individual earnings. Otherwise, marriage would be meaningless. Necessary steps in this direction should be taken after careful consideration." (*Vivekodayam*, April-June 1909). The Ezhava Law Committee decided to exclude the sections following *Makkathayam* system of inheritance from the ambit of its proposed legislation owing to opposition from that section. A common law covering those who followed the *marumakkathayam, misradayam,* and *makkathayam* was considered to be too radical a step at that moment (Ezhava Law Committee (1919) : 6).

III

As low castes struggling to assert their identity and dignity, the Ezhava social reform movement's campaigns were directed not only towards enhancing the Ezhavas educational and occupational status but also towards freeing them from social shackles or customs, many of which appeared to have been imitations of the upper caste norms. The latter had an important bearing on Ezhava women. From its inception, therefore, the SNDP Yogam called for ending the elaborate and expensive customs such as *talikettu kalyanam* (pre-puberty rite), *tirundukuli* (ceremonial bath after first menstruation), *pulikudi* (a pregnancy related rite), and called for a new code of marriage. "*Talikettu kalyanam* was an expensive affair for most Ezhavas and had led to tensions and litigation within Ezhava *tarawads* as the ceremony was considered a *tarawad* necessity justifying alienation of property for meeting its expenses."(Ezhava Law Committee (1919) : 9). As early as in 1904, Kumaran Asan noted the "interest that has been generated among our people on the question of reforms in the customs.....The Yogam activist have two main objectives: one is to eliminate, to the extent possible, the impediments to the progress of the community caused by the enormous expenses and other difficulties that have to be incurred in order to maintain several meaningless customs and practices: secondly, to protect the dignity of the community which gets eroded and became an object of ridicule...it has been the esteemed opinion of our respected Guru Swami that the practice of *kettukalyanam* is unnecessary and an unworthy practice...this practice cannot be found in Hindu scriptures or religious practice. Marriage by nature occupies an important place in human life and among Hindu customs it has a prominent place. If we are a community with real self-respect and pride, we should feel sorry that we have not so far felt ashamed of reducing an event of such importance to mere child's play celebrated with much pomp and show..."(Velayudhan (1978)).

The Ezhavas in Travancore appeared to follow two forms of marriage: the traditional *mundukoda/pudavakoda* and the new form introduced by Sree Narayana Guru known as *vivaham*. The customary marriage or *sambandham* as practised by the Ezhavas, the Ezhava Law Committee held, "was not based on Hindu laws such as the *Smritis* to which the Ezhavas owe no allegiance.... The unilateral declaration or act of one of the parties which is neither communicated or assented to by the other, was considered insufficient for dissolution of *sambandham*. For the children of the *sambandham*, the sense of paternity in husbands is quite as developed as in the case of *makkathayam* (patrilineal) communities." Elaborating its ideal of a patriarchal, monogamous marriage, the Committee stated, "The Ezhavas maintain a high standard of conjugal fidelity and that they are keenly alive to the sacredness of the marital tie are clear, alike from the undivided opinion of the community in favour of a law enjoining strict monogamy in future and from the rarity of instances of divorce. In the generality of cases, the Ezahava wife lives with her husband and under his protection." (Report of the Ezhava Law Committee (1919) : 9).

Vivaham or the new form of marriage, propagated by Sree Narayana Guru through the SNDP Yogam's reform committees, involved a simple ceremony to be held in a temple or open courtyard (in the presence of priests and elders), the handing over of the bride by her father/parental authority, the tying of the *mangalyasoothram* (the bridal string) around the neck of the bride by the groom. These acts are accompanied by the chanting of *manthrams*. (Ezhava Law Committee (1919) : 8; see also *Vivekodayam* 1904 and Geroge (1972)).

Though this form of marriage had been spreading and taking the place of the old, both forms need to be recognised as ignoring the old form may result in "bastardizing a large per cent of the present Ezhava population," the Committee noted. Opposing compulsory registration of marriage on the ground that it would go against the sentiment of the community, the Committee suggested legalising marriages between sub-divisions and within members of the community in Travancore and outside. Among the propertied sections of the Ezhavas, marriages between members of the community from different regions were becoming a possibility. Thus "it was possible for an Ezhava born near Shoranur in south Malabar to become manager of a cash-crop trading company in Alleppey and marry a woman from a family based at Quilon, which in turn prospered by ferrying coconut husks and coir yarn from central Travancore to Alleppey." (Jeffrey (1993) : 51). With the Ezhavas moving into the several niches in the economy being created by commercialisation and growth of industries, there was interaction among sub-sections within the caste.

The Committee moved in an even more emphatic way to elaborate its ideal of the patriarchal family norm, terming it "natural" and "conforming to the line and tendency of civilisation," interpreting both Brahmanical precepts, including Manu, as well as the liberal ideas of Bentham and Mill for this purpose. Opposing both polygamy and polyandry which prevailed among sections of the Ezhavas, as barriers to "moral development and the tranquillity of domestic life," the Committee emphasised that monogamy favoured "both the cultivation of self-restraint and the elimination of female jealousy, a fruitful source of breach of domestic peace. Says the popular Malayalam poet of old, Kunjan Nambiar a keen observer of social life in Kerala: "the wretch who takes to himself two wives never tastes the blessings of comfort...."

IV

Faced with increasing internal tensions and litigation for divorce (Ezhava Law Committee (1919) : Appendix) within its matrilineal property groups in Travancore, the Ezhava Law Committee was forced to pay attention to the investigation of customary practice which prevailed. Customs concerning divorce varied. Judicial decisions on the question of the conditions of divorce were often conflicting. An account of the customary practice of divorce among the Ezhavas revealed that if either party wanted a divorce, relatives and village elders were informed. If a compromise was not effected, the husband had to pay the wife *azhivu* (a "compensation for damage to the youthfulness and health of the woman"), *chilavu* (cost of marriage) and *Ozhivu Pudava* (the `release' cloth which the husband presented to his wife to mark the end of the relationship). Another form of divorce was that effected through mutual consent, through the "wish of the husband supported by the decisions of the caste assembly" and the wife receiving a share of the husband's property or 101 "fanams" or a deed for 101 fanams by the husband.

The Ezhava Law Committee suggested that instead of the caste assembly which interpreted the conditions of divorce in differing ways, the District Munsif's Court should effect divorce as was the case of the Travancore Nair Regulation. In contrast with the Nair Regulation which provided for the payment of compensation by the husband alone, the Ezhava Law Committee held that the majority of the witnesses questioned on the point (the men mainly) were for making the wife also liable to pay compensation and therefore, compensation should be paid by the party seeking divorce—husband or wife. A sum of Rs. 500 was fixed as the maximum payable by the wife. Here, it may be noted that over 94 per cent of the petitioners seeking divorce were women.

The focus of the legislation concerned self-acquired property and the committee went to great lengths to stress that it did not wish to alter the rules of matrilineal succession of *tarawad* property. Here too, it had to reckon with the varied customs prevailing among the Ezhavas in Travancore. Some had been recognised through judicial decisions. The customs followed by Ezhavas included one known as *Valsaravakasam* the enjoyment of the whole of the self-acquisition of a person by his wife and children for a year before a division is made. Another custom, *Cherunettam* or *Cheruthettum*, provided an additional share in the acquisition given for the marriage and ceremonies for minor children.

Judicial decisions regarding the origin of these two customs, however, varied and the debate centred around the recognition or not of woman's contribution and entitlements to self-acquired property. The Saddar Court held that the wife's right to one-half of the husband's self-acquisition originated from the contribution of labour. It stated, "In the enterprising community of Ezhavas, the wife generally helps the husband in his business, whether industry or trade". In a case, the Saddar Court referring to the origin of the custom ruled. "The reason is that, among the Ezhavas, when a member of a *tarawad* makes a self-acquisition, his wife contributes partly to the same by her labour and the wife being non member of the *tarawad*, her progeny is entitled to the benefit of that labour to the extent thereof, that is, to a moiety and the rule, therefore, is that half the self-acquisition goes to her heirs who are not heirs of her husband. The children received to father's self-acquisition not as his heirs but as the heirs of their mother who was a co-owner with the father owing to the labour she put for the self-acquisition. (Ezhava Law Committee (1919)).

The High Court questioned the Saddar Court's interpretation of the custom based on the theory of joint labour and stated that it was not certain whether joint labour or "natural affection" formed the basis of the custom. Later, the High Court rejected the theory of joint labour and entitled the children to one-half of the self-acquisition, irrespective of whether the self-acquisition was made before or after the marriage of the mother. The Ezhava Law Committee viewed the High Court's rejection of the theory of joint labour as striking a blow to the very foundations of the *misradaya* or mixed system of inheritance. The High Court's decision had, for a time, led to the demand among them for a law vesting the title in the son. The High Court emphasised that the legal rights of the children arose from the relationship with the father. The Committee held that there was a growing tendency among the Ezhavas following the *marumakkathayam* system to give the self-acquisition to the wife and children although customary practice denied them such rights.

The right of the wife and children to the self-acquisition was upheld by the SNDP Yogam and 60 out of 70 other Ezhava organisations. Among those who supported the High Court's version were Karnavars of wealthy Ezhava *tarawads*.

The leaders supporting such a viewpoint included SNDP Yogam's leaders such as Sree Narayana Guru, Dr. Palpu, Madhavan Vydian of Trivandrum, Kunjushankaran Vydian, Kochukunju Channar, a Karanavar of a wealthy *tarawad*, and two other influential and wealthy Ezhavas, Narayana Panikkar and Ayyappan Raman. Among smaller sections who opposed the same were C.O. Madhavan, Komathu Kunju Panikkan, C.V. Kunjuraman, B. Parameshwaran and Shankara Panikkar. Their opposition was based on the view that such a right of devolution of self-acquisition to the wife and children combined with individual partition of property would destroy the *marumakkathayam* family and the development of *makkathayam* which would go against minors and women in the community (Ezhava Law Committee (1919) : 15).

In the Committee's view, the conjugal union was held in the community as sacred and inviolate as in any other and the sense of paternity was deeply ingrained. The wife generally lived with the husband in his house along with their children. The father acted as the guardian of his children and educated them. He lived and worked for his wife and children and the latter, whether they contribute or not to his self-acquisition, are in the generality of cases made to expect the fruits of his labour. When he died, his children 'observe' pollution and perform his funeral obsequies and *sradha*. Thus has come into existence a species of property derived from the father on which the father's *tarawad* has no right and this had contributed not a little to stimulate enterprise for which the community is well known.

The Committee emphasised that its goal was to move towards *makkathayam* (patriliny) which was the *natural course* as the Ezhavas, it felt, had developed a high sense of duty, paternal and filial which followed from "the natural consequence of the condition". However, the proposed legislation concerned only the "self-acquired and separate property of an Ezhava male left undisposed of at his death", and would apply to only those self-acquisitions made after the enactment of the law (Ezhava Law Committee (1919)).

As the large majority of the Ezhavas were labourers, the number of *tarawads* with over one acre of land was estimated, by the Ezhava Law Committee, to be not more than 5000. However, self-acquisitions were many. Increasing employment opportunities had an impact on the Ezhava joint families following the *marumakkathayam* system. The early recognition given to entitlements in self-acquisition may also have been due to the disinclination of the earning members of the *tarawad* to share the fruits of their labour. The need for separate residence and management could be another such reason. While the Committee supported the idea of individual partition on the ground that individual ownership would be an incentive to expand more capital and labour on land and lead to improved methods of cultivation, an increase in the productiveness of the soil, it advocated caution on making a law on individual partition as it may expose the landed property of an agricultural community to the risk of outright alienation.

Conclusion

This Chapter has examined the discourse around the Ezhava Law Committee's attempts to enact laws of inheritance, succession and marriage. The discourse signified both an attempt to build the 'reputation' and 'status' of a community as well as the subordination of women by controlling relations between the sexes within the family. The chapter focuses on the elements which went into the creation of new social roles for women. While avoiding the pitfall of viewing this as the sole site for the construction of a gendered identity for Ezhava women, the chapter, none the less, argues that this formed the contours within which varied contests emerged within the Ezhava social reform movement.

In its efforts to enact common laws of succession and marriage for Ezhavas, the reformers formed a complex association with the State. While judicial pronouncements on customary practices of the Ezhavas were often conflicting, the reformers concurred with a particular ruling or approach which indicated a well-defined move towards a patrilineal system of inheritance. When the reformers find themselves in a situation where working out a common law is contentious, as in the case of the role of the caste assemblies in deciding divorce, it permits the State to mediate, i.e. the Munsif's court replacing the caste assemblies. This, in a way, undermines the power relations between a property group and the wider caste group.

The concerted attempt of the Ezhava social reform movement led by the SNDP Yogam to end matrilineal practices is evident from the writings, newspaper reports and reports of women's meetings (Kesavan (1968)). The Ezhava matrilineal *tarawad* were themselves under stress owing to the changes in the wider economic processes. The Ezhava Law Committee's moves to enact a common law of succession and marriage for Ezhavas involved the strengthening of the emerging patrilineal structures as a legal and ideological construct. This construct weighed heavily against women. It projected women as dependent and subordinate members in the family and men as heads of household and argued that the male authority was derived from "natural law" and that was "the way civilization moved".

REFERENCES

Aiyappan, A. (1944), *Eravas and Cultural Change*, Government Press, Madras, 122.

Arunima, G. (1996), 'Multiple Meanings: Changing Conceptions of Matrilineal Kinship in Nineteenth and Twentieth Century Malabar.' *The Indian Economic and Social History Review*, vol. 33, no. 3, Sage, New Delhi.

Ezhava Law Committee (1919), *Report of the Ezhava Law Committee* with Draft Bill and Appendices p i.

Ganesh, Kamala and Carla Risseeuw (1993), 'Gender: Between Family and State', *Economic and Political Weekly*, October 23, p 2332.

George, K.M. (1972), *Kumaran Asan,* Sahitya Akademy, Delhi, p. 47.

Isaac, Thomas (1983), 'The Emergence of Radical Working Class Movement in Alleppey', CDS Working Paper No. 175, Trivandrum.

Jeffrey, Robin (1993), *Politics, Women and Well Being, How Kerala Became A Model,* Oxford University Press, Bombay, p 9.

Kesavan, C. (1968), *Jivitasamaram,* National Book Stall, pp 40-41.

Morris, M.D. and M. McAlpin (1982), *Measuring the Condition of India's Poor,* Pramilla, New Delhi, p. 104.

Mehra, Rekha and K. Saradamoni (1983), *Women and Rural Transformation.* ICSSR-CWDS, Delhi, p. 38.

Ratcliffe, Jhon (1978), 'Social Justice and Demographic Transition: Lessons from India's Kerala State', *International Journal of Health Service,* vol 8, no 1, pp 139-41.

Schneider, David M and Kathleen Gough (eds). (1962), *Matrilineal Kinship,* University of California Press, Berkeley, Los Angeles, pp. 405-06.

UN Department of Economic and Social Affairs (1977), *Poverty, Unemployed and Development Policy: A Case Study of Selected Issues with Reference to Kerala,* Orient Longman, Bombay, pp. 5, 142-53.

Velayudhan, Meera (1991), 'Caste, Class and Political Organisation of Women in Travancore', *Social Scientist,* vol. 19, nos 5-6, May-June, Delhi.

Valayudhan, P.S. (1978), *SNDP Yoga Charithram,* Quilon SNDP Yogam, p 124.

Vivekodayanm, November 15, 1904 and April-June 1909.

SIX

DEVELOPMENT EXPERIENCE OF COLONIAL KERALAM

RAJAN GURUKKAL

The chapter seeks to perceive the specificity of the development experience of Malabar, Cochin and the princely State of Travancore within the overall pattern of modernity under colonialism. Its goal is to understand the manifold reconstructive effects of colonialism on the people of the region.

The principal focus of the chapter centres around the multiple modes of cultural preparations under the norms of colonial modernity. It sets out to unravel the operational processes of the various strategies of subjectification at different sites where the people of Keralam were discursively reconstructed as colonial subjects.[1] We propose to examine the ways in which colonial modernity operated as a new world-view effecting an ontological transmutation of the indigenous way of life. It also attempts at understanding the ways in which the colonised were represented; the strategies through which colonisability was made acceptable as natural; and the sources with which structures of domination were made legitimate.[2]

The chapter takes up five sites, viz, evangelicalism, schooling, printing press, economy and administration, to visualise the phenomena of socio-cultural reconstruction. These are arbitrarily chosen sites but sufficient to represent the mechanisms of the production and circulation of the discourse of colonial modernity. The sites reveal how the people were trained to seek the truth about themselves in the colonial representations and constitute their self-image exactly as construed by the colonisers.

The chapter has three parts : (a) the initial one characterising the immediate pre-colonial social formation and the traditional world-view of Keralam; (b) the part discussing the sites of production and circulation of what in a summating metaphor can be expressd as colonial modernity that supplanted the traditional world-view; and (c) the subsequent part examining how in the process of epistemic shift society and culture of Keralam developed. The themes covered being very vast, the chapter is more conceptual than empirical.

There are studies on the political and economic processes of colonial Keralam, focusing on the subjugative and exploitative dimensions respectively. Apart from incidental references to the enmeshed state of culture, there is no study as such on cultural processes under colonialism. Even a survey of the various aspects of colonial cultural preparations and social transformation is entirely new to the historiography of Keralam. This justifies the introductory outline attempted here.

The history of the emergence of colonial modernity and the operation of its multiple strategies is too huge a project to be comprehended in a chapter like this. How modernity became an inescapable mode of perception and hegemonic representation is equally incomprehensible. What the chapter attempts to provide is only an overview of four major sites of the transformation of subject positions. The first wave of cultural invasion by the West on the region's traditional world-view dates back, plausibly, to the Portuguese times. Nevertheless, it was in the latter half of the 19th century with the hegemony of the English that these ongoing cultural preparations by different ethnic groups such as the Portuguese and the Dutch arrived at a point of perceptible difference.

The pre-colonial social formation was an aggregate of garden land economy, crafts production, trade and shifting cultivation structured by the dominance of wet-land agriculture. Excepting for the high ranges and coastal tracts where the pattern of settlements differed, the entire arid and arable terrain had innumerable scattered settlements, all organised into agrarian villages of a recurring pattern. The pattern recurred, for it emerged out of uniform social processes of labour under relatively similar eco-types of the villages. Each village was a self-sustaining agrarian unit with all essential arts, crafts, productive labour and other services localised.[3] The control of resources including both labour and its objects signified a hierarchically structured tenurial relations and entitlements interlocking the domestic segments of hereditary occupations (*jatis*) within a historically contingent hierarchy of wealth and powers. The temples, as well as their *uralar namputiris*, the ruling aristocracy, the warrior headmen, the big traders and the other privileged groups in the hierarchy could appropriate as their legitimate right the unpaid surplus labour of the lowlier social orders, as was sanctioned by convention. There, were many *allodials* as well with small holdings (*kanam*) mainly in the terrain of garden lands. The surplus from the lower strata moved up in kind to the top from where it was transmuted into money. It was a monetised economy though barter continued to be the common mode of exchange in the villages.

A system of numerous levels of hereditary rights and entitlements, this arrangement of land control in spite of its built-in hierarchy of power relations, meant a collective operation without absolute ownership. The higherups in the hierarchy monopolised the juridico-political level with varying degrees of power as determined by their wealth and tradition. But by and large power operated at every level almost autonomously though there existed a running thread of royal control across the levels. This was particularly true of the Zamorins of Kozhikode who had better institutional structures to maintain their chiefs and nobles under subordination. They had a more systematic arrangement for periodic exaction in cash from their subordinates and had better control over the movement of trade goods on which duties were levied. There were a large number of chieftains all over the region, showing subservience to one of the principal ruling families.

The juridical conventions and administration of justice were primarily based on *sastraic* jurisprudence institutionalised as *desamaryada* or local conventions. Since the *Namputiris* were the hegemonic group with enormous economic and cultural control, their Vedic *sastraic-puranic* adaptations constituted the chief tradition of wisdom for representing the socio-political processes.

The institution of *Jati* based social stratification was the major effect of the *sastraic-puranic* mode of representation of the hereditary social division of labour. Though there existed all kinds of non-brahmanical institutions, ideas, values and conventions in the society, the *sastraic-puranic* idiom had enmeshed them all through a syncretic process. The Vedic-sastraic-puranic cosmology, ethics, and eschatology provided an encyclopedic compendium for the traditional society to generate knowledge. This encyclopedic wisdom as such never entirely filtered down to the lower strata. Its influence on ethnic groups in the coastal tracts and forests was marginal. Nevertheless, the larger society's dominant world-view did certainly derive from the aggregate of the *Vedic*, *itihasic*, *sastraic* and *puranic* wisdom.

As it is impossible to recount all the features of the traditional world-view, no attempt at a comprehensive definition of it is made here. The already constituted definition characterising it as introspective, other-worldly, unchanging, and spiritualistic, is Orientalistic. This definition is representational rather than historical.[4] The region's cultural milieu made up of its own systems of signs, symbols, language, script, arts and other structures of communication can be distinguished as *desi* against *margi*. The *desi* structures are different from their *margi* sources of origin and collectively signify a common semantic horizon wherein they derive meaning and make sense. Below the broad linguistic identity and semiotic milieu, there were several community specific sub-cultures with their own local slangs and clusters of signs.

The traditional society in the region had numerous channels and structures of communication that facilitated the reproduction of the cultural conditions of social existence. There were considerable variations in the social strata's accessibility to them which was determined by the requirements of each one's functional space in the social structure. Most of the cultural channels and structures were tied to the practice of hereditary specialisation of *jati* exclusiveness which precluded universalisation. Contemporary society hardly required universal accessibility to all kinds of cultural skills and knowledge forms since skills and knowledge were functionally specific, and function hereditary as well as caste-oriented. So the production and transmission of each form of knowledge was a task normally confined to the caste concerned. There was no commonly instituted means for social education which obviously is anachronistic in a system of hereditary specialisation of arts, crafts and skills with little or no scope of caste mobility. Transmission of knowledge in hereditary trades was the responsibility of the elders of the *jatis* concerned who undertook to train their youngsters in the respective art, craft or skill. All arts and crafts in those days did not require education of a general nature and therefore generalisations based on modern assumptions of literacy would be meaningless. Excepting for the category of primary producers and menial servants, most of the people had accessibility to the use of writing based on alphabets or signs or symbols. Alphabetical writing skill and reading faculty of an elementary level had a wider clientele reaching out even to the lower rungs of artisanal *jatis*.

The theoretical knowledge of all trades was pursed generally by the leisurely *jatis* who were unencumbered by other obligations. Astronomy, Mathematics, Grammar, Architecture and Philosophy of a high order were pursued mostly by intellectuals belonging to such *jatis* who engaged themselves in the production of new texts as well as the re-interpretation of old ones. Anybody could take lessons in them if the *jatis* encumbrances did not impede. However, the *Vedic* and *sastraic* knowledge was the monopoly of the *Namputiris*.

It was a document-minded society that used written texts as a source of legitimacy and validation. Writing and accounting were crucial in the maintenance of a system of resource control involving multiple rights, obligations, entitlements, periodic appropriation and diverse transactions. The numerous local chronicles, the *granthavaris*, vouch for the faculty of meticulous recording of events and accounting of returns in minute fractions. They are the best indicators of the craft of contemporary documenting in precise prose. The documents, mainly the *granthavaris,* constituted the most legitimate instrument of domination in contemporary society of transactional relationships. The local conventions and customs like *urmura* and *desamaryada* rooted in the legitimacy of the *sastraic* tradition proliferated differences over the years and required to be documented. Transactions of rights and entitlements relating mainly to mortgaging and pledging (*orri* and *panayam*) leading to the alteration and occasional dispossession of traditional privileges too necessitated documentation. Documents served the purpose of guarding the traditional rights as well as validating their alterations. Among other instruments of domination were the various socio-political institutions, religious sensibilities and cultural practices.

What emerges from the foregoing discussion is the outline of a social formation of hierarchical land relations and hereditary occupations interlocked by the institution of caste with: (a) the unilineally recurring structures of political power relations, (b) historically contingent relationships of communication, and (c) cultural mechanisms of domination overlapping—not as three separate regimes but as mutually reinforcing and appropriating within the semantic horizon of the *Vedic-sastraic-puranic* values and norms. This pre-colonial social set-up underwent the gradual process of radical transformation during the 18th and 19th centuries of colonization by the British.

Contacts with the alien civilizations were not new to the history of the sub-continent in general and the region in particular. There is recorded history of the Jewish, Christian and Arab settlements dating back to the 9th, 10th centuries and what their tradition claims is a much greater antiquity.[5] These communities co-existing and interacting with the local people for a few centuries hardly had any features of separate religious and cultural identities. It was hard for the Portuguese missionaries to distinguish the local Christians from the heathens. But for their separate faith in the *Bible* or in the *Kuran*, these communities were very much identical with others of the region in terms of social and cultural practices. What is significant is the absence of an epistemic order that would enable the construction of new identities for these communities.

The Portuguese missionary activities were the first to induce the beginnings of a shift in the world-view of the Christians in the region. Their imposition of a series of restrictions on them in the name of christianization rather forced a construction of differences and the unconscious acceptance of a new subjectivity.[6] There was strong resistance to the form of submission which, however, marked the beginnings of the new identity consciousness and sense of difference among the local Christians. The evangelical movements led by the Protestant missionaries in the subsequent centuries made the dichotomy of the 'self' and the 'other' sharper. This change was not confined to the Christians of the region since the process was not merely the making of the Western religious subjectivity, but a much wider and massive operation of an enormously powerful discourse, the effect of which was a profound epistemic shift. Evangelicalism was just one of the many sites that facilitated the production and circulation of the new world-view. The colonial processes represented a myriad of strategies, objectives, institutional structures and technologies which as a vast terrain of knowledge/power relations could set in the historic transformation of the traditional epistemic order.[7]

This historic transformation of the traditional epistemic order opened up a new regime of meanings and visibilities. We name it here as the discourse of colonial modernity. An extensive range of knowledge that claimed to be scientific, the discourse of colonial modernity began to encompass every aspect of human existence and produce truth about everything in an extremely influential mode of perception. It operated simultaneously at various site and through various strategies.

There were several sites and forms of submission that belonged to the totalising domain of colonial modernity. The subjectivities under the sites like evangelicalism, colonial administration, education and reform were all different but were only apparently so. Fundamentally, they all signified the subject position within colonial modernity. A common epistemic foundation discursively united them. The evangelical ethics, administrative essence, educational goals and reformist perspectives like any other structure of contemporary Western civilization, on a closer look, lay bare how they converged on the totalising power relations of colonial modernity.

There are no sequential or correlative implications in the order followed here for the review of sites, strategies and subject positions. It is hard to conceive any historically valid priority in their discussion since they all overlap with one another. We choose to discuss the site of evangelicalism first and subsequently colonial administration, education, printing press, and reform. This does not mean that these are mutually exclusive domains. In fact, they are interconnected and reciprocally supporting one another. However, each one of them is a relatively independent field of activities, techniques and processes of domination. This justifies their individual discussion.

Evangelicalism

The field of evangelicalism with its programmes, methods and processes became significant during the 16th century when the Portuguese Jesuits following their brethren trading in the Indian Ocean world got established in the region.[8] They founded their monasteries and churches at certain strategic centres convenient for missionary work. Though the history of Christianity in the region goes far anterior to the Portuguese times a subjectivity linked to the Christian religion was born much later as the effect of the evangelical movement under the Portuguese Jesuits. Their pastoral power surcharged with the ecclesiastical responsibility of leading people to salvation in the other world, operated as an imposition on the local Christians who, according to the Western criteria of Christianity, were hardly different from the pagans. The task of the Portuguese missionaries was, therefore, either to kill them and thereby ensure entry in heaven or to forcibly christianise them.

In the name of Christianisation, the Portuguese Jesuits imposed a series of Decrees called the Synod of Diamper in 1599 dictating Western socio-religious terms of Christian existence. The Synod brought the local Christians forcibly under the control of the Roman Catholic church declaring many of their rites, rituals and customs heretical. What they brought and spread was a code of ethics fundamentally different from that of the traditional communities in the region. What made the Decrees different from the local faith was their link with the truth of the individual that stood in contradistinction to that of the community. It was a set of new power relations, order of communication, and strategies of domination constituting an individualising subjectivity. The missionary activities marked the beginnings of the organised distribution of individualising power. In short, the effect of evangelicalism was the shaping of an individuality which submitted itself to a pattern utterly different from that of commonality. This powerful effect imposing the form of submission almost entirely unknown to the communitarian life in the land, naturally excited a rebuttal in the minds of the local people.

The local Christians put a strong resistance against the Decrees of the Synod of Diamper which in the name of true Christianity banned their age-old socio-cultural practices. The resistance manifested itself in the form of an organised protest by a group of the Syrian Christians who took an oath neither to follow the Decrees nor to obey the ecclesiastical authorities of Rome. The oath is known in history as the *Kunan Kurisu Satyam,* an oath taken by holding a rope tied to a cross that consequently developed a bend. This was a spontaneous reaction against a kind of subjection that the people were not willing to agree to.

But the passion of resistance and the urge for identity marked actually the birth of a new subjectivity, a process which the local Christians never realised. This is not to say that the local Christians had no identity of their own and that they had not distinguished themselves from the other local communities.[9] The Christians in the region had indeed distinguished themselves from the other communities, but only within the parameters of the *jati* society wherein this distinction meant only a *jati* identity. The *jati* consciousness was so deep-rooted that even towards the end of the 19th century when the first Christian community organization was born it was called *nasrani jatyaikkya sangham.* The efforts of those who fought to differentiate themselves from the Western

Christians, in fact, made them more and more Western. It was a process of modernisation, but overtly taken for traditionalisation by the concerned people. The Syrian Christians were in the contradictory state of being both the subject and its rival. They rivalled with the form of submission imposed on them without recognising the subject position that made rivalling possible.

The *Kunan Kurisu Satyam* divided the Syrian Christians into two factions, one recognising the papal sovereignty in Rome and the other recognising the locally represented authority of the patriarch of Antioch. Further, the new converts were divided among themselves as high and low castes. Even those who agreed to abide by the Synod differentiated themselves as Syrian or St. Thomas Christians from the low caste converts.

The resistance to new power relations, the consequent identity constructions and differentiations had manifested as ecclesiastical debates and theological viewpoints. Nevertheless, across these differences, a Christianity of the absolute type as the unifying force was getting established as the point of reference and as the basis for each one's identity. It is this notion of the absolute where the differences converged that we identify as the centre of discursive power relations transferring all of them into Christian subjects. The world-view they use for recognising the truth about themselves and differentiating them from others was of colonial modernity. The mentality of the Syrian Christians to postulate what was absolutely Christian as opposed to what was heretical, helps us unravel their Western subjectivity. The ultimate unity at the fundamental level of subjectivity is clear in the oneness the Syrian Christians tended to construct by imagining themselves as the subjects of the Portuguese King. A petition the Syrian Christians submitted to the Portuguese King said that although they lived in the country of pagan kings, they were loyal subjects of the King of Portugal.[10] When confronted by the new power relations represented by the Portuguese Jesuits, the Syrian Christians in the struggle to maintain their identity got encapsulated by the Western Christian identity of the ecumenical nature.

At the level of actual being, there existed objective conditions constituting the Syrian Christian difference from the Western other. But the truth of Christianity postulated in the absolute by the Portuguese as the reference point to determine what is Christian and what is heretical compelled them to prove how closer they were to the truth through their apostolic origins. The result was the fabrication of a tradition that would enable them to stake better claim on a truth that was Western. This was the process through which the modernity discourse subsumed them, compelling to seek their identity as construed under the Western truth of Christianity which they as well as others were to recognize in them.[11]

The conflicts between the Syrian Christians and the Portuguese Jesuits that continued till the 18th century lost their relevance with the spread of the Protestant ethics. Under the Protestant system the apparently different subject positions were drawn closer to one another under the hegemonic concept of absolute Christianity. The evangelical movement acquired a popular dimension with the erosion of the pastoral secrecy, mysticism and the biblical monopoly of the Jesuits. The Protestants made the Bible accessible to all. The pastoral power now began to spread beyond the ecclesiastical domain. It got linked with the colonial state and the various non-religious institutions such as education, printing press, publication, library, hospital, orphanage and so on that were born as effects of the discursive practices under review.

The post-Portuguese Syrian Christian identity constituted in the wake of this resistance was both an outcome and a reflection of what it resisted. What they claimed traditional in justification to their being different from the other was Western. It is this inescapable mode of constituting truth upon which the subjects wield no control that Michel Foucault calls discourse.[12] In the hope of preserving what were traditional, the local Christians were building up new systems of symbols and signs, but without knowing that they were under the rules of Western relationships of communication—a game theoretical situation with the rules and norms laid down by the European 'other'.

Colonial Administration

The new form of power was continuously developing at the site of colonial administration giving birth to various institutional structures. It was a kind of political power transcending individuals. Its focus was on citizenry and its procedures meant a combination of individualisation and totalisation. Foucault located this new political structure in the post-renaissance European state.[12] Identified as the Western integration of ecclesiastical power techniques and modern political procedures, the State is the new pastoral power. Through colonial relations the powers penetrated into the whole social body of the region through a multitude of institutional devices.

Colonial administration did not directly encompass the entire region at a stretch. During the 16th and 17th centuries it was not altogether free of ecclesiastical preoccupations. But the officials and institutions of the new pastoral power proliferated in the 18th-19th centuries giving rise to newer forms of colonial administration as it spread out. Even in the 19th century direct colonial rule was confined to the British Malabar where an administrative system run by the British bureaucracy got established. In the princely States of Cochin and Travancore the colonial rule was indirect. Nevertheless, this made little difference since the British residents in the princely States wielded substantial control over their administration.

Administration represented an array of institutions of juridical, legislative, and disciplinary functions affecting the people's conditions of social existence. It affected the landscape, resources, production, productivity of labour, conditions of labour realisation, social relations, communication, health, urban growth, hygiene, education, planning, transport and so on. Its procedures which were at once individualising and totalising tended to transform the people into colonial citizenry. The mechanisms of colonial subjection got integrated to the traditional mechanisms of economic exploitation and domination. As a result of this, the traditional social arrangement for surplus expropriation from the peasants became more oppressive, for it meant an additional exaction for the new lords, namely, the British. Fresh norms, values and obligations began to be thrust upon the peasant.

Under the tutelage of colonial administration and legality the traditional seigneurial jurisdiction became more harsh. The landlords began to exercise transactional rights with the intention of absolute ownership of property that was a creation of the colonial administration. It was during the colonial period the process of the subordination of *kanam* (allodial of *jenmam*) started long ago became complete. Large-scale eviction (*olippikkal*) and dispossession of peasants through over-lease (*melcarttu*) and arbitrary transactions of land made their life miserable. There were numerous court cases against such arbitrary acts of the landlords (*janmis*) but these were mostly decided in favour of the landlords. Between 1862 and 1880 there were about 20,015 of such favourable judgements.[13] Apart from the class of the actual tillers who were landless, a near landless peasant category called the *verumpattakkar* (mere share-croppers) proliferated. There was resistance to the new form of power from the oppressed peasants. They struggled against the various forms of oppression, the instances of which are abundant in the history of the region as testified by the series of insurrections between 1836 and 1921.[14] These were not overtly anti-colonial struggles. What the peasants fought was the form of submission under the traditional agrarian system which had become unprecedentedly oppressive because of its integration with the colonial administration. The series of peasant uprisings of the 19th century related to the miserable plight of the Muslim *verumpattakkar*. Though directed against the landlords who constituted the immediate enemy, the peasant struggles were ultimately counterpoised to challenge the colonial domination. These were struggles for a new subjectivity outside the agrarian relations of domination which virtually brought into existence a non-traditional self-perception for the peasants. This non-traditional perception is typical of the self constructed under colonial modernity.

At different levels of the social strata the people's perception changed under the administrative impact that reached them through traditional agencies and institutions of control. Obviously all members of the society had not directly encountered the transforming power. The landlords indulging in indiscriminate transactions of land rights through leasing (*carttu*), over-leasing (*melcarttu*) and releasing (*policcucarttu*) on one side and the consequently evicted or dispossessed peasants on the other would form the examples. But everyone had a feel of difference either in the form of enhanced power or in the form of enhanced oppression depending upon the nature of one's position in the relations of power. The peasants felt the ever-intensifying oppression by the landlords who in turn could exercise power differently under the colonial land system and civil administration.

Even the kings were brought into a form of submission despite the fact that theoretically kingship symbolizing sovereign power precluded the subordination of royal authority. Though at different points of time, all the ruling dynasties came under British paramountcy. The initial phase of colonial interaction with ruling families was characterised by friendly and protective relations which facilitated the penetration of Western ideas and institutions into the royal administration. Even armed confrontations often ended up in the acceptance of Western methods. The capture of the Dutch Army chief D'Lanoy and his subsequent appointment as the Travancore Army chief by Marthanda Varma is a good example. Much before the formal subordination of royal authority, the princes had been transformed into new subjects. They were in a better position to have meaningful interactions with the colonial authorities, and had greater access to the Western culture, and to the Western modes of learning and the new relationships of communication than the rest of the society.

Unknowingly, the princes sought apprenticeship under the Western craft of administration and became its practitioners. They were also able to fashion their capacities and aptitudes which emboldened them to resist the alien power, though in vain. In both the cases they proved to be colonised subjects. The princes were exposed to the tradition of royal authority in the Western world. This accounts for their transformation into the colonial subjectivity than expressed itself through acts of resistance to the British paramountcy and demands for reforms of a socio-economic nature. Bureaucracy, secular jurisprudence, regular secretarial system, budgetary planning and developmental scheming that became part of the palace rule virtually reconstituted the royal administration. Most of these found their way into the royal governments of the region through Tipu Sultan, a better transformed subject who had led a campaign across the domains of the Kozhikode and the Cochin royal houses. Tipu Sultan had already become a ruler of the reconstituted subjectivity in the kingdom of Mysore. His vigorous resistance to the British rule, concept of authority and advocacy of reform indicate a non-traditional subjectivity.

The subject positions of the numerous petty chieftains who were suppressed by the Zamorins and the Travancore kings in their respective domains were also likewise not uniform. Some of them put up armed resistance to the new relations of power. The princes who were forcibly subjugated and controlled through institutional devices in the wake of colonial development, fought simultaneously their traditional overlords as well as the British power. Those who constituted the most prominent of the ruling aristocracy tried to assert themselves by all means. The examples of Pazhassi Raja in Malabar and Veluttampi Dalava in Travancore may be recalled here.

In short, when the power relations operated directly through the establishment of colonial administration and indirectly through traditional ruling authorities, new subject positions were born at the different levels of socio-political order. The birth of subject positions at the site of administration opens before us the inter-related functioning of communication, power and dominating capacity. The site built up new relationships of communication through fresh lessons, interrogations, responses, imperatives, exhortations, and values. There happened a whole series of power processes manifesting in the form of a new hierarchy, and patterns of disciplining, surveillance, reward and punishment. There emerged new technologies of domination too. All sections of society including the kings, chieftains, landlords, traders, peasants, artisans, craftsmen, and tillers acquired, in varying measure, non-traditional informations and meanings. They were made to play a game of communication within the relationships of different subjectivities.

The hierarchy of agrarian relations superimposed on bureaucracy dissociated these multiple state of people from the traditional system of allegiance. In addition to the seigneurial subjection confined to the agrarian villages, new processes of domination enmeshed the larger society demanding obedience as citizens and not as functionaries of the *janmi* system. The Namputiri *janmis* tried to maintain a kind of exclusiveness with their temple-centred *yogam* (a local body) governing the agrarian villages. The British administration did not directly interfere with their system. But, both the Namputiri *janmis* and their peasants as reconstituted subjects resorted to the British jurisprudence for settling the disputes of land rights issuing out of colonial domination. The Namputiris who turned away from education and reform refused to internalize colonial values. Except for the colonial legal system that was added on to their seigneurial jurisdiction, there was practically nothing that seems to have affected the Namputiris in a radical way.

But the rest of the society absorbed colonial values, often with an emancipatory urge generated by the miserable conditions of their social existence. The territorial resource management, jurisdiction, legal structures and the pervasive means of surveillance brought the people directly under the control of administration. Through the various forms of institutionalisation, types of objectives, systems of differentiations, means of generating power relations and degrees of rationalisation, the colonial powers transformed the people as subjects of modernity.

The differentiations that the colonial power relations brought into being were mainly the traditional ones relating to caste status, economic entitlements, social hierarchy and ritual privileges. All the differentiations immanent in the labour processes and resource appropriation remained the same despite the administrative measures adopted to ban slavery and improve the conditions of peasants. In fact, the new power relations brought into existence, both as conditions and effects, various other differentiations based on language. religion, ethnicity, culture, knowledge and competence. These additions ensured the colonial objectives of maintaining domination for resource control and profit accumulation. Though use of arms was part of the means of bringing colonial power relations into being, more sustaining were the strategies of education and reform leading to total shift in the world-view of the people. A silent but profound operation, this procedure of transformation received voluntary submission from the people who often courted the new subjectivity with an emancipatory urge. Both education and reform built upon ecclesiastical infrastructure under the umbrella of pastoral power enabled the historic breakdown of tradition and the phenomenal establishment of colonial modernity.

The strategic distribution of power relations across the new subjectivities in the traditional social system was a significant aspect of the institutionalisation of colonial power. Penetrating into the framework of traditional predispositions and *sastraic* jurisprudence, there happened a new institutionalisation of legal practices. Dissociating the various social segment from the traditional systems, the new relations brought into existence specialist groups of separate hierarchies. Numerous people including teachers, clerks, constables, soldiers, technicians, labourers and so on, were made part of new hierarchies under the general rules and surveillance of the colonial administration. The demonstrative domination was reinforced by various other means of institutionalisation.

One cannot exaggerate the role of arms in the process of colonial domination. The rifles, indeed, symbolised the superiority of the Western army, but much more crucial was the army's rigorous disciplining and its strategic deployment that often guaranteed success. The military intervention in terms of colonial strategy was always the last resort because of its economic implications and its possible unfavourable fallout. So the colonial strategies happened to be predominantly centred around the question of cultural confrontation. The strategies of education and reform made the people accept their colonizability that rendered open resistance impossible. This is not to visualise a confused situation where the power relations of tradition and colonial modernity merged together without the tension of resistance. The potential of struggle was certainly there since tradition never phased out despite its modification through relationships of confrontation. The reconstituted traditional identity, however modern, zealously guarded a line of demarcation separating modernity from it. This ensured the potential of resistance in the colonial processes themselves.

Education

In the process of subjectification, perhaps education played the most decisive role. The school, an institution where the power relations, activities and systems of communication converged, was a wonderful site where the people as colonial citizens were moulded. The school was a well-defined space of meticulous regulations and disciplinary mechanisms comparable only to military barrack or a police battalion. It functioned not merely as a pedagogic institution, but a regimenting station moulding the future citizenry. As centres transmitting the elements of colonial world-view the schools not only moulded the students but also transformingly influenced the local societies. The values, norms, meanings and measures not known to the traditional society spread informally to the areas surrounding the schools.

An institution like the school with enormous transforming power combining individualisation and totalisation never existed in the pre-colonial society. Traditional society had known only personalised institutions imparting knowledge relevant to hereditary specialisations of caste exclusiveness. There were temple centred institutions called *ghatikas* and *salas* for Vedic-cum-martial learning accessible only to the Namputiris.[15] The Vedic learning being quite extensive, it allowed for exegetical specialisations suitable for scholarly pursuit transcending the ritual milieu. There were diverse forms of knowledge and specialised branches. But the traditional pedagogic practice never presupposed a socially accessible institution comparable to the school. In the pre-colonial society there seem to have existed several personalised educational institutions called the *pallikkutams*, probably a relic of the pedagogic practice attached to the Jain and Buddhist monasteries. This institution must have imparted literacy among the non-Brahmins as the *kutippallikkutams* of the later period indicate.[16]

The establishment of schools was mainly an outcome of the Protestant missionary activities. The first school in the region was established as early as in 1806. Several schools were established in the 19th century by the CMS missionaries who took care of the education of girls and of children belonging to the lower castes. The Christians and *ilavas* (also written as Ezhavas) were the major beneficiaries of the pedagogic missionary work. However, the education of the lower castes was not an easy task since they were tied to their hereditary occupations under caste obligations. In Travancore the situation was a little different because of the reforms effected in the system of land relations.[17] As early as in 1816 the *ilavas* got royal land on lease, and that accounts for their relatively unencumbered status that enabled some of them to go to schools. Similar reforms were not adopted in Malabar which might help us understand the background of the peasant struggles there. Compared to the chances of the lower castes of Travancore to join grammar schools and village schools the chances of their counterparts in Malabar were extremely marginal. However, a large number of schools were established there also under the initiative of the British government.

Introduction of the Printing Press

The introduction of the printing press by the missionaries facilitated the circulation of information more widely and systematically.[18] As a totally non-traditional technique of making reading materials, the printing brought about a radical change in the sensibility of the readers. The expansion of printing brought about orthographic modifications and proliferation of narratives. However, the general belief that the missionary literature was instrumental for the birth of prose in the region is incorrect. It is true that the missionaries developed and promoted a specific kind of prose narrative. But it is inferior to the prose of the pre-colonial *granthavaries* in terms of spontaneity and precision. There was tremendous speed in the process of subjectification, once printed materials began to circulate among the school-educated. The emergence of books, a convenient alternative device to the *granthas*, marked the spread of the skill of reading. The circulation of printed periodicals and books revolutionised the scene of knowledge dissemination. The books and periodicals published by the missionary centres carried mainly biblical stories and didactical narratives, the effects of which went far beyond their evangelical goals. They gave rise to the institution of reading rooms and libraries at various places as manufacturing points of the subjects of colonial modernity.

The proliferation of schools, growth of literacy, circulation of books, expansion of the vernacular press and development of indigenous book-publishing provided the essential prerequisites for the objectification of the subject of colonial modernity. The schools and the printing press gave rise to the English-speaking and English-reading subjects across the region. The books of literary genres, grammar, linguistics, sciences and the social sciences objectivised the speaking, thinking and living subjects. Translation, historiography and Census were the most powerful strategies of objectification. Translations particularly of English novels acted as a very powerful vehicle carrying the dialogical world of the West to the minds of the reading subjects. Western historiography provided for the local people not only a non-traditional mode of appropriating the past, but also a new way of seeking the truth about themselves. The decennial Census objectified the people as grouped, classified, tabulated, defined and divided subjects. Several social segments went into a sort of amalgamation under these groupings and classifications. The Census made a few new *jatis* and unmade many in the classificatory process. Translation, historiography and Census appeared to be encompassing a commendable range of authentic knowledge in which the reading subjects discerned their mirror images. Anthropology, ethnography, geology, etc., added to the forms of objectification. People soon accepted the characterisation in them and began to live it. They could only treat this official knowledge final and reconstruct themselves accordingly.

Reform

Though reform was part of the activities of evangelicalism and colonial administration, its discursive effect had a relatively autonomous dimension when it picked up the dynamism of a movement. Reforms as evangelical actions upon traditional practices began at the very inception of the relationship of confrontation between the region and the West. The socio-religious reform imposed by the Portuguese Jesuits through the Synod of Diamper for 'Christianising' the local Christians set in the first wave of Reform. Since the process of subjectification was yet to advance, there was as already noted strong resistance to it. With the coming of the Protestant movements, reforms took a more persuasive turn towards conscientisation through exhortations. The Protestant missionaries carried along with the gospels a call for socio-economic reforms addressed to the public. Compared to the politico-religious impositions of the earlier. Jesuits, the popular exhortations of the Protestants with sympathy and openness proved to be highly effective. In fact, the making of the colonial subject began with these social reform campaigns that acquired the semblance of a popular movement.

The reform as administrative action in the region had its beginning in British Malabar with Tipu Sultan's bold interventions aimed at reforms. As soon as the English took over as the rulers in 1792, regulations were made to stop slave trade. In 1819, they stopped the practice of selling agrestic slaves. Regulations were adopted in 1836 to liberate the tillers attached to the government lands. The traditional trials by ordeal and crude forms of punishment were banned through orders. In Travancore and Cochin too reforms were introduced by the Kings at the behest of the British residents.

Reforms came also as a result of popular demands, which in turn would explain the nature of the subjectivity behind such demands. The demand for the right to wear upper garments by the Cannar women of the Christian converts in Travancore in 1829 is a case in point. There were riots between the Upper castes and the Christians on the Cannar women issue and army intervention became necessary to quell them. The Resident Colonel Munroe persuaded the King of Travancore to grant permission to the Cannar women to wear jacket. But the women had demanded a covering *dotti (melmuntu)* over the jacket which was not permitted. They began wearing it on their own which led to much more violent riot in 1875. The Canner women submitted a petition to Lord Harris, the Governor of Madras who acted through Munroe and persuaded the King to accord sanction for it.

A reform movement of the ÏÓavas likewise acquires a wider socio-economic dimension in the context. The movement was initiated by the English-educated ÏÓavas who, in spite of their wealth and learning, enjoyed no social status owing to the stigma attached to their caste. It was this lowlier order in the caste hierarchy whose economic status improved towards the middle of the 19th century with the *pÈ—am* proclamation conferring fixity of tenure and permanence of occupancy rights and labour market.[19] The opening of schools by the Christian missionaries had provided them with opportunities to educate their children. Schooling and the subsequent absorption of many in colonial Government service enhanced their economic status. Empowered by the missionaries, schools, and print media the Western passions and values reconstructed the educated among them as subjects of the new world-view. They owed the urge for reform to this new subjectivity which enabled them to objectively realise their social condition.

In fact, English education was not that indispensable for sharp minds to follow suit since contemporary intellectual atmosphere was surcharged by the variously objectified Western worldview. The historic emergence of Sreenarayana Guru, a traditional yçgi, as the leader of the social reform movement in Kerala exemplifies it. That the core of the teachings of the Guru corresponded to the spirit and sobriety of contemporary Western discourse of progress is not altogether accidental but historically contingent. [20] The role of the educated and enlightened Ïóava elites like Dr. Palppu was crucial in bringing a spiritual leader like the Guru to head the social reform movement. The source of the rational principles of reform was certainly colonial modernity. However, the movement owed its success solely to the genius of the Guru who sought indigenous cultural sources to articulate his strategies. The stir of reform eventually acquired the dimension of an anti-caste movement in the Guru's insightful social praxis.

A series of other reform movements seeking to extricate the various caste groups sprang up at the turn of this century. What is to be noted as relevant to the context is the presence of a transformed people capable of upsurges against traditional forms of submission. All reforms were mainly reformulations of tradition into colonial modernity through the joint efforts of colonized subjects who could carve out a political space for themselves in the existing relations of power[21]. Even the Namputiri caste underwent the process with the catastrophic triggering of a protest with (in) tradition. A Namputiri woman charged with infidelity and subjected to *sastraic* trial (*smÈrttavicÈram*) in 1905, articulated her protest within tradition by implicating a wide-ranging people of high status and ranking. The reaction from the accused was too grave and influential for the jury (*smÈrttan*) to proceed with excommunication and the predicament called for royal intervention. Contrary to the traditional practice, the king ordered *puu-avicÈram* a counter-trial of the accused. The *sastraic* jurisprudence thus received a fatal blow. It was an eventful shift of even the most orthodox from the traditional jurisprudence to the Roman laws for individual freedom. The ascendancy of common laws was a crucial development in the process of the making of a citizenry in the region.

The reforms did not remain confined to social groups and social processes alone. They swept through the entire realms of life in the region. There were innumerable incidents of public assertion showing the maturing of a culturally reconstructed people recognising new visibilities of freedom. To conclude, the central argument of the chapter is that the generative force behind the series of social and cultural developments which went into the making of modern Keralam, was colonial modernity.

NOTES AND REFERENCES

1. The insights borrowed are mainly from the concepts of subjectification and mechanisms of subjection. The study of the subject and the procedures of subject-change is central to most of the studies by Foucault. For the fundamentals of subjectification see his *Archaeology of Knowledge,* A.M. Sheridan Smith, New York, 1982. But the concept grows along with the various writings of Foucault. The works like *The History of Sexuality: An Introduction,* New York, 1978. Also, *Power/Knowledge,* ed. by Colin Gordon, New York, 1980. For a detailed study of the birth of different subjectivities see his book: *The Birth of the Clinic: An Archaeology of Medical Perception,* London, 1973. For fresh recapitulations of the ideas by Foucault himself, see H.L. Dreyfus and P. Rabinow, Michel Foucault: *Beyond Structuralism and Hermeneutics*, 2nd edn. Chicago University Press, 1983.
2. In fact, any historical work on modern Kerala can exemplify this. P.K.K. Menon, *History of Freedom Movement in Kerala, 1885-1935, vol. I & II,* Trivandrum, 1979; K.K.N Kurup, *Tellicherry Fort,* Calicut, 1979; K.N. Panikkar, *Against Lord and State,* New Delhi, OUP, 1989.
3. For a long time the Indian villages were studied by scholars in the orientalist perspective. Generally the concept of Asiatic mode provided the basis for their conceptualisation. A change in the perspective was introduced first by D.D. Kosambi. See his *Introduction to the Study of Indian History,* Bombay, 1958. Also R.S. Sharma, *Indian Feudalism* Calcutta, 1962. A historiographic appreciation of the colonial perception of Indian villages is given in R. Thapar, *Ancient Indian Social History,* New Delhi, 1982, p. 9ff. For the specific situation of the villages in Kerala, see the discussions in Raghava Varier, "The Pattern of Village Settlements in Kerala", unpublished paper, University of Calicut, 1986.
4. The beginnings of the study of the representational effect can be seen in Albert Memmi, *The Colonizer and the Colonized,* Boston, 1967. The question of representation as a mode of domination is discussed at length in Edward Said, *Orientalism,* New York, 1985, p. 3ff. He defines Orientalism as "a Western style for dominating, restructuring and having authority over the Orient ...." Also see his *Culture and Imperialism,* London, 1993, pp. 230ff.
5. For the details of the recorded history of the Jews, Christians and Islam in the region, see M.G.S. Narayanan, *Cultural Symbiosis of Kerala,* Trivandrum, 1972.

6. See the discussions in Biju Mathew, "Strategies of Identity : The Case of the Syrian Christians of Kerala", Unpublished M. Phil. dissertation, School of Social Sciences, Mahatma Gandhi University, 1993, pp. 12ff.
7. Michel Foucault, Colin Gordon ed. *Power/Knowledge*, Selected Interviews and other Writings 1972-1977, New York, 1980, p. 101. Also Gordon's "Politics and the Study of Discourse", in Graham Burchell *et. al.* eds. *The Foucault Effect*, University of Chicago, 1991, p. 53ff. See what has been given by way of recapitulation by Foucault himself about his main concerns in H.L. Dreyfus and P. Rabinow, eds. *Michel Foucault: Beyond Structuralism and Hermeneutics*, 2nd edn, Chicago University Press, 1983. For a detailed study of the concept of discourse in Foucault see, G. Deleuze, *Foucault*, University of Minnesota Press, 1987, pp. 20ff.
8. See the discussions in M.N. Pearson, *Before Colonialism: Theories on Asian European Relation 1500-1750*, New Delhi, 1988. See the concept of World System formulated in Immanuel Wallerstein, *The Modern World System I & II: Capitalist Agriculture and the Origins of the European World Economy in the 16th Century*, New York, 1974.
9. Biju Mathew, *op. cit.*, pp. 30ff.
10. *Ibid.*
11. See the relevant concepts in Foucault, *Language, Counter Memory, Practice*, Cornell University Press, 1977. Also *Power/Knowledge*, New York, p. 98ff. 1980. See the question of nation discussed in its discursive historical context in Partha Chatterjee, *The Nation and Its Fragments*, Delhi, 1994, p. 95ff.
12. See the discussions on Foucault's concept of governance in "Politics and the Study of Discourse", in Graham Burchell *et.al.* eds. *The Foucault Effect*, Chicago, 1991, p. 53ff. Also see the note by Foucault on the matter in H.L. Dreyfus and P. Rabinow eds. *Michel Foucault : Beyond Structuralism and Hermeneutics*, Chicago, 1983, p. 213ff.
13. William Logan, *Malabar Manual*, vol. I, rpt. Madras, 1951, pp. 581-84.
14. See the latest discussions on the structure and processes of the struggles in K.N. Panikkar, *Against Lord and State*, New Delhi, 1988. Also M. Gangadharan, *Mappila Rebellion*, Delhi, 1990. The struggles in the context of land relations are examined in P. Radhakrishnan, *Peasant Struggles, Land Reforms and Social Change : Malabar 1836-1982*, New Delhi, 1989, p. 42ff.
15. For details see M.G.S. Narayanan, "Bachelors of Science", in *Aspects of Aryanization*. Trivandrum, 1973 pp. 21-42.
16. See Michael Tharakan, "Socio-economic Factors in Educational Development : Case of 19th century Travancore", *Economic and Political Weekly*, vol. XIX, no. 45, 1984. Also Mary Kurien, "English Schools and Colonial Subjectification", Unpublished M. Phil. dessertation, School of Social Sciences, Mahatma Gandhi University, 1993.
17. The details of matters relating to land rights in late medieval and early modern Kerala are yet to be studied. For general observations see T.C.

Varghese, *Agrarian Change and Economic Consequences: Land Tenure in Kerala, 1850-1960,* Bombay, 1970.

18. For a study of the arrival of printing in Kerala from this perspective see C.I. Isaac, "Printing Press in Colonial Travancore: Aspects of Subjectification", Unpublished M.Phil. dissertation. School of Social Sciences, Mahatma Gandhi University, 1993.
19. For the details of the Sreenarayana Movement, see Chandramohan, "Popular Culture and Socio-religious Reform: Narayana Guru and Ezhavas of Travancore", *Studies in History: New Series,* vol. 2, no. 1.
20 For a detailed study of the *Elavas* and their Movement see P. Chandramohan, *Social and Political Protest in Travancore: A Study of the Sreenarayana Dharma Paripalana Yogam (1900-1938),* unpublished M. Phil. dissertation, Jawaharlal Nehru University, 1981.
21. For an analysis of the discursive dimensions of Reform in the context see S. Raju, "Discourse of Reformulation: Soul and Body of the Society", paper in *Lateral Study Series,* 3, School of Social Sciences, Mahatma Gandhi University, 1993.

SEVEN

COALITION POLITICS

The Kerala Experience

K. RAMAN PILLAI

The Socio-Political Milieu

Kerala situated at the land's end of India has been the meeting place of ancient religions, cultures and traditions. Though there was a common culture, it had been influenced by the Christian and Muslim cultures which flourished under the patronage of the tolerant Hindu princes. Over the centuries, Kerala had remained 'a living museum of ethnology, culture and religion, presenting every stage of development'.

Following the footsteps of Jews and Christians, Muslim religious leaders visited Kerala. Joseph Rabbon, the Jewish leader, St. Thomas the Christian missionary and Malik Ibu Dinar, the Messiah of Islam, constituted the religious trio responsible for the popularisation of the message of the respective religions in Kerala. Among the Indian religions both Buddhism and Jainism had their impact on Kerala though the subsequent Brahmanical revival swept them away as in the rest of India.

The history of Kerala is replete with instances of religious tolerance and harmony. The Hindu princes and nobles vied with one another in extending favours to Muslims and Christians. While the relationship between Hinduism, Islam and Christianity had been one of equality and mutual respect, this was not visible between different castes within Hinduism.

The hierarchical character of Hinduism and its emphasis on 'purity' and 'pollution' as existing between castes was rigorously enforced by the upper caste Hindus, the Namputiris and the Nairs. 'Lower castes' were not allowed even to use public roads where even dogs and cattle could stray. Each major caste had its own code of behaviour and rules relating to marriage, property and inheritance rights. Social stratification was at its peak by the beginning of the 19th century.

The establishment of British rule over Kerala witnessed the beginning of a gradual change in the social order. The gradual enforcement of English civil and criminal laws encroached upon the age-old privileges of the upper caste Hindus. The encouragement to education which Kerala and especially Travancore and Cochin received through their rulers and through missionaries had exposed a considerable section of the population to liberal Western ideas and enabled them to assess their social position in relation to it.

Social Reform Movements

The caste-ridden social order underwent changes under the impact of the Social Reform Movement launched by pioneers in the field like Sree Narayana Guru, Chattampi Swami, Ayyankali and others. While the Hindu backward communities were organising themselves for improving their social status, the forward communities also did not lag behind. The SNDP Sangham, Sadhujana Paripalana Sangham, the Yoga Kshema Sabha and Nair Samajam were formed in the wake of the Social Reform movements. Each of these organisations tried to protect the interests of people belonging to the particular community and thus became sectarian in outlook and functioning.

The Social Reform Movements made considerable impact on the politics of Kerala. Chattampi Swami and Sree Narayana Guru revolted against Brahmin ascendancy and campaigned effectively for the mitigation of the rigours of caste. The most important achievement of NSS (Nair Service Society) on the plane of social reform was the change over of Nairs from matriliny to patriliny and division of family property replacing the joint family system. The legislation abolishing the matrilineal system was passed in 1925 leading to the partition of large estates held by joint families.

The Vaikom Satyagraha (1924-25) and the Guruvayur Satyagraha (1931-32) were important episodes in the struggle for the eradication of untouchability in Kerala. The untouchables were not allowed to enter the temples nay even walk along the roads adjoining the Vaikom temple. It was against this evil custom that Vaikom Satyagraha was started in March 1924. Although the Satyagraha failed to achieve the desired goal, the movement electrified the whole country on the question of caste discrimination. The Guruvayur Satyagraha was launched to throw open the temple for all castes. As a result of these movements, the temples were thrown open to all classes in 1936 by an edict of the Maharaja of Travancore.

The Social Reform Movements exposed the people of Kerala to new ideas in the realm of politics as well as social structure. The old value system based on matriliny, landlordism and the hierarchical caste system had declined. The search for new values led to radical political movements as well as new trends in literature.

The Hindu society can be broadly categorised into two sections-the high castes (Savarnas) and the low castes (Avarnas). The Namputiris, the Tamil Brahmins, the Kshatriyas and the Nairs formed the Savarnas. The 'low castes' included the Ezhavas, the Pulayas, Parayas and Kuravas. Each caste had its own subcastes.

Among the Christians the following denominations are prominent—Anglo-Indians, Latin Catholics, Syrian Catholics, Marthomites, Jacobites and Church of South India. The Muslims of Kerala form two distinct groups: the descendants of the Arab traders and the Keralites who were converted voluntarily because they wished to escape from the social disabilities of belonging to low Hindu castes or converted forcibly during the invasions of Hyder Ali and Tipu Sultan in the late 18th century.

Kerala has rightly been called the 'political laboratory' of India. Communalism as it finds expression in casteism had always been considered the bane of politics in Kerala. The Christians and Muslims represent the religious minorities and the Hindu backward classes and castes constitute the majority in Kerala. The battle for economic and political advantage is based on this social stratification.

The main contenders for economic and political power in the erstwhile Travancore-Cochin area were the Christians and the Nairs having powerful communal organisations. Ezhavas jumped into the fray later. The rivalry among these communities has been a chronic problem of Kerala politics.

The representatives of the Christians, Nairs and Ezhavas kept aloof from the nationalist movement in the initial stages. Later the Christian leadership found it more profitable to hover round the Congress as it facilitated the fight against the establishment then represented by C.P. Ramaswamy Iyer, former Dewan of Travancore who favoured the Nair community. At one stage, the Nairs and Ezhavas ganged up against the challenge of Christians under 'Hindu Mandalam'. Slowly the Congress in Travancore-Cochin area became a confederation of communal and caste forces. The rivalry between the Nairs and Ezhavas got relegated to the background in the face of the challenge of their combined political power, spurred by the leftist forces spearheaded by the Communist Party. The economically weaker communities and classes chose to remain on the side of the left progressive parties: the privileged sections irrespective of caste or religion sided with the Congress or Kerala Congress a break-away group of the Indian National Congress.

The political situation in Malabar an integral part of the Madras State until 1956 was entirely different. The Congress movement in Malabar in its formative period was more or less representative of the privileged sections of the caste Hindus. Politics underwent radical changes when the message of the national movement reached the masses. The Congress was forced to turn left; its leadership at all levels went to the Congress Socialist Party. These leaders later on went over to the Communist fold becoming the pioneers of the party in the State. They made the first major attempt to break the barriers of casteism and communalism while consciously forging mass organisations of the working class.

It was the backwards among Hindu communities that constituted the majority of the rural masses. They rallied round the Communist Party while the Muslim masses, though economically backward, kept aloof or preferred the Muslim League to the Communist Party.

Coalition Politics

The term 'coalition' as employed in the political sense commonly denotes a cooperative arrangement under which two or more political parties unite to form a government or ministry. It is a combination of political parties none of which has an absolute majority in the legislature and which put aside their political differences to form a government with a minimum programme acceptable to all partners.

A coalition is in essence a system of government in which actual policies are the result of an attempt to synthesise the conflicting views of different political parties.

No other State in India has experimented coalition government in its different shapes and different forms, with all sorts of permutations and combinations in successive periods as it was done in Kerala. A retrospective analysis of the working of coalition governments in Kerala will throw a good deal of light on the practical problems associated with the working of coalition governments. Such an analysis will be relevant in the present context in which coalition governments have come into being not only in other States but also at the Centre.

As has already been mentioned, the root causes for the formation of coalition governments in Kerala can be traced to some of the sociological and historical factors that dominated the society and politics in Kerala. In the pre-independent period the native States of Travancore and Cochin had their political groups mainly based on caste and religious communities. Kerala is an example of a plural society in which no religious or caste group is in a dominant position. In such a situation various groups represent communal interests. The dominance of a majority party is always taken to mean the predominant influence of a particular regional or communal group. Therefore the majority party system has never worked in the socio-political milieu of Kerala.

Communalism as it finds expression in casteism, regionalism, the small size of the State and the system of education are factors contributing to multiplicity of parties and instability of government which ultimately result in coalition governments in Kerala. Each small group, communal or regional, based on some other interest gains undue importance in the context of multiplicity of parties.

Coalition Politics in Kerala

With the fluid political climate that prevails in Kerala with a proliferation of political parties, coalition politics has become inevitable. In the Kerala situation coalitions are not characterised so much by ideological affinities as by narrow partisan interests. The making and breaking of coalitions were a regular feature of Kerala politics till the 80s. Thereafter they have become more or less stable.

Coalition politics made its begining in 1960 with the victory of the non-communist alliance of Congress, the PSP and the Muslim League. This alliance collapsed within two years. In the 1965 elections no party or a group of parties could manage a majority. A long spell of President's rule was an inevitable consequence.

In the 1967 elections the seven-party United Front comprising Communist Party of India (Marxist), (CPI (M), Communist Party of India (CPI), Revolutionary Socialist Party (RSP), Samyukta Socialist Party (SSP), Muslim League (ML), Kerala Socialist Party (KSP) and Karshaka Thozhilali Party (KTP) swept the polls securing 113 seats in a House of 133. A United Front Ministry under E.M.S. Namboodiripad assumed office in March 1967. Consequent upon the infighting among the coalition partners, the ministry bowed out of office in October 1969. A mini front under the leadership of the CPI leader, C. Achutha Menon came to power in 1969. This marked the beginning of the CPI-led coalition in Kerala. The CPI-Congress alliance came out victorious in the 1970 elections and remained in power for more than six years—an all-time record in Kerala's coalitional politics. The period, 1977 to 1980 witnessed four coalitions mainly anti-Marxists headed respectively by K. Karunakaran (Congress), A.K. Antony (Congress), P.K. Vasudevan Nair (CPI) and C.H.

Mohammed Koya (Muslim League). While Karunakaran's Cabinet lasted for only one month that of Mohammed Koya remained in power for 51 days.

The 60s and 70s witnessed splits in almost all political parties as well as the emergence of communal political parties. In the 1980 elections the Left Democratic Front (LDF) secured a majority and assumed office under the leadership of the CPI (M) leader E.K. Nayanar. But within two years it also collapsed as a result of the withdrawal of the Congress (A) and the Kerala Congress (M) from the LDF Government. The next elections in 1982 went in favour of the Congress-led United Democratic Front (UDF) consisting of Indian National Congress, Muslim League, Kerala Congress (M), NDP and Janta Party (G). However the political balance tilted in favour of the LDF in the 1987 elections. For the first time since 1970, the LDF formed a government without the support of Kerala Congress and Muslim League thereby creating history in the electoral politics of Kerala. All the regional and communal parties were kept at bay by the LDF. The UDF again came to power in the 1991 elections.

K. Karunakaran formed a Government in June 1991 but he had to bow out of office in May 1994 in deference to the protests by the coalition partners including INC against his arbitrary style of functioning. A. K. Antony was brought in as Chief Minister and he reconstituted the Cabinet which continued upto April 1996. In the elections held in April 1996, LDF bagged 80 seats out of 140 and came to power. After the decisive victory of the LDF in the elections the mantle of chief ministership had fallen once again on E.K. Nayanar for the third time. His choice had come as a surprise due to the fact he did not enter the election fray on grounds of health and inability to carry the workload both as the party's State secretary and as a legislator giving the impression that he would prefer to keep the party position. He contested the by-election from Thalassery and his astounding victory has indicated his popularity as a leader. Thus, in all, Kerala witnessed 16 coalition governments since 1960 with periods ranging between one month and six years and five months and constituent parties varying between two and seven. Table 7.1 indicates the duration and composition of the 17 coalition governments in Kerala.

Table 7.1 Duration and Composition of Ministries in Kerala.

Sl. No.	*Chief Minister*	*Duration From To*	*No. of Ministers*	*Constituent Parties*
1.	E.M.S. Namboodiripad	Apr.1957-Jul.1959	11	CPI & Independents
2.	Pattom Thanu Pillai	Feb.1960-Sep.1962	11	INC and PSP
3.	R. Sankar	Sep.1962-Sep.1964	10	INC and PSP
4.	E.M.S. Namboodiripad	*Mar.1967-Oct.1969	13	CPM, CPI, PSP, RSP, ML, KTP, and KSP.
5.	C. Achutha Menon	Nov.1969-Aug.1970	8	CPI, INC, PSP, RSP, ML and KC
6.	C. Achutha Menon	Oct.1970-Mar.1977	14	CPI, INC, PSP, RSP, ML and KC
7.	K. Karunakaran	Mar.1977-Apr.1977	15	INC, CPI, RSP,ML, KC, NDP, and SRP
8.	A.K. Antony	Apr. 1977-Oct.1978	15	INC, CPI, RSP, ML, KC, and NDP**
9.	P.K. Vasudeven Nair	Oct.1978-Oct.1979	14	INC, CPI, RSP, ML, and KC
10.	C.H. Muhammed Koya	Oct.1979-Dec.1979	6	INC, ML, KC, NDP, and PSP
11.	E.K. Nayanar	Jan.1980-Oct. 1981	17	CPM, INC, (A), RSP, CPI, KC (M), KC (P) and AIML
12.	K. Karunakaran	Dec.1981-Mar.1982	8	INC, (I), INC (A), ML, KC, (M), KC (J), NDP and JP (G)
13.	K. Karunakaran	May. 1982-Mar.1987	19	INC, ML, KC, (M) NDP, JP(G), KC (J) & SRP.

Table 7.1 (*contd.*)

Sl. No.	*Chief Minister*	*Duration From To*	*No. of Ministers*	*Constituent Parties*
14.	E.K. Nayanar	Mar.1987-Jun.1991	19	CPM,CPI, Cong (S), RSP and Janata
15.	K. Karunakaran	June.1991-May.1994	19	INC, ML, KC, (M) KC, (P), NDP, CMP and KC(J)
16.	A.K.Antony	May.1994-Apr.1996	17	INC, ML, KC (M), KC (J) and CMP.
17.	E.K. Nayanar	May 1996-	14	CPM, CPI, RSP, Cong, (S), KC (J) and Janata Dal.

* Assembly elections held in March 1965 were declared infructuous.

** NDP later withdrew support to A. K. Antony.

An analysis of the functioning of coalition governments in Kerala since 1960 reveals the salient features of coalition politics in Kerala.

1. No single party can hope to secure a clear majority in the State Assembly.
2. Even if a party forms a government either by itself (with the support of others) or in coalition with other parties, it can never be certain that the support will continue till the end of the term.
3. The alignments and realignments among political parties keep on changing before and after every election be it to the State Assembly or to the Lok Sabha. The two major combinations of political parties in Kerala since the 60's are the United Democratic Front (UDF) under the leadership of the Congress and the Left Democratic Front (LDF) under the leadership of the Communist Party of India (Marxist). In fact political parties in Kerala other than the Congress and the CPI (M) align with the UDF or LDF from time to time and the nature

of this alliance determines the power structure in Kerala. The possibility of changing sides and entering into an alliance that comes to power has really enhanced the bargaining capacity of some of the political parties more especially the regional and communal parties like the Kerala Congress, the Muslim League, the National Democratic Party (NDP) and the Socialist Republican Party (SRP). The followers of these parties especially those of Kerala Congress (with four splinter groups) and Muslim League have been the major beneficiaries of the administration. The course of every election and the final outcome will be influenced by the nature and character of the respective alliances. The votes secured by an individual candidate are not exclusively votes given to him, they also include the votes of the political allies.

4. More often than not, the United Fronts are formed on a negative platform either anti-Congress or anti-Marxist. Coalitions are often 'marriages of convenience' to be broken on petty issues.
5. Socio-economic developments are considerably hampered because of political instability. More time is spent on setting the coalition house in order than towards formulating and implementing peoples' welfare programmes. Administration has come to mean division of spoils among the coalition partners. As a result, the State's common problems like unemployment, slow industrialisation and decay of traditional industries like handloom, coir and cashew remain unattended for most of the time.
6. In the political struggles in Kerala, one finds a strong undercurrent of ideology but in coalition ministries this is conspicuous by its absence. Political expediency has gained acceptance over all other considerations.
7. Each decade since the 60's had contributed its own share to the destabilisation of Kerala politics. During the 60's splits occurred in the Indian National Congress and the CPI. Kerala Congress was formed by the dissidents of the INC in 1964. The 70s was marked by coalitions based on the plank of anti-Marxism. The Marxist party was kept at bay by five coalitions.

This decade also witnessed the emergence of two communal parties the NDP and the SRP. By the end of the decade, splits took place in almost all political parties. This phenomenon of splits continued unabated in the first half of 80s. There is not a single political party which has not split during this period be it the Cong (I), CPI, Kerala Congress, Muslim League, NDP and SRP. 'Split within a split' can be appropriately used in the Kerala context. The splinter groups are known after the name of their leaders indicating clearly the basis of the split. These groups get a chance to join the government because of the coalitional nature of the government.

8. The lure for power has done considerable damage to the body politic of Kerala. It has prompted major political parties to pamper minor parties out of proportion with the result that these minor parties thrive on the shoulders of the major partners in the coalition. The minor parties have always been the beneficiaries of the administration. Hardly a week passes without some political crisis brewing up causing considerable damage to the administration.
9. The political struggle often tends to become a game of numbers. What permutations and combinations will enable a major party to come to power? This seems to be the most important consideration before and after the elections . Kerala has tried all kinds of experiments in running a democratic government, one-party majority rule whether of the Congress or the Communist party, minority government, a coalition government limited to two parties and multi-party coalitions. The only coalition that has not been tried so far is the one between the Congress and the CPI (M)—a difficult but not an impossible proposition.
10. The success of a coalition depends on the presence within it of a central political force, a mature leadership, a common goal, the restraint displayed by the constituent parties in pursuing their own individual policies and above all the ability to be on the same wavelength with the central force. Most of these factors were absent in many of the coalitions in Kerala and hence their failure.

11. Stability of a coalition government by and large depends upon the leadership of the Chief Minister. The policies that are adopted by the coalition government are formulated by the coalescing parties and merely finalised by the Chief Minister. But in a conflictual coalition game, each party opposes every other party, each party seeks its own maximum ministerial advantage. Hence the Chief Minister's ability is much counted in the working of a coalition government. The leadership must be able to solve the differences between parties in the coalition. A considerable amount of time is spent in sorting out inter-party differences.

Kerala : A Pace-Setter

In spite of various difficulties and problems, Kerala has made headway in making distinctive contributions to coalition politics. It has been able to explore new concepts through parliamentary coalitions. The role of the cabinet has yielded place to co-ordination committee and liaison committee to be prominent in the decision-making process. Inter-party differences are settled in these committees. Kerala's political solution seems to be in coalition government which has sprouted mainly from the stratified social structure. In fact Kerala's experience with coalition politics can serve as a pace-setter for the rest of the country.

In the ultimate analysis, the success of a coalition depends on the commitment of the coalition partners to a pre-election common minimum programme, the self-restraint on the part of the constituent parties in not trying to push their partisan interests at the expense of the common interest and above all the ability of the leader of the coalition in resolving amicably the intra-party and inter-party conflicts.

EIGHT

SOCIAL STRUCTURE AND SOCIAL CHANGE*

T.K. OOMMEN

The Working Group on social structure and social change had five sessions and ten presentations which dealt with a wide variety of themes and several social categories. The social categories analysed include Adivasis, Dalits, Thiyyas, Syrian Christians and Hutment Dwellers. The themes too were varied : popularisation of science, Ravi Varma's painting, Kathakali, use and misuse of secularism and the inadequacy of Kerala's current education system. Admittedly a review of these papers will produce only a pot pouri and hence I desist that attempt.

As the intent of this working group was to analyse Kerala's social structure and social change in the context of development experience, it is necessary to identify a few specificities of Kerala. These, I am aware, are widely known but perhaps inadequately recognised and hence the moment for recounting.

First, the linguistic homogeneity of Kerala as compared to most other States is substantial: 98 per cent of the residents in Kerala are native speakers of Malayalam. This makes communication at the grassroots level an eminently viable project.

Second, the people of Kerala share a common myth of origin and collective memory notwithstanding the fact that Kerala is a product of amalgamation of three disparate parts—Travancore and Cochin (the two erstwhile principalities) and Malabar—the Malayalam-speaking part of the former Madras presidency. This imparts a unique ethos to the Kerala society, not easily found in several other societies of India.

* This is the full text of the presentation given by T. K. Oommen at the plenary session in his capacity as Chairperson of working session II on Social Structure and Social Change.

Third, while Kerala is uni-lingual, she is utterly multi-religious. Kerala's three major religions—Hinduism, Islam and Christianity—coexist in a situation of balance because of their numerical size and socio-economic standing. Further, Kerala Christianity is a pre-colonial and Kerala Islam is a pre-conquest phenomenon. This historicity and rootedness makes it nearly impossible to stigmatise Christians and Muslims as 'outsiders' as is the wont in much of the rest of India. This produces a social ethos which reduces communal conflict.

Fourth, missionary influence made possible early developments, particularly in the sectors of education and health. This had a demonstrative effect on all communities to initiate projects and programmes in these fields. The caste and community associations of Kerala are not only identity-seeking but also development-promoting instruments.

Fifth, the incomplete *varna-jati* system, particularly the absence of Vaishyas provided an opportunity structure not only to Jews, Muslims and Syrian Christians to fill this structural vacuum but also rendered entrepreneurship a caste-neutral enterprise, to a large extent. This facilitated individuals and families with a wide variety of background to pursue economic activities.

Sixth, the absence of rural-urban dichotomy and the pattern of dispersed village habitat made the location of economic and social infrastructural facilities in Kerala a viable proposition providing for ready-made catchment areas. This provides considerable economies of scale to infrastructural facilities.

Seventh, thickly populated Kerala was always in the forefront of spatial mobility within India and across the world. The proverbial Malayali diaspora not only encouraged spatial mobility but also social and ideological mobility. While a substantial section of the Kerala immigrants settle down at the point of destination, if it were legally and culturally possible, the tendency to repatriate one's earning back to Kerala is widespread among Malayalis. This provides for an instant visible economic prosperity in Kerala.

Eighth, prevalence of hypergamy between Nair women and men drawn from Brahmins and Kshatriyas created an ethos of caste fluidity and facilitated circulation of wealth among these social categories. Further, matriliny among Nairs, the dominant caste of Kerala, not only provided for certain juridical advantage to Nair women but also created a social milieu which rendered Kerala women socially visible and legally conscious.

Ninth, Kerala's is a 'movement society' par excellence; protest is ubiquitous and even institutionalised. Kerala is famous for its literacy movement, agrarian movement, left movement, science movement and the like. But even the right of lower caste women to cover their breast and the right to keep mustache by lower caste men were achieved through organised protests. This tendency to wrest one's rights through struggles substantially contributed to the social development in Kerala.

Tenth, if the starting of printing in Malayalam came through missionary initiative, the stupendous spread of the press in Kerala is the result of competition between different political parties and communities. One can clearly identify newspapers and magazines in terms of their communal and political identifications. This in turn led to the creation of an intellectual ethos which promoted intense debates of ideas and ideologies. In the rural areas, the ubiquitous coffee shop played an important role in spreading current ideas among the poor and the lowly placed.

Finally, crystallisation of two political blocks ensuring stability both to governance and opposition makes the continuation of development projects possible without much interruption. It seems that there is a broad consensus regarding the shaping of Kerala society among all political parties.

I venture to suggest that unless we take cognizance of the combination of these factors it will not be possible to understand and situate Kerala's development experience. Having said this, let me provide you with a flavour of presentations and discussions in the working session on social structure and social change.

It was argued by S. Mohan that notwithstanding the fact that Kerala has achieved high levels of literacy and education, the prevailing pattern of education does not respond to the demands of the market, resulting in high level of unemployment. In turn, the present education also undervalues production orientation and needs of skills and creates a wedge between manual and non-manual occupations. Thus, while social transformation in the socio-political sector is apace, the change in the economic context is lagging behind. This economic lag can be partially rectified through change in values and attitudes and orienting production and marketing to niches appropriate to Kerala.

Kerala is in the forefront not only in regard to general education but also in other respects. Two such examples are the struggles for *Kudikidappu* (hutment dwelling) rights and the popularisation of science by Kerala Shastra Sahitya Parishad (KSSP). However, these projects also reflect the lag between different sectors of Kerala society. For example, while *Kudikidappu* has a deeper meaning than mere economic gains achieved through it by the landless, even the economic gains are not translated into social relations; 'feudal' social relations have not disappeared argued Jai Sen. Similarly, the presentation on KSSP by Shoma Choudhary unfolded that notwithstanding the movement's monumental achievements in grass-roots communication, it has not addressed adequately the issues of ethno-science and the autonomy of civil society vis-a-vis the State.

Development always raises the issue of distributive justice. Are the wretched of the earth any better in Kerala as compared with the condition of their counterparts elsewhere? Not quite. Francis Kulirani discussed immigration of Travancore peasantry to the tribal belt of Wayanad and demonstrated that it has initiated social change among the tribals by linking them with the urban milieu. However, de-tribalisation did endanger their identity. Further, colonisation of the tribal belt is leading both to pauperisation and proletarianisation of the tribal population.

The issue of identity is much more germane to the Dalits as brought out by Sanal Mohan in his presentation. A variety of identity constructions are in vogue in Kerala. While self-constructed identities such as Cherumar and Sambavan are anchored to past glory and confined to Kerala, those of Dalits and Adi Dravidas are self-constructed all-India identities which are emancipatory. There are other all-India identities which are imposed on Dalits either by the State (e.g., Scheduled Castes) or by co-religionists (e.g., Neo-Christians and Neo-Buddhists) of upper caste origin. Thus, there are both consolidating and fractionating as well as emancipatory and stigmatising identity constructions. Be that as it may, when it comes to equality, particularly economic equality, the situation of Kerala Dalits is not very different from that of Dalits elsewhere, in fact it is worse. Thus, the material fruits of development barely trickle down to the traditionally disadvantaged-Adivasis and Dalits—notwithstanding the gains in the socio-political realm.

The problem of identity assumes a wider canvas both substantively and conceptually in Kerala as elsewhere in India. The context of this is the juxtaposition between communalism and secularism, a theme discussed by Saji Jacob. There are two articulations in this context. First, Kerala is a den of the politics of casteism and communalism because mobilisations for distributive justice are anchored to castes and religious communities. In this view, even the State practises communal politics. The second view is that caste and religious community politics is essentially secularising because the deprived are being organised for inter-group equality. The problems here are mainly two; (i) differing conceptualisations of secularism and (ii) disagreement regarding the units of distributive justice—the individual or the group.

There is another context in which the problem of identity surfaces—self-definitions versus other definitions, as brought out by Susan Visvanathan and Janaki Abraham through the recounting of their field work encounters and experiences. The hyphenated identity of the two researchers provided a fascinating opportunity towards conceptual clarifications. Criss-crossing identities such as Hindu-Christian, Tamil-Malayali, Caste-Hindu-Tiyya, Marxist-Christian, Hindu-Gandhian and above all the gender identity cutting across all these exist in the everyday life-world. How does one negotiate with these variegated identities? Is there a possibility of mutation or syntheses?

It seems the answer is in the affirmative if we look at Kerala's art forms. Arjun Raina contended that Kathakali is highly structured and yet the possibility of improvisation is enormous; it combines the religious and the secular, the folk and the classic, freedom and restraint. It can be seen in part or in full, it can be performed with or without an audience! Indeed, Kathakali provides an acute representations of the astute Malayali ambiguity.

But this effort at syntheses is not without its strains and stresses as is evident in Ravi Varma's paintings. Arunima postulated that the tension between the search for national modernity as against colonial modernity, the tension between national authenticity versus imitation of the West, and the insistence on cultural sovereignty and autonomy bordering on cultural relativism are all present in Ravi Varma's paintings. Pursuantly, the crisis of modernity is the crisis of self itself. But one is not sure which brand of modernity is involved here. The modernity of structural differentiation, of rationalisation, of making history or of decolonising the life-world?

My inadequate and indeed tangential references to the variety of themes and categories dealt with in the working group on social structure and social change do not unfold the richness of presentations made and discussions ensued. Let me, however, conclude by referring to the creative and critical tension that permeated the deliberations in the five sessions.

I suggest that there were two essential tensions emanating from social structure and articulated in the ongoing process of social change in the context of Kerala's development experience. First, the tension between the politics of equality and politics of identity. Those who pursue the politics of equality tend to stigmatise those who pursue the politics of identity as communal and conservative and privilege themselves as the torch-bearers of progress and secularism. Those who pursue the politics of identity insist that those who uphold the politics of equality ignore the ground reality; they are promoting elitism in the name of merit.

There is a serious problem here. Those who pursue the politics of identity belong to two diametrically different sets: those who insist on reinforcing their dominant identity and those who are searching a new and dignified identity, the traditionally disadvantaged. These two varieties of identity politics are qualitatively different; if the first is hegemonic the second is emancipatory. One must understand and squarely recognise this difference before privileging the politics of equality.

The second tension that I am referring to is that between the individual and the group as objects of distributive justice. Occasionally, it takes the form of caste versus class. The self-righteousness of those who argue for individual and pursuantly for class as the unit of distributive justice is all too evident. But those who argue for the group and therefore caste or communities as the unit of distributive justice insist that there is a colossal co-terminality between caste and class in India.

Let me stop by alerting ourselves that if we do not recognize these seminal issues it only indicates our incapacity to learn from our experience, I mean Kerala's Development Experience.

NINE

IS THE KERALA MODEL SUSTAINABLE?

Lessons from the past: Prospects for the future

RICHARD W. FRANKE & BARBARA H. CHASIN

Is the Kerala Model sustainable? To answer this question adequately, we must pose several others:

1. What do we mean by sustainability?
2. What is the Model that is to be sustained?
3. What forces brought the Model into being?
4. Why is the question of sustainability being asked now?
5. What are the principal forces threatening the Model's sustainability?
6. What resources are available to sustain the Model? Can the forces that created the Model in the first place be used to sustain it, or will new forces be necessary?

To attempt an answer to these questions we propose a formal definition of sustainability and of the Kerala Model. We shall then elaborate the definition of the Kerala Model to identify those elements that are most critical to the question of sustainability. This will be followed by a consideration of the Model's major failures and shortcomings that threaten its sustainability—what many scholars now call, 'The Crisis of the Kerala Model'. The present world political and economic structure favours models based on private accumulation and growing inequality over Kerala's emphasis on public services and egalitarian ideals. Out of the complex present-day conjuncture of events and processes, Kerala's activists and intellectuals have fashioned the elements of a new Kerala Model based on decentralization and high levels of local participation. Can the New Kerala Model preserve what is best from the old? Can it overcome the major failures of the old model? Can it foster local structures strong enough to survive in the hostile world of international capitalism? Can it lead to meaningful environmental preservation? Can it empower people to achieve these difficult goals just as they once achieved public services and redistribution of wealth?

Sustainability

Sustainability is one of the most widely discussed concepts in the developed world at present.[1] Most proponents see it primarily in ecological terms. We suggest a broader conceptualisation. We consider a development model sustainable to the extent that it:

1. Improves or at least maintains the material quality of life of the population.
2. Expands or at least maintains access to any entitlements necessary for economic security and personal dignity, particularly of vulnerable groups.
3. Expands or at least maintains the number of people obtaining access to production resources adequate for a decent life or employment at reasonable wages.
4. Reduces the level of social and economic inequalities, or at least does not exacerbate them.
5. Expands or at least maintains basic political and individual rights.
6. Improves or at least maintains productive resources including land, water, flora and fauna.[2]

For many years, the Kerala Model has met most of these criteria. Few models elsewhere have come so close to fulfilling all the demands of sustainability. This results from the features of the Kerala Model.

The Kerala Model

We define the Kerala Model as:

1. A set of high material quality of life indicators coinciding with low per capita incomes, both distributed across nearly the entire population of Kerala.

2. A set of wealth and resources redistribution programmes that have largely brought about the high material quality of life indicators.
3. High levels of political participation and activism among ordinary people along with substantial numbers of dedicated leaders at all levels. Kerala's mass activism and committed cadre were able to function within a largely democratic structure which their activism has served to reinforce.

Quality of Life Indicators

The most obvious component of the Kerala Model is the set of statistical quality of life indicators putting Kerala closer to high-income developed countries than to its counterparts in the low-income world. The most recent figures we could locate are mostly from 1993 and reflect Kerala's continuing success as shown in Table 9.1.

It is important to emphasize Kerala's continuing lead among low-income areas and the rest of India. Recent criticisms of the Kerala Model suggest that Kerala is losing its lead within India. K.K. George (1993:119) cites figures indicating that Punjab now spends more per capita on education, and that both Rajasthan and Punjab now spend more per capita on health than Kerala. He also compares Kerala unfavourably with Maharashtra, Haryana, Madhya Pradesh, Nagaland, Rajasthan, and Uttar Pradesh in pension payments to destitutes. These weaknesses should not be overlooked, though they remain minor compared with Kerala's continuing overall ability to deliver a high basic material quality of life to its people as the indicators show. Oommen and Anandaraj's district-level profile (1996) found 9 of Kerala's 14 districts among the top 12 in all of India on a composite of literacy, life expectancy, and several economic variables. Kerala's lowest district of Malappuram was 31st on a list with 372 entries.

Table 9.1 Comparison of Quality of Life Indicators, 1993

Indicator	*Kerala*	*India*	*Low-Income Countries*[a]	*United States*
Per capita GNP ($)	[b]180	300	300	24,740
Adult literacy rate (%)	[c]91	48	51	96
Life expectancy in years		61	56	76
	[d]73 (Male)			
	79 (Female)			
Infant mortality per 1,000	13	80	89	9
Birth rate per 1,000	17	29	40	16

Sources: GOK 1995:3, 21; Bose 1991; World Bank 1995: 162-63, 212-15.

Notes:

[a] Low-income refers in 1993 to 45 economies with per capita GNP of $695 or less. With China and India excluded, it refers to 43 countries, almost the same as the 37 countries used to Franke and Chasin 1989: 11 for 1986 data and the 38 countries used in Franke and Chasin 1994:ii for 1991 data.

[b] We estimated the $ figure for Kerala by multiplying the State Government's 1993 figure of Rs. 6,009 (GOK 1995:3) by 30, the approximate number of rupees per dollar over the past three years. Based on the World Bank (1995:162) estimate of $300 for India nationally in 1993, this implies a 1993 all-India per capita income of Rs. 9,000.

[c] Kerala's adult literacy rate for 1991 is taken from the 1991 Indian Census, prior to the literacy campaign. By the end of 1991, Kerala's rate was near 100%, but weaknesses in the follow-up may have reduced the rate again.

[d] The latest figures (1996) relevant for male and female are taken from Irudaya Rajan *et.at.* vol. II. (Editor)

It is also important to note that Kerala's performance on the basic indicators has continued to improve since the early 1980s. Generally, the rest of India and the low-income countries have made only sluggish progress. Kerala's infant mortality rate dropped from 27 in 1986 (Frank and Chasin 1989:11) to 13 in 1993 (see Table 9.1). This is a 52 per cent drop. By contrast, the all-India rate appears to have gone from 86 in 1986 to 80 in 1993, a decline of only 7 per cent. The closest Indian State to Kerala was Punjab, with an IMR in 1992 of 56 (GOK 1995:S14), more than four times the 1993 Kerala rate. Furthermore, Kerala continues to maintain a nearly even distribution of its indicators when compared with the rest of India. The all-India IMR for 1992 was 53 for urban areas versus

85 for rural areas, a 38 per cent difference. For Punjab the rural figure was 60 versus 41 for the cities, a 32 per cent difference. In Kerala, the rural rate of 17 contrasted only with an urban rate of 13, a 23 per cent difference (computed from GOK 1995:S14). Birth rates show similar patterns.

What is the significance of Kerala's continuing ability to improve literacy, birth rates, infant mortality, and life expectancy? It simply means: the Kerala Model is still valid and relevant as an alternative to growth-only development strategies. Despite the many problems the Model faces, it seems to continue to function, even in times of crisis. This important fact should not be overlooked when assessing the sustainability of the Kerala Model.

Redistribution Programmes: Case Study of Nadur Village

Behind Kerala's statistical indicators lies a century-long process of struggle for redistribution of wealth and the expansion of public services that would benefit most people rather than a small elite. In 1986-87, we conducted research in the central Kerala village of Nadur ("Centreville") to ascertain the effects of these struggles at the local level. Our first goal was to assess the effects of the land reform.

Nadur village has many typical features of Kerala, historically, geographically, and sociologically. Nadur lies in the former princely state of Cochin. In terms of land reforms, Cochin lies between the former princely State of Travancore, now southern Kerala in which many changes took place in the 19th century, and Malabar, now northern Kerala, where the most protracted and bitter land struggles occurred. Nadur was the scene neither of intense battles between tenants and landlords in past decades nor of land occupations by radical peasant groups in the late 1960s as took place in some other villages. At the same time, Nadur has had its share of land reform militants and Communist organisers so that it represents a kind of midway point in terms of land reform struggles in Kerala.

Geographically, Nadur is in the lower foothills of the Western Ghat mountains and contains intensive wet-rice paddy fields typical of the lowland areas of Kerala, as well as cashew and coconut gardens and hillside fields more common in the central midlands.

It also contains some upland rubber and forest lands more like the parts of Kerala in the higher elevations to the east. In both history and geography, Nadur is thus in the middle of the range of types found in Kerala.

Nadur's 5,000 plus residents include representative numbers of all the major castes of Kerala except the Christians. Like many Cochin villages, Nadur has a higher than average percentage of Namputiri Brahmins, one of the most important former landlord groups in Kerala. It also has Nair caste members in several occupations, craft castes, Ezhavas, and Pulayas. The Nadur sample in 1987 contained only two households with workers sending large remittances from the Persian Gulf States. Nadur's near absence of such households makes it a controlled case in which the redistribution of the land reform should show up more clearly than in areas where remittances have flooded the village economy.

The Field Research

Nadur had been studied by Professor Joan Mencher who kindly made available to us copies of her 1971 household survey. Although the Kerala land reform was enacted in 1969 and went into effect in 1971, land titles in 1971 were still held by landlords and several households were paying rent. The 1971 survey, with a few assumptions, can be taken as pre-land reform, while our 1986-87 survey describes the situation 15-16 years later, after all land reform transfers had been completed. By comparing the two surveys we can describe how the land reform affected land ownership, income distribution by caste and class, and upward and downward income mobility of selected households.

The Findings

In the Nadur sample, abolition of Paddy land tenancy resulted in the transfer of 52.25 acres of land from 10 large landlords (6% of the sample) to 47 tenants (29% of the sample) who became fully entitled small holders. The former tenants received on average 74 cents each. One hundred and three landless households (64%) were not affected by the rice land reform.[3]

The abolition of house compound tenancy benefited 92 per cent of households. Rights to 47.87 acres were transferred from 7 households (4%) to 156 households (92%). The average tenancy in 1971 was 51 cents while the average owned in 1987 was 54 cents. The poorest labouring families gained title only to small and often inferior plots. Rents and interest dropped from 7 per cent of total sample income in 1971 to 1 per cent in 1987 (Franke 1993:110)

Declining Land and Income Inequality

We used the Gini Index to measure inequality. A decline in the Index means a decline in inequality. In Nadur, the Gini Index for Paddy land ownership inequality dropped 13 points. For house compound land, the Gini dropped 39 points between the two surveys. During the same 16 years period, the Gini Index for income inequality declined by 5.3 points. Although forces outside the land reform pulled both toward greater and less inequality, land reform must have caused much of this decline in income inequality. The 1974 Kerala Agricultural Workers' Protection Act may also have played a role in these figures.

Declining Caste Inequality

In Nadur, a reduction in caste inequality is one of the clearest consequences of the land reform. The Namputiri Brahmin's hold on land and high incomes was broken. In 1971, 12 Namboodiri caste households had incomes that correlated 0.86 with rice land and 0.89 with paramba owned. In 1987 the figures changed to -0.09 and -0.19. Namputiri incomes rose far less rapidly than those of other castes. Nair and Mannan caste households gained the most while the lowest caste Pulayas raised their relative position only slightly. Mannans and Pulayas probably gained more from programmes other than the land reform such as the reservation policies. The political conditions for these programmes, however, included the power of tenants and their allies in the land reform movement. Land reform struggles reinforced the leverage for these lowest caste groups to move upwards economically.

Class Inequality

Nadur's class structure was altered dramatically by the elimination of landlord and tenant classes. Former landlords dropped from garnering 6.5 times the sample average income in 1971 to 1.5 times the average in 1987. Former tenants did not gain much on average, but several occupational groups slightly improved their economic positions. Households depending primarily on farming raised their relative share of income from 60 per cent of average to 90 per cent. Land reform played an important but not determining role in these class changes.

Social and Economic Mobility

In Nadur upward mobility occurred in 16 households that gained land but only one that lost land. Downwardly mobile households included 2 that lost land and 5 that gained. Overall, changes in income levels correlated 0.19 with changes in Paddy land ownership, and 0.21 with changes in house compound land. Both associations are statistically significant. Many other factors interacted with the reform. These include access to highly paid wage labour, age and health of household head, number of wage earners in the household, and access to reservation and targeted development programmes. Land reform in Nadur helped foster upward mobility in conjunction with other social and economic processes.

Exploitation

One of the most effective components of Kerala's land reform was to end the threat of eviction of tenants by their landlords from either Paddy land or house compounds. The success of the land reform, however, has produced new tensions. In place of the struggle between tenants and landlords, former tenants are now at odds with their hired agricultural labourers. Where once the poor were pitted against the rich, now the poor are pitted against the slightly less poor. This development may present an obstacle to progressive forces in Kerala in rallying small landowners to their programmes.[4]

Landlord Response to the Land Reform

Nadur's Namputiri caste landlord households adopted various strategies to prevent the land reform from depriving them of high incomes and good future for their children. One strategy was to send their children for higher education to make professional employment the chief landlord response to the reform. This response has benefited Nadur because formerly parasitic landlords have become teachers, administrators, and small business people who contribute to the economy in ways their ancestors did not. Kerala's high unemployment of the educated, however, threatens the former landlords' escape route.

Other Redistribution Programmes in Nadur

Our Nadur study found that other Kerala programmes also had measurable effects. School and nursery lunches added 3 per cent to the incomes of the poorest households with children in school and raised their calorie intake by 5 per cent. The lunches improved the distribution of calories and income by caste, class, income, and land ownership groups (Franke 1993a:360).

Nadur's ration shop effectively reduced income inequality by 5 per cent in 1987, providing 10 per cent more income for the bottom two quintiles which include mostly agricultural labour and low caste households. The lunches and the ration shop became particularly important in July, near the end of the long lean season before the August harvest. By making available subsidised food, they probably reduced the need for borrowing by many poor households. Even so, 11 per cent of Nadur sample households reported food shortage so severe that, at least once during the reference year, they had to reduce food intake. Although 46 per cent reported eating less, borrowing money, or borrowing food at least once in the year (Franke 1993:176).

Agricultural labour pensions played a small but significant role in reducing inequality and bringing up the income levels of the poorest groups. Our research showed that 91 per cent of Pulaya caste households received at least one pension, that the pensions raised the average incomes of all households, by 17 per cent. The ration shop, school lunches, and agricultural labour pensions benefited female-supported households more than male-supported households. They thus contributed to reductions in one aspect of gender inequality (Franke and Chasin 1996:628).

Literacy in Nadur rose from 60 per cent in 1971 to 74 per cent in 1987. Among members of the age cohort 15-29 years, the average years of schooling was 8.1 for males and 7.6 for females. The age cohort 61+, by contrast, had below 2.5 years of school (Frank 1993:228). Every caste and class group experienced increases in the percent literate and the average years of education between 1971 and 1987. Muslims and Pulayas experienced the greatest increase in years of education, thus tending to improve their position vis-a-vis the other castes. The rate of passing the SSLC also improved, but remained low, with only 14 per cent of the cohort 15-29 having passed. Those included 75 per cent of Namputiris but only 5 per cent of Pulayas, 14 per cent of Nairs, and no Nadur Muslims in that cohort in the sample. The challenge for Nadur's educational system clearly comes in creating conditions favourable to real school success for those groups most disadvantaged in the past. The Nadur sample displays the same characteristics as have been noted in other parts of Kerala with regard to education, late marriage, and declining birth rates. A regression equation shows that after age has been controlled for, age of marriage and years of education play statistically significant roles in accounting for the number of births of females in the sample (Franke 1993:239).

Overall, our research in Nadur strongly suggests that redistribution has been beneficial to the lowest castes, lowest income groups, agricultural labourers, and female-support households. During the 16 years period between the two surveys, several poor households experienced upward social mobility (Frank 1993:241-264). The percent of tiled roofs went from 59 per cent to 91 per cent, and the average number of rooms per house increased by one (Frank 1993:267). Electricity went up from 8 per cent to 23 per cent of houses and the economic advantage of electricity users dropped (Frank 1993:270). Still, Nadur residents have few household furnishings or consumer goods (Frank 1993:270-71). Only 22 per cent had enough cots for all household members; the average household income was Rs 6,871 ($529), in 1987 (Frank 1993:112), an increase of about 10 per cent over 1971 when adjusted for inflation. Most people remain very poor by international standards.

Implications of the Nadur Study

Our evaluation of Kerala's redistribution programmes in Nadur appears to be the only local-level study of its kind. The research seems to show that redistribution lies behind many of Kerala's material quality of life indicators. As we noted above in the section on the statistical indicators component, when village-level redistribution is considered, *the Kerala Model is still valid and relevant as an alternative to growth-only development strategies.*

Political Participation and Activism

We believe the Nadur study supports the contention that Kerala's statistical indicators result from redistribution. But why has redistribution occurred in Kerala? Enlightened 19th century Maharajas provide part of the answer. Kerala's intense exposure to Christian missions provides another part. We would argue, however, that the main factor is Kerala's popular movements that have sustained themselves for nearly a century.[5] These movements have gone through many stages, from caste improvement associations to trade unions and peasant associations to Communist parties to the Kerala People's Science Movement. Whatever the stage popular movements in Kerala have displayed, a combination of characteristics that—taken together—make them especially powerful and enduring.

1. Kerala's movements have often (though not always) contained very large numbers of members overall. Kerala's activists have shown an ability to mobilise very large numbers of people for a variety of causes. In 1957 the membership of the *Kerala Karshaka Sangham* (Kerala Peasants' Organisation) reached 190,000 (Sathyamurthy 1985:189). With just 3.5 per cent of India's people, Kerala had 20 per cent of all the unions in the country (7,836) in 1984. Kerala's union membership accounted for 7.5 per cent of total Indian union membership (Thampy1994:291). Left-oriented unions appear to have a slight majority of the total membership in Kerala (Thampy 1994:292-93). In `1983, 44 per cent of workers in Kerala's

factory sector were trade union members (Thampy 1994:291). In 1988, CPM-organised events in Alappuzha involved 750,000 participants (Franke and Chasin 1989/1994:27). The 1989-91 all-Kerala Total Literacy Campaign recruited 350,000 teachers.

2. Kerala's movements have often achieved nearly total representation in strategic geographical or economic areas so that their influence far outweighed their total numbers. During the period 1935-84, the *All-Malabar Karshaka Sangham* (Peasants' Organisation) had a paid-up membership of 5,000 in Kasargod, and 10,000 in Chirakkal (Sathyamurthy 1985:156). The Shertellai Coir Factory Workers Union in 1946 had 98 per cent of the workers as members. Six other unions in the areas had above 80 per cent membership (Kannan 1988:118). Similar concentrations existed in recent years for toddy tappers in Thrissur (Kannan 1988:145-92) and agricultural labourers in Kuttanad and Palakkad (Kannan 1988:249).

3. Kerala's movements have often been very militant and creative in finding ways to challenge authority. The birth and success of the Kerala Dinesh Beedi Workers' Cooperative in Kannur depended on the concentrated union membership, militancy, and history of mobilisation of the beedi workers in the area, and the class solidarity of other workers across Kerala who became the cooperative's initial market (Thomas Isaac, Franke, and Raghavan 1997). The workers' creativity in sending out marketing teams to other unions and to community organisations was matched by their capacity to set aside party disputes and focus on the cooperative's survival. In so doing, they may have laid a basis for the present-day LDF approach of trying to free certain development activities from interparty fighting. The KSSP in Kerala is known for its innovative communication style that includes street theatre, puppet plays, songs, and an emphasis on making political struggle interesting to make it more effective.

4. Kerala's movements have thrown up an unusually large number of dedicated and self-sacrificing middle and top leaders, thereby creating a cadre structure of unusual strength,

> endurance, and ability to generate new ideas and actions to adjust to changing local, national, and even international circumstances. It seems unlikely that movements with the features described above could sustain themselves for so long without a strong and viable cadre structure of leaders who for the most part do not succumb to corruption and privilege. Why did popular movements develop this set of characteristics in Kerala? In our view, one of the most critical and compelling issues in the historical study of Kerala would be to come up with a convincing explanation.

Some pieces of the puzzle may already be in place. We suggested in our first book that Kerala's location might play a role. As a transfer point on many ancient trading routes, Kerala has experienced influences from many other cultures, for the most part peacefully. This has led to cosmopolitan outlook on the part of many of Kerala's people, rendering them keenly aware of the possible value of such ideas (Franke and Chasin 1989/1994:23-25). Today, Kerala maintains national and international ties of extraordinary strength: 50 per cent of the gross output of the primary and secondary sectors of the economy is exported to other parts of India and overseas, while around 65 per cent of consumption expenditure goes for imports (Thomas Isaac 1994:368). In the 1980s, over 682,000 of Kerala's people worked overseas altogether (GOK 1988:12-13), with as many as 187,000 in the Gulf States in 1980 alone (Nair 1994:104), possibly contributing as much as 19 percented to the state SDP in 1981 and remaining above 12 per cent through 1989 (Thomas Isaac 1992:24).

Based on ideas proposed by other researchers, we also advanced the argument that Kerala's ecology might play a role. The mostly undifferentiated access to water led to an evenly dispersed settlement pattern that makes it easier to protect against water-borne bacteria and parasites. This means Kerala starts with an advantage in combating many infectious and parasite-driven diseases—the main diseases of underdeveloped areas. Another advantage is political: rural and urban workers can more easily interact and support each other's struggles. Furthermore, Kerala's elected progressive governments could more easily supply public services to a population fairly evenly distributed: there were few special costs associated with isolated, distant, politically weak groups (Franke and Chasin 1989/1994:22-23).[6]

Another probable factor is the set of historical conjunctures that produced a modern rural proletariat in Kerala. Cool, well watered, and close to ocean transport lanes, the Western Ghats were ideal for tea and rubber plantations that British colonialists set up eagerly in the late 19th and early 20th centuries. Coir mat-weaving factories, cashew nut processing, tile factories, and sawmills were added. In a parallel process, the supply of cheap labour in northern Malabar seems to have stimulated the rise of beedi production under the direction of Indian capitalists (Thomas Isaac, Franke, and Raghavan 1997).[7] More sharply than any other part of India, Kerala experienced rupture of traditional ties of kinship, caste, and locality with the potential for intensified class consciousness.[8] The dissolution of traditional ties in Kerala coincided with one of the most radicalising periods of world history: the Russian and Chinese revolutions, the class struggles in Europe, and the independence movement in India and other Western colonies. The combination of these several factors and their timing may be part of the answer to Kerala's apparently unique constellation of radical movements with such power and endurance.

The Crisis of the Kerala Model

Since the late 1970s, many scholars and activists within Kerala, and a few from outside, have been sounding an alarm: the Kerala Model faces several problems and shortcomings that, taken together, can be called a crisis (Thomas Isaac and Tharakan 1995:1995). In 1990, the *Economic and Political Weekly* devoted two issues to the theme *Kerala Economy at the Crossroads* (EPWM 25:35-36 and 37, 1 and 8 and 15 September 1990). The Crisis of the Kerala Model was the major theme of the August 1994 *First International Congress on Kerala Studies,* held in Thiruvananthapuram. Hundreds of papers and discussions at the Congress reaffirmed suspicions and elaborated on the nature of the problems Kerala faces. In our view, the crisis of the Kerala Model has eight major components.

1. Kerala's SDP has grown at a much slower rate than the Indian national average since the late 1970s.
2. Stagnation in agricultural production until the late 1980s coincided with a decline in the area planted in rice. This led to increasing vulnerability to outside sources for the major food crop—rice—which was already substantially dependent on outside markets.
3. Escalation of prices for raw materials and competition from cheaper labour sources in other areas have sent traditional industries such as coir, cashew, and handloom into a tailspin (Thomas Isaac and Tharakan 1995:1995).
4. Industrial growth since the mid-1970s has been sluggish in general and even negative in some years (Mohan 1994; Subrahmanian 1994; Thomas Isaac and Tharakan 1995:1995).
5. Unemployment—already high enough to be the major blight on the Kerala Model—has remained at about three times the all-India average (Prakash 1994:22, Thomas Isaac and Tharakan 1995:1996).
6. The State government has experienced a series of fiscal crises that threaten to undermine many of the Kerala Model redistribution programmes (George 1993). Threatened programmes include the agricultural labour pensions, educational and health spending, and the public distribution system for food. The price of ration shop rice has been rising relative to the open market price. Furthermore, subsidised supplies are declining. In 1993, subsidised rice purchases declined by 9 per cent from their 1992 level (GOK 1994:21).[9]
7. Up to 15 per cent of Kerala's people may have been left out of the Model. These include fishing people (Karuna 1994; Kurien 1994), female stone cutters (Ukkuru *et al.*, 1994), female domestic servants (Subramony 1994), some female agricultural labourers (Mencher 1994), at least some tribal peoples (Devi 1994; Corrie 1994), migrant workers from Tamil Nadu, and

many head load and other casual labourers (Pillai 1992;1996).[10] Extending the Model to these groups becomes increasingly difficult while the other elements of the crisis noted above continue to worsen.

8. Finally, Kerala—like most places on earth at present—faces an environmental crisis of large proportions. Kerala's environmental damage directly threatens the quality of life and both directly and indirectly reduces the economic potential that must be tapped to sustain the main elements of the Model. The best documented component of Kerala's environmental destruction is the loss of forest cover, down from 44 per cent in 1905 to 27 per cent in 1965, 17 per cent in 1973, and 10% in 1983 (Kannan and Pushpangadan 1988: A125-126; Chattopadhyay 1985). Loss of forest cover has resulted in substantial soil erosion and may also play a role in water-logging of lowland areas where drainage is impeded by excess water and soil runoff from higher elevations. Additional environmental problems include various kinds of water and air pollution, and possible overfishing of some offshore regions (Kurien 1991). Repairing environmental damage is among the costliest of human endeavours, adding difficulty to a stagnant economy with little surplus to invest in renewal. Kerala's ecological problems are exacerbated by the State's high population density and its intense land-use that make it difficult to set aside protected areas. Poverty becomes a further source of pressure on the environment when it reaches certain proportions. In Kerala, poverty drives settlers onto hillsides too steep for sustainable cultivation and forces people to cut the dangerously depleted forests for firewood to sell.

The Problem of Sustainability in the Present World Situation

At the beginning of this chapter, we asked what forces threaten the sustainability of the Kerala Model. Clearly, the several components of the Crisis of the Kerala Model described in section 6 above threaten the model. But outside forces are also threatening the

Model. Sustaining the Kerala Model requires surmounting several important national and international obstacles.

The New World Order and Structural Adjustment

One of the behind-the-scenes strengths of the Kerala Model has been the (limited) power of the State government to align features of the economy with the demands the of the poorest groups. The collapse of the Soviet Union led to the emergence of an essentially one-power world in the early 1990s. The New World Order threatens even limited local government powers. Structural adjustment, privatisation, downsizing, and associated policies will have complex and sometimes unforeseen effects on Kerala, but a few features of the New World Order seem to be taking shape: (1) the protectionist policies that helped today's capitalist economies once developed will be denied to today's underdeveloped nations, (2) public expenditures are considered inefficient and inflationary—pressure is being exerted to reduce them, and (3) inequality is accepted as a natural result of market forces and seen as beneficial to development. Without directly saying so, advocates of the one power New World Order seem to have accepted Simon Kuznets' 1955 paper on the need for an entrepreneurial phase of development in which inequality increases in order to raise production, and is followed by a period of increased output, leading to eventual better lives for all with (relatively) reduced inequality. Kuznets' scenario takes about 100 years to unfold.[11] In the meantime, India may witness a bifurcation of prosperity in which the upper 10 per cent of the population enjoys the benefits of liberal investment opportunities and unrestricted imports, while most of the rest of the population is threatened by diminished benefits and increased insecurity (C.T. Kurien 1994).

Structural adjustment may be new to India, but its effects in other parts of the world have already been described. Much of Africa and Latin America have been in structural adjustment programmes since the 1980s. Between 1984 and 1990, average per capita incomes in Africa decreased by 12.5 per cent, in Latin America they dropped 9.1 per cent (Pinstrup-Anderson 1993:87). Official poverty levels in Latin America rose from 25 per cent in

1980 to 31 per cent by the end of the decade (Pinstrup Anderson 1993:88). In Costa Rica between 1971 and 1983, the poorest 10 per cent of the population lost 20 per cent while the richest 10 per cent gained 15 per cent relative to prices (Pinstrup-Anderson 1993:88-89). In Ghana, a long-term trend of falling infant mortality rates was reversed by a 20 per cent increase from the mid-1970s to mid-1980s (Pinstrup-Anderson 1993:105); in Abidjan, Ivory Coast Neonatal mortality rates went from 37 per 1,000 in 1977-1981 to 81 per 1,000 in 1982-86 (Pinstrup-Anderson 1993:106). In Brazil, 60,000 "extra" child deaths are attributed to the 1980s recessions. Brazil has previously been labelled an economic miracle. The Third World generally absorbed more than 500,000 excess deaths in 1988 alone than might have been expected. War-related deaths are not included in these estimates (*The New York Times*, 20 December 1988:1; Grant 1989:1). Despite a long term trend of declining child deaths, 13 million children died in 1993, 98 per cent of them in the Third World. At least 8 million of them could have been saved by oral rehydration therapy, vaccinations, and public health action to prevent diseases such as malaria, meningitis, respiratory ailments, and certain kinds of diarrhoea (Brown *et al* 1993:96). To the best of our knowledge, no study has yet shown that structural adjustment or any other programme of the New World Order has benefited the poorest groups. Nor has any study shown that the policies of the New World Order fit logically, theoretically, or empirically with the concept of sustainability.[12]

In the context of statistics and trends such as those just noted, we consider it appropriate to reassert that, despite its crisis, the Kerala Model is still valid and relevant as an alternative to growth-only development strategies. As the brutality of the New World Order imposes itself on nations and cultures unprepared or unable to defend their most vulnerable groups, Kerala, for all its shortcomings, might become even more of a model.

The very survival of the Kerala Model is in question, however. Structural adjustment and related processes threaten to undermine past achievements, replacing them with policies benefiting only affluent consumers and freewheeling investors. Fewer restrictions on investment may lead to more investment going out of the State—

the precise opposite of what people from all political persuasions seem to think is necessary. Abolition of subsidy protections to domestic agriculture could undermine Kerala's spice, cashew, and other cash crop exchange earnings, thereby worsening the subsistence base that depends on such earnings. Protection of small firms may also be lost—a potentially catastrophic blow to an economy with high unemployment in which hundreds of thousands who are employed work in cottage industries. A market takeover of health, education, and social welfare could price the poor out of the process. M.A. Oommen (1994:15) has characterised these trends as "euthanasia" for the Kerala Model.[13]

The International Environmental Crisis and the Problem of Sustainability

Structural adjustment and New World Order domination are not the only perils to the sustainability of the Kerala Model. International environmental developments also pose serious hazards of unpredictable nature and scope. The 20th century has generated so much output that numerous "sustainable yield thresholds of natural systems" (Brown 1995:4) have been crossed. At current and likely future levels of abuse, any area can be affected by another area's practices. Forest cover, topsoil, range lands, and 13 of the world's 15 main oceanic fisheries are on decline. Fresh water tables are dropping all over the world. In 1996, international grain stocks were expected to decline for the third consecutive year, to as low as 49 days—the lowest level recorded since the system was set up (Brown 1995:6-8). Declines in area planted and fertilizer use have combined with stagnation in irrigation water availability to threaten an impending food crisis. Worldwide, grain prices in 1995 rose by one-third (Brown 1995:8-9). Atmospheric warming from massive developed country carbon emissions—with the U.S. by far the worst offender—has probably brought on local weather changes all over the world.[14] High winds, floods, droughts, and other weather extremes may be harming food production and threatening lives in many areas.

Kerala could well be influenced by international grain decline, fish catch losses, and climate irregularities. With no direct bargaining power in international forums, and dependent on India's influence, which seems limited vis-a-vis the U.S. and other rich countries, in the short run, Kerala can only try to react locally to the several world-system ecological sustainability wildcards.

Is the Kerala Model Sustainable?

The answer to the question requires drawing up a balance sheet with Kerala's internal shortcomings along with the worldwide threats. Against these, we must weigh Kerala's traditional and current resources. What are Kerala's strengths in the current situation?

The Old Kerala Model Still Matters

The old Kerala Model fostered a literate, fairly healthy, motivated population with a sense of purpose, involvement, commitment to ideals, and a generally optimistic orientation to the future. These achievements—along with the expectation of high material quality of life indicators and willingness to organise and carry out mass actions—give Kerala weapons with which to build a new model appropriate to today's circumstances.

Let us return briefly to Nadur Village. In 1971 Joan Mencher found that only 25 per cent of sample respondents believed that the village "had made progress." Following the several radical reforms, we found in 1987, that 59 per cent believed their lives were better than those of their parents, and 71 per cent thought life for their children would be even better (Franke 1993:273). Several respondents volunteered observations about the important role of community actions in making life better. Eight years later, Thomas Isaac and Tharakan (1995:1997) observed in their report on the First International Congress on Kerala Studies that "It is the consciousness and struggles of the masses and not the manipulations of the politicians that will ultimately determine" whether the Kerala Model survives and is renewed.

Redistribution still matters too. A study by Cereseto and Waitzkin (1988) found that for any given level of average per capita income, countries with more equality provided better education, longer life, and lower infant mortality. In other words, the Kerala

Model holds cross-culturally. But does redistribution work at cross-purpose to production? Economists Bowles, Gordon, and Weisskopf (1990:223) found that among advanced industrial countries, both productivity growth and investment performance are strongly and positively correlated with equality. *The New York Times* (8 January 1994:A39) reported that "many economists [have] begun to see greater income equality as compatible with faster growth—and perhaps even contributing to it." And the US magazine, *Business Week*, led its issue of 15 August 1994 with a story entitled "Inequality: how the growing gap between rich and poor in America is hurting the economy." Among the studies cited in the article was one showing that in 26 US cities, those with the least inequality between suburban and inner city incomes had job creation significantly greater than those with greater inequality. Another study cited was a summary of 54 other studies from which the author, Harvard economist Richard B. Freeman, argued that market strategies and privatization tend to raise inequality while government programmes are essential to reducing it.

The exact mechanisms leading to the correlations between equality, productivity, investment performance, and job creation, are not spelled out in these reports, but surely they deserve closer attention. Taken together, they imply that Kerala's strategy of redistribution is not the likely cause of the State's high unemployment and sluggish economic growth. On the contrary, they imply that the Kerala Model is valid and relevant as an alternative to development strategies emphasising growth by means of or along with increasing inequality. The gains made in Nadur—that we cited earlier—may be a less an outmoded left wing chimera and more a reasonable basis from which to launch sustainable development.

How will this sustainable development come about? In their review of the discussions at the First International Congress on Kerala Studies, Thomas Isaac and Tharakan (1995:1997) pointed out that ". . . the Left needs to draw up a new agenda that is more responsive to the changed reality of contemporary Kerala.:" At the same time veteran CPM leader E.M.S. Namboodiripad pointed out the need to "accelerate economic growth without sacrificing the welfare gains and the democratic achievements of the past"

(Thomas Isaac and Tharakan 1995:1997). Without jettisoning past achievements, the left today proposes a set of initiatives that, in our view, constitute reasonable extensions of the programmes of the past, that seem to offer possible solutions to past shortcomings of the Kerala Model, and that create at least the initial elements of a type of sustainability that has real chance to succeed.

The programmes to which we refer are currently underway, so we cannot evaluate them empirically. But we can consider their main features and offer reasons why they might or might not work, based on the points made in earlier sections of this chapter.

A New Kerala Model?

The Left's "new agenda" is the *People's Campaign for the Ninth Plan.* This campaign seems to have been drawn up on the basis of the discussions at the First International Congress on Kerala studies and discussions at several follow-up conferences in 1995 and 1996. It is also based in part on the *New Democratic Initiatives* of the 1987-91 LDF Ministry. These included elected district councils—which are being brought back to life for the new campaign—the Total Literacy Programme, the installation of high-efficiency chulahs, some untied funds to local panchayats, and the People's Resource Mapping Programme. Each of these programmes had met with modest success in 1987-91. The Congress-led UDF victory in the 1991 elections brought the programmes to a near halt (except for the panchayat unrestricted funds), but forces had been set in motion that could be reactivated after the LDF election success of April 1996: the New Democratic Initiatives had mobilised many activists and had given them experience, and LDF leaders and middle level cadre may have learned lessons about the potential for grassroots development action aimed more at community integration and increasing production than at class struggle to spread existing wealth.[15]

The current campaign aims at giving panchayats and urban communities local control over 40 per cent of the development budget.[16] Prior to taking this control however, they are participating in what seems to be a massive educational and discussion programme to help them make informed choices. The education programme involves training 400 State-level instructors from among the most educated groups with experience in organising, 6,000 district level instructors, and 50,000 local level facilitators (Namboodiripad 1996, GOK 1996, 1996a).The content of the training includes a shortened version of resource mapping, knowledge of KSSP environmental publication, cost-benefit analysis, how to lead a meeting, and similar skills.[17] Plans called for an attempt at one-third female representation in the leadership, along with special attention to mobilising Scheduled Caste and Scheduled Tribe activists as well. The early phases of the campaign witnessed promising initial signs of over 30 per cent female participation, which has tended to drop off in the secondary phases to about 15 per cent. A women-focused campaign to overcome pockets of poverty is being considered as an additional means to involve women more actively in future political action.

Training of facilitators was followed in September-December 1996 by local seminars leading to the creation of local task forces that developed proposals to raise production while maintaining the environmental base of the community. To involve the largest number of people, the campaign carried out most mass meetings on holidays. Printed invitations with agendas were delivered to every house, *jathas, padayatras,* street theatre, and other KSSP-like activities were utilised, and a development quiz was organised in most schools (GOK 1996).

The People's Campaign for the Ninth Plan appears to be a giant composite of the earlier New Democratic Initiatives. Atleast on paper, it is an integrated programme to foster a high degree of interaction between government and ordinary people with a focus on the particular issues that make up the Crisis of the Kerala Model. As such, it also becomes a conscious, organized attempt both to keep the Kerala Model alive, and to throw up local shields of resistance against the most harmful elements of the New World Order. To the best of our knowledge, Kerala is one of the very few places in the world at present with such a massive, organised, conscious campaign aimed at an alternative to market-only development. Can it succeed? Based on the earlier sections of this chapter, on reading of several *Ninth Plan* documents, on visits to eight panchayats in December of 1996 and January of 1997, and on participation in one of the campaign's training sessions in January 1997, we offer the following tentative assessment of, and questions about the *People's Campaign*. First, let us consider the apparent negative elements :

1. The Campaign will only help Kerala's people and succeed in its own terms if it leads to increases in agricultural and industrial production and productivity. It is not clear from the process so far whether a strategy for evaluation of these crucial outcomes has been prepared.
2. The Campaign does not clearly protect agricultural labour pensions, fair price shops, and health and education spending that are all necessary for maintaining the quality of life indicators of the Kerala Model. Many elements of the old Kerala Model require statewide mobilisation of resources. How are the new programmes going to protect state-wide policies?

On the positive side—·

3. The Campaign seems to follow a logical process in extending the earlier Kerala Model. Redistribution of wealth is being followed by and supplemented by redistribution of power. Kerala's earlier mass movements could thus be reinvigorated and redirected. We saw evidence for this rejuvenation in several panchayats in 1996-97 and in the enthusiasm of participants at the training session in Calicut on 10-12 January 1997.
4. Better use of local resources might ease Kerala's unemployment crisis if the local development plans can be made labour-intensive.[18]
5. Local self-sufficiency to a reasonable extent may be a smart survival tactic in a world of unpredictable climate change and possibly erratic grain prices.
6. Local self-sufficiency (to a reasonable extent) could provide a shield against some elements of structural adjustment.

7. Local, democratically planned development is less likely to lead to extreme forms of inequality than the market would otherwise inevitably promote. People who work together to create their panchayat or urban district development plan are less likely to accept exploitative economic relationships with each other. Several cooperative interactions among the better-off and most impoverished villagers that we witnessed in December 1996-January 1997 support this observation.
8. Participation in meaningful democratic development planning and actions could conjure up a new generation of Kerala activists.

Is the Kerala Model sustainable? As we noted earlier, Oommen has argued convincingly that unchecked penetration by the forces of the New World Order will mean an answer "no". An attempt by left forces in Kerala to simply continue the old Kerala Model as it is, will probably also mean an answer "no". But perhaps the forces that created the old Kerala Model can be reinvigorated and can be directed into a new model in which the shortcomings of the old are addressed. And if sustainability becomes a conscious part of the New Kerala Model and a conscious element of planning and thinking throughout the society, the New Kerala Model might just have a chance for success. In a world needing every possible experiment in sustainability, we all stand to benefit from their attempt.

NOTES

1. A subject search of the Harvard University Library Union Catalogue brought up 180 books with (non-military) "sustainability" as one of the key words. Most were published since 1993.
2. These adapted from Franke and Chasin 1983:11. Daly (1996:195) gives more detailed and technical definition: "An economy in sustainable development adapts and improves in knowledge, organisation, technical efficiency, and wisdom; it does this without assimilating or accreting an ever greater percentage of the matter-energy of the ecosystem into itself but rather stops at a scale at which the remaining ecosystem can continue to function and renew itself year after year. The non-growing economy is not static—it is being continually maintained and renewed as a steady state sub-system of the environment." Daly goes on to specify how particular

elements of the economy should operate, but does not directly take up the question of distribution of wealth, political rights, and material levels of living.

3. See Franke (1993), chapter 7 (pp.121-122) or Franke (1992), for details of the analysis of the land reform that follows.
4. Thomas Isaac and Tharakan (1995:1996) see this conflict as a possible reason for the heavy election losses of the LDF in 1978 in Palakkad and Alappuzha, two of its traditional strongholds. Herring (1989;1991) surveys many aspects of the conflict with particular reference to Palakkad.
5. Jeffrey (1993), appears to agree with this point, though his explanation for how the movements grew differs somewhat from ours. Casinader (1995), offers a view similar to ours in the context of a comparison between Kerala and Sri Lanka. Herring (1983) argues that mass movements and their level of militancy were the keys to the enactment of the Kerala land reform.
6. See also Franke (1993), pp. 19-21 where the overview cites Cohn (1971), Fuller (1976), and Mencher (1966). The recent study by T.T. Sreekumar (1993), adds new dimensions to the discussion.
7. Beedi production in northern Malabar is otherwise difficult to account for since none of the raw materials is available there.
8. Robin Jeffery (1993), has suggested that the decline of the *marumakkathayam* system and the breakup of the Nair *taravad* may also have played a role. His point is well argued, but we think larger forces also had to be at work. For one thing, Nairs make up only about 14 per cent of Kerala's population, and while many Ezhava households also practice *marumakkathayam*, this hardly seems enough to produce such widespread class mobilisation as occurred in 20th century Kerala.
9. The State Planning Board report (GOK 1995:26-28) does not give a final figure for subsidised rice distribution for 1994, but the figures for the first 10 months indicate a drop of 29 per cent over 1993 (computed from GOK 1995:28). An increase in the amount of wheat of about 20 per cent may offset some of the rice losses.
10. Pillai (1996, p. 2099), reported that about 4,600 headload workers are covered by a Kerala-Model type scheme to regularize their work relations and create a modern benefit structure. The 4,600 workers appear to represent only about 2 per cent of the total estimated headload and casual labourers in the State.
11. Franke (1993, pp. 9-10), summarises and documents the Kuznets approach that still seems to lie at the basis of capitalist thinking about development.
12. A full-scale attack from almost every angle appears in Mander and Goldsmith, eds. (1996).
13. The other elements mentioned in the paragraph are also taken from M. A. Oommen's paper.
14. US emissions in 1994 were 1.4 billion tons, almost double those of second place China with 835 million. Per person emissions in the US were 5.3 tons, also a first place rating (Flavin 1995:30).

15. Tornquist (1995), has produced a critical overall assessment of the New Democratic Initiatives. Although his criticisms have apparently been considered too harsh by some LDF activists, the foreign reader is likely to be struck by the evidence he presents of LDF leaders and middle cadre being able to engage in rather impressive analysis and criticism of their own programmes.
16. M. A. Oommen (1995) provides an overview of the legal basis for decentralisation to panchayats in the all-India context.
17. More elaborate resource mapping is planned for the near future. It has been found that panchayats with resource mapping from the earlier period were able to produce better quality development documents. The 1996 campaign utilized a technique called the "transect walk." Development volunteers attempted to identify a cross-section of the panchayat with the greatest geographical and geological variation, and walked this transection, noting geological forms, land types, elevations, and other phenomena. An overview of the programme structure appears in Thomas Isaac and Harilal 1996.
18. Kalliasseri Panchayat's experience in reducing seasonal unemployment with a dry-season vegetable garden project suggests grounds for optimism in this regard. In the dry season of 1993, 21 cooperative groups of unemployed youth got medium harvests and broke even on their investments. A total of 2,500 unemployed got work experience and pay. More than 6 acres became productive in a new way (Gangadharan 1993). Our one-day visit to Kalliasseri on January 8, 1997 revealed an expanded vegetable garden programme and several other smaller employment-generating schemes based on local initiatives.

REFERENCES

Alexander, William (1994), Exceptional Kerala: Efficient and Sustainable Human Behaviour. Unpublished Manuscript.

Bose, Ashish (1991), *Population of India: 1991 Census Results and Methodology.* Delhi, B.R. Publishing Corporation.

Bowles, Samuel, David M. Gordon, and Thomas E. Weisskopf (1990), *After the Wasteland : A Democratic Economic for the Year 2000,* Armonk, N.Y.M.E. Sharpe, Inc.

Brown, Lester (1995), The acceleration of history. In Brown, Lester, *et al. (1995), State of the World: A Worldwatch Institute Report on Progress Toward a Sustainable Society.* New York, W.W. Norton & Company, pp. 1-20.

--Christopher Flavin, and Hal Kane (1993), *Vital Signs 1996: The Trends That are Shaping our Future,* New York. W.W. Nortern & Company.

Casinader, Rex (1995), "Making Kerala Model more Intelligible: Comparisons with Sri Lankan Experience." *Economic and Political Weekly,* vol. 30, no. 48, pp.3085-3092.

Cereseto Shirley, and Howard Waitzkin (1988), "Economic development, Political-economic System, and the Physical Quality of Life", *Journal of Public Health Policy* (Spring 1988), pp. 104-120.

Chasin, Barbara H. (1990), Land reform and women's work in a Kerala village, Michigan State University, Working Papers on Women in International Development no. 207, East Lansing.

Chattopadhyay, Srikumar (1985), "Deforestation in parts of Western Ghats Region (Kerala), India", *Journal of Environmental Management* pp. 20:219-230.

Cohn, Bernard S. (1971), *India: The Social Anthropology of a Civilization*. Englewood Cliffs, N.J. Prentice-Hall.

Corrie, Bruce P. (1994), The Kerala Model of Development from the Perspective of the Dalit Child in Kerala, Paper presented at the First International Congress on Kerala Studies, Thiruvananthapuram, August 27-29, 1994.

Daly, Herman E. (1996), "Sustainable growth? No thank you", In Mander, Jerry, and Edward Goldsmith, eds. (1996), *The Case Against the Global Economy and for a Turn Toward the Local*, San Francisco. Sierra Club Books. pp. 192-196.

Devi, T. (1994), "Sexual Abuse and Poverty: Tribal Women of Wayanad". Paper presented at the First International Congress on Kerala Studies., Thiruvananthapuram, (August 27-29, 1994).

Economic and Political Weekly, *Kerala Economy at the Crossroads—vol I.* (no. 35-36). (1-8 September 1990).

Economic and Political Weekly, *Kerala Economy at the Crossroads—vol. II.* (no. 37). (15 September 1990).

Flavin, Christopher (1995), Facing up to the Risks of Climate Change, In Brown, Lester, *et al.* (1995), *State of the World: A Worldwatch Institute Report on Progress Toward a Sustainable Society*, New York. W.W. Norton & Company, pp. 21-39.

Franke, Richard W. (1992), "Land reform versus inequality in Nadur village", Kerala. *Journal of Anthropological Research* vol. 48, no. 2. pp. 81-116.

—— (1993). *Life Is a Little Better: Redistribution as a Development Strategy in Nadur Village Kerala* (1996), New Delhi. Promilla and Company, Publishers. [Malayalam translation to be published in 1997].

—— (1993a. "Feeding Programmes and Food Intake in a Kerala Village". *Economic and Political Weekly* vol. 28, no. 8-9, pp. 355-360. February 20-27, 1993.

—— Barbara H. Chasin, (1983), "Asking the Critical Questions". Development Watch column in *The Global Reporter: a Journal of People, Resources, and the World* 1(1):11, Boston, The Anthropology Resource Center.

—— Barbara H. Chasin, (1989), *Kerala: Radical Reform as Development in an Indian State*, Oakland, California, Food First, Second edition (1994), Also

(1991), New Delhi. Promilla and Company Publishers. Second edition, 1994.

—— (1996), Female-supported Households: A Continuing Agenda for Kerala Model? *Economic and Political Weekly,* vol. 31, no. 10, pp. 625-630. March 9, 1996.

Fuller, C.J. (1976), *The Nayars Today.* New York, Cambridge University Press.

Gangadharan, T. (1993), Report on Kalliasseri People's Mapping Project at the National Level Orientation Course on Drinking Water and Sanitation Programme with People's Participation IRTC Mundur, October 1, 1993.

George, K.K. (1993), *Limits to Kerala Model of Development: An Analysis of Fiscal Crisis and its Implications,* Trivandrum, Centre for Development Studies, Monograph Series.

Government of Kerala (GOK). (1994), *Economic Review 1993,* Thiruvananthapuram, State Planning Board.

—— 1995. *Economic Review (1994),* Thiruvananthapuram, State Planning Board,

——(1996), People's Campaign for Ninth Plan: An Approach Paper. Thiruvananthapuram, State Planning Board.

—— (1996a), Power to the People. People's Plan—Ninth Plan: A Note, Training Programme for Resources Persons, Thiruvananthapuram, State Planning Board.

Grant, James. (1989), *The State of the World's Children: 1989.* Oxford. Oxford University Press, Published for UNICEF.

Herring, Ronald J. (1983), *Land to the Tiller: The Political Economy of Agrarian Reform in South Asia,* New Haven: Yale University Press.

—— (1989), Dilemmas of Agrarian Communism: Peasant Differentiation, Sectoral and village politics, *Third World Quarterly* vol. 11, no.1. pp. 89-115.

—— (1991). From Structural Conflict to Agrarian Stalemate: Agrarian Reforms in South India. *Journal of Asian and African Studies* vol. 26, no.3-4. pp. 169-188.

Jeffrey, Robin. (1993), *Politics, Women and Well Being: How Kerala Became 'A Model'.* Delhi. Oxford University Press.

Kannan, K.P. (1988), *Of Rural Proletarians: Mobilization and Organization of Rural Workers in South-West India,* Delhi, Oxford University Press.

——, and K.Pushpangadan (1988), "Agricultural Stagnation in Kerala: An Exploratory Analysis". *Economic and Political Weekly,* vol. 23, no. 39, pp. 120A-128A.

Karuna, M.S. (1994), Socio-economic Status of Fishermen Families in Thiruvananthapuram District. Paper presented at the First International Congress on Kerala Studies, Thiruvananthapuram, August 27-29, 1994.

Kurien, C.T. (1994), *Global Capitalism and the Indian Economy,* New Delhi. Orient Longman Limited, Tracts for the Times/6.

Kurien, John (1991), *Ruining the Commons and the Responses of the Commoners: Coastal Overfishing and Fisherman's Actions in Kerala State, India.* Geneva, United Nations Research Institute for Social Development. Discussion Paper 23.

Kurien, John (1994), Kerala's Marine Fisheries Development Experience, in Prakash, B.A. (ed.) *Kerala's Economy: Performance, Problems, Prospects,* New Delhi, Sage Publications pp. 195-214.

——, and T.R. Thankappan Achari, 1989, On Ruining the Commons and the *Commoner: the Political Economy of Overfishing*, Trivandrum, Centre for Development Studies, Working Paper No. 232.

Mander, Jerry, and Edward Goldsmith, (eds.) (1996), *The Case Against the Global Economy and for a Turn toward the Local,* San Francisco. Sierra Club Books.

Mencher, Joan P. (1966), Kerala and Madras: A Comparative Study of Ecology and Social Structure, *Ethnology* vol. 5, no. 2, pp. 135-171.

—— (1994), The Kerala Model of Development: the Excluded Ones. Paper presented at the First International Congress on Kerala Studies. Thiruvananthapuram, August 27-29, 1994.

Mohan, V. Nanda (1994), Recent Trends in the Industrial Growth of Kerala, in Prakash, B.A. ed. *Kerala's Economy: Performance, Problems, Prospects.* New Delhi. Sage Publications, pp.217-236.

Nair, P.R. Gopinathan, (1994), Migrations of Keralites to the Arab World. In Prakash, B.A. ed. *Kerala's Economy: Performance, Problems, Prospects.* New Delhi. Sage Publication, pp.95-114.

Namboodiripad, E.M.S. (1996), A Kerala Experiment: Planning from Below—and Above. *Frontline,* October 18, 1996, pp. 91-92.

Oommen, M.A. (1994), Kerala and the New World Order: Some Tentative Hypotheses. Paper presented at the First International Congress on Kerala Studies. Thiruvananthapuram, August 27-29, 1994.

—— (1995), Devolution of Resources from the State to the Panchayati Raj Institutions: Search for a Normative Approach, New Delhi, Institute of Social Sciences. Occasional Paper Series. No. 18.

—— and R. Anandaraj, (1996), A District Profile of Human Development Index in India, New Delhi, Institute of Social Sciences, Unpublished paper.

Pillai, S. Mohanan. (1992), *Social Security Schemes for Workers in the Unorganised Sector: A Case Study of Headload Workers Welfare Scheme in Kerala.* Dissertation, Master of Philosophy in Applied Economics, Trivandrum, Centre for Development Studies.

—— (1996), Social Security for Workers in Unorganised Sector: Experience of Kerala. *Economic and Political Weekly* vol. 31, no. 31. pp. 2093-2107, August 3, 1996.

Pinstrup-Anderson, Per. (1993) Economic Crisis and Policy Reforms During the 1980s and their Impact on the Poor in *Macroeconomic Environment and Health: With Case Studies for Countries in Greatest Need.* Geneva. World Health Organization.

Prakash, B.A. (1994), Kerala's economy: An overview. In Prakash, B.A. ed. *Kerala's Economy: Performance, Problems, Prospects,* New Delhi, Sage Publications, pp. 15-40.

Sathyamurthy, T.V. (1985), *India Since Independence: Studies in the Development of the Power of the State, volume 1, Centre-State Relations, the Case of Kerala,* Delhi, Ajanta.

Sreekumar, T.T. (1993), Urban Process in Kerala, 1900-1981, Trivandrum, Centre for Development Studies.

Subrahmanian, K.K. (1994), *Some Facets of the, Manufacturing Industry in Kerala.* In Prakash, B.A. ed. *Kerala Economy: Performance, Problems, Prospects.* New Delhi, Sage Publications, pp. 237-258.

Subramony, Dhanalakshmy (1994), A Profile of Urban Poverty: the Case of Domestic Servants in Thiruvananthapuram City. Paper presented at the First International Congress on Kerala Studies. Thiruvananthapuram, August 27-29, 1994.

Thampy, M.M. (1994), Development of Organised Small-scale Industries: Some Issues. In Prakash, B.A. ed. *Kerala's Economy: Performance, Problems, Prospects,* New Delhi, Sage Publication, pp. 279-297.

Thomas Isaac, T.M. (1992), *Economic Consequences of the Gulf Crisis: A Study of India with Special Reference to Kerala.* New Delhi, Asian Regional Team for Employment Promotion, International Labour Organisation. Publication No. RAS/88/029.

—— (1994), The Trend and Pattern of External Trade of Kerala, in Prakash, B.A. ed. *Kerala's Economy, Performance, Problems, Prospects.* New Delhi, Sage Publications. pp. 368-393.

—— and P.K. Michael Tharakan, (1995), ''Kerala: towards a new agenda.'' *Economic and Political Weekly* vol. 30, no. 31-32. pp. 1993-2004, August 5-12, 1995.

—— and K.N. Harilal (1996), ''Planning for Empowerment: People's Campaign for Decentralised Planning Kerala.'' *Economic and Political Weekly,* vol. 32, no. 1-2. pp. 53-58.

—— Richard W. Franke, and Pyaralal Raghavan (1997), *Kerala Dinesh Beedi: The Dynamics of Work and Democracy in an Indian Industrial Cooperative.* Ithaca, New York, Cornell University Press.

Tornquist, Olle, with P.K. Michael Tharakan (1995), *The Next Left? Democratisation and Attempts to Renew the Radical Political Development Project. The Case of Kerala.* Copenhagen, Nordic Institute of Asian Studies, Report Series, no.24.

This book also appears serialized in *Economic and Political Weekly,* vol. 31, no. 28, pp.1847-1858 and vol. 31, no. 29, pp. 1953-1973.

Ukkuru, Mary P. Jyothi Augustine, Prema L., and Sujatha A. (1994), Working Pattern and Nutritional Profiles of Women Engaged in Stone Breaking. Paper presented at the First International Congress on Kerala Studies. Thiruvananthapuram, August 5-12, 1994.

World Bank (1995), *World Development Report 1995: Workers in an Integrating* World, New York, Oxford University Press.

TEN

SUSTAINABILITY OF KERALA'S DEVELOPMENT EXPERIENCE

C.T. KURIEN

The distinguishing feature of Kerala's development experience of the post-independence period, as is well known, is the fact that at rather low levels of per capita income—lower, indeed, than the low all-India level—it was able to achieve human development, in terms of health and education, of a very high order, not only higher than what prevails in the rest of the country, but comparable to that in the advanced countries. Several aspects of this phenomenon were critically considered at the International Congress on Kerala Studies held in Thiruvananthapuram in August 1994. What is being attempted here now need not be and should not be a repeat of what was done in Thiruvananthapuram, but a kind of necessary follow-up. The title of our symposium suggests that the emphasis is on the sustainability of the experience of the past.

What I propose to do in this brief presidential presentation is to pick up the issues that figured prominently at Thiruvananthapuram to provide a kind of launching pad for our deliberations.

The title of our symposium makes a reference to the Kerala Model and hence let me make a couple of observations about it. For three reasons, I suggest that we do not get too preoccupied with the "Model". Nobody really knows what that term is supposed to communicate. When the expression "The Kerala Model" came into currency late in the 1970s or early in the 1980s, it was probably meant to imply that Kerala's development experience was a "model" worth emulating. If so, the euphoria did not last for long. By 1990 the mood had changed completely as indicated by the common title of a series of studies that appeared that year, "Kerala Economy at the Crossroads".[1] Since then the question has been not whether the

Kerala Model could be replicated elsewhere, but whether it could be sustained in Kerala itself, though the admiration for what Kerala was able to achieve still continues unabated in certain quarters.[2]

Second, it is well known that the expression "Kerala Model" was initially associated with the study, *Poverty, Unemployment and Development Policy* with reference to Kerala conducted by the scholars at the Centre for Development Studies (CDS) and published by the Centre and the United Nations.[3] At the Thiruvananthapuram Congress, K.N. Raj, the coordinator of that study, explained its background and the major conclusions and went on to say: "At no stage, however, has the Centre described its findings on the set of issues as constituting in effect a Kerala Model".[4] The same view was expressed in a piece that the late T.N. Krishnan (who had closely collaborated with K.N. Raj in the preparation of the CDS study) prepared after the Thiruvananthapuram Congress. He said: "The CDS study showed how the implementation of social programmes, like public distribution of foodgrains and public support for education and health care, made significant contributions to raising the welfare of the community and in reducing social inequalities. Unfortunately, international scholars launched a "Kerala model of development" using the CDS study as its foundation. The authors of the CDS study never claimed that Kerala presented a model of development and they were already aware of the various problems of, and constraints operating in the Kerala economy. Their misgivings were reinforced by the findings of subsequent research at CDS on the Kerala economy."[5]

Third, though the positive aspects of Kerala's development performance have been quite striking, they have not been exceptional or unique. If achieving high levels of human development at low levels of per capita income is what is meant to be conveyed by the "Kerala Model", the same has been achieved elsewhere also. It is well known that Sri Lanka has been an instance of that kind. The UNDP's Human Development Report 1996 which makes a global cross-country comparison of the relationship between per capita income and its growth on the one hand and its own human development index on the other, lists apart from Sri Lanka, Costa Rica, Jamaica and Peru in that category.

Thus if the so-called "Kerala Model" does not relate to Kerala alone and is not much of a model, why continue to celebrate it or criticise it? I suggest, therefore, that for our purpose we concentrate on Kerala's development experience itself in its own historical context, and draw lessons from it for the future development of Kerala. In so doing, I will not be surprised if we arrive at some issues which may be of significance to other parts of our country or even beyond.

I do not propose to make an inventory of Kerala's past achievements or of its contemporary problems. I take it that the wealth of material on these aspects presented at Thiruvananthapuram is familiar to those who are participating in the symposium.[6] I shall select a few themes and pose a few questions.

One of the constant refrains about Kerala's development experience is that it must be viewed in historical perspective going back at least a century prior to Independence. In terms of education a landmark that is identified is the 1817 Royal Rescript of Travancore which declared universal education, paid for by the State, to be the objective of State policy. It has been recorded that State-sponsored schemes of public health were initiated early in the twentieth century "in an earlier era before the concepts of development, not to speak of policies towards the same, became articulated."[7] In a recent review of Kerala's development achievements, V.K. Ramachandran identifies State-sponsored reforms, missionary activities, caste-based reform movements, the role of the Left parties and of women activists as contributory factors for whatever Kerala was able to achieve.[8] I shall come back to this "agency" question later. But in terms of history itself a question has to be raised. While acknowledging the historical processes, T.N. Krishnan draws attention to the fact that they are the legacies, largely, of Travancore and Cochin and that Malabar that formed part of Kerala in 1956 lagged far behind Travancore and Cochin in literacy levels and in access to health care. Krishnan goes on to say: "The history of social development since the formation of Kerala State is really a story of how these differentials were eliminated or narrowed and what policies and programmes were adopted for this purpose."[9] Krishnan is of the view that the basic strategy was the same: extension of the policies and programmes followed earlier in Travancore and Cochin to Malabar region. Even granting that such is the case, it is important to consider how Malabar was able to achieve in three decades or so what took Travancore and Cochin well over a century.

Such an enquiry into the reduction in the regional gap in achievement may yield some clues to the understanding of why other pronounced gaps still exist within the State in terms of the indices of human development. John Kurien's paper at Thiruvananthapuram featured an issue which, surprisingly, had not received enough attention in the discussions on Kerala's socio-economic performance.[10] Kerala has come to be used prominently in inter-State comparisons of gaps in socio-economic achievements within the country. But how valid it is to concentrate on Kerala's "central" tendency", as Kurien puts it, ignoring the "outliers"? The one "outlier" instance that he examined is quite revealing. The literacy level (1981) of female fishworkers was as low as 44 compared to the State average of 85 for all workers. Again, compared with the all-Kerala infant mortality rate of 40 per 1000 in 1981, the rate for the fishing communities was 85 per thousand. The 1991 Census report shows that the literacy rate in the Palakkad district for Scheduled Caste males was 63.32 and for Scheduled Caste females was 51.07 and that in the case of Scheduled Tribes the rates were far lower 34.31 for males and as low as 25.10 for females. In other words, if there is a small pocket called Kerala among the Indian States that is an exceptionally bright spot in terms of human development, that same Kerala may have within it little pockets of Bihar, Orissa, M.P. or U.P. with exceptionally low levels of human development. Existence of such outliers must be brought out through a social disaggregation of what is frequently treated as the Kerala totality. When that is done, I am sure it will be seen that Kerala too has promises to keep and miles to go.

Similarly, it is important to note that Kerala's achievements are generating new kinds of problems. The most prominent among these is unemployment, especially unemployment among the educated in both of which Kerala now leads the country! The less widely known, but equally disturbing, has been the fall in the quality of primary education: at least one study has claimed that the performance of children at the primary levels in Kerala is lower than that of children at that level in Bihar.[11] There is also the alarming fiscal crisis about which much has been written by scholars like K.K. George and M.A. Oommen, reflected in the growing inability of the State to finance precisely those social aspects that had become the glory of Kerala. As has been pointed out, ironically Kerala earned the dubious distinction of being the only State in India whose real social expenditure had decreased during the 1985-86/1991-92 period compared to the decade 1974-75/1984-85.[12]

The picture that emerges is certainly not that of a model to be emulated even in terms of the human development aspect. It also raises the question of the sustainability of the experience of the past in Kerala itself. It is on this question, the attention must turn from the human development aspect to the material development aspect. What is implied is not that material development is more important than human development. There is no question that human development, the development of the capabilities of every member of society, should be the aim of development policy . But concentration on the development of human capability sometimes leads to the neglect of some of the crucial but less obvious means to its achievement. At Thiruvananthapuram it was E.M.S. Namboodiripad (EMS) who forcefully reminded the gathering about the possibility of such a neglect and pointed out that the progress of Kerala has to be through increases in material production and productivity. "Although important advances have been made in respect of what are now called human development indicators", he said. "Kerala today faces an intense economic crisis in the spheres of employment and material production, agricultural and industrial . . . Let not the praise that scholars shower on Kerala for its achievements divert attention from the intense economic crisis that we face."[13]

There is no set pattern linking human development and material development. UNDP's Human Development Report 1996 makes a four-fold classification of countries in terms of the link between the two. There are countries where the link between the two is strong reinforcing each other through policy links. Japan, Malaysia, the Republic of Korea and Singapore are cited as examples. The opposite case is where the link between the two is weak, where slow growth accompanied by slow progress in human development undermine each other. Examples are Bangladesh, Niger and Tanzania. The third category is one of unbalanced links consisting of two types. One of them consists of cases of rapid economic growth but slow human development exemplified by Egypt and Pakistan. The other is where slow economic growth is associated with high human development. These cases that are similar to Kerala have been referred to already, Sri Lanka, Costa Rica, Jamaica and Peru. The unbalanced categories cannot remain in that State for long. With respect to the last that share Kerala's experience, the high human development can be sustained only if supported by economic growth. If not, over a period, they will degenerate into the weak case of low economic growth and low human development.

That is the scenario that Kerala must avoid. The discussion on that issue cannot be done in the abstract. We must take into account the specific context of Kerala. Two aspects of Kerala's post-independent situation deserve special attention. The first is the fact that Kerala has not been an independent country, but part of the Indian Union, a federal constituent of it. Though the federal relationship has led to some irritants, there is no doubt that the link has been to the advantage of Kerala. In my presentation at Thiruvananthapuram, I pointed out a major positive aspect—the Indian Union accepted the responsibility of providing foodgrains to the people of Kerala at concessional prices. It enabled Kerala whose per capita foodgrain production was extremely low and rapidly declining (62 kg per year in the triennium 1969-70 to 1972-73 compared to the all-India figure then of 186 kg, but falling to 38 kg in the triennium 1989-92 compared to the all-India figure of 203 kg) to have an assured supply of foodgrains of around 60 kg through the public distribution system covering practically the entire population. The assured supply of foodgrains at reasonable prices provided the material basis for Kerala's experiments in human development.

The second contextual factor in Kerala's development was, of course, foreign remittances, in the region of 20 per cent of the state domestic product (SDP) in the early 1970s, rising to about 30 per cent by the end of the decade and declining somewhat thereafter.[14] This flow of resources from outside, not entering into the calculations of the state domestic product enabled a consumption level much higher than was warranted by the low and in the 1980s declining growth of SDP.

The combination of these two factors was responsible for shaping Kerala's economy into a commercial-cum-service economy. It could have been and should have been directed into a more healthy and sustainable pattern of material growth with emphasis on infrastructural development. But that did not happen for reasons that I do not propose to enter into here. The fact remains, however, that what did happen in Kerala was a lopsided pattern of development which cannot be maintained any more, not even the human development component of it.

That is where Kerala had arrived by the end of the 1980s and that rang the alarm bells of a crisis in Kerala's "model" economy. I get the impression that those who have made it a habit of propounding and propagating the "Kerala Model" have not taken sufficient note of this aspect possibly because the achievement of "total literacy" and the 1991 Census figures have led to a greater celebration of the State's human development.

Be that as it may, the real issue is how Kerala's development is likely to turn out in the future. We may note, first, that the two contextual factors that influenced the State's pattern of development during the last three or four decades are unlikely to continue, certainly not likely to be as dominating as they were hitherto. The economic reforms initiated in 1991 had contemplated radical changes in the matter of making foodgrains available to the population, preferring to leave it largely to market forces. The government that came to power in June 1996 has yet to make its position clear in this regard. But it seems fairly certain that Kerala's foodgrain requirements will not continue to be as heavily underwritten as was done in the past. There is no doubt also that market forces will have their impact on Kerala's commercial agriculture also. Foreign remittances are also not likely to be as favourable as they were in the immediate past. It is, therefore, reasonable to envisage that in the decades ahead the development of Kerala will be within a different all-India context and a different global context.

This is not to imply that conditions will necessarily be unfavourable to Kerala's human and material development. In fact, on the material front, things have begun to change for the better. The growth of per capita net domestic product which had remained extremely low in the 1970s and 1980s (annual rate of a mere 0.06 in the 1970s and just 1.40 per cent in the 1980s, both way below the national averages of these decades) is recorded to have been 6.16 per cent per annum during the 1986-87 to 1991-92 period, well above the national figure of 3.79 per cent.[15] The how and the why of this significant change are yet to be analysed and when taken up may yield some clues regarding the possibilities for the future. One hopes that the States' Ninth-Five year Plan, now under preparation, will throw some light on this aspect.

It is significant, though not surprising, that in the preparation of the Ninth Plan, Kerala has once again decided to turn to popular participation as the guiding factor, starting the exercises from the Panchayat level and moving up. It is a further affirmation that development should not only be for the people, but meaningfully by the people also. There is no doubt that Kerala' achievements of the past were the result of public participation—social intermediation, public action, people's participation or whatever other designation is given to it. At Thiruvananthapuram, while emphasising the need for material growth, EMS was equally emphatic in pointing out, "our great assets are our mass organisations and the democratic consciousness of our people", that people themselves are the primary agency in the development process. I have no doubt that what is needed in Kerala is more people's participation and not less.

I would, however, add that it is easier to convince people about the need for health and education and even to pay for such services than to make them aware of the significance of increasing material production or of infrastructural improvements. But this time around that is precisely what needs to be done. Decentralisation of decision-making certainly can be helpful to achieve the task, but the fact remains that most aspects of material development do not have the visibility and immediacy of benefits or the emotional appeal that health and education have. Hence, channelling popular participation and enthusiasm into processes of material development will be more difficult. Yet I would repeat what I said in Thiruvananthapuram, that unless the commercial revolution that Kerala has experienced and is still going on is directed into an appropriate form of industrial revolution, it will dissipate itself. The people of Kerala cannot afford to let that happen. I am sure they will not let it happen.

NOTES AND REFERENCES

1. See *Economic and Political Weekly*, Sept.1, 8, 15, 1990 (vol. XXV, nos. 35 and 36 and 37).
2. For instance, see Jean Dreze and Amartya Sen (1995), *India - Economic Development and Social Opportunity*, Delhi, Oxford University Press.
3. Centre for Development Studies (1975), *Poverty, Unemployment and Development Policy: A Case Study of Selected Issues with reference to Kerala*, New York, United Nations.
4. K.N. Raj. "Has There Been a Kerala Model?" International Congress on Kerala Studies, Abstract, vol. I, p.13.
5. T.N. Krishnan (1995), *The Route to Social Development in Kerala: Social Intermediation and Public Action*, Thiruvananthapuram, Centre for Development Studies, Preface.
6. International Congress on Kerala Studies, Abstracts, five volumes (1994), Thiruvananthapuram, A.K.G. Centre for Research and Studies; Also Social Scientist nos. 260-62 which carries some of the papers presented at the Congress as well as an overview of the Congress by T.M. Thomas Isaac and P.K. Michael Tharakan.
7. P.G.K. Panikar and C.R. Soman (1984), *Health Status of Kerala: The Paradox of Economic Backwardness and Health Development* (1984), Trivandrum, Centre for Development Studies, p.46.
8. V.K. Ramachandran (1995), *Kerala's Development Achievements, A Review* Bombay, Indira Gandhi Institute of Development Research.
9. T.N. Krishnan, *op. cit.*, p.10.

10. John Kurien, "The Kerala Model: Its Central Tendency and the Outliers", Reproduced in *Social Scientist*, pp. 260-62.
11. Varghese N.V. (1994), "School Quality and Student learning: A study of Primary Schooling in Kerala", *NIEPA*, New Delhi.
12. M.A. Oommen (1994), "Kerala and the New World Order: Some Tentative Hypotheses", paper presented at the International Congress on Kerala Studies cited by T.M. Thomas Isaac and P.K. Michael Tharakan, "Kerala, the Emerging Perspective: Overview of the International Congress on Kerala Studies", Social Scientist, nos. 260-62.
13. E.M.S. Namboodiripad, Presidential Address, International Congress on Kerala Studies, Abstracts, vol. I, p.4.
14. These estimates by T.N. Krishnan are quoted by V.K. Ramachandran, *op. cit.*, p.15.
15. V.K. Ramachandran, *op. cit.*, Table 1 (Statistical Tables).

(This paper is the full text of the Presidential address by the author in Symposia 1 : on *The Kerala Model and Sustainable Development*).

ELEVEN

KERALA MODEL

Time for Rethinking

K. SARADAMONI

There is no need to describe Kerala Model as much has been written on the subject. Its essence without significant development on the economic front, the State has attained remarkable progress on social front—has entered the minds even of ordinary Keralites. It is a matter of happiness for them to know that we are better off in many respects than our counterparts elsewhere in India as well as in several other countries. Despite this sense of pride, there is growing doubt[1] about the 'model' and concern over the contradictions and paradoxes in Kerala. It can also be thought that the halo around the 'model' obstructs a clear view of Kerala.

This chapter may be treated as a preliminary effort to understand Kerala society as it evolved during the last fifty (since independence of India) or forty (formation of the present State of Kerala) years. Fifty years back the region of Kerala comprised of the Malabar province of Madras Presidency of British India and the two princely States, Cochin and Travancore. By and large the people living in the area had a common history and they shared the same language and culture. The social reforms movement in the decades prior to independence affected the people living in the region alike.

The above period saw the people of Kerala making determined efforts to break away from the past, particularly the rigid caste distinctions and unfair and exploitative socio-economic conditions. The leadership in the struggles filled with enthusiasm, commitment, honesty and willingness to sacrifice could transmit to the people idealism to dream of a beautiful, fair and just Kerala and struggle to fulfil that dream. The result, a new person emerged, defiant and with a heightened sense of rights. That was fifty years back..

Talking about Kerala Model two questions arise; one, are we accepting the achievements of U.S.A. and other industrially developed countries of Western Europe as the model to emulate ? Two, can we make a distinction between economic and social development? Any discussion on Kerala Model today can take place only in the global context of growing unemployment, widening disparities in income, wealth, life-style and opportunities.

Keeping these in mind let us examine some of the key elements[2] in the Model as well as some important factors which have influenced the moulding of present Kerala.

Literacy and Education

Between 1901 and 1991 literacy rate in Kerala rose from 19.15 and 3.15 to 93.62 and 86.17 for men and women respectively. It is no small achievement. In the matter of education too the State has made impressive advancement. It has to be kept in mind that the State started with some advantage over other regions. Nagam Aiya who was Dewan Peishkar and the Census Commissioner wrote as early as 1875 that there was no reason to suppose that any British pressure had been brought to bear on the people in Travancore to persuade them to send their daughters to school.[3] Aiya was quoting an English officer. What happened as a result is that the institutions increased, not just clustered in and around cities and towns. Except in some tribal and fisher peoples' pockets most students can today walk to a school. Colleges, including professional institutions, have come nearer home to many more students when compared to the situation in 1956. Though fees paid by the students at the various institutions are relatively small, educating wards has become costlier for the parents. Private tuition has become an inevitable part of education. The number of years spent in the name of education has also increased. The Education Commission sponsored by the Kerala Sastra Sahitya Parishad, (K.S.S.P.) in their preliminary report, observed that students who successfully complete one stage of education appear to go to the next higher stage as a matter of course in the absence of useful occupations or avenues. "Thus no stage is terminal except for those who drop out of the system on account of failure" (Kerala Education Commission (1997) : 143). The Commission also agreed with the disturbing view prevailing in the State that the education system, despite its positive aspect had deficiencies in terms of content, societal relevance, quality and management. That all is not well with education comes out in seminars and conferences, and newspapers publish investigative reports on the matter quite regularly.

We may examine a couple of points more on these issues. One is the emergence of a large number of elite schools catering for the rich and not so rich who can somehow manage to find the huge expenses needed in these institutions. In terms of the present system of performance, the students of these schools have better chance to enter academics, bureaucracy, policy-making places and even politics. Another fact regarding education is the difference in the background of the students which we cannot ignore. A sizeable number of them come from families where four-five generations have already had some form of education, if not higher education itself. There are still students who are the first generation to seek education from their families.

Kerala has also been following a system by which students are upgraded up to tenth class without examination. So those who do not leave school out of sheer boredom, can reach up to class ten without much effort. Recently a woman Panchayat president openly said that most of the children who reach that level do not know even to write their own names. In the examinations held for class ten and pre-degree failure is abnormally high. So moderation has become an integral part of the system.[4]

In brief we may say that the majority of students are not getting anything from the system to develop curiosity, critical faculties and to give expression to their creative energies.

Though for the sake of convenience we examine education, employment, and health independently, they are not exclusive topics. For example, the pressure on the children to 'excel' or 'perform' comes from the family and society and the resulting health problems mainly psychological fall on the students and the family members, especially mothers. The ultimate solutions to such problems do not lie within the family as these are vital societal problems. The parent teacher associations and other concerned citizens can initiate debates on the very important problem of education. It has already begun, but has to cover larger sections.

Health

Health is another area which the supporters of Kerala Model have applauded. The general level of health awareness of the people, their sense of right in getting primary health care etc. are highlighted by them.

It has to be emphasised that the data from the official statistics on health available is actually data on ill-health; we come to know about the number of hospitals, doctors, beds, patients etc. True, more people go to hospital today than even thirty years back. People's trust in the 'modern' medicine or allopathy as a speedy relief giving system has been rising.

Just as in the case of education, concerned observers have been expressing their distress over the health care systems. As two eminent scholars remark : "Kerala's health-status has emerged as a low mortality high morbidity syndrome. As for the morbidity pattern the diseases of poverty are seen to co-exist with the so-called diseases of affluence" (Panikar and Soman (1984) : 146).

Newspaper reports and television programmes have come up with severe criticism of the medical system which is becoming more and more commercialised and market oriented. As the people are trapped into quick-healing system, and as the power relation between the doctor and the patient is rigid and hierarchical, most people remain without a clear understanding of their ailment. And they are very often over-medicated. True, there are organisations working to create awareness regarding cancer, AIDS etc., but they cannot be expected to reach out to all people. It is now established that heart problems among young people is on the increase in Kerala. So also stress related diseases. The increasing number of super-speciality hospitals with advanced technologies like scanning, ultra-sound and the like thrive on the above developments.

We do hear some voices against the unnecessary, thoughtless and even inhuman medicare arrangements. The need for clean air and water, proper food, and stress-free life is also heard. But people by and large have been made to forget the idea 'prevention is better than cure'. It cannot be said that all people have forgotten how to lead a healthy life. Ayurveda, homeopathy and siddha systems still attract patients, many among whom would have tried allopathy initially. Naturopathy also has good following. But these are limited to a minority. They are people who are generally knowledgeable about the ways and means for a healthy living with associated outlook on life. They try not to be competitive, go for regular walks, do exercise or yoga and prefer peace in life. But who can afford to do so ? But the majority who are trapped in a meaningless and hurried existence, sometimes for mere survival, find all these a luxury which they cannot afford.

In the whole process we have lost our time-tested simple remedies for common ailments like common cold, ordinary stomach pain, indigestion and so on.

Women's health needs special attention. It is generally taken along with family planning or under women and children. This in a way assumes that women's health problems are related to family planning and childbirth. Much data have been generated in many parts to show that this is not so. It is fairly established that women suffer from back pain, pain in the joints and other stress-related diseases.

In most of the work places including government offices, clean and hygienic toilets are not guaranteed. It will not be an exaggeration to say that one can find women even among those who commute long distances, who do not urinate the whole day. But such things are not discussed in public or taken up at their Union level.

Kerala government's much acclaimed success of the family planning programmes would not have been achieved without the cooperation of women, who irrespective of class or caste, wish to give a `better life' to their children. They are also aware of the cost of bringing up a child. However they cannot be said to have sufficient and necessary knowledge about their body, sexuality and possible linkage between the family planning methods they adopt and their ailments, physical or mental. As a result, they have not succeeded in demanding continuous monitoring of these, as is done in other countries.

It is now a known fact that caesarean deliveries have come to be accepted as normal in Kerala. The business aspect of this is also known. Yet women and women's organisations have not raised their voice against the trend or tried to understand why pregnancy has come to be treated as an ailment which needs medication from the beginning. The author has dealt with these in an earlier paper. (Saradamoni (1994), 501-509).

Unemployment and Development

According to the *Economic Review,* 1996 published by the Government of Kerala, the number of job seekers as per the live register in the employment exchange rose from 32.26 lakhs to 32.99 lakhs between 31-12-1995 and 31-8-1996. Seventy-five percent of these job seekers have educational qualification S.S.L.C. and above, 2.85 lakh pre-degree certificate holders, 1.57 lakh graduates, 31,044 post graduates are found among them (see Table 11.1).

The number of professional and technical job seekers increased from 1.16 lakhs in 1990 to 1.30 lakhs as on 31.8.1996. The other information, the *Economic Review* provides are very brief paragraphs on employment in the organised sector, placement through employment exchange, placement through ODEPC, self-employment assistance scheme and unemployment assistance scheme. The numbers given under each heading, whether in terms of people or money, do not tell much about the unemployment situation and its meaning for the people. The unemployed also do not form a homogeneous community. Unemployment is not a situation about which anybody is happy. But there are middle and upper middle-class households which can afford to support the

Table 11.1 Number of Work Seekers and Employment between 1980 and 1996

Period (year at the end of December)	*Total Work Seekers*	*% Below SSLC*	*% Above SSLC*	*Employment*		
				Public Sector	*Private Sector*	*Total*
1980	1579164	48.45	51.55	496659	526459	1023118
1985	2574074	46.95	53.05	568713	507395	1076008
1990	3320035	36.97	63.03	634379	512034	1146413
1996	3298581	25.00	75.00	620068	552474	1172542

Source: *Economic Review*, 1989 and 1996 (from the Directorate of Employment and Training).

While the total work seekers who have registered with the Employment Exchange and renewed their names in time made a rise of 209 per cent between 1980 and 1996 the total number of persons absorbed in public and private sector has been only 115 per cent. It has to be noted that all those who seek work do not register with Employment Exchange or renew their names in time.

unemployed wards for a relatively longer period. At the same time there are those households for whom immediate employment is necessary for survival.

The efforts our country followed to bring about economic development through the Five Year Plans never treated employment generation as a top priority. It was seen as a by-product of the form and size of development we accepted. Certainly we tried the trickle down theory and development with social justice ingrained in it. But we never asked, what sort of policies should we follow to absorb the millions with uneven levels of education and skill. As far as Kerala is concerned employment-unemployment appear to be non-issues to the authorities. The government makes tall claims about unemployment benefit schemes and social security initiatives.

There was a poignant statement made by Krishnaji in the Delhi conference on Kerala's Development experience and I wish to record it here. His observation was that the absence of a class of small peasants was a disturbing feature of Kerala agrarian scene. This was not accidental. This is also something which no other country has experienced. Depletion of paddy lands has not only reduced paddy production, but eliminated the women and men labourers who had combined in them a way of life and culture and skill inherited through generations. However neither the labourers who were in the forefront of many a struggle nor the leaders who organized them could see the above reality as it was, or avert the conversion of paddy fields into residential areas and for other purposes.

Coconut was the second major crop. In this Kerala has come down from its premier position to a rank lower than the neighbouring States of Tamil Nadu and Andhra Pradesh. Rubber which was allowed to substitute many other crops is in a crisis. Even in the case of spices which had earned Kerala a name prior to the advent of the European powers and modern trade the State does not enjoy the old pre-eminent position. In fact the much publicised land reform measures in Kerala and their impact need a thorough and objective study.

Though Kerala depends upon the neighbouring states for practically everything, from rice, provisions and vegetables to jaggery, flowers and plantain leaves, the State still has award winning cultivators, and horticulturists who export ornamental flowers and fruits. The government schemes to promote the cultivation of mushroom, medicinal plants, etc., are welcomed by the people especially by women. What is lost is the respectability and sense of pride any farming community would wish to cherish and a population who can make decent living from agriculture.

If this is the State of affairs in agriculture it is better not to examine the industrial sector. Apart from specialized studies and articles, anyone interested in this topic can have a cross-section of views from the volumes of abstracts brought out during the International Congress on Kerala Studies held in Thiruvananthapuram in August, 1994. As in many other parts, the traditional industries like cashew processing, coir making, handloom weavning are facing crisis. Then how do people live? Migration is one way.

It is not wide of the mark to note here that the Keralites have come to believe that works based on manual labour cannot resolve the unemployment problem. They also believe it below their dignity to engage in such works.

When a group of young women planned to organise something along the pattern of Self-Employed Women Organisation (SEWA) in Ahmedabad, they decided against any production-based units but have succeeded in providing women for home nursing, dusting and cleaning household and office premises including libraries, and running canteens. Domestic help is in great demand. Another new sight is group of young and even middle-aged women going from home to home to sell ordinary things needed to satisfy day-to-day demands or special company products. The items may include biscuits, pickles, pappad, and under-garments. It is generally young men who come to sell more durable and costly items, like vacuum cleaner, gift packets etc. They are also engaged in the increasing number of market surveys. All these people travel long distances, and it is not always easy to sell all these things. Some have a salary, others a commission based on the volume of sales. Units set up by private agencies to make use of the modern methods of communication, FAX, e-mail as well as computer and electronic type writers also offer employment to some people. Tourism is projected as a big employment generating sector,but this is yet to be seen. In the whole process the people have come to belive that the old-type of jobs with security may not be available in the future, hence, they accept any job. There are plenty of women in this category and the employers find all these to their advantage.

It is not difficult to collect information on the type of work people are engaged in different parts of the State. Some of them can be ingenious.[5] But these cannot be thought of as answers to our unemployment problem.

It can come only when our development provides employment with decent wages a top priority and our agricultural and industrial growth geared to that.

Migration

To many people migration from Kerala is associated with the exodus to the Gulf countries. At one time this migration was seen as solving the unemployment problem, and supporting our economy through the money coming in. Then sceptics came forward to find fault with the Gulf migration for raising the cost of everything here, including taxi charges, wages to carpenters and masons. The migrants were accused of wasting hard earned money in non-productive investment like houses.[6] But of late the story has changed. These migrants to the Gulf are not a homogeneous category. There are many success stories, but there are many who have had only harassment, and sense of loss and failure which they do not wish the outside world to know.

The story of internal migration, especially of young women who go in search of jobs, to cities like Delhi or are recruited by agents to the prawn peeling centres in the coastal regions of Gujarat, Maharashtra and Karnataka is not in any way enthusing.[7]

The migration of highly qualified professionals to the U.K., then USA and lately to Australia mainly with the idea of settling down in those countries bring more money and greater comforts to those persons. It may take another two or three decades or more for Kerala to feel the impact of this kind of migration.[8]

There is yet another type of migration. For quite some time well-to-do Keralites have been settling down in places like Bangalore or Madras. A young friend of mine studying the Thiyyas of north Kerala was astounded by the number of well off Thiyyas who have left Kerala. This cannot be compared to the migration to Israel of the Jews who had contributed much to the social and economic fronts.

Those Keralites who were employed in places like Bombay or Delhi used to return after retirement. This trend has changed of late, the main reason being not having a joint family or property back at home, as well as the absence of job opportunities for the children.

Can Kerala be proud that it cannot offer a sense of belonging to its people who are compelled to make a living outside their home land?

Family and Status of Women

Kerala family has undergone big changes since the beginnig of the century. Matrilineal joint families were through legislative interventions, transformed to nuclear, male-headed families. This brought about changes not only in the size and composition of the family but also kinship bonds which was an essential part of the former system. Subsequent policies on family planning, large scale outmigration etc. have resulted in further changes in the family structure. Along with all these, longevity has also been on the rise resulting in the proportion of elderly population.

The demographers and the government see this as the result of the health and welfare policies followed by the State. There is no doubt that the ageing or the aged population receive attention. They have a day when programmes are arranged on them and for them. Articles are written about them and seminars and conferences are organised too. Geriatrics wards are opened in the hospitals. Despite all this the elderly in general continue to wonder why they are continuing to live so and get annoyed with the God above for not calling them.

If the elderly are not getting all the love, care and attention they wish or deserve it is not entirely because the children or others who are expected to look after them are unwilling. They have other responsibilities which they have to deal with. Their life is filled with tension. This can be caused by a child who lost the first rank by one mark in a class test, unemployment or alcoholism of any member of the family or due to other causes. One serious cause for tension in the family is when they cannot keep up with the Jonses.

All this affects women who are not only stressed out, but do not very often try to understand the happenings outside the home. The women who are said to be advanced in literacy and education are by and large ignorant about public affairs, even in the immediate surroundings.

Violence

Any attempt to understand contemporary Kerala has to take note of increasing violence. The State is having the second highest crime rate in India (*Hindu,* December. 16, 1996). In 1994 crimes against women itself were reported to be 1,609—193 rape cases,

105 kidnappings, 550 cases of torture, 679 cases of molestation, nine dowry deaths, 16 cases of indecent representation of women and 54 cases of immoral traffic.

Cheating, theft and burglary are also on the increase. In 1994 property worth Rs. 9,364.4 lakhs was stolen and the recovery rate of 58 per cent was the lowest in the country (*ibid.*).

All these naturally fill people's mind with fear, apathy or indifference and helplessness. Women's groups occasionally organise protests and demonstrations against atrocities on women. But increasing violence has not evoked the alertness and concern it warrants, though the authorities are well aware of it.[9] One does not see a genuine attempt at understanding the root causes of this phenomenon. It is not something which can be seen as "it was there always but is being reported more now".

What we have discussed above does not include domestic violence which is also on the increase in the State. It can be physical abuse, mental torture or even absence of any communication between the members of the family, particularly husband and wife. While the poor women from low income groups shout and retort when they are beaten by drunken husbands, the middle class women generally suffer in silence.

Coming back to the question why violence and crime are increasing we can make a few speculations. One can again argue that this is a global phenomenon. True, but when we explore the reasons for increasing violence in Kerala we are not denying that. What do the people here want? We are not engaged in the process of creating a peaceful, harmonious, contented society. The essential simplicity which was the hallmark of traditional Kerala has been replaced by extravagance and vulgarity, supported by the philosophy of unending greed and unnecessary wants.

It has to be remembered that it is not only the middle class and those who can afford that have fallen prey to the above. Thanks to the incessant pressure of advertisements and demostration effect, discriminative judgement appears to have lost its relevance in deciding what one needs or otherwise.

The large number of the unemployed are subjected to complex psychological pressure. Many of them experience repeated setbacks in their attempts to get a job either in Kerala or outside. Even among the employed there is so much of discontentment, lack of commitment to work, and indifference to the people who come to them with requests and petitions. One important reason for this is that the society has come to give undue emphasis to success and excellence depending on the money one amasses and the affluent life style one leads. This naturally results in a sense of failure to which any normal person would find it difficult to come to terms. Alcohol—foreign, desi, and spurious—and drugs, scenes of violence reaching them constantly through the media, reports in newspapers and also through cinema, T.V. serials etc. find vulnerable preys among the above categories of people. Another equally important reason for discontentment among the people is that a good number of the employed are in much lower positions than they should have been. For example, there are among bus conductors many who have postgraduate degrees and sometimes even Ph.D degree. Many are talented in other ways too.

In conclusion what shall we make out of Kerala society? Development measured by certain indices can give only partial if not distorted view of a region's progress or change. At the same time we have to admit that we have yet to evolve dependable tools of analysis to study people. Yet we are not far from truth to say that despite apparent well-being Kerala society and people are disturbed by various facts. Each of the factors we have examined has left the people discontented and helpless. Many people try to seek help from gods, godmen and godwomen and astrologers when they are torn by problems they cannot resolve. All this is happening along with growing individualism and alienation. A statement showing sample headlines collected at random from newspapers is given at the end of this chapter as an Appendix.

Is there not a way out? A large section of people are silent but that does not mean that they do not wish for change for the better, to feel less competitive, more relaxed and safer. We find many among the same people joining protest marches and demonstrations, going to women's commission, Family Courts and Neeti melas and this is indicating their sense of deprivation or injustice even if they are not clear about what they want.

Kerala can emerge as a Model if the same sense of injustice can be converted to an urge to fight for fairness and justice. This would bring back the hopes and aspirations of the pre-independent era. In the present context it means promising the people security of food, shelter, employment with decent earnings, clean water and air, gender justice, protection of environment from destruction and community supports as their rights. The people have also to be made to take the responsibility in preserving these rights.

If we succeed in creating an environment where people would start wishing for a peaceful, contented and harmonious life, we would have more to offer to the world, much more than the myths around the Model.

APPENDIX

SOME TELLING HEADLINES FROM NEWSPAPERS

22 September 1996 M.	Old Woman raped
22 September 1996 M.	Howsewife raped
25 September 1996 M.	Two women found hanging
26 September 1996 M.	Unidentified woman's dead body on the beach
13 October 1996 M.	Woman thrown off on the wayside from car
13 October 1996 M.	Daughter's marriage broken : father dies of heart attack
17 November 1996 M.	Mother who along with children jumped before running train dies: both children hurt
17 November 1996 M.	Tragedy after drinking poisoned alcohol, death toll rises to four
2 March 1997 M.	Santosh murder case: Mother under arrest
2 March 1997 M.	Life sentence for son for killing mother
9 March 1997 M.	Suicide by the entire family: economic reasons hinted
30 June 1997 M.	Suicide on the increase in Kerala

30 June 1997 M.	Four member family dead after taking poison
31 July 1997 H.	Housewife gangraped
30 September 1997 H.	Priest kills wife, kids: commits self-immolation

M—"Matrubhumi Malayalam Daily"
H—"Hindu"

NOTES

1. See the volumes of abstracts published after the International Congress on Kerala Studies, held in Thiruvananthapuram, August 1994.
   K. Saradamoni (1996), "Kerala Model: Do Figures Tell the Whole Truth?" Paper submitted to Sixth International Karl Polanyi Conference held at the Concordia University, Montreal, November 7-10, 1996.
   ———, (1997), Kerala Model: Can Economic and Social Development Be Distinguished? Workshop during International Institute, Centre for popular Economics, Amherst, USA August 6, 1997.
   — "Kerala Matrukayum Streekalum" (Kerala Model and Women) Kerala Padhanangal, July-September 2, 1993, pp. 225-245.
2. Apart from literacy, education and health, sex-ratio, falling infant mortality, rising life expectancy, efficient public distribution system, politically conscious people demanding their rights form part of the indices measuring the Kerala Model. To these can be added any number of achievements like the number of post offices, telephones and so on for specific number of people etc.
3. Census of Travancore, 1875, p. 238.
4. Moderation has become a common feature of all examinations conducted by the Kerala University. In the process the standard of examinations is lowered cited in "Moderation—a necessary evil?" The *Hindu* October 6, 1997.
5. When the author was doing field work in connection with another study she found a large number of plastic cans arranged in rows in a house compound in Vypeen island in Cochin. We found out that the cans were full of water collected from taps.They were sold to others especially boat men. This may not be possible today with aggravated watershortage. The young women there were washing, starching and ironing the clothes of boatmen who came that way for payment. They were not dhobis. Kerala is not a place endowed with traditional handicrafts like some other States. Prostitution has increased in a big way to such an extent that women appeared on the television and said that it was their occupation to bring up their children. They did not want to be masked.

6. Many of them may be people who never had owned a house for generations. They are not the only people who spend lavishly on houses. It is time for some kind of restriction on the expenses on houses taking into consideration demographic changes and changing size and composition of families. It can also reduce the visible disparity in income and wealth.
7. The harrowing tales of young women who were attracted to the coastal regions to work in the prawn peeling centres especially in Gujarat attracted media attention several years back. The governments of Gujarat and Kerala took up the matter, but nothing has been done so far. Many young girls with no special skill go to places like Delhi in search of jobs. Women go to the Middle East too, though their number is not as big as women migrants from Sri Lanka or Philippines.

   Male migration especially to the Middle Eastern countries is not evenly successful. People go through financial and psychological stress and strain to reach there. Of late thousands had to come back either because they had not obtained proper papers or for other reasons.
8. Many of these highly qualified professional migrants are from relatively well-off propertied families. So far an aged parent or a relative would have looked after their land and other properties. There can come a stage when there would be none to do that, and create legal problems regarding ownership, inheritance of property and other assets..
9. Recently the Mayor of Thiruvananthapuram admitted that there are three or four underworld groups functioning in this small city.

REFERENCES

Goverment of Kerala (1989), *Economic Review*,1989.

———— (1996), *Economic Review*, 1996.

Kerala Education Commission, Preliminary Report, Sastra Sahitya Parishad, 1997.

Panikar, P.G.K. and C.R. Soman (1984), *Health Status of Kerala*, Centre for Development Studies, Thiruvananthapuram.

Panikar P.G.K. and C.R. Soman, (1984), *Health Status of Kerala*, Centre for Development Studies, Thiruvananthapuram.

Saradamoni, K. (1994), "Women Kerala and some development issues", *Economic and Political Weekly*, February 26, 1994.

TWELVE

THE SOCIAL ROOTS OF KERALA'S DEVELOPMENT DEBACLE

JOSEPH THARAMANGALAM

Introduction

According to a well-known and influential scholarly view, Kerala offers many valuable lessons, if not a model, to other States in India and to poor Third World countries (Franke and Chasin, 1989; Alexander, 1995; Radcliffe, 1978; A.K. Sen, 1993, 1994; Amin, 1991). The point to Kerala's impressive achievements in literacy, health and other indicators of quality of life—all spread relatively evenly across the population. It is particularly noteworthy that the State has reached the third stage of the demographic transition with fertility rate lower than those of "upper middle income" groups of countries (Gita Sen, 1992) and China, but achieved without compulsion, that the survival chances of Kerala's people are better than those of African Americans (Amartya Sen, 1994) and that female literacy rates are higher than those of every province in China (Amartya Sen, 1994). The key to these achievements was not through focussing on economic growth, but through social and political mobilisation and social policies promoting distributive justice and quality of life. It has now become apparent, however, that there are major weaknesses in the model that have begun to gnaw at its very achievements raising serious doubts about its sustainability. While these issues have been widely discussed by scholars, the debate has so far been dominated by economists and Left intellectuals who have generally been unable or unwilling to examine possible endogenous and inherent social causes of the malaise. Is it possible that Kerala's weaknesses may, in fact, stem from tendencies and constraints inherent in the model ? (Tharamangalam, 1985a, 1985b, 1991). Answering this question requires us to invert the model and to ask, not how Kerala achieved social development despite economic stagnation, but how and why it experiences such prolonged economic stagnation despite social development contrary to the experience of many, dynamic and high growth societies (see also George, 1993,1994).

This chapter attempts to explore the basic economic, social, political and cultural roots of Kerala's development experience and to critically assess the nature and causes of the current crisis.

The Historical Background

The Malayalam-speaking nation of Kerala became a State in 1956 when most Indian states were reorganised on the basis of language. The two princely States of Travancore and Cochin and the Malabar district of the Madras Presidency of British India were united to form Kerala. Some of the essential elements that make up the Kerala model have a long history and have evolved over a long period of time. Travancore was long known as a model native State, apparently since 1867 when a Secretary of State for India proclaimed it as such in Britain's House of Commons. And Cochin followed closely behind with respect to the things that made Travancore a model State. To be sure, the Rajahs of Travancore had established a British style administration and had even encouraged the activities of European missionaries who were apparently attracted to the region in large numbers because of the presence there of a significant community of ancient Christians. More important, they initiated economic enterprises such as plantation agriculture, agri-based industries and generally encouraged and even subsidised commercial and capitalist developments. They also pioneered progressive social policies especially in education and public health. The State, in particular developed a successful school system that integrated both the traditional and the new, both Malayalam and English and both government schools and government-aided private schools.

The new educational system was open to large sections of the population, including many previously disadvantaged groups.

A tradition of what has been referred to as public politics (Jeffrey, 1993) and public action (Dreze and Sen, 1989) struck roots in Kerala in response to these changes. If growing education and social consciousness among the previously disadvantaged challenged the old order, the new resources that were made available by the growing commercial-capitalist economy and expanding educational opportunities demanded changes in the caste-based ascribed status system of Kerala and radical changes to the old rules of the game. The first movements were the social reform and the protest movements of castes and communities who had suffered deprivations under the old system. Ironically, it was the upper caste Nairs who set the ball rolling with the Malayalee Memorial of 1891 submitted to the Dewan (Prime Minister) protesting against the dominance of Tamil Brahmins in Government service. This was followed by the most significant social reform or protest movement of Kerala, led by Sree Narayana Guru of the numerically largest caste as well as the most important of the lower castes, the Ezhavas. Originally intended as a non-sectarian movement open to all, the Sree Narayana Dharma Paripalana Yogam or SNDP eventually became an influential caste association. There followed a series of similar movements and caste organisations among the Pulayas, the Syrian Christians and among the Nairs. In the 1930s, the issue that dominated Kerala was the demand of the Ezhavas and other lower castes to enter the Hindu temples and the temple premises which led to the famous temple entry proclamation of 1936.

From 1888 on, Travancore, the model State, also began to experiment with popular assemblies which became more and more democratic by the 1920s and the 1930s. Intense mobilization and agitations by communal and caste organizations led to an arrangement of proportional representations or quotas for them in the legislative assembly. Eventually, however, the communal road seems to have led to secular politics as argued by George Matthew (1989) in a book by the same title. To the extent that caste and "communal" conflicts have persisted, they have generally been fought within the framework of the democratic political game and with relatively little inter-religious violence or strife. Recent reports (Isaac and Tharakan, 1989), however, suggest a retrogressive trend in this respect. It is probable that the resurgence of casteism and communalism is at least partly caused by the current developmental and social crisis.

In the 1930s, Malayalees began to organise new kinds of social movements—nationalist movements for "responsible government", and rapidly spreading socialist and communist movements. Radical political parties organized various sectors of the working classes into trade unions, especially in Travancore and a strong peasant movement, especially in Malabar. When elections were held in the newly created Kerala State in 1957 Kerala achieved international fame by democratically electing the communist party to power. It was this government that initiated some of the most radical and comprehensive reforms and social welfare measures including the much discussed land reforms. A "liberation struggle", spearheaded by the Christian churches and the Nair Service Society, led to the dismissal of this government by the Central Government. Kerala's politics have since fragmented, but a variety of parties are broadly grouped into two alliances led by the Communist Party of India-Marxist (CPM) and the Congress party, respectively giving the appearance of a two-party system.

Historians have generally stressed the connection between a tradition of continuous struggles and the trajectory of Kerala's development. The evolution of public politics in Kerala was a response to social forces such as an earlier and more thorough penetration of capitalist and commercial relations in society than elsewhere in the country (Tharamangalam, 1984), and the disintegration of matriliny which, according to Jeffrey, led to a "Social collapse more complete than anywhere in India" (1993:2). By the end of the Second World War, Kerala's people believed strongly that they had entitlements, that they had a right to protest about social conditions and to demand redress. Such involvement intensified in post-independence Kerala. The other side of this "public politics" was the evolution of a State that had to respond to popular demand. As the politics of agitation and struggle led to increasing fragmentation of politics in Kerala, the imperative to respond to such demands became even more urgent. The result was the creation of one of the most extensive welfare States by Third World standards—an important dimension of the Kerala Model. The welfare State has other roots, of course, especially the influence of socialist and communist ideologies that saw such State intervention as ideal and desirable.

The Nature of the Current Debacle

It has become apparent to many observers that the Kerala Model is unsustainable because of a three-fold economic crisis: a progressively worsening fiscal situation, prolonged economic stagnation and even decelerating growth, and the continuing inability of the economy to generate employment for Kerala's people. What is worse, these economic problems appear to be inherent in the model, and not anomalies that can be easily overcome.

The Fiscal Crisis

K.K. George (1993) has made an excellent study of the fiscal problems of Kerala for a period of 16 years from 1974 to 1990. He has clearly brought out the systemic nature of these problems and convincingly demonstrated the fiscal unsustainability of the Kerala Model. Basically, Kerala's problem is that it does not and cannot generate enough revenue to finance and maintain its social development with the result that it has progressively increasing budget deficits. These deficits are not only substantially higher than those of other Indian States, but are different in origin and nature. First, the deficits are largely in the revenue account that finances current consumption. The government has been attempting to finance these deficits by using capital receipts and public accounts. According to George, in 1986-87, 1987-88 and 1989-90 revenue deficits absorbed more than a quarter of the total capital receipts. This severely reduces the government's ability to incur capital expenditures. The government has also been dipping into its public accounts such as savings deposits and insurance and pension funds with the result that it is even unable to meet its fiduciary obligations—behaviour for which private trustees of such funds are liable to be severely punished. Second, the revenue expenditures are inherently liable to increase over the years not only due to inflation but also because of second generation requirements of social development. For example, expenditure on health care and pension payments have been going up as the increase in life expectancy has been significant. Third, the Kerala government's ability to raise resources is severely constrained by a variety of factors including stagnation in the tax base, and control of taxation policy by the Central Government. For example, the State Government has no control over Gulf remittances. Fourth, Kerala's public undertakings have become a serious economic liability. Fifth, Kerala has been unable to obtain its fair share of Central Government transfers which are distributed according to rules and priorities that do not take into account the specific nature of Kerala's problems. For example, Kerala does not receive its share for social development since it is seen as having reached the national targets despite the fact that the State is unable to meet the recurring expenditures needed to sustain these achievements.

Those who celebrate the Kerala Model generally suggest, or at least imply, that Kerala may have made a morally superior choice for human development and quality of life in place of economic growth. More will be said about the false paradox below; the idea that there is such a choice needs to be quickly laid to rest. For, as George has shown clearly, Kerala cannot sustain its achievements and is losing its lead in social development itself. For example, it has been pointed out that since the mid-seventies Kerala has been reducing its share of expenditure on social development such as education and health both because of the fiscal crisis and apparently also shift in government priorities (George, 1994 : 8). And since most of the available funds on education and health are spent on salaries, very little is left for current inputs or modernising the facilities. Similarly, the social security system is put under severe strain by the growing number of the unemployed and the pensioners. More serious is the erosion of the subsidy for the public distribution system since Keralites are now more dependent on food imports than at any time in the past. Kerala has already lost its lead in education and health; Punjab has overtaken Kerala in per capita expenditure on education and both Punjab and Rajasthan in per capita expenditure on health (George, 1993, 1994).

Economic Stagnation

Kerala's fiscal crisis must be seen as reflecting a deeper structural crisis of continuous stagnation in the productive sectors of its economy since the mid-1970s. The experts who have examined Kerala's economy have shown a remarkable consensus in arguing that the stagnation is both all-pervasive and deeprooted. Kerala's per capita income is not only significantly lower than India's but has been steadily declining in relative terms since the 1970s. Between 1970-71 and 1985-86 it increased only from 594 to 636 (in 1970-71 prices) while the corresponding figures for the country were 718 and 798, respectively (Oommen : 154). In fact, Kerala's per capita income as a percentage of India's declined from 93 per cent in 1970-71 to 90 per cent in 1980-81 and 73 per cent in 1987-88 (George, 1993 : 6) and to 70 per cent by the 1990s (Oommen, 1993 : 210). The gap between Kerala and Punjab widened steadily, and by 1987-88 Kerala's per capita income was only a little more than two-fifths of the latter's (George, 1993 : 6). Similarly, growth in Kerala's State domestic product (SDP) has been quite dismal. Kannan (1990) shows that between 1974-75 and 1985-86 the SDP grew only by 1.76 per cent while in the period 1962-65 to 1974-75 the corresponding figure was 3.2 per cent. Between 1980-81 and 1989-90 the share of Kerala's SDP in the GNP declined from 3.3 to 2.6 (Oommen, 1993 : 210). Kannan regards 1975 as the crucial year in which the economy began receiving large amounts of remittances. But apparently this was also the year in which economic performance began to show real decline. The modest growth registered since then was largely due to a spurt of growth in the tertiary sector. The secondary sector grew by 2.15 per cent compared with 4.71 per cent during the first period while the primary sector showed negative growth of 0.70 as against a growth rate of 2.23 per cent during the first period.

Kannan and Pushpangadan's study (1990) of the performance of agriculture found that from the mid-1970s to the mid-1980s rubber was the only major crop that showed an increase in output. There was a decline in the output for paddy, tapioca, banana, coconut, cashew and arecanut, and stagnation in the case of pepper and cardamom. It is significant that in the case of the two main food crops, paddy and tapioca, the decline has been the result of a fall in area while in the case of banana and cashew, fall in production was due to a decline in yield. As will be seen below, this was also accompanied by a fall in the absolute number of independent 'cultivators' (Kurien, 1994 : 27). As this has also resulted in a significant fall in employment in agriculture what has happened to the traditional class of agriculture labourers remains a moot question.

More alarming for Kerala is the deceleration in industrialisation, especially the poor performance of the manufacturing sector in the second period. According to Subramanian (1990 : 2023) "Kerala's industrial performance measured by any parameter—annual growth of its manufacturing sector, share of manufacture in the State domestic product, value added in the factory sector or any like measure—has been on a low side". Thus by the 1980s Kerala with 3.7 per cent of the country's total population accounted for only 3.07 per cent of the number of factories, 3.12 per cent of employment, 2.61 per cent of fixed capital, 2.56 per cent of gross output and 2.90 per cent of net value added in the factory sector of the country. Between 1980-81 and 1987-88 Kerala recorded only a pitiable 1.73 per cent growth in value added by manufacture as against the annual compound growth rate of 10.56 per cent for all-India (2053). Kerala's share of exports, well above the all-India average in the past, has also been falling; it fell from 17 per cent in 1966-67 to less than 5 per cent in 1989-90 (Oommen, 1993 : 211). As India forges ahead with accelerated industrialisation in the 1990s, Kerala is inevitably slipping farther behind the rest of India and such industrially dynamic neighbouring States like Karnataka and Tamil Nadu. In fact, Kerala stands with Bihar and Uttar Pradesh as the three States which have lagged behind the most in investments after liberalisation (George, 1994). The plight of

Kerala is brought into sharp focus when we note, that in 1950 per capita manufacturing product in the erstwhile State of Travancore (Rs. 48) was significantly higher than in India as a whole (Rs. 37).

Unemployment

The third dimension of Kerala's economic crisis is the State's acute and ever-increasing levels of unemployment which too has its own Kerala-specific characteristics. From every possible parameter of measurement Kerala has the worst record of unemployment in the country. With 3.4 per cent of India's population it accounted for nearly 16 per cent of the country's unemployed (Oommen, 1993 : 108). In terms of relative intensity of unemployment, Kerala's figure of 4.63 was way above that of any other State. The second highest, Tamil Nadu, registered 1.2. In absolute numbers the unemployed increased from 144,000 in 1965 to 1,879,000 in 1987-88. As must be expected, a large number of Kerala's unemployed are graduates and post-graduates. The greatest paradox, however, is seen among the uneducated unemployed such as coconut pickers (tree climbers), construction workers and, especially, agricultural workers. Here high levels of unemployment coexist with a widely reported "shortage" of labour.

A "Nation" of Migrant Labourers?

As everyone in Kerala knows, this is not the whole story, however; nor do the figures above represent the real per capita disposable income of Kerala. Had this been so, it is very unlikely that there would have been any admirers of the Kerala Model today since Kerala would have long sunk into widespread poverty. Kerala has been rescued from such a disaster by the very substantial remittances of Keralites employed outside, especially in the Arabian Gulf, and also by the rapid fall in population growth. Kerala's real per capita income, therefore, is almost certainly higher than the Indian average. This has triggered a major consumer boom and significant growth in the tertiary sector of the economy.

Since the early 1970s consumption levels in Kerala have steadily moved in a direction exactly opposite to the various indices of economic development. From a position of less than the national average it moved to exceed the national average by 1983-84. By 1987 consumption expenditure exceeded SDP, obviously due to the influx of remittances, estimated to be in the order of some 1000 to 1500 million rupees during the past two decades (R. Krishan, 1994 : 147). According to T.N. Krishnan (1994:58), during the same period annual remittances have ranged from 15 to 30 per cent of the SDP. He also estimated Kerala's per capita consumption in real terms in 1994 to be about double that of 1960-61 (*Ibid* : 59). It is important to note that the vast majority of these Keralites working abroad are employed in low level jobs and are subject to exploitation, racial discrimination and denied many fundamental human rights such as religious freedom and the right to organise trade unions. There seems to be an irony in the fact that a people who have so valiantly struggled against capitalist exploitation at home are now so happily sending their sons and daughters to work under such humiliating conditions. But then what is the choice of a people whose prosperity and high consumption are based on the largesse of international employers and on the ability of societies with different models of development to produce the goods so widely sought after today?

More Paradoxes of the Kerala Model

It is clear that the economic and the social structure of Kerala has some unique features and is radically different from that of every other State in India. A few basic features that are central to understanding the specific nature of Kerala society are outlined here. First, Kerala's agrarian economy has undergone radical and far-reaching changes, so that Kerala can no longer be classified as an agrarian society without important qualifications. Today the production of food for consumption, is only a minor activity for Kerala people. During the past two decades, Kerala saw a decline in foodgrains production at an annual rate of 1.09 per cent, and Kerala is unique in India in this respect. Area under foodgrains fell from 960,000 hectares in 1970-71 to 560,000 hectares in 1990-91. The share of cultivators in the total work-force declined from 17.8 per cent in 1971 (against the all-India figure of 43.3) to 13.06 per cent in 1981 (India 41.46) and to 12.24 in 1991 (India 38.41) (Kurien 1994 : 27). The fact is that agriculture is neither a subsistence activity nor a viable economic enterprise except for a limited number of plantation crops, especially rubber. The phenomenal rise in land prices has little to do with their value for agriculture; land is real estate, needed for residence and status and also generally seen as the safest and best investment given the still volatile nature of the stock market. This has also led to a radical transformation in the nature of agricultural activities, employment and life styles. Second, a substantial number of "agricultural families" have non-agricultural sources of income, mainly remittances or employment in the highly bloated service sector of Kerala. Third, a variety of traditional economic activities including the cultivation of many seasonal crops and many small businesses are no longer seen as economically viable as they do not provide what is regarded as an adequate return. Fourth, there is the coexistence of labour shortage with high unemployment levels partly because these jobs are not economically "worthwhile" and more importantly because low status and physically irksome jobs are not culturally desirable options any longer. Fifth, the Kerala economy exists and functions as an integral part of the Indian economy and polity and in the underdeveloped periphery of a world economic system that at this stage needs the cheaply available unskilled, semi-skilled and skilled labour of Malayalees.

State, Society and Politics : A Kerala Model of Socialism?

Reference has been made above to the dialectics of a patronizing State that implements reform and welfare, and distributes the collective pie to various demand groups on the one hand, and political mobilisation and struggles by organised groups continuously putting pressure on the State on the other. It is widely acknowledged that Kerala's gains could not have been achieved without extensive state interventions. While such state intervention in Kerala has been effective by Third World standards, it has not necessarily been efficient; nor has its beneficiaries been mainly the poorer sections of the population. It is nevertheless true that it has had a significant effect in reducing poverty in Kerala. For example, Kannan (1995) has shown that state intervention has been mainly responsible in significantly reducing poverty in Kerala since the mid-1970s. He estimates (*ibid*:721) that by 1983-84 the income effect of the various poverty alleviation programmes represented 26 per cent of the income of rural labour households. However, this model of state intervention and politics too seems to have reached its limits today, and become disruptive of Kerala's economic and social development.

One consequence of this kind of development has been that politics became over-emphasised and over-developed and people began to place undue reliance on politics and the State to achieve all their goals, including economic ones. Significantly, the tradition of self-help that was evident earlier when communities mobilised investment capital through local mutual funds (such as kuries and chitties), and banks, and built educational institutions and hospitals with their own local resources, had practically disappeared by the 1960s. The goals of mobilisation and organised activities became extracting benefits from the government, the patronising State government—land, rice, jobs, roads, schools, hospitals, and other varieties of welfare and subsidies. The means to obtain all this were typically mobilization and agitation which were not always confined to peaceful and democratic methods, but included gheraos, sit-ins, stoning of public buses and other violent methods. This also led to the fragmentation of politics and to destructive competition among rival parties and trade unions preventing the articulation and pursuit of basic collective goals of the people and the State. Weak and short-lived State Governments (between 1951 and 1970, Kerala elected a new government every three years) were unable and unwilling to address some of these long-term goals or to secure Kerala's legitimate interests vis-a-vis the Central Government. Furthermore, over-politicisation and bureaucratic State interference have adversely affected the orderly functioning of civil society and systematically undermined the autonomy and efficiency of other spheres such as economic enterprises, and educational institutions. Public sector enterprises do not function in conformity with the ordinary norms of economic rationality nor educational institutions with norms of academic standards and priorities. Government loans become euphemisms for hidden subsidies since these are not backed by adequate mechanisms for recovery (George, 1993:35-37). Let us look at public sector enterprises and education, two crucial areas controlled by the State.

The Kerala Government is one of the biggest entrepreneurs in the State (Pillai, 1990). In 1989-90 there were 80 public enterprises excluding the State Electricity Board and Transport Corporation accounting for 9.7 per cent of the total 823 enterprises in all States and 6.7 per cent of total investments in these enterprises. But of these, only 32 units made a profit, a total of Rs. 370 million. Against these were the losses of the other 48 units, which amounted to Rs. 990 million resulting in a net loss of Rs. 760 million to the State. Further, 65 units had carried forward losses of Rs. 6530 million and 37 enterprises had negative net worth. The problem of mismanagement and lack of accountability is brought into sharp relief when it is seen that audits of 63 enterprises were in arrears; one of them had not conducted any audits after 1982-83 (George, 35). The problem is a systemic one, quite basic in understanding the Kerala Model's present crisis.

The educational system, particularly post-secondary education, is similarly entrapped in a web of institutional, political and cultural constraints from where the road to any form of rationalization is difficult to see. Undoubtedly, mass education has been one of Kerala's greatest success stories and the root of its major achievements. But today post-secondary education in Kerala is frozen into an unsustainable burden which does not and cannot meet the economic and social needs of society. The great expansion in college education began in the 1960s when government began to build or sanction colleges offering degrees in arts and sciences in response to organised demands from various constituencies. By 1989-90 the number of students in these colleges rose from about 36,000 to 330,000 and the number of teachers from 2170 to 13,900. This does not include the privately registered students who are allowed to take the examinations of the universities, roughly half the number of the registered students, nor those of the 331 "parallel" colleges revealed in a 1989 survey, the 2952 tutorial colleges catering to both university and secondary school students nor the 1318 parallel-cum-tutorial colleges (1990 figures) (Oommen, 1993 : 118). By the 1980s, Kerala was spending more than 6 per cent of its SDP on education, the only State to meet the norm recommended as desirable by the Kothari Commission (Oommen, 1993 : 119). In 1988-89 the percentage for all States was 3.65 and for the richest State (Punjab) 3.26. During the past three decades Kerala's expenditure on education ranged from 30 to 40 per cent of its total revenue receipts.

What returns does Kerala receive from such massive investments? Clearly, primary and secondary school education has been a success story in terms of promoting general literacy and quality of life and in providing Keralites with a definite comparative advantage in obtaining employment abroad. But higher education tells a very different story. To begin with, "affiliated colleges" spread to the towns and villages of Kerala in response to a great demand for degree, B.A.s, B.Sc.s and later M.A.s and M.Sc.s which, in a bygone era, were useful in obtaining prestigious and comfortable jobs in government and the teaching profession. These institutions provided and continue to provide a type of education completely unrelated to the manpower requirements of the economy or of the development needs of the State. The results have now come home to roost. First, Kerala has the worst record of educated unemployment in the country and probably in the world. When in 1989 the Kerala Public Service Commission advertised a few vacancies for the post of bus conductors for which the minimum qualification was a high school diploma, the commission received 2,68,000 applications. Of the 6000 who qualified for the interview 80 per cent had qualifications beyond the S.S.L.C., and 20 per cent of these were postgraduates (including one doing Ph.D. in Laser Physics). The list also included several graduate engineers (Oommen, 1993 114). Vast number of graduates are not only unemployed but nonemployable. Degrees for women are seen as qualification for the marriage market; it is not surprising that the unemployment rate among educated women in the rural areas in 1990 was a whopping 57 per cent. Given Kerala's dependence on employment outside the State and the country, one would have expected the educational system to cater to the needs of these job seekers. In fact, however, Kerala's facilities for providing the needed training are meagre and underdeveloped forcing large number of Malayalees to go outside the State for the required training. For example, at least since the 1950s Kerala's nurses have sought and found employment in many parts of India and abroad including Germany, Canada, USA and the Arabian Gulf. Yet, the majority of these young women had to seek the needed training in other Indian States and not Kerala, facing many difficulties in the process. The issue of vocational and professional training is receiving some serious attention in Kerala only recently. Second, Kerala shows an inverse relationship between growth in education and economic development. In particular, the inverse relationship between education of rural population and agricultural growth during the past quarter century despite many favourable circumstances and considerable government investment has been contrary to all expectations and predictions. Third, the quality of higher education has deteriorated. Kerala students are illequipped to compete in national competitive and entrance examinations making Kerala's unemployment problem even more acute. Of course, they provide employment to those who offer them "coaching" in the hundreds of private tutorial colleges at a substantial price.

The problem is not that the system has failed, but that any restructuring or rationalisation of the system is precluded by entrenched interests and a political system and culture that support these interests. Suppose, for example, that a decision were made by Kerala's educationists to abolish the largely useless and wasteful postgraduate courses offered in the hundreds of colleges in favour of, superior programme in the university departments which have better resources. It can be safely predicted that such a decision will be effectively thwarted. The unions that represent the thousands of teachers and non-academic staff and function under the auspices of several political parties can be expected to resist any change to the *status quo*, and in this they are likely to be successful. The most destructive of these activities may be carried out by the non-academic staff who have a total lack of commitment to the main business of the universities, yet exercise power through unions as well as through the other highly politicized bodies such as Senate and Syndicate. On the other hand, those concerned with higher education—politicians, bureaucrats and academics, are unlikely even to contemplate any radical measures given Kerala's political culture and their entrenched vested interests in the system. The very terms of the discourse would have. Kerala-specific characteristics—issues such as employment security gaining prominence vis-a-vis academic issues. In the end, when spending cuts are forced upon the government by the fiscal crisis without ever having made a rational ordering of priorities, to the great detriment of Kerala's future development and wasting vast investments already made.

Though only a State in India, Kerala reveals a syndrome of a bureaucratic, "socialist," welfare State system that is proving to be unsustainable at least within the new world order of the late 20th century. At least one writer (Nossiter, 1982 : 289) has unflatteringly referred to Kerala as "a degenerate form of feudalism in which managerial barons, their retainers, and marauding contractors pillaged the public treasury." Nossiter greatly overstates his case, but draws attention to the still "feudal" character of the State and its predominant role as a distributor of the dwindling State resources to various mobilised and organised constituencies as well as to the political and bureaucratic-managerial elite. This characterisation, however, ignores what is perhaps Kerala's greatest achievement—a remarkably successful welfare State and a social democracy that has allowed the Left and the Right to compete and come to power with very little violence by any standards in the world. In an interesting recent examination of the relationship between States and industrial transformation, Peter Evans (1995) characterises State-society relations in Kerala as almost the mirror image of the East Asian "developmental state". In both cases, a well-developed and relatively effective state apparatus stands in a relationship of "embedded autonomy", a combination of close relationship an insulation, with particular constituencies. Kerala is a "redistributive State" where the connection is with mobilised groups, while in the East Asian "growth states" the connection is mainly with industrial capital. Given this motif, Kerala's ". . . idiosyncratic version of 'embedded autonomy' (was) extremely well suited to accomplishing a transformative project aimed at increased levels of welfare" (p. 237). Evans' conclusion is that ". . . the Kerala case reinforces the idea that reconstruction must involve a more encompassing definition of embeddedness."

The discussion about State, society and politics above leads us to two general conclusions. First, it shows that State intervention in such institutions of civil society as education and industry has now the effect of severely constraining their autonomy and rationality, and these need to be restored if progress is to be made. Second, the Kerala State makes little contribution to economic growth so that it can be characterised as a "no-growth" if not an "anti-growth" State. Not only does it contribute little to the task of capital accumulation, it does even less by way of "inducing" growth as most modern "developmental States" do. At least this is so from the conventional perspective of economic growth. Popular movements and democratic initiatives for total literacy or local self government, laudable and necessary as they are, cannot compensate for economic growth, at least within the framework of the world system in which Kerala is embedded. This failure is all the more damaging since the Central Government too has not been particularly helpful to Kerala in this respect.

A Cultural Crisis?

The set of values, norms and goals (the collective habits of minds and heart) that have come to prevail in Kerala and that has a bearing on Kerala's development experience may be called the culture of the Kerala Model of development. What needs to be asked now is whether and to what extent the economic stagnation, social dysfunction and political atrophy that afflict Kerala are indicative of a crisis at the cultural level. I shall argue that there indeed is such a crisis which has resulted in the society's failure to effectively articulate and pursue collective goals in a sufficiently disciplined manner, to promote adequately a social ethic that informs public life, and to generate and maintain an adequate degree of enterprise and creativity in its individual members. There are probably other aspects of this cultural crisis as reflected in such phenomena as rising suicide rates, new religious movements and cults, mental illness, crime, and alcoholism, but these are outside the scope of this chapter. The failure referred to here must also be seen as an end result of a recent process of development since the earlier social reform movements and the socialist-communist movements that followed were infused with high ethical values and commitments to collective goals just as Malayalees had also shown a relatively high degree of entrepreneurship in that earlier period, perhaps up to the 1950s. The cultural crisis seems to have become aggravated in the aftermath of the ideological vacuum created by the decline of the left parties following the rapid collapse of socialist and communist states and ideologies internationally.

One dimension of the culture that is worth examining is what may be called the economic ethic of society, by which I mean culturally defined and culturally induced orientation of people towards everyday economic activities. Two aspects of this which are important here are the work ethic and entrepreneurship. There is hardly anyone today who discusses Kerala's economic failure without referring to the erosion of the work ethic. While this concept has many complex meanings, it can be broadly defined as referring to a systematic and disciplined approach to one's work as a duty and a responsibility and even as an ethical idea. Every society, feudal, capitalist, socialist or any other kind, must ensure that members of society develop a certain degree of commitment to work, and carry out their duties with a sense of responsibility and accountability. In modern industrial societies where economic activities are carried out in organised enterprises in a highly coordinated and rationalised manner in order to meet standards of efficiency and productivity, these values take on greater importance. Our discussion above has shown that in Kerala the erosion of the work ethic, and the lack of accountability is particularly acute in all matters that are considered government or "sarkari" business. Both the administrators and the recipients of State-sponsored welfare measures share such attitudes. Those who distribute "sarkari" patronage and benefits such as agricultural loans share a part for themselves as bribes and easily write off the other share. This provides a perspective in understanding another one of

Kerala's paradoxes—relatively easy availability of agricultural loans, low rates of recovery and low productivity in agriculture at the same time. A second aspect of the economic ethic is another much discussed puzzle about Kerala, the very low levels of entrepreneurship despite the high degree of human resource development and despite the early rise here of a commercially minded middle class, Jeffrey (1982) has noted that only Punjab was comparable to Kerala in this latter respect. It is an irony that Kerala which had the highest number of banks per capita in their towns and villages by the 1930s must today have their remittances pooled and utilized by financial institutions based outside the State. In place of individual or collective initiative, they prefer the security of government jobs or other similar occupations, and preferably "Gulf jobs".

The question that arises at this point is whether the Left in Kerala has played a role in creating and promoting these cultural patterns that have had a detrimental effect on economic development. I would suggest that it has, although I cannot elaborate this point here. A whole generation of Keralites, particularly those who were socialised within the mass movements, internalized values and goals that have been, to say the least, unhelpful to economic growth. For example, it was taken as a self-evident "socialist" axiom that socialist production was not only ethically superior, but economically more rational and efficient. This was because it released the suppressed energies of the people, that state ownership was an effective means for rationalising the economy and accelerating growth, that land reforms would lead to significant increases in agricultural production, that maintaining employment was not merely more humane, but also economically more rational than introducing technological innovations that reduced employment. My own field notes collected in the 1970s abound in such expressions by the rank and file in the left movements. Faced with overwhelming empirical evidence that belies these beliefs, people do not necessarily turn to alternative theories or belief systems. One result of this discrepancy between cultural expectations and empirical realities has been widespread cynicism about politics and a loss of faith in politicians. This, in turn, has contributed to the erosion of collective ideals and goals, and to the fragmentation of politics. In the Paddy field or industry, trade unions working under different political parties can paralyse not only the functioning of the organization but also work at cross purposes undermining the collective interests of the workers themselves. When I observed this tendency among the highly successful agricultural labour unions in Kuttanad in the 1970s union mobilization had reached its plateau and just begun to stagnate.

Conclusions

The paradox of Kerala is that it has achieved exceptionally high levels of social development while slipping behind the rest of India in economic development. Such social development has involved a commitment of fiscal support by the State Government which cannot be maintained without an adequate productive base or other revenue resources for the State. This means that the State is not only unable to invest in further social development, but it is also unable even to maintain the gains already achieved. Paradoxically, Kerala has also been experiencing an unprecedented consumption boom and increasing standards of living thanks to the foreign remittances. The remittances contribute to inflation, but do not help to ease the fiscal problems because the State Government has no control over these. This, in economic terms, is Kerala's dilemma.

The question then is no longer how an economically backward society achieved such high social development, but how a society with such levels of social and human resource development and at least some favourable economic factors could not attain even the minimum degree of economic development that would have enabled it to sustain its social achievements. Whatever be Kerala's limitations, it does have such advantages as high saving rates comparative advantages in areas such as plantation agriculture and a rapidly falling population.

The political Right blames the Left for the debacle, in particular, its land reform, militant unionism and over-politicisation. While this is an over-simplification, the argument is not without merit. Although there is no evidence that land reforms affected agricultural productivity negatively, it is clear that they did not lead to the anticipated increase in productivity. Again while unions *per se* may not have hindered Kerala's economic development there is strong evidence that the many restrictive practices, disruptive politics of competing unions, some unions' ability to prevent modernisation and technological innovation have had a detrimental effect on the State's industrialisation and economic development. More important is the impact of a tradition and culture that placed a patronising State as the central institution in initiating and managing increasingly larger spheres of economic and social activities while at the same time discouraging private enterprise and devaluing institutions of civil society. The initiative and enterprise of the community associations that had earlier played such a crucial role in the development of Kerala society became undermined as they got inextricably entangled in the scramble for state patronage. The fragmentation of politics and the erosion of collective purposes and commitment now characterising Kerala society is, in no small part, a consequence of this.

The Left generally tends to attribute Kerala's failures to external factors, in particular, to Kerala's historical development of under-development and constraints imposed by the imperialist, world capitalist system and its institutions, and to discriminatory treatment by the central government, especially in investing in the State. To be sure, these are not untrue, but are no longer useful in explaining Kerala's basic problems. Today we need to explain why the State with all its advantages has not been able to transcend its colonial condition and join a resurgent Asia.

REFERENCES

A.K.G. Centre for Research and Studies (1994), International Congress on Kerala Studies, Abstracts (ICKS-A), vols. 1-5. Thiruvananthapuram.

Alexander, William M. (1995), "Exceptional Kerala: Efficient Use of Resource and Life Quality in a Non-Affluent Society", GAIA-Ecological Perspective in Science, Humanities and Economics. Postfach, Basel (Schweiz).

Centre for Development Studies (1975), Poverty, Unemployment and Development Policy: A Case Study of Selected Issues with Reference to Kerala, New York, Department of Economic and Social Affairs, United Nations.

Dandekar, V.M. and N. Rath (1971), "Poverty in India", *Economic and Political Weekly*, vol. 6, no. 1, January 2.

Dreze, Jean and Amartya Sen (1989), *Hunger and Public Action*, Oxford: Clarendon Press.

Economic and Political Weekly (1990), "Kerala Economy at the Crossroads". Special Issue on Kerala, vol. 25, nos. 35-36.

Evans, Peter, (1995), *Embedded Autonomy: States and Industrial Transformation*. Princeton University Press.

Francis, Shaji K. (1993), "Institutions and Dynamics of Rural Labour Markets: Labour Shortage in a Labour Surplus Agrarian Economy of Kerala," *The Indian Journal of Labour Economics*, vol. 36, no. 4.

Franke, Richard W. (1993), *Life Is a Little Better: Redistribution as a Development Strategy in Nadur Village*, Kerala. Boulder, Westview Press.

—— and Barbara Chasin (1989), *Kerala: Development Through Radical as Development in an Indian State*, San Francisco, The Institute for Food and Development Policy.

——(1994), Kerala: *Development Through Radical Reform* (Updated version of the above), Promila and Co. in collaboration with Institute for Food and Development Policy, San Francisco.

George, K.K. (1993), *Limits to Kerala Model of Development: An Analysis of Fiscal Crisis and Its Implications*, Thiruvananthapuram: Centre for Development Studies, Monograph Series.

—— (1994), "Wither Kerala Model", paper presented at the International Congress on Kerala Studies, AKG Centre, Thiruvananthapuram.

——(1996), "Economic Liberalization : What It Foretells Different States" paper presented at the Conference on Regional Disparities in India, Guwahati.

Isaac, Thomas and Michael Tharakan (1989), "Kerala : Towards a New Agenda", *Economic and Political Weekly*, vol. 30, nos. 31-32.

Jeffrey, Robin (1992), *Politics, Women and Well Being*. Delhi, Oxford University Press.

Kannan, K.P. (1990), "Kerala Economy at the Cross Roads?" *Economic and Political Weekly*, vol. 30, nos. 35-36, September 1-8.

——(1995), "Public Intervention and Poverty Alleviation: A Study of the Declining Incidence of Rural Poverty in Kerala, India," *Development and Change*, vol. 26, no. 4, pp. 701-727.

Kannan, K.P. and K. Pushpangadan (1990), Dissecting Agricultural Stagnation in Kerala: An Analysis Across Crops, Seasons and Regions," *Economic and Political Weekly*, op. cit.

Krishnan, R. (1994), "Kerala: A Fall From Grace", *India Today*, November 15.

Krishnan, T.N. (1994), "Foreign Remittances, Consumption and Income", *ICKS-A*, vol. 2, pp. 58-59.

Kurien, C.T. (1994), "Kerala's Development Experience : Random Comments About the Past and Some Consideration for the Future." *ICKS-A*, vol. 1, pp. 20-34.

Mathew, George (1989), *Communal Road to Secular Kerala*, New Delhi, Concept Publishing House.

Ram Mohan, K.T. (1991), "Understanding Keralam : the Tragedy of Radical Scholarship." *Monthly Review*, vol. 43, no. 7, pp. 18-31.

Monthly Review (1991), vol. 42, no 8, Review of the Month on Kerala.

Nair, P.R. Gopinathan (1981), *Primary Education, Population Growth and Socio-Economic Change*, New Delhi, Allied Publications.

——(1983), "Educational Reforms in India : Universalization of primary Education in Kerala, Trivanadrum, Centre for Development Studies. Working Paper No. 156.

Namboodiripad, E.M.S. (1994), "Presidential Address," *ICKS-A* vol, 1, pp. 1-5.

Nossiter, T.J. (1988), *Communism in Kerala*. Delhi, Oxford University Press.

Oommen, M.A. (1993) *Essays on Kerala Economy*, New Delhi, Oxford and IBH.

Pillai, Mohanan, P. (1990), "Some Aspects of Performance of State Sector Enterprises in Kerala", Working Paper No. 234, Centre for Development Studies, Thiruvanthapuram.

Sen, Amartya (1994), "D.T. Lakadawala Memorial Lecture" Institute of Social Science, New Delhi.

Sen, Gita (1992), "Social Needs and Public Accountability : The Case of Kerala", Development Policy and Public Action, *OUR*.

Subrahmanian, K.K. (1990), "Development Paradox in Kerala", *Economic and Political Weekly*, September 15.

Tharamangalam, Joseph (1981), Agrarian Class Conflict : the Political Mobilization of Agricultural Labourers in Kuttanad, South India. Vancouver, UBC Press.

——(1984), "The Penetration of Capitalism and Agrarian Change in Southwest India, 1901-1941 : A Preliminary Analysis", Bulletin of Concerned Asian Scholars, vol. 16, no. 1, pp. 17-21.

——(1985a), "From Class Struggle to the Politics of Accommodation: Social Change and Politics in Kerala ", paper presented at the 2nd World Congress on Malayalam Language, Kerala Culture and Development, Washington DC, August 24.

——(1995b), "The Quiet Revolution in Kerala : An Anthropologist's Look at a Kerala Village", Annual meeting of the AAA, Washington DC, December 5.

——(1991), "People, Society and Culture: the Making of Modern Kerala", chapter prepared for the Kerala State Gazeteer, vol 2, nos. 30, 31-32, pp. 1993-2004

Zachariah, K.C. *et. al* (1994), Demographic Transition in Kerala in the 1980s. Tiruvanthapuram, Centre for Development Studies.

Zachariah, Mathew and R. Sooryamurthy (1994), Science for Social Ravolution? Acheivements and Dilemmas of a Development Movement—the Kerala Shastra Sahitya Parishat, New Delhi, Vistar Publication.

THIRTEEN

THE SOCIAL PATH TO KERALA'S HEALTH

N.H. ANTIA

The uniqueness of the achievements of Kerala in the field of health stands out not only from the rest of India but also in the world. Kerala has demonstrated what can be achieved by a high level of social development supported by modest medical service. It has achieved at a cost of less than $15 per capita a health status as measured by Infant Mortality Rate, Life Expectancy, Birth and Death Rates which is almost comparable with that of the wealthiest country of the world expending about $4000 per capita. Even allowing for the difference in purchasing capacity of the rupee as compared to the US dollar, Kerala provides a vivid demonstration of the real cost of health and its care, which all countries whether rich and poor can seek to emulate.

And yet, this provides no cause for complacency to Kerala since it is itself in a state of economic and social transition due to both internal as well as external influences. This needs to be considered in the future planning for its health which will be influenced as much or more by non-medical than medical forces. A major difference in the health status of Kerala and of the countries of the West is the morbidity rate which according to Soman and Panicker (1984) seems to be more than even the rest of India. This may be due to the increased health awareness in a State with high education and consequent awareness. The high morbidity rate in all 'need based' countries is the result of the poor economic status resulting from poor housing, inadequate water supply, sanitation and environment as compared to that of the affluent countries. About 20 per cent of Kerala's population still lives below the poverty line and consequent inadequate nutrition which can also play a role in the high morbidity rate. The low mortality despite high morbidity indicates the ready access and utilisation of medical services which up to now is available at relatively affordable cost in both the public and even in the private sector.

It is well known that the morbidity of a population is greatest in the below five age group as a result of immaturity of the immune system to communicable diseases like gastroenteritis and acute respiratory tract infections which are not amenable to immunisation. These are nevertheless amenable to treatment at remarkably low cost if detected and treated at home or on outpatient basis in the early stages.

The morbidity of the older age group which is more common in affluent countries, and now increasingly seen in Kerala, is mainly the result of degenerative diseases like cancer, heart-stroke and arthritis which are increasingly treated with high cost medical interventions in tertiary care hospitals. In a market economy this has resulted in exponential increase in the cost of health care with only marginal increase in life span and that too of a relatively poor quality.

With the increase in life span, Kerala will be increasingly subjected to morbidity of both the younger as well as that of the older age groups. This will consist of communicable diseases due to increasing poverty resulting from increasing polarisation of its society and inadequate resource allocation to improve water, sanitation and nutrition. Together with the problems of aging this will further divert the people's meagre resources to the rapidly increasing for-profit private health sector which often promotes unnecessary expensive over-medicalisation and over-hospitalisation of the diseases at both ends of the demographic spectrum as is sbeing observed in the cities and small towns in other States of our country. This is especially when the public health system fails to meet the demands.

Together with the problems at both ends of the life span, there will also be an increase in the problems of the middle age group such as trauma due to increasing traffic on narrow roads, industrial injuries, diseases such as asthma, dermatitis and poisoning due to pollution of air, water and food from excessive use of fertilizers and pesticides as well as mental illness resulting in increase of suicide and violence as a result of increase in the number of educated unemployed.

It will neither be feasible nor desirable to merely increase the expenditure on health on the existing medical lines for treatment of these problems. An entirely new approach is essential. The answer lies increasingly in the field of social medicine which by and large has been ignored to the present but could play the dominant role in the newly emerging scenario.

Contrary to the affluent countries, the predominant problems of health of our society are the result of poverty and the diseases associated with it. Western medical science and technology together with our traditional systems of medicine like ayurveda, including locally grown herbal medicines, and homeopathy provide an efficient, safe, cheap and readily available care for the majority of these diseases if they are not medicalised. Contrary to common belief this is not second rate health care for the poor left to their own resources, but is based on sound available medical knowledge and technology. This approach is not only rational and highly cost-effective but also more humane than the existing over professionalised services. It is also socially and culturally acceptable to both the individual as well as the community.

The ICSSR/ICMR report, *Health for All : an alternative strategy*, (while reiterating the Bhore Committee's report which was the basis of the national health strategy for independent India) has clearly stated that, with experience, about 80 per cent of all promotive, preventive as well as curative health care can be best undertaken at the village level (the Ward in Kerala) by specifically trained local women if they are provided a graded supportive service at the sub-centre, PHC and the Community Health Care Hospital at the 100,000 population level where medical, obstetric and surgical services can be provided and tailored to local requirements. This would take care of over 95 per cent of all medical and surgical problems in this population at a cost of approximately Rs. 150 per capita per annum.

Based on sound epidemiologic, technical knowledge and practices, evident in the past decade, in various parts of the country has confirmed the feasibility as well as the high cost-efficiency of such a decentralised people-based health care of which the Tata Tea Estate in Munnar in Kerala is a vivid example. There is no reason why such a model for achieving Health for All should not be made available for all when at 6 per cent of our GDP, the overall spending on health in India is over Rs. 650 per capita per annum, three quarters of which is unfortunately in the for-profit private sector. What is being promoted by the World Bank is a diametrically opposite model based on a profilerating for-profit curative-oriented privatized health care which is being promoted together with a resource starved centralised and bureaucratised public sector to provide minimal health care to the poor masses.

Fortunately, Panchayati Raj now provides the possibility for the people to demand the resources to operate a health service in which they will play the dominant role and of which they will be the chief beneficiaries. All infrastructure, manpower production, training, distribution, production of drugs and equipment must conform to achieve this, and not in reverse as is at present. Only thus can a cost-effective, humane and accountable health service be provided which is funded and operated by the Panchayat with technical assistance of the health professionals. The available public health resources can be augmented by those who can obtain better services of their own rather than spending on private curative service. This system involves the entire community and especially the women in their own health, not only in curative care but even more so in health education as well as the prevention and control of the diseases which originate in their own environment. They have the greatest interest in improving the conditions which affect them and their children. This would also be an impetus to the overall improvement of their community of which they are a part.

Let us take the example of the commonest cause of morbidity that affects our people namely water-borne diseases such as diarrhoea, dysentery, worms, cholera, infective hepatitis and typhoid. Ensuring adequate and safe water supply varies from village to village and is primarily the role of the local community such as the cleaning of wells, repairing the hand-pumps, drainage of stagnant water and sanitation. In this the professionals can only provide technical advice. Their attempt to take over people's functions has failed even after 50 years and has only created a sense of dependency while water-borne diseases continue to take their unremitting toll of disease and death. The answer lies squarely in the hands of the local community. This would not only drastically reduce the need for medical attention but the people themselves are also the best functionaries for prompt treatment of conditions like dehydration by ORT. This would reduce the need and cost of professionalised medical care which can be restricted to the care of a few difficult problems. The problem of water-borne diseases is hence amenable in a most effective and low-cost manner to people's own social action if the necessary awareness and encouragement together with the necessary graded supportive professionalized care is provided rather than creating dependency through primary professionalised intervention. This applies for most communicable diseases such as malaria, acute respiratory infections and even tuberculosis and leprosy.

Even for the disease of the older age group the majority of the conditions, especially under the existing socio-economic and cultural conditions, a simpler more cost-effective and humane approach consists in prevention by the adoption of a better personal life style, and community action such as reducing air and water pollution. Symptomatic treatment for alleviating discomfort and pain using all available systems of medicine and even religious solace together with the family for loving support is not only cheaper but far more humane than aggressive hospital-based medical and surgical intervention at far greater cost. Acceptance of ageing and death is a part of our holistic culture which should not be eroded by imported Western concepts. The evaluation of the cost-effectiveness and humaneness of various technologies is essential before their utilisation.

Even the problems of the middle aged such as accidents, mental illness and diseases of pollution need reflection for return to a more civilized and humane form of development than what is being thrust on us under the guise of imitative 'modernity', for the hall-mark of civilization is how society looks after its aged, disabled, weak and underprivileged.

Kerala's health care is presently at the cross-roads. The present mode of development if unchecked will lead to a variety of problems of both the young and the aged, of the rich, middle class as well as of the poor. The uncontrolled expansion of Western medicine and even of Ayurveda in a market economy will make unsustainable demands for resources in a field where consumer resistance is at its lowest.

And yet health can be achieved at relatively low cost if we return to a people-based and people-operated decentralised form of care using all available cost-effective and humane methods as recommended by the Bhore Committee which was reiterated by the ICSSR / ICMR report and even by the National Health Policy of 1983 which quotes as follows: "The existing situation has been largely engendered by the almost wholesale adoption of health manpower development policies and the establishment of curative centres based on the Western models, which are inappropriate and irrelevant to the real needs of our people and the socio-economic conditions obtaining in the country. The hospital-based disease, and cure-oriented approach towards the establishment of medical services has provided benefits to the upper crusts of society, specially those residing in the urban areas. The proliferation of this approach has been at the cost of providing comprehensive primary health-care services to the entire population, whether residing in the urban or the rural areas. Furthermore, the continued high emphasis on the curative approach has led to the neglect of the preventive, promotive, public health and rehabilitative aspects of health care. The existing approach, instead of improving awareness and building up self-reliance, has tended to enhance dependency and weaken the community's capacity to cope with its problems. The prevailing policies in regard to the education and training of medical and health personnel, at various levels, have resulted in the development of a cultural gap between the people and the personnel providing care. The various health programmes have, by and large, failed to involve individuals and families in establishing a self-reliant community. Also, over the years, the planning process has become largely oblivious of the fact that the ultimate goal of achieving a satisfactory health status for all our people cannot be secured without involving the community in the identification of their health needs and priorities as well as in the implementation and management of the various health and related programmes."

Panchayati Raj provides the necessary milieu for the operation of this highly cost-effective and humane approach where the people and not the professionals will be the chief beneficiaries—a social approach to health. Kerala is eminently qualified to lead the way towards a social path to health care.

REFERENCE

Panikar. P. G. K. and C.R. Soman (1984) *Health Status of Kerala,* Centre for Development Studies, Thinivananthapuran.

FOURTEEN

KERALA MODEL

Prospects and problems

M.P. PARAMESWARAN

Kerala a tiny State on the southwest corner of India has made world news a number of times. It was in this State that a communist ministry was voted to power through democratic election for the first time in the world. It was this State which successfully mounted a mass campaign for eradication of illiteracy under a non-revolutionary situation.

Kerala Model has again become a subject of discussion in the world development debate. To many it is, still, a topic for seminars and discussions, but it is something more—perhaps a possible way out of the present global madness. Humanity is in the grip of a violent wave of consumerism. Capitalism has defeated the socialist experiments of this century. But it does not know that it is defeating itself and destroying the entire humanity. It cannot sustain itself wave continuously expanding production and exchange of goods and services, without exponentially increasing consumption of limited natural resources. It is in the path of a divergent chain reaction and is bound to explode sooner or later.

In the struggle for the limited resources on this earth, humanity is increasingly getting divided into a minority of rich, very rich and a majority of poor. The gap between the poor and the rich has been increasing continuously, both internally within every country and internationally between countries. It is a mad race for resources and markets. It was the root cause for the two World Wars, for the mass killing of the Jews, the Vietnam war, the Korean war, the Ethiopian famine, the Chechenian and Yugoslavian massacres, the

Khalistan and Kashmir terrorism, the ethnic killings in Rwanda, the decimation of Africa, the Intellectual Property Rights, the World Trade Organisation and scores of similar atrocities on humankind. And all these for what purpose? Progress? Development? And for whom?

Human Development

What is progress? What is development? It has been, for long, accepted that per capita income of a country is not an index of the welfare of its people. Welfare depends not only on wealth but also on equity, justice and wisdom—wisdom of using resources and wealth. Any living organisation has two basic attributes: resistance to death and tendency to procreate. The vigour or health of a species can be measured by it longevity and population. However, human beings have cultural-ethical existence over and above the physical-material existence. Some of these elements are captured by the Human Development Index (HDI) developed in UNDP reports on human development. However, it is short of many aspects of human life, especially the cultural-ethical aspects, which are often considered to be unquantifiable. Yet, if one has to plan and implement actions designed to improve the quality of life, every quality where improvement is aimed at should be quantifiable.

I have attempted elsewhere (Parameswaran (1994)) to define a total quality of life composed of a Physical Quality of Life (PQL) and a Spiritual Quality of Life (SQL) whose essential elements are:

Physical Quality of Life

(a) High effective life expectation (biological life expectation less life time integrated morbidity period).

(b) Freedom from excessive hard manual labour—a reasonable ratio between manual and intellectual labour—say 30 : 70 or 50 : 50.

(c) Sustainability: Use of lesser and lesser natural resources to obtain the same life expectation and same freedom from hard labour.

Spiritual Quality of Life

(a) Social quality: Continuous decrease in—tending to zero—universally accepted social vices like murder, crime, suicide, rape and other atrocities against women, child labour, consumption of alcohol and narcotics, expenditure on police, army and weapons, and the like.
(b) Cultural quality: A high level of literacy and education, high reading rate, high participation in cultural and sports activities, etc.
(c) Economic quality: A high degree of participation of the average citizen in the economic and political life of the society—leading to a continuous reduction in economic and political disparities—an inversion of the power pyramid.

All these are, theoretically, quantifiable and comparable.

Kerala Model

Compared to the developed countries Kerala is a poor State, even poorer than the average of Indian states. But in most of the human development parameters Kerala ranks with developed countries. The same is the case with Sri Lanka, China and Costa Rica. All these peoples have shown that it is possible to achieve a high level of human development with much less per capita income. Table 14.1 compares the achievements of these four countries with those of a few developed countries and some "oil rich" countries. Equally important, as the national averages, are the disaggregated achievements. As far as rural-urban differences and male-female differences are concerned, the status of Kerala is even higher than that of many developed countries.

The essence of the Kerala model lies in proving the principle that more than the quantity of income of a country, its distribution and wise utilisation contribute to the quality of life.

That a people can attain a fairly high degree of Physical Quality of Life without expending too much of natural resources is an important factor. If it was necessary to consume as much natural resources—coal, oil, iron, copper, etc. as an average citizen of USA or Japan is consuming presently to attain an equivalent life

Table 14.1 Per Capita Income and Human Development Indicators

Country	*Per Capita Income $*	*Life Expectation (Years)*	*Literacy %*	*Under Five Mortality*
USA	23,760	76.0	99.0	9
Switzerland	22,580	78.0	99.0	6
Japan	20,520	79.5	99.0	5
Qatar	22,380	70.5	78.5	20
UAE	21,830	73.8	73.8	20
Oman	11,710	69.6	35.0	20
Costa Rica	1,960	76.00	93.00	14
Sri Lanka	540	71.9	89.3	18
China	470	68.5	79.3	31
KERALA	300	72.00	93.00	15

expectation etc., it would not be possible for two-thirds of the humanity to "progress". Simply there are not enough resources on this earth and whatever there exist have been appropriated by the rich nations. The Kerala experience gives hope to the poor countries and the poor people. Despite their present poverty they can aspire for a higher physical quality of life. As far as spiritual quality of life is concerned it is interesting to note that beyond a certain minimum level the income-quality correlation is negative ! This is not to say that a country can attain and maintain a high level of human development with very poor economic development. In fact Kerala is at a critical juncture. It is too poor to assure steady maintenance and gradual improvement of its achievements. Its economic foundation is very weak. Its cultural foundation too is tottering.

Threats to the Kerala Model

The achievements of Kerala are under threat from several quarters:

1. An almost stagnant economy
2. Widening gap between the aspirations of the people and actual achievements
3. Increasing economic polarisation

4. Unbearable fiscal strain
5. Increasing threat of falling gulf remittance and return of "foreign" Malayalees.
6. Increasing bondage to the "global" economy
7. Increasing inflow of migrant labour, who cannot be provided with minimum facilities and who bring with them different cultures
8. Increasing anarchy in administration and in society
9. Growing cultural degradation
10. Growing apathy to manual work
11. Growing consumerism
12. General lack of realisation of the threat, both by the people and their leaders.

Kerala economy is almost stagnant—tertiary growth is not real growth. Agriculture is stagnant for the past 15-20 years. Gross area under paddy has come down from 8.9 lakh hectares to 5.0 lakh hectares in 20 years. Paddy production has fallen from 13 lakh tonnes to 9.5 lakh tonnes. Coconut plantation is affected widely with root wilt disease. So is the case with pepper, cardamom, etc. Only rubber has shown some improvement. But its market is being increasingly subjected to "global" threats. Cardamom and pepper too face the threat from import. Even tapioca production has gone down drastically. Per capita fish consumption has gone down. Food insecurity is more severe today than twenty years ago.

Industrial growth is stunted because of a variety of reasons:

(i) An almost hostile administration (multiple windows, multiple corruption)
(ii) Shortage of electricity and poor infrastructure like roads and communication
(iii) Fragile environment
(iv) High cost of land
(v) Spectre of labour indiscipline
(vi) Lack of local entrepreneurship

Reasons can be multiplied. The point is how to overcome them. Environmental limitations and human power opportunities are to be properly taken into account. Enough political will has to be shown to overcome (i) and (ii). A sense of optimism has to be cultivated amongst the people about industrialisation instead of the present cynicism.

The consumer-culture onslaught through a variety of media on the one hand and the influence of foreign remittance (nearly 30 per cent of State Domestic Product) on the other hand has made Kerala an international market for consumer goods. This together with the distorted values instilled by our education system has made the new generation totally averse to manual work. They want only "white collar jobs". Even radicals and leftists think that ultimate development goal is—to be like USA, Germany or Japan. In these societies the share of agriculture in GDP is about 2 to 4 per cent, of industry 25-35 per cent and of the tertiary sector 60-75 per cent. This is an unrealisable world model because it requires too much of energy. A healthy mix of manual and intellectual labour is required. This has to be understood. It is the disdain of Keralites towards manual labour on the one hand and the prevalent high wage rate on the other hand that has attracted labourers from other States, "Kerala" is their equivalent of "gulf". This has led to a large increase in migrant population living in virtual slums even in rural areas. The ills of urbanization are affecting the entire State.

Administrative bcttlenecks can be removed only with an enlightened political leadership and rationalised procedures.

During the past ten to fifteen years there is a marked increase in wastage of resources in Kerala. This is seen not only in durable consumption goods like scooters, cars, T.V. sets, domestic appliances, etc. but also in oversized dwellings. Bulk of the gulf remittance and a good part of the domestic savings go for house construction—about 1.5 lakh houses, costing about Rs. 2000 crores per year. Unoccupied and under-occupied houses abound in Kerala. Isolated buildings and fully detached houses surrounded by their own compound has made provision of services like electricity, water supply and approach roads costly. Poor Kerala has begun to compete with the rich nations in wastage of resources. This is a sure way to defeat the achievements of the "Kerala Model" and the model itself.

In achieving the desirable aspects or indices of Kerala Model, there was an element of conscious intervention on the part of government and society—in education, in health, in building infrastructure, in public distribution, in enacting land reforms, and so on. The ability of the government to respond to these requirements has been continuously eroded for the past two decades. The Government is in a constant fiscal crisis. It is not able to balance income and expenditure. Its expenditure has been increasing at a rapid rate partly due to the expansion of services and partly due to the increase in the unit cost of providing these services: electricity, education, health—everything. On the other hand the economy of the State has been expanding only at a very slow rate, not commensurate with the increased in pressures on it. The government responds to this situation by gradually withdrawing from these responsibilities, by allowing commercialisation of the social sector. Though still protesting weakly, out of old habits, the society too is increasingly accepting this commercialisation process as something inevitable. This lack of will to safeguard the achievements of Kerala, the lack of appreciation of the importance of collective action except for individual economic gain, and increasing reliance on the individual competition mode are other threats to the achievement of Kerala.

There are people who argue that the Kerala Model is just an illusion, a result of four or five decades of "dependent economy, a result of lopsided development (in social sector) neither sustainable nor desirable in itself". It has been, according to them, partly the cause for the economic underdevelopment of Kerala—because it ate up all the surpluses and left nothing for the productive investment. This criticism comes both from extreme Left and extreme Right. The solutions offered are different. The extreme Left insists that unless the capitalist system is smashed and replaced by a socialist system nothing can be achieved. But not knowing how to do it or not being able to do anything they slowly graduate into post-modernistic debaters or into Right wing activists or into spiritual charlatans. The criticism from the Right wing is that competition is the motive force of development and that the State should not intervene in the economic or social life of the society. They are open supporters of liberalisation and the new economic policies.

Among the conventional Left too, there are people who question the Kerala Model. The achievements in health, education, and the like are welcomed by them. But they consider them to be not very important. For them economic growth is primary, its importance is over arching. They believe that under a new political situation, under socialism, all countries can afford the present wastage level of the affluent nations. They do not even consider it as wastage but only as increased consumption. In their dream to provide "each according to their needs" they do not recognise the necessity to differentiate real needs from pseudo needs created by capitalism. For them greed is a subjective terminology characterised by the present inability to satisfy them. Today's greeds actually become tomorrow's needs.

Redeeming Features

Yet, all is not lost. Kerala has begun to fight back. This fight was initiated and led by a movement called Kerala Sastra Sahitya Parishad—belonging to a genre now popularly known as People's Science Movement. Starting with pre-Stockholm and post Stockholm conferences on environment in 1972-73, going on to an astonishingly predictive analysis of Kerala's energy situation (Parameswaran (1975)) and resources of Kerala (Shyamasundaran Nair et al (1976)) it went ahead with a grand project : making democracy real-creative and participative. For this it helped the formation of Rural Science Fora, which were conceived as informal Village Planning Boards, argued for decentralization of economic and political power and strengthening of panchayats, strived to make people's representatives at these lowest levels capable of assuming and using such powers. In the process it had to become active and creative in almost all fields of human endeavour—irrigation, land and water management, local area planning, energy, transport and communication, education, health, and environment (KSSP (1988)).

It is interesting to note that while the Nation was preparing for the "great surrender" during the end of eighties and the beginning of the nineties, Kerala initiated the "great fight back". It started with the Total Literacy Campaign in Eranakulam district which attracted more than 23,000 volunteers in one district alone and later spread to the whole of Kerala and the entire country—involving till now nearly 6-7 million volunteers and 60-70 million learners. This shows that there is still optimism. There are lessons to be learnt and causes to be fought for.

Many ideas initially propounded by the Kerala Sastra Sahitya Parishad but rejected either as utopian or as reformist by political parties and other mass movements—are currently becoming more and more acceptable to the mainstream political and economic thought. The result is the on-going People's Planning Campaign, inaugurated on the 17th August 1996. Formally initiated by the State Planning Board and supported by the State government it started off as an experiment in the formulation of the State's Ninth Five Year Plan from bottom upwards by the people. In the process the campaign has transformed itself into one for people's real empowerment, for participative and creative democracy. In the endeavour to enhance people's capabilities to take power in their own hands, the campaign had to develop and train tens of thousands of resource persons at State, district and local levels, involve about one-third of the entire households—nearly two million out of six million households in *Grama Sabhas.* Concepts like micro watershed management, increasing local self-sufficiency in primary and simply secondary goods, networking of small-scale units, etc. are becoming popular. Local initiatives in drinking water, sanitation, health care delivery, education, energy generation and distribution, are becoming discernible. The consciousness about weak economic base, the necessity of integrated approach, ills of consumerism etc. is spreading, albeit slowly. The experiment is still in the preliminary stage, built on a weak foundation. There is no widely shared grand vision or theory to support it. Results of an attempt by the present author to develop such a vision and to formulate a programme of action to realise it are given below.

A vision for the future

Society

I would like to call the future society a "Participative and Creative Democracy". It means:

(i) Each able-bodied citizen undertakes some societal responsibility or other which is not dictated by any direct benefit for self or any immediate kith and kin.

(ii) Each citizen is given education adequate to run the affairs of the society—i.e. besides being word literate—to be literate in numbers, in technologies, in science, in development planning, and the like.

(iii) Democracy is not the obligation to give an "irrevocable power of attorney" to some individuals—a panch, an MLA or an MP—to lord over them for a period of five years.

(iv) It gives them an enforceable right to recall their representative, it gives them the right to know anything done in the name of the society.

(v) It understands that very large undertakings like our present steel plants, fertilizer plants, oil refineries, and for that matter the by transnational corporations are inherently violent—as Gandhiji used to repeat—against the poor majority of the people. Every production activity should be subservient to the people.

(vi) The present structure of the power pyramid has to be inverted. Citizens and their small groups—tola, mohalla, neighbourhood should be sovereign. Larger formations, the district, state and nation shall enjoy the powers conferred on them at the "pleasure of the citizens".

(vii) The overall economy should be so structured that individual citizen's life should become increasingly free from "Global" controls and events. Smaller and smaller regions/groups should become more and more "self-sufficient" not only "Self-reliant". Production of goods and services are to be, increasingly, for consumption than for exchange and profit.

(viii) This is not to deny global connections or reversal of human history. It implies a system of production which is much less hierarchical in nature than today.

(ix) In the long run (this may be considered as too utopian) there shall not be "national boundaries" which are to be protected by military. Humanity has to come out of the "National Security Straight-Jacketing". Wars should become unnecessary.

(x) This is not possible under a capitalistic societal organisation. Capitalism requires a continuous increase in production, exchange and consumption of goods and services. This world has got enough to satisfy everybody's needs but not their greeds as Gandhi used to say. But capitalism manufactures, above everything, else, greeds, or pseudo needs as Marx put it.

(xi) One can conceive of a future, a post-capitalist society based on "private-social" enterprises. They are private in the sense that they are not run by the State but by individuals and groups. They are social in the sense that profit maximisation is not the objective, instead maximisation of social good is the objective. Needless to say that such enterprises should be financially, technically and ecologically viable and sustainable. But this condition need not be contradictory to societal good.

(xii) Human progress in whatever way one may define it, does not require exponentially increasing consumption of material goods and services. The limited experience of Kerala and Sri Lanka has shown that it is possible to increase longevity, decrease IMR, death rate, achieve universal education, and the like even at very low levels of material production and natural resources utilization.

Technology

(i) Any technology which cannot be applied for small-scale production has the potential to become oppressive. So bulk of the material production world over should be based on technologies which are viable on small scale.

(ii) So, going beyond Schumacher one can say that "Small has to become powerful, not only beautiful". (Beautiful things are always appropriated by the powerful !)

(iii) We have to arrive to a commonly agreed hierarchy of "needs" both basic and optional. Depending upon one's role in the productive activity of the society, tools required will be different. Such tools will, or are, sometimes, likely to be construed as luxuries. This mistake should not be committed.

(iv) The present sectoral inversion in economy has to be rectified. Primary sector has to become PRIMARY, and secondary sector only SECONDARY. It is the malignant growth of secondary sector that has created the cancer of consumerism.

(v) Tertiary sector will have to be viewed in a different manner. Health care, education, arts, sports, etc. cannot be equated to economic production activity. Most of it is enjoyment or consumption than production.

(vi) A society cannot live on tertiary sector alone neither on secondary sector too. It has to produce, first and foremost, food required for all. The present technology of agricultural production is not sustainable. (Neither is the case with industry.)

(vii) Humanity cannot live on non-renewable fossil fuels indefinitely. A stable and peaceful global society can be realised only when we learn to live depending solely on solar energy. Technologies will have to be developed

— to tap solar energy more effectively, cheaply and abundantly,

— to extract desired metals and other materials from highly diluted sources making use of very little energy and much more of knowledge and ingenuity,

— to convert materials from one to another in form and content, again with very little energy expenditure.

One may term this as "a universal solar economy" —where sun is the only energy source and anything, soil under your feet or water in the ocean, becomes your raw material. It is a far cry from the present, but that is the direction into which we should consciously guide our R & D efforts.

Politics

What sort of a "politics" will be prevailing in those days of "solar economy" it is difficult to imagine now. But what sort of a "politics" we should have now so that society can be oriented to a more desirable direction one can think of :

(i) Capitalism cannot be sustained. This is quite understandable. As Eric Hobsbaum has bemoaned in his latest book on "*The Age of the Extremes*" even capitalists have lost control over capitalism. Anarchy reigns supreme in every department of human activity !

(ii) The first post-capitalist experiment of building socialism too has failed. Reasons may be many—lack of democracy, distorted understanding of development, specific historic circumstance of encirclement of USSR, pressures of cold war, lack of criticism and so on.

(iii) It is certain that a new form of post-capitalist society will have to be thought of. According to me it will have elements of Gandhian and Marxist thoughts in it. A system whose economic, political and philosophical ideas are fully compatible among themselves will have to be worked out fully with all its nuts and bolts.

(iv) Instead of a United Front of political parties what we require is a United Poeple's Front with a clearly spelt out programme which can attract bulk of the people who today are subscribing to various political parties, out of habit or out of lack of anything better.

(v) Our Constitution demands serious revision. It has got many elements which are radical, progressive and sympathetic to people at large. We have to safeguard all of these. It has got also a lot of deficiencies—some of them outright anti-people, quite a few anti-federalistic, and several serious omissions. It is suggested that a new Constituent Assembly (CA) may be formed to draw out such changes as required in the Constitution.

(vi) This CA can be elected through a rather protracted procedure of people's consultation. Each party/independents/non-party organisations should bring out its version of the Constitutional Amendments—in full details and allow six months to one year for people to debate on it before the actual election of the members to the CA. People will be voting the programme or draft constitutional amendments. Parties/independents/non-party organisations who put forward the programme will be given seats in accordance with the principle of proportional representation. There will not be any "constituency" as such. All citizens will vote. Each party/non-party organisation/individual will register in advance their list of candidates in the order of priority to be sent to the CA in proportion to the votes they obtain.

(vii) This may look a bit too far-fetched. But we have to understand that whatever may be the sincerity of our purpose and earnestness unless people actively participate, democracy will be only in name. Right and ability to "lead" does not automatically confer right to "rule". Societies would require leaders but not "rulers". They have to learn to "rule" themselves at all levels.

(viii) The "political formations" in India are disintegrating based on individual, caste and small group loyalties. As mentioned earlier a United Front of the People has to be built up, based on a PROGRAMME which is understood by them and owned by them.

Programme of Action

There are innumerable organisations, groups, disillusioned individuals who are deeply pained by the present happenings in India and elsewhere—with almost total criminalisation of politics and the helplessness of the major national parties in checking the growing empire of the underworld. According to me two major streams of activities are to be initiated.

(i) Preparing a programme to restore and strengthen participative and creative democracy in India. This would involve three components :

— *Economic*: from local neighbourhood to international division of labour.
— *Political*: from neighbourhood groups/grama sabhas and

gram panchayats to blocks, districts/states/centre and international relations.
- *Philosophical*: wisdom to differentiate greed from need, acceptance of limits to natural resources, necessity of ecological and environmental considerations, redefining human development and quality of life including both physical-biological and spiritual-ethical qualities.

This will require the formation of a large number of working groups, preparation of drafts, innumerable consultations, revision and re-revision of drafts, besides attempts to induct maximum number of existing political formations into this process and finally arriving at a "draft" ready to be placed before the people of India for informed and involved discussion.

(ii) Initiation of a process wherein people in large numbers start accepting responsibilities as citizens in a democratic society. Here, the current experiment going on in Kerala, with all its weaknesses and limitations, can offer a practical starting point. The All India People's Science Network (AIPSN) has decided to initiate such experiments in a few thousand gram panchayats all over India. But a few thousand in two lakhs is too small a number, but that is all the AIPSN is capable of doing today.

(iii) This experiment, to involve a large number of people in each village, in a process of exploring their own history, their current plight, their natural resources, the current controls on these resources, the best way of using these resources in a sustainable way for the benefit of the maximum, preparation of an area development plan for their own village/panchayats, attempts to get it incorporated in the actual Five-Year Plan using the rights conferred under Panchayati Raj and Nagarpalika Acts, suggest amendments required to these acts and in the various rules and regulations issued by each State government so that the spirit of decentralisation up to the level of individual citizen is not lost—all these can, perhaps, initiate the process of a more enduring "alliance building", and also emotional integration with unified "visions".

REFERENCES

An Introduction to a Critique on Eighth Five-Year Plan (1988), Kerala Sastra Sahitya Parishad, Thiruvananthapuram.

Parameswaran, M.P. *(1994), A New World —A New India—* Bharat Gyan Vigyan Samiti, New Delhi.

Parameswaran, M.P. (1975), *Electricity and Industrialisation of Kerala*, paper presented at the 10th Annual Conference of Kerala State Electricity Board Workers' Association.

Shyamasundaran Nair K.N. and M.P. Parameswaren (1976) (eds.), *Wealth of Kerala* (KSSP 1988), Kerala Sastra Sahitya Parishad, Thiruvananthapuram.

RETHINKING DEVELOPMENT
Kerala's Development Experience

About the Author

Professor M.A. Oommen, currently Senior Fellow, Institute of Social Sciences, New Delhi is an economist with a rich collection of professional papers and books to his credit. He has taught in the Universities of Kerala, Calicut and Botswana, besides being the Director of the Institute of Management in Government, Thiruvananthapuram.

RETHINKING DEVELOPMENT

Kerala's Development Experience

Volume 2

Editor

M. A. Oommen

INSTITUTE OF SOCIAL SCIENCES

CONCEPT PUBLISHING COMPANY

ISBN 81-7022-764-X (Vol. 1)
ISBN 81-7022-765-8 (Vol. 2)
ISBN 81-7022-766-6 (Set)

First Published 1999

Printed and Published by
Ashok Kumar Mittal
Concept Publishing Company
A/15-16, Commercial Block, Mohan Garden
New Delhi-110059 (India)

Phones: 5648039, 5649024
Fax: 091-(11)-5648053

DEDICATED TO

RASHTRAPATIJI SHRI K. R. NARAYANAN

PROUD SON OF KERALA

Editor's Note

The introductory chapter in Vol. I is a comprehensive essay on the theme: "Towards rethinking development in the context of Kerala's development and social experience". The twenty nine papers in the two volumes examine various dimensions of the evolution and shaping of what has come to be called 'Kerala Model', besides critiquing it with special reference to its sustainability and continued relevance. The papers in both the volumes are chosen to fit in with the basic theme.

The second volume starts with a thorough review of the socio-economic implications, especially the second generation problems in a futuristic perspective, of the momentous demographic transition Kerala has been experiencing for sometime now. This is followed by an empirical analysis of the question of labour shortage in the labour surplus Kerala economy. Sectoral development issues relating to environment, resource management, agricultural development, education, healths care, housing, energy planning, public distribution system and transport are examined in the following chapters. Women's agency, hailed as a vital component of Kerala's social transformation, is interrogated in the last but one chapter. The volume ends with an account of the Peoples' Planning Campaign widely held out even by the World Bank as a promising social experiment in the context of Kerala's quest for sustainability and new development paradigms.

CONTENTS

CONTRIBUTORS

C. GASPER is Associate Fellow, Centre for Development Studies Thiruvanathapuram.

C. P. GEEVAN is Senior Scientist, Gujarat Institute of Desert Ecology, Bhuj—Kach, Gujarat

K.N. HARILAL is Expert State Planning Board, Thiruvanathapuram.

T.M. THOMAS ISAAC Member, State Planning Board, Kerala, and Associate Fellow, Centre for Development Studies, Thiruvanathapuram.

AMMU JOSEPH is Freelance Journalist, Bangalore

V. RAMAN KUTTY is Associate Professor, Achuta Menon Centre for Health Science Studies, Thiruvanathapuram. He is a Doctor (M.D.) who specialises in Health Economics.

R. V. G. MENON is Director Integrated Rural Technology Centre, Palakkad. He was Professor of Mechanical Engineering, Government Engineering College, Thiruvanathapuram.

M. K. SUKUMARAN NAIR is Professor, Department of Applied Economics, Cochin University of Science and Technology.

K. N. SHYAMASUNDARAN NAIR is Vice-Chancellor, Kerala Agricultural University, Thrissur and Distinguished Fellow M. S. Swaminathan Research Foundation, Chennai.

K.R. NAYAR is Associate Professor, Centre of Social Medicine & Community Health, School of Social Sciences, Jawaharlal Nehru Univerisity, New Delhi.

K. NARAYANAN NAIR is Associate Fellow, Centre for Development Studies, Thiruvanathapuram.

M.N. PRASAD is Former Chairperson, Railway Board, Government of India.

S. IRUDAYA RAJAN is Associate Fellow, Centre for Development Studies, Thiruvanathapuram.

V. SANTHAKUMAR is Visiting Scholar, Centre for Development Studies, Thiruvanathapuram.

M.H. SURYANARYANA is Associate Professor, Indira Ghandhi Institute of Development Research, Mumbai.

T.K. SEBASTIAN is Lecturer in Economics, Nirmalagiri College, Kannur.

T.A. THOMAS is Lecturer, Department of Economics, Government College, Kottayam

JOSEPH A. THOMAS is Lecturer, Department of Economics, Government College, Kottayam.

N.V. VARGHESE is Senior Fellow and Head, SNS Unit, NIEPA, New Delhi.

K.C. ZACHARIAH is Honorary. Fellow, Centre for Development Studies, Thiruvanathapuram. He was Senior Demographer World Bank (1972-87).

FIFTEEN

LONG-TERM IMPLICATIONS OF LOW FERTILITY IN KERALA

S. IRUDAYA RAJAN & K. C. ZACHARIAH

In recent years, Kerala has made remarkable progress in its demographic transition. The State has achieved below replacement level of fertility two decades ahead of the all-India target year of 2011. The total fertility rate (TFR) declined from a high level of 5.6 in 1951-61 to about 1.7 in 1993, a level which is very much below the replacement level of 2.05. The State's infant mortality rate (IMR) has touched a low level of 13 in 1993, a level comparable to that of some of the developed countries of the world. The population growth rate has declined to about 1 per cent per annum in 1995 from a high level of 2.3 per cent per year during 1961-71.

A number of factors and policies have contributed to these remarkable achievements in Kerala's demographic transition. The high population density is one such factor. So is the peculiar settlement pattern of population in the State. But a very much larger role was played by the State's policies and programmes in bringing about the rapid transition in fertility and mortality rates. Policies in the areas of education, especially female education, health care, especially child health and universal immunization programme, family planning programme, land reforms, etc. (Nair, 1974; Krishnan, 1976; Zachariah, 1984; Nair 1986; Mari Bhat and Irudaya Rajan, 1990; Zachariah *et al.*, 1994).

Achievements on the demographic front, however, have not yet brought any real solution to the economic problems in the State. Unemployment, especially unemployment among the educated, is still a very serious problem in the State. Data on unemployment are not very reliable. According to the 1987-88 National Sample Survey, more than 10 per cent of the unemployed in India are in Kerala though Kerala accounts for only 3.4 per cent of the country's population. Educated unemployment in Kerala has assumed alarming proportions. Its rate increased from 29.3 to 35.0 per cent and the number of educated unemployed from 3.5 to 6.3 lakhs during 1983 to 1987-88.

It is, however, important to note that unemployment is not evenly distributed among all age groups. On the contrary, it is concentrated in the age group 15-29 (Mathew (1996)).

A very glaring manifestation of the unemployment problem in the State is the large number of migrants from the State. Firm figures are not available, but according to our own estimate, there were about 618,000 emigrants from Kerala in 1991 (Zachariah *et al.* (1994)). The rate of net migration from Kerala stood at – 0.16 in 1971,. 0.22 in 1981, and 0.31 in 1991 (Mari Bhat and Irudaya Rajan (1990)); (Zachariah and Irudaya Rajan (1997)).

Thus, the State's success in moderating fertility, mortality and population growth has not yet succeeded in solving the pressing economic problems of the State. It is perhaps a little too early to expect major changes. In the coming years the demographic changes will have their repercussions on the social and economic conditions in the State. If TFR remains below replacement level, the rate of population growth is bound to become negative and the population of the State will ultimately start declining. If fertility and mortality rates remain at the current levels, the age distribution of the State's population will undergo dramatic changes with far reaching consequences in the social and economic sectors. The objective of this chapter is to examine some of these implications: the social and economic consequences of a below replacement level of fertility rate, a declining mortality trend at very low levels and a moderate rate of emigration from the State.

An essential tool for such an analysis is a set of population projections using probable trends in fertility, mortality, and migration. This chapter includes three sets of projections. The assumptions on future fertility and mortality trends and future migration trends are based on data on recent trends in fertility, mortality and migration, our understandings on the determinants of demographic transition in the State, and international experience in fertility transition in many developed countries. As studies on these determinants are plenty in the literature, we are not attempting to review them here (Zachariah and Irudaya Rajan (1997)). However, as a back drop, we shall review the mortality and fertility transition in some detail.

Mortality Transition

Kerala's health conditions are the best among the various States in India, a conclusion well supported by a variety of data sources. Tables 15.1 and 15.2 give the mortality data for Kerala from the Census and the Sample Registration System (SRS). Kerala consistently had lower levels of mortality than that of India as a whole even for the period 1951-61. The crude death rate declined from 19.7 to 8.6 per thousand between 1951 and 1981. It declined further to about 6 in the first-half of the 1990s.

Table 15.1 Estimates of Mortality, Kerala 1951-81

Decade	*Crude Death Rate*	*Life Expectancy at birth*		*Life Expectancy at age five*	
		Male	*Female*	*Male*	*Female*
1951-61	19.7	44.3	45.3	50.9	49.6
1961-71	12.2	54.1	57.4	58.1	57.7
1971-81	8.6	60.6	62.6	59.6	61.5

Source: P.N. Mari Bhat, 1987; P. N. Mari Bhat and S. Irudaya Rajan, 1990.

Infant mortality rate is considered as an index which measures the quality of life in any given population. Of all changes in the demographic sphere that have occurred in Kerala, the decline in the infant mortality rates is the most remarkable. In reviewing the last 70 years, it is found that the infant mortality rate which stood at 242 per thousand live births (1911-20) has been reduced to 66 in 1961-70. Annual series on IMR provided by the SRS also reveals the similar decline throughout the last 20 years and the current IMR in Kerala is 13 per thousand live births. Both the neo-natal and post-natal mortality have declined but the decline is impressive among the post-natal mortality.

Table 15.2 Mortality Indicators, Kerala

Year	*Crude Death Rate*	*Neonatal Mortality*	*Post-Neonatal Mortality*	*Infant Mortality*
1971	9.0	21	37	58
1972	9.2	26	37	63
1973	8.5	27	31	58
1974	7.8	23	32	54
1975	8.4	20	34	54
1976	8.1	22	34	56
1977	7.3	19	28	47
1978	7.0	15	27	42
1979	6.9	13	30	43
1980	7.0	11	30	40
1981	6.6	12	26	37
1982	6.6	09	22	30
1983	6.7	10	23	33
1984	6.4	08	21	29
1985	6.5	09	22	31
1986	6.1	08	19	27
1987	6.1	09	19	28
1988	6.1	10	18	28
1989	6.4	14	07	21
1990	5.9	12	05	17
1993	5.9	10	03	13

Source: K.C Zachariah and S. Irudaya Rajan et al., (1997)

'Expectation of life at birth is an important indicator for assessing the overall health situation of any population. There has been a remarkable improvement in the expectation of life in Kerala among males and females. Interestingly, even at the turn of this century, expectation of life at birth was not very different for men and women. Between 1911 and 1960, the expectation of life had increased by 21 years for males and by 23 years for females. We also provide decennial estimates made by Bhat for the period 1951-81. These estimates show that the expectation of life at birth has been consistently higher among females in Kerala whereas it is not true for India as a whole. In the period 1951-61, the expectation of life at birth was 44.3 years for males and 45.3 years for females. Thus it would appear that people in Kerala have all along been enjoying a better and healthier life than people in other parts of the country (Irudaya Rajan, Mari Bhat and Tim Dyson (1997)). The expectation of life at birth for females is higher than males, as is the pattern in developed countries. In the period 1971-81, the expectation of life at birth was 60.6 years for males and 62.6 years for females. The percentage increase in the expectation of life at birth between 1951-61 and 1971-81 was 37 per cent for males and 39 per cent for females. Among all the States of India, longevity is highest for Kerala, both for men and women. As of 1991-96, the expectation of life at birth for males is 73 years and 79 years for females. Interestingly, the difference between the rates in the life expectancy between males and females was 1 year during 1951-61, 2 years in 1971-81 and almost 6 years in the recent periods.

Fertility Transition

Reliable data on fertility trends of Kerala are available only for the period since the introduction of the Sample Registration System (SRS). However, estimates made by several authors using the Census data are available for different periods. The Census based estimates shown here are taken from Bhat (1987). These estimates are presented in Table 15.3. The annual series of fertility indicators derived from the Sample Registration System are provided in Table 15.4. A few conclusions are drawn from these figures.

Table 15.3 Estimates of Fertility, Kerala, 1951-81

Decade	*Crude Birth Rate*	*Total Fertility Rate*
1951-61	43.9	5.6
1961-71	37.1	5.0
1971-81	28.1	3.4

Source: Same as Table 15.1

Table 15.4 Fertility Indicators for Kerala

Year	*TFR*	*GRR*	*CBR*
1971	4.1	2.0	31.1
1972	4.2	2.1	31.2
1973	3.9	1.9	29.2
1974	3.3	1.6	26.8
1975	3.4	1.6	28.0
1976	3.4	1.7	27.8
1977	3.1	1.5	25.8
1978	3.0	1.5	25.2
1979	3.1	1.5	25.8
1980	3.1	1.5	26.8
1981	2.8	1.4	25.6
1982	2.7	1.3	26.2
1983	2.6	1.2	24.9
1984	2.6	1.3	22.9
1985	2.4	1.2	23.3
1986	2.3	1.2	22.5
1987	2.3	1.1	21.7
1988	2.2	1.1	20.3
1989	2.1	1.0	19.8
1990	2.1	1.0	19.0
1991	2.0	1.0	18.0
1992	1.9	1.0	17.0
1993	1.7	1.0	16.6

Source: Same as Table 15.2

Firstly, over the last 40 years or so, the fertility has been on a continuous decline. Crude Birth Rate (CBR) declined from 43.9 during 1951-61 to 28.1 in 1971-81. Total Fertility Rate (TFR) has declined from 5.6 children to 3.4 during the same period. According to the SRS, the CBR declined from 31.1 in 1971 to 25.6 in 1981 (5.5 points) and to 16.6 in 1993 (9.0 points). The TFR has also registered the same decline throughout the period under study. For instance, the TFR was 4.1 children per woman in 1971, 3.1 children in 1980 and 2.1 children in 1990. Kerala has achieved the replacement level of fertility in the beginning of 1990s. At this stage many demographers in India and abroad thought that further decline is unlikely. Against their predictions, Kerala's TFR declined further to 1.7 by the year 1993.

Birth rates by districts are also available from the Sample Registration System and other sources (Tables 15.5 and 15.6). Mari Bhat has estimated fertility rates of all districts of Kerala using 1991 and Censuses (Bhat (1996)). According to these estimates, the TFR varied from 1.6 in Ernakulam to 3.4 in Malappuram during 1984-90. In the beginning of 1990, only five districts (Palakkad, Malappuram, Wayanad, Kannur and Kasaragod) in Kerala have registered TFR above the replacement level. The remaining districts had already achieved below replacement level of fertility. One major conclusion from the district-wise analysis is that all the districts have contributed towards the State-wise fertility decline. A CDS study has shown that the decline in TFR in Malappuram District was as sharp as in Ernakulam and Palakkad Districts (36%) between 1975-80 and 1986-91 (Zachariah *et al.*(1994)).

Table 15.5 Crude Birth Rate by Districts

	83-88	*1983*	*1988*	*74-80*	*84-90*
Trivandrum	21.5	20.8	20.5	22.8	19.6
Kollam	19.8	20.2	16.1	23.3	18.5
Alappuzha	17.7	18.1	14.8	21.0	16.7
Pathanamthitta	18.7*	n.a	17.3	n.a	17.2
Kottayam	18.5	18.1	16.8	20.1	16.6
Idukki	22.2	24.5	17.9	26.7	19.8
Ernakulam	17.9	21.0	15.8	21.4	16.9
Trissur	19.1	17.9	18.7	22.2	18.7
Palakkad	21.9	22.0	18.9	22.5	18.8
Malappuram	33.5	33.8	28.4	33.6	29.5
Kozhikode	23.7	24.3	20.0	26.3	20.5
Wyanad	25.7	31.8	19.4	31.4	23.4
Kannur	26.5	31.4	25.2	28.8	20.5
Kasargod	28.4*	n.a	26.8	n.a	24.4
Kerala	22.6	24.9	20.3	25.0	20.3

* Average from fewer years

$ First 3 columns based on SRS data; Last 2 columns from Mari Bhat, 1996

Sources: K C Zachariah *et. al.*,(1994); P N. Mari Bhat, (1996)

Table 15.6 Levels and Trends in Fertility in the districts of Kerala

	Total Fertility Rate		
	1974-80	*1984-90*	*% Decline*
Thiruvananthapuram	2.3	1.8	21.7
Kollam	2.7	1.8	33.3
Alappuzha	2.3	1.6	30.4
Parhanamthitta	—	1.7	—
Kottayam	2.4	1.7	29.2
Idukki	2.9	1.8	37.9
Ernakulam	2.4	1.6	33.3
Trissur	2.5	1.9	24.0
Palakkad	3.4	2.4	29.4
Malappuram	4.3	3.4	20.9
Kozhikode	3.0	2.0	33.3
Wayanad	3.8	2.3	39.5
Kannur	3.5	2.1	40.0
Kasaragod	—	2.5	—
Kerala	2.9	2.0	31.0

Source: P N Mari Bhat, (1996)

Table 15.7 Percentage Distribution of Population by Five-year Age Groups and Sex for Kerala, 1961, 1991 and 2021.

	Males			*Females*		
	1961	*1991*	*2021*	*1961*	*1991*	*2021*
0-4	15.29	09.53	5.20	14.61	08.79	4.44
5-9	14.84	10.16	5.58	14.07	09.43	4.84
10-14	13.48	11.00	5.85	12.97	10.38	5.11
15-19	08.25	10.30	5.69	08.70	10.50	5.20
20-24	08.11	10.33	5.12	08.84	11.07	5.08
25-29	07.22	08.83	5.96	08.04	09.46	5.96
30-34	06.24	07.31	7.01	06.45	07.18	7.15
35-39	06.06	07.08	7.35	05.89	07.01	7.40
40-44	04.55	05.34	7.55	04.36	04.90	7.76
45-49	04.31	04.60	8.01	04.12	04.59	8.00
50-54	03.33	03.66	8.68	03.29	03.65	8.32
55-59	02.63	03.66	8.24	02.60	03.45	7.63
60-64	02.18	02.93	6.75	02.28	03.08	6.72
65-69	01.42	02.28	5.02	01.48	02.53	5.64

Table 15.7 (*contd.*)

	Males			*Females*		
	1961	*1991*	*2021*	*1961*	*1991*	*2021*
70-74	00.97	01.40	3.55	01.05	01.57	4.33
75+	01.09	01.76	4.41	01.22	02.14	6.38

Source: Calculated by the authors from the 1961 and 1991 Census data; 2021 data are taken from the projections made by K. C. Zachariah and S. Irudaya Rajan of the Centre for Development Studies, Trivandrum.

Table 15.8 Components of Population Growth, Kerala, 1901-1991

Census Year	*Population (000s)*	*Intercensal Growth*	*Rate of Net Migration*	*Rate of Natural Increase*	*Percentage to Total Population of India*
1901	6,398	—	—	—	2.68
1911	7,148	1.11	0.03	1.08	2.84
1921	7,802	0.88	0.04	0.84	3.10
1931	9,507	1.98	0.12	1.86	3.41
1941	11,032	1.49	-0.01	1.49	3.46
1951	13,549	2.06	-0.11	2.16	3.75
1961	16,904	2.21	-0.20	2.41	3.85
1971	21,347	2.31	-0.16	2.47	3.89
1981	25,454	1.75	-0.22	1.97	3.72
1991	29,099	1.32	-0.31	1.63	3.44

Sources: P. N. Mari Bhat and S. Irudaya Rajan (1990); K. C. Zachariah and S. Irudaya Rajan *et. al.* (1997)

Population Projections

Three sets of population projections are made by the authors using various assumptions about fertility and mortality trends. The starting point is the 1991 Census age-sex distribution. All the three projections are made for the next 60-year period from 1991 to 2051.

Mortality assumptions are the same for the three sets. The expectation of life at birth of males is projected to increase from 73.43 years during 1991-96 to 77.15 during 2021-26 and 78.85 during 2046-51. The corresponding changes in the female expectation of life at birth are from 79.43 to 83.15 and 84.85 (for more details, see Table 15.10).

Table 15.9 Fertility Assumption Assumed in the Various Projections

	Projection 1 (Low)	*Projection 2 (Medium)*	*Projection 3 (High)*
1991-1996	1.7	1.7	1.7
1996-2001	1.6	1.7	1.7
2001-2006	1.5	1.7	1.7
2006-2011	1.4	1.7	1.7
2011-2016	1.4	1.7	1.8
2016-2021	1.4	1.7	1.8
2021-2026	1.4	1.7	1.9
2026-2031	1.4	1.7	1.9
2031-2036	1.4	1.7	2.0
2036-2041	1.4	1.7	2.0
2041-2046	1.4	1.7	2.0
2046-2051	1.4	1.7	2.0

Table 15.10 Expectation of Life at Birth Assumed in the Projections

	Expectation of	*Life at Birth*
	Males	*Females*
1991-1996	73.43	79.43
1996-2001	74.47	80.47
2001-2006	75.20	81.20
2006-2011	75.78	81.78
2011-2016	76.29	82.29
2016-2021	76.74	82.74
2021-2026	77.15	83.15
2026-2031	77.53	83.53
2031-2036	77.89	83.89
2036-2041	78.23	84.23
2041-2046	78.55	84.55
2046-2051	78.85	84.85

In 1993, Kerala's total fertility rate was 1.7. We have examined the implications of the three alternate courses of fertility trend.

In the alternative, we have assumed that fertility will remain constant at a TFR of 1.7 for the entire projection period (Projection 2). The second alternative is a continuation of the recent fertility decline. We assume that TFR will decline further to about 1.4 during the next 10 years and will remain at this low rate indefinitely (Projection 1). The third alternative is a declining fertility to a TFR of 1.4 as in projection 1, followed by an increase in fertility after 2001-05 (Projection 3). The assumed TFRs are given in Table 15.9.

[*In deciding on these fertility assumptions, we were governed mostly by the trend in fertility in Kerala in recent years, the social and economic progress the State has been making and the international experience in fertility decline. According to United Nations sources, there were nearly 40 countries with a TFR of less than 2.0 in 1990-95 including large countries like China, Russia, Australia, UK, Japan, Italy, etc. Nearly 10 of them have a TFR of 1.5 or less. Among the countries of this latter group are Japan, Hong Kong, Italy, Spain, Germany, Greece, etc.*].

In all the three projections we have assumed that Kerala will continue to experience a moderate level of net emigration. The assumed rate —0.25 is less than the observed rate of —0.31 per cent (for more details see Table 15.8). A migration rate of —0.25 is kept constant throughout the projection period. Much of the discussions in this chapter are based on projection 2.

Population Stabilization and Zero Population Growth

The current population of Kerala is estimated to be about 30.4 million and the decadal growth during 1981-91 was about 3.5 million. It is unlikely that future decades will see anything like the growth of the past decades. During 1991-2001, the population growth is unlikely to be more than 2.5 million (see Table 15.11). (The population growth in Kerala during 1961-91 and projected growth according to the three alternate projections are shown in Chart 15.1).

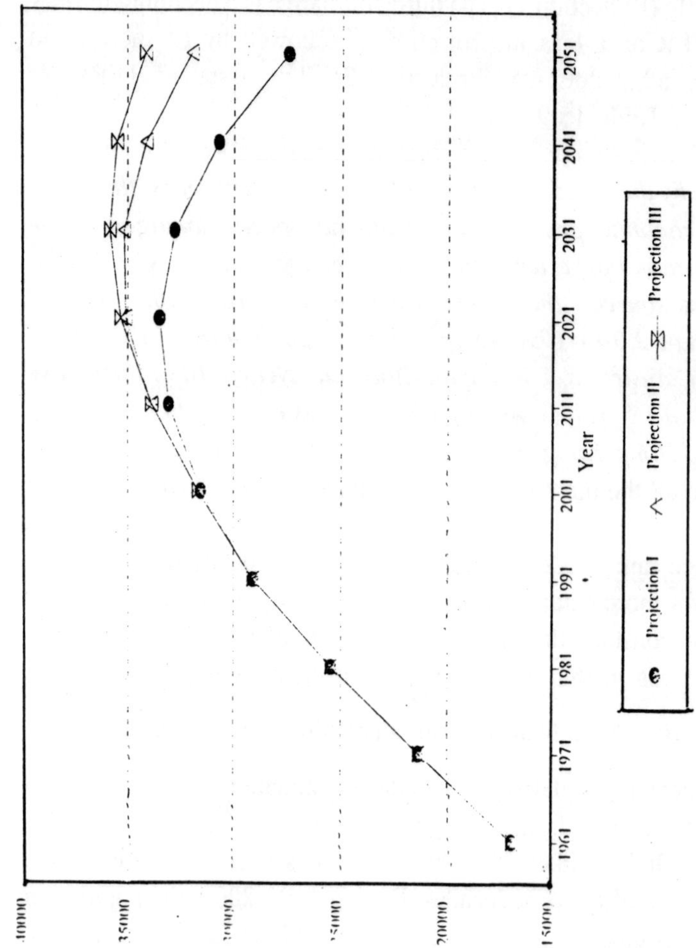

CHART-15.1 Population Growth in Kerala

CHART-15.1 Population Growth in Kerala

These figures indicate that Kerala's population growth has lost much of its momentum. The present indications are that the total population of the State is unlikely to cross 35.5 million. Kerala is likely to achieve zero population growth (ZPG) in 25 to 30 years from now. It is not impossible that Kerala will have short periods of negative growth rates. Thus the demographic situation of the State in the next half a century will be very much different from that of the previous half a century. The socio-economic impact of population growth will be vastly different. Some of these are examined below in detail.

Table 15.11 Population Projections for Kerala

	Proj 1	*G Rate*	*Proj 2*	*G Rate*	*Proj 3*	*G Rate*
1991	29099	—	29099	—	29099	—
1996	30391	0.81	30391	0.87	30391	0.87
2001	31553	0.75	31692	0.84	31692	0.84
2006	32460	0.57	32875	0.73	32875	0.73
2011	33054	0.34	33869	0.60	33869	0.60
2016	33421	0.22	34615	0.44	34741	0.51
2021	33511	0.05	35073	0.26	35316	0.33
2026	33299	-0.13	35249	0.10	35715	0.22
2031	32765	-0.32	35158	-0.05	35842	0.07
2036	31892	-0.54	34786	-0.21	35798	-0.02
2041	30688	-0.77	34112	-0.39	35476	-0.18
2046	29196	-1.00	33148	-0.57	34899	-0.33
2051	27489	-1.20	31961	-0.73	34127	-0.45

Changing Age Structure

One way by which demographic trends affect the socio-economic conditions is through changes in the age composition of the population. Trends in fertility rate, mortality rate and migration have some repercussion on the age structure of the population. (Chart 15.2 gives the age pyramid of Kerala's population in 1961,

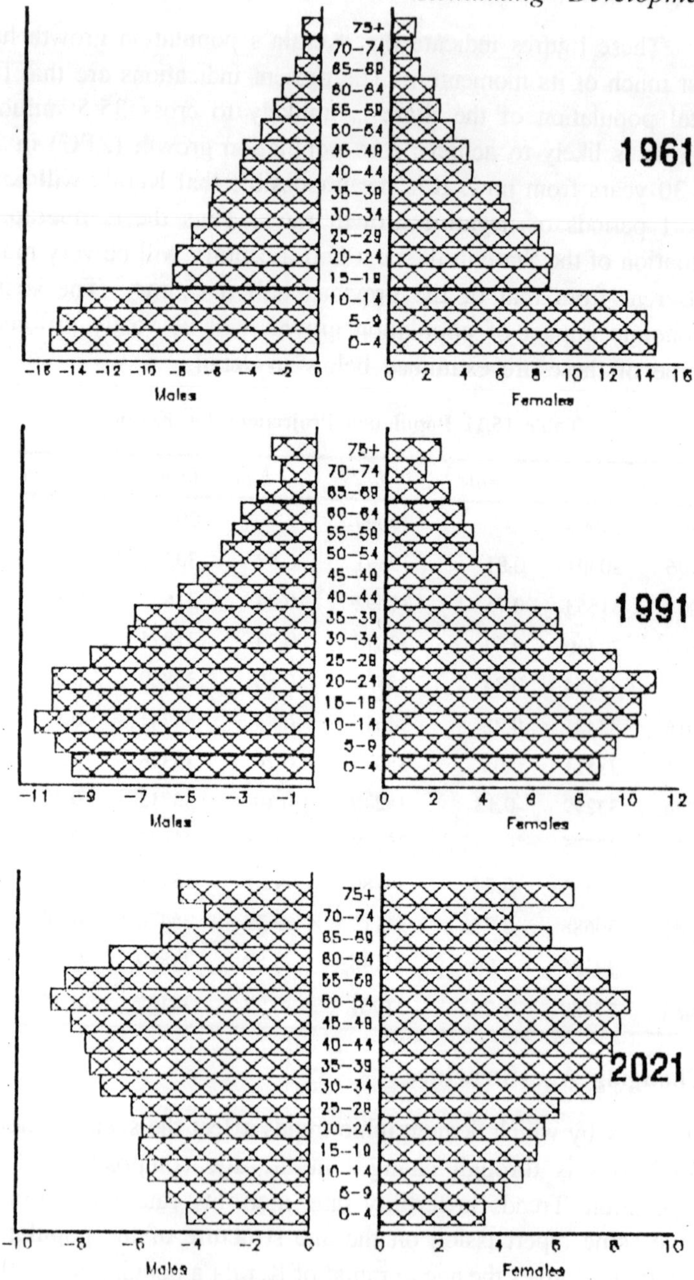

CHART-15.2 : Age Pyramids for Kerala

1991 and 2021.) The changes in the proportion of children in Kerala's population, the proportion of working age population, and that of the elderly are very clearly brought out in these pyramids (see also Tables 15.7 and 15.12). We begin this analysis by taking up the changes in the number and proportion of children in Kerala. These numbers are directly relevant for the State's educational planning.

Table 15.12 Demographic Scenario: Past and Present

		Number(000)	
	Total	*Children*	*Aged*
1961	16904	7205	986
1971	21347	8595	1328
1981	25451	8901	1910
1991	29074	8617	2573
2001	31692	7243	3426
2011	33869	6862	4767
2021	35073	6290	7012
2031	35158	5567	9686
2041	34112	5147	11100
2051	31961	4671	11283
		Growth Rate	
	Total	*Children*	*Aged*
1961-71	2.33	1.76	2.98
1971-81	1.76	0.35	3.63
1981-91	1.33	0.32	2.98
1991-01	0.86	1.74	2.86
2001-11	0.66	0.54	3.30
2011-21	0.35	0.87	3.86
2021-31	0.02	1.22	3.23
2031-41	0.30	0.78	1.36
2041-51	0.65	0.97	0.16

Table 15.13 Decomposition of Children under 15 years

Year	*Children under 15 years (,000)*	*Proportion to Total Population*	*Children 5-9 years (Primary)*	*Children 10-14 years (Secondary)*
1961	7205	42.62	2443	2235
1971	8595	40.26	2876	2864
1981	8901	34.97	2922	3258
1991	8617	29.64	2847	3108
2001	7243	22.85	2252	2636
2011	6862	20.26	2301	2310
2021	6290	17.93	2103	2207
2031	5567	15.83	1833	1937
2041	5147	15.09	1718	1755
2051	4671	14.61	1554	1632

Educational Planning

Children are defined as those under 15 years in this discussion. The number of children in a population is mostly by the contribution of number of births and to a lesser extent by mortality among children. As birth rate has declined very considerably (from about 40 in 1950s to about 17 in 1993), dramatic decline in the number of children should be expected. Part of the expected changes in the number of children is, however, cancelled by the increase in the number of mothers and the decline in the death rate among the children. Table 15.13 gives the number of children under 15 years according to the various Censuses since the formation of Kerala and the Projection 2.

Between 1961 and 1981 there was an increase of about 1.7 million children under 15 years, but since then the number has been on the decline. By the end of the century, the increase would have been almost negligible. The number of children in 2001 would be the same as of 1961.

Decomposition of the total by 5-year age group indicates that the decline will be the largest in the very young age group. School age population will shrink considerably in the coming decades. Children in the primary school ages (taken as 5-9 years for convenience) will decline from 2,847,000 in 1991 to 1,554,000 in 2051. In the secondary school ages also (taken as 10-14 years for convenience) similar decline is observed.

The implication of such drastic decline in school population has been evident for quite some time in Kerala. A decline of 32 per cent in school age population will necessitate a corresponding decline in the number of class rooms, number of teachers, etc. Policies and programmes taking these major demographic shifts might take some time to be implemented, but the adjustments are inevitable (more details, see Government of Kerala (1994)); (James (1995)).

Apart from schooling, the repercussion of decline in children's population will be felt in many other areas of economic activity—children's clothing industry, toy manufacturing, health professionals involved in child birth and children's health maintenance, etc. Economic activities catering for children and pregnant women are bound to shrink and will require considerable structural adjustment in the coming years. One saving factor is that not all children make use of these services now, and an increase in the proportion of children using these services will partly compensate for the decrease in the number of children. Children are likely to get a better deal in the coming years.

One aspect of the Census statistics on the number of children in the school-going age deserves special mention. The number of children enumerated in the Censuses of 1971, 1981 and 1991 has always been larger than the corresponding cohort (after adjusting for the intercensal mortality) in the previous Census (Table 15.14). Thus the number of children in the 10-14 age group in 1971 was in excess of the survivors of children 0-4 years enumerated in 1961 by as much as 766 thousands (Table 15.14). This is not an isolated incident of the 1961 and 1971 Censuses. Similar anomaly is observed in the 1981 and 1991 Censuses and the differences are 904 thousands and 866 thousands respectively. A number of explanations could be given for this anomaly: underenumeration of children in 0-4 years, misstatement of age, etc. But since the differences are very large (32%) and there is considerable correspondence between the number of children under 5 years and the number of births in the previous 5 years, other explanations are needed. One hypothesis is that Keralites living outside Kerala send their children back to Kerala for school education. This is only a hypothesis, but, if found correct, could have some policy implications.

Table 15.14 Some Special Features Observed in Census among Children

Actual 0-4 in 1961	Expected Survivors as 10-14 in 1971	Actual Enumerated as 10-14 in 1971	Difference
2527160	2097084	2863885	766801
Actual 0-4 in 1971	Expected Survivors as 10-14 in 1981	Actual Enumerated as 10-14 in 1981	Difference
2855404	2353260	3257922	904662
Actual 0-4 in 1981	Expected Survivors as 10-14 in 1991	Actual Enumerated as 10-14 in 1991	Difference
2720731	2240651	3107600	866949

Labour Force

As mentioned above, unemployment, especially unemployment among the educated is one of the major economic and social problems of Kerala. A number of factors are involved in the emergence of unemployment as a very serious problem and rapid population growth since the 1950s is one among them. Efforts to find a solution of the unemployment problem is hampered by the demographic explosion in the State.

In 1961, there were only about 764,000 persons in the working ages 20-64 years in Kerala (Table 15.15). This number has increased to about 1,566,000 by 1991 (a 104 % increase). Our projections indicate that the number of persons in the working age would increase further to about 21329127 by 2021 (a 36% increase), and then decline (by 24%) to about 1,572,000 by 2051 (it may be noted that most of the persons above 20 years in 2021 were already born before the 1991 Census and therefore our projections of working age population for 2021 are quite realistic). Thus the accentuation in the employment problem in the State is partly due to the demographic pressure. In spite of the very rapid decline in the birth rate in the State for the last two decades, the demographic pressure on the labour force will not disappear for quite some time. It is only after 2021, that we may expect a real decline in the number of persons in the working ages.

Table 15.15 Population in Working Ages in Kerala

	Numbers			
	20-64	*20-34*	*34-49*	*50-64*
1961	07639624	3798636	2474651	1366337
1971	09568105	4586988	3234650	1746467
1981	12312589	6290800	3709377	2312412
1991	15660910	7878650	4871010	2911250
2001	19261650	8274484	7122387	3864779
2011	21298707	7417236	8175520	5705951
2021	21329127	6311121	7493965	7524041
2031	17579497	5900615	6481781	5197101
2041	17761857	5307853	5674699	6779305
2051	15722320	4568788	5401216	5752316
	Growth Rate			
	20-64	*20-34*	*34-49*	*50-64*
1961-71	2.25	1.89	2.68	2.45
1971-81	2.52	3.16	1.37	2.81
1981-91	2.41	2.25	2.72	2.30
1991-01	2.07	0.49	3.80	2.83
2001-11	1.01	-1.09	1.38	3.90
2011-21	0.01	-1.61	-0.87	2.77
2021-31	-1.93	-0.67	-1.45	-3.70
2031-41	0.10	-1.06	-1.33	2.66
2041-51	-1.22	-1.50	-0.49	-1.64

There will, however, be a significant decline in the growth rate of the labour force beginning with the first decade of the next century and some actual decline after 2021. Equally important will be the change in the structure of the working age population.

In 1961 and 1991 the proportion of the working age population in the young working ages (20-34 years) was nearly half of the total: 49.7 in 1961 and 50.3 in 1991. But after 1991, the proportion of the young will undergo a dramatic decline to less than 30 per cent. Between 1991 and 2021, the actual number of such young workers will decrease by 1.6 million. Thus the unemployment problem among the young will greatly ease in the coming years. Other things being equal on the economic front such an easing of the employment problem is almost inevitable.

Just the opposite is the case among the older workers (those above 50 years). The proportion of the population in the 50-64 year bracket will increase from 18.6 in 1991 to 35.3 by 2021. The actual number will also increase very considerably, from 2,911,000 in 1991 to 7,524,000 by 2021 (a 158% increase). Finding suitable employment for the older working age population will be a major challenge on the employment front in the early part of the next century.

The population in the middle ages (35-49 years) will also increase very considerably in absolute terms (2,622,000) during 1991-2021, but in relative terms their share changes very little (from 31% to 35%).

Marriage Squeeze

One consequence of a rapidly declining fertility rate is its effect on the parity between the number of girls and the number of boys in the marriage age groups. As girls are married at relatively younger age, the number of girls in the marriage market usually exceeds the number of eligible boys. However, the situation changes considerably if fertility were to fall rapidly as in Kerala in the last two decades. The effect of fertility decline is felt first in the number of girls in their usual ages at marriage. As boys usually get married at higher ages, the effect of fertility decline on their size is felt 5 to 6 years later.

In Kerala, most of the girls get married when they are in the age group 20 to 24 years and most of the boys get married when they are in the 25 to 29 age group. The difference between the number of girls in the 20-24 age group and the number of boys in the age group 25 to 29 years is a measure of the marriage squeeze in the State. These numbers are given in Table 15.16 for the years 1961 to 2051.

Table 15.16 Population in Marriageable Ages in Kerala

	Girls 20-24 Years	*Boys 25-29 Years*	*Difference*	
			Absolute	*Percentage Increase*
1961	0755227	0604244	150983	19.99
1971	1012032	0664365	347667	34.35
1981	1364026	1005881	358145	26.26
1991	1634240	1263540	370700	22.68
2001	1385865	1345003	040862	02.95
2011	1268763	1218104	050659	03.99
2021	1093301	0963048	130253	11.91
2031	1042004	0990320	051684	04.96
2041	0910941	0891204	019737	02.17
2051	0822690	0754468	068222	08.29

Girls in the age group 20 to 24 years have always outnumbered boys in the age group 25 to 29 years. The excess of girls was as much as 20 per cent of the number of boys in 1961. It increased to 34 in 1971 greatly increasing the marriage squeeze. Since then it has been on the decline. In the coming years, girls will have a much wider choice in finding a suitable groom than they ever had in the past in Kerala. The number of girls in the 20-24 year age group will be more or less the same as the number of boys in the 25-29 year age group. This is a welcome consequence of the decline in fertility in the last two decades. One could speculate a decline in the age at marriage of girls in the coming years!

The Elderly

One of the inevitable consequences of demographic transition is population ageing. Being ahead in the demographic transition, Kerala is expected to increase the number of elderly and the proportion in the years to come (Irudaya Rajan (1989)). The ageing population is defined as those above 60 years of age. According to the 1961 Census the number of elderly was just one million, which increased to 2.6 million in 1991 Census (a 161% increase). According to our projections, the number of the elderly is expected to reach 7.0 millions by 2021 (a 173% increase) and 11.3 millions by 2051 (a 61% increase). The change in the proportion of the elderly is even more dramatic. Their proportion was around 9 per cent in 1991 but it is expected to increase to 20 per cent in 2021 and 35 per cent in 2051 (Table15.17).

The decomposition of elderly by age and categorizing them as young old (60-74) and old old (75+) provides additional information on the old age problem in the State. Among all the age groups of the population, the fastest growing group is the old old. Additional demographic information on the elderly is provided in Table 15.17.

Table 15.17 Composition of Young Old and Old Old in Kerala

	60-74 Nos.	*75 + (000)*	*60-74 Proportion*	*75 +*	*60-74 Growth Rate*	*75+*	*Proportion to Total 60 +*	*70 +*
1971	1060	267	79.87	20.13	—	—	06.22	1.25
1981	1519	391	79.52	20.48	3.59	3.81	07.50	1.54
1991	2005	568	77.92	22.08	2.78	3.74	08.85	1.95
2001	2575	851	75.14	24.86	2.49	4.05	10.81	2.69
2011	3497	1269	73.37	26.63	3.06	3.99	14.07	3.75
2021	5235	1776	74.66	25.34	4.03	3.36	19.99	5.07
2031	6962	2724	71.87	28.13	2.85	4.28	27.55	7.75
2041	7101	3998	63.97	36.03	0.20	3.84	32.54	11.72
2051	6535	4747	57.14	42.08	-0.83	1.72	35.30	14.85

In 1995, Kerala administered more than 30 social security and assistance schemes for the elderly and disadvantaged groups. The annual budget provision for all schemes is more than Rs. 100 crores. In addition, more than Rs. 400 crores are spent on the pensions every year for the retired government employees numbering around Rs. 3 lakhs.

The old age pension scheme was first started on 1st November 1960 and the widowed and destitute pension scheme was added on 1st January 1964. The scheme provides pension to the old age destitute and widowed/divorced destitute subject to fulfilment of the following eligibility conditions: (a) The destitute person has been residing in Kerala for a continuous period not less than two years; (b) The destitute person is above 65 years of age. However, the age limit does not apply to a widowed or divorced destitute. A recipient under this scheme is entitled to Rs. 80 per month. An additional amount of Rs. 5 per month is paid to a widow if she has a minor child to support.

The 1981 Census revealed that divorced/widowed/deserted population accounts for about 15 lakhs or 6 per cent of the population. Calculations based on the 1991 census data are given below:

Number of widows in Kerala (1991)	Rs.17.15 lakhs
Number of widows above 60 years of age	Rs.08.05 lakhs
Proportion of widows in the total population	10.55 per cent
Proportion of old age widows in the total	22.49 per cent
Proportion of widows among old	67.40 per cent
The widow pension beneficiaries (1991)	Rs. 9.78 lakhs
The cost of the scheme (1991)	Rs. 144 lakhs
Actual coverage	9.78 per cent
If all elderly widows of 1991 are covered by the scheme, the estimated cost	Rs. 644 lakhs
If all widows in Kerala of 1991 to be covered, by the scheme, the estimated cost	Rs. 1372 lakhs
If at least 75 per cent of the widows are to be covered, the estimated cost	Rs. 1029 lakhs

Thus 67 per cent of the elderly women are widows as per 1991 Census. The actual coverage of the scheme is only 9.78 per cent. The cost is expected to increase from Rs. 144 lakhs to Rs. 644 lakhs, if all elderly widows are covered in the scheme. In 1991, all the schemes existing in Kerala covered only 25 per cent of the 60+ population. The cost is approximately Rs. 100 crores. If the government could cover the entire elderly, the approximate cost works out to Rs. 400 crores. In 2021, if the government extend its benefits to all elderly persons numbering around 7.0 millions, then the estimated cost is around Rs. 1388 crores, at constant prices.

The issue of the social support for the elderly needs to be addressed in the context of not only the ageing population but also the overall change in the age structure. The political economy will also change and other efficient system of support are expected to emerge.

There is still one more point to be noted. In 1996, the proportion of old voters in Kerala was 14, about 1 in 7, a respectable proportion by any standards. The proportion is expected to increase to 1 in 5 in 2021. Thus the elderly will be a formidable vote bank in the next century.

Conclusion

Kerala's demographic trends in the first half of the 21st century will be dramatically different from those of the second half of the 20th century. Whereas the total population of the State increased by 270 per cent in the second half of the last century (from 11,723,000 in 1951 to 31,553,000 in 2001), the growth (if any) in the next half a century will be very negligible. The crude death rate declined from about 20 to about 6 in the last half a century, but it is likely to increase from 6 to 13 in the next century. The crude birth rate decreased from 40 to about 16 in the last half a century, but it is likely to remain more or less stable in the next half a century. While Kerala experienced varying degrees of net out-migration and net emigration in the last half a century, migration trend in the next half a century is somewhat uncertain. It will depend more on socio-economic developments than on demographic trends.

The socio-economic implication of the demographic trends will be far-reaching. To begin with, the pressure on schools and colleges will be a thing of the past, giving ample opportunities for the educational system to concentrate on the quality of education rather than on quantity.

This is also true of hospitals and health personnel catering to the health needs of the children. It will be easier to bring about the needed improvement in the quality of their services.

In the transitional period, parity between the number of girls and boys in their respective marriage ages will be maintained. But this is a temporary respite.

Other things being equal on the economic front, unemployment among the young working age population will be reduced. The educated young workers can almost pick and choose the job they want. But this is not the case with older workers. The number of older working population would almost double in a short period of 20 years between 2001 and 2021.

In the last half a century the major socio-economic problems were related to the schooling, maintenance of health and nutrition and finding employment to the youngsters. In the next half a century, the major socio-economic problems would be finding gainful employment to the older working age population, maintenance of the health and nutrition of the elderly, and providing them with means of subsistence through social security and pension.

In 1991, all the schemes existing in Kerala cover only 25 per cent of the 60+ population. The cost is approximately Rs. 100 crores. If the government could cover the entire elderly, the approximate cost required works out to Rs. 400 crores. In 2021, if the government extend its benefits to all elderly persons numbering around 7.0 millions, then the estimated cost is around Rs. 1388 crores, of course at 1991 prices.

REFERENCES

Government of Kerala (1994), Report of the Expert Committee on School Age *Group Population in 2001 A. D. and its Implications on Educational Policy and Planning*, State Planning Board, Trivandrum.

Irudaya Rajan, S. (1989), Aging in Kerala: One More Population Problem? *Asia Pacific Population Journal*, volume. 4, no. 2.

S. P. N. Mari Bhat and Tim Dyson (1997), *Fertility and Mortality Transition in Kerala: A Historical Investigation*, Hindustan Publishing Corporation, New Delhi.

James, K. S. (1995), Demographic Transition and Education in Kerala, *Economic and Political Weekly*, volume 30, no. 51, pp. 3274-76.

Krishnan, T. N. (1976), Demographic Transition in Kerala: Facts and Factors, *Economic and Political Weekly*, vol. 11, no. 31-33, pp. 1203-24.

Mathew, E. T. (1996), Employment and Unemployment Trends in Kerala : A Study Based on National Sample Survey Data. *Review of Development and Change*, volume 1, no 2, July-December, pp. 197-218.

—— (1990), Demographic Transition in Kerala Revisited, *Economic and Political Weekly*, volume 25, nos. 35 & 36, September 1-8, pp. 1957-1980.

Mari Bhat, P. N. and S Irudaya Rajan (1992), Demographic Transition in Kerala: A Reply, *Economic and Political Weekly*, volume 26, no. 23, June 6.

Mari Bhat, P. N. (1996), Contours of Fertility Decline in India: A District Level Study Based on the 1991 Census, Chapter 4, pp. 96-177 in K. Srinivasan (eds). *Population Policy and Reproductive Health*, Hindustan Publishing Corporation, New Delhi.

Nair, P. R. G. (1986), Decline in Birth Rate in Kerala: A Hypothesis About the Inter-relationship between Demographic Variables, Health Service and Education, *Economic and Political Weekly*, vol. 9, pp. 323:336.

Nair, P. K. B. (1986), Factors in Fertility Decline in Kerala. In K Mahadevan (eds). *Fertility and Mortality: Theory, Methodology and Empirical Issues*. Sage Publications, New Delhi.

Zachariah, K. C. (1984), *The Anomaly of the Fertility Decline in India's Kerala State : A Field Investigation,* Staff Working Paper No. 700, The World Bank, Washington DC.

Zachariah, K. C. et al. (1994), *Demographic Transition in Kerala in the 1980s,* Centre for Development Studies Monograph Series, Trivandrum, Kerala.

Zachariah, K. C. and S Irudaya Rajan (1997), Kerala's Demograaphic Transition: An Overview. Chapter 1 in K. C. Zachariah and S. Irudaya Rajan (eds.) 1997, *Kerala's Demographic Transition; Determinants and Consequences,* Sage Publications, New Delhi.

SIXTEEN

LABOUR SHORTAGE IN A LABOUR SURPLUS ECONOMY?

A Study of the Rural Labour Market in Kerala

M. K. SUKUMARAN NAIR

Kerala has had a unique development experience whose salient features have been the subject matter of academic discourse in India as well as abroad for more than two decades now. However, the implications of this for the labour market dynamics have not drawn enough attention. This chapter makes an attempt to understand the phenomenon of labour shortage in rural Kerala. Though it is not made explicit in the chapter, the context of analysis is the so called Kerala Model with all its ramifications.

The pattern of land distribution and the nature of the crops grown are, *inter alia*, two key determinants of rural labour market dynamics. Most of the existing literature on rural labour markets has a skewed distribution of land and the predominance of annual crops as their behavioural assumptions. But none of the theories developed against the backdrop of these assumptions, as argued in this chapter, is able to explain the labour market behaviour in rural Kerala where agriculture is characterised by the predominance of small holdings and perennial tree crops. These two characteristics have substantially altered the structure of the labour market from the stylised model and hence theories based on the dominant norm fail to explain the labour market behaviour in Kerala.

When it is claimed that rural unemployment is rising in Kerala, there are reports to the effect that there is a shortage of rural labour especially in the agricultural sector in the sense that employers are willing and are actually seeking to hire additional workers at the going wage rate, but find no more available at that rate. The objective of the present study is to offer an alternative explanation to the paradoxical behaviour of rural labour market in Kerala. It is hypothesised that there is a situation of relative labour shortage in rural Kerala caused by the small holder tree crop character of the agricultural sector accompanied by high transaction costs due to the various imperfections and segmentation of the rural labour market.

The rural sector in Kerala has the following typical features:

1. The average size of holdings is relatively low. Consequently, land distribution is less skewed and even labourers possess some land.
2. The cropping pattern is characterised by the predominance of commercial and tree crops.
3. The labour market is fragmented by villages and the village market is further segmented by skill and type of tasks.
4. Wage rates are high and do not significantly vary with seasons and across the villages.
5. Government subsidies, welfare measures and other transfer payments keep the real wages high as also the reserve price of labour.

While the small farmers are unorganised, the rural labourers are highly organised either in trade unions or informal groupings so that they can considerably influence the supply decisions in the labour market. But the small holders, as they are unorganised, are not able to influence decisions regarding labour demand. Unlike their counterparts in the inter-linked markets, the small holders are very weak. This makes a lot of difference in the labour market dynamics in rural Kerala.

The available secondary data, though do provide considerable insight into the macro-economic characteristics of the labour market, do not shed adequate light on the micro dynamics of the situation. Therefore, a detailed household survey was carried out in the Pathanamthitta District of Kerala in 1989. Five villages, viz., Travon, Vallicode, Kodumon, Koipuram and Ranni were selected at random for detailed investigation. The necessary data were collected in two rounds, one during the peak season and the other during the lean season from 241 labour and 241 cultivating households.

Demand for Labour

The holdings in the sample village are medium-sized. The average size of holdings is only 3.09 acres. Such a distribution pattern may generate a greater labour demand, if accompanied by certain concomitant characteristics. Of the several factors that may influence the demand for labour, the two closely connected with land distribution are cropping pattern and cropping intensity. Only 26 per cent of the area under cultivation accounts for paddy. Rubber is the predominant crop. The rest of the area is devoted to other crops which are largely commercial. Thus the degree of commercialisation is relatively high in the sample. Except in the lowest size class, paddy is not the major crop in any holding.

Rubber and other tree crops are not generally considered to be labour absorbing. They generate demand for labour during the initial three to four years. After that, nurturing of the trees requires lesser quantum of labour. Once the trees are grown, the major source of demand for labour is harvesting for coconuts and arecanuts, and tapping for rubber. These tasks are highly skilled and specialised and hence the labour market is segmented.

The predominance of tree crop agriculture does not, however, imply a lower labour demand. It is quite unlikely that the trees on all holdings in the villages have crossed their early stages when the labour demand is at the peak. In Kerala the transition to tree crop agriculture has been a slow and staggered process. This has been because the holdings are small in size and the number of holdings numerous and hence cropping decisions are made in a discrete fashion. As a result, the labour demand remained more or less stable over the years. Another demand augmenting factor is that these trees are removed and replanted after 25-30 years. Thus the cutting of old trees and their replacement and the consequent nurturing for a period of 3-4 years generate further demand for labour. These processes take place in different holdings at different time periods. Consequently, the demand for labour either has increased or remained steady. Further, tasks associated with tree crops are not season-specific as in the case of paddy. This helps to wipe off the large gaps in labour absorption between the peak and off season. We do not have data on the age distribution of the trees to arrive at any estimate of the level of labour absorption at various stages in the tree crop life cycle. Tree crops along with paddy provide a seasonal balance in labour demand. However, it may be argued that it need not *per se* generate any greater demand for hired labour given the fact that a majority of the holdings are of smaller size where the labour use pattern is likely to be characterised by the predominance of family labour.

Table 16.1 Percentage Distribution of Family Labour and Hired Labour Employed by Size of Holdings During the Preceding Week of the Survey

Size of holdings	*Percentage of family labour*	*Percentage of hired labour*	*Total*
0.00-0.49	25.0	75.0	100.00
0.50-0.99	23.3	76.7	100.00
1.00-1.99	13.8	86.2	100.00
2.00-4.99	10.1	89.9	100.00
5.00-9.99	5.8	94.2	100.00
10.00 acres and above	7.4	92.6	100.00
Total	10.3	89.7	100.00

Table 16.1 presents data on the labour use pattern. It is seen that only 10 per cent of the total demand for labour is met through family labour. Even in small holdings a large proportion of the labour requirement is met through hired labour. This is mainly due to the relatively smaller household size of cultivators. The average household size is only 4.95 in the sample (see Table 16.2). Together with this, we may consider the fact that those engaged in farming constitute only 23.2 per cent of the total number of members of the cultivating households. On an average only 1.15 persons per household are available for farm work. This figure is 2 in the lowest size class and less than 2 in all other size

classes. These figures show that in the medium and large size classes, the involvement of family labour is not very significant. It is by and large of a supervisory nature. Family labour is not adequately forthcoming, much of which is employed in the other sectors of the economy.

Table 16.2 Occupational Distribution of Members of Cultivating Households by Size of Holdings

Size of holdings (in acres)	*Occupations*				*Total*
	Farming	*Business industry and trade*	*Salaried employees*	*Others*	
0-0.49	2.00	1.30	0.03	1.00	4.33
	(46.2)	(30.0)	(0.01)	(23.1)	(100.0)
0.50-0.99	1.73	1.00	0.40	1.58	4.71
	(36.7)	(21.2)	(8.5)	(33.5)	(100.0)
1.00-1.99	1.20	1.21	0.61	1.90	4.92
	(24.4)	(24.6)	(12.4)	(38.6)	(100.0)
2.00-4.99	1.05	1.77	1.00	1..08	4.90
	(21.4)	(36.1)	(20.4)	(22.4)	(100.0)
5.00-9.99	1.07	1.92	1.03	1.17	5.19
	(20.6)	(37.0)	(19.8)	(22.5)	(100.0)
10 acres	1.53	1.97	1.43	1.67	6.60
and above	(23.2)	(29.8)	(21.7)	(25.3)	(100.0)
All	1.15	1.59	0.87	1.34	4.95
holdings	(23.2)	(32.1)	(17.6)	(27.1)	(100.0)

Further, about 60 per cent of the members of the cultivating households are having educational qualifications of the level of SSLC and above (Table 16.3). Nearly 17 per cent are graduates or postgraduates or professionally qualified. Only 38 per cent were found to be below SSLC level. It is generally found that the educated are not available for farm work despite being unemployed.

When considering the distribution of household members by educational qualifications and size of holdings, it is seen that only households possessing less than 2 acres account for more than two members having lower educational qualifications. In higher classes the number of such persons is less than two. Even in the lower classes, if one out of the two happens to be the housewife who generally looks after the household duties, only one person is effectively available for farm work. All these indicate that even smaller holdings have fairly high demand for hired labour.

Table 16.3 Distribution of Members of Cultivating Households by Educational Status and Size of Holdings

Size of holdings (acres)	*Educational Level*				
	Less than Standard V	*Less than SSLC*	*SSLC & above, but below graduation*	*Graduation & above*	*Total*
0-0.49	0.98 (22.6)	1.62 (37.4)	1.70 (39.3)	0.03 (0.7)	4.33 (100)
0.50-0.99	0.90 (19.1)	1.50 (31.8)	2.20 (46.7)	0.11 (2.3)	4.71 (100)
1.00-1.99	0.94 (19.1)	1.56 (31.7)	2.22 (45.1)	0.20 (4.1)	4.92 (100)
2.00-4.99	0.83 (16.9)	1.13 (23.1)	2.11 (43.1)	0.83 (16.9)	4.90 (100)
5.00-9.90	0.70 (13.5)	1.17 (22.5)	2.40 (46.2)	0.90 (17.7)	5.19 (100)
10 acres & above	0.52 (7.8)	1.11 (16.8)	3.47 (52.6)	1.50 (22.7)	6.60 (100)
All holdings	0.74 (15.0)	1.23 (24.8)	2.18 (44.0)	0.80 (16.2)	4.95 (100)

A surer way of gauging the true nature of demand for labour is the availability of labour per acre within the cultivating households. The available number of adult males and adult females per acre per household are 0.74 and 0.68 respectively. As expected, these ratios fall sharply with size of holdings (Table 16.4). In holdings of the size of 2 acres and above, the number of adult males as well as females per acre is less than one and in the largest size class these ratios are 0.20 and 0.23 respectively.

Another significant dimension of the problem is that only 21 per cent of the cultivating households depend on agriculture as their major source of income. Only in the case of 16 per cent of the farmers agriculture has a greater than 50 per cent share in their total income.

There are also certain other factors which have contributed to the increase in the demand for hired labour. Now a days bullock labour is increasingly being replaced by human labour as far as possible. This possibly has two effects. One is that it can lead to mechanisation of agriculture; but the relatively smaller size of holdings does not permit large scale mechanisation. The other effect is an increase in the demand for human labour which is in fact happening in Kerala at present. Moreover, the practice of direct seeding, extensive weeding, direct application of weedicides, fertilisers and pesticides etc. also seem to have increased labour demand.

Table 16.4 Distribution of Adult Males and Females per Acre per Household by Size of Holdings

Size of holdings (acres)	*Adult males per acre*	*Adult females per acre*	*Total*
0-0.49	6.47	3.69	10.16
0.50-0.99	2.41	2.24	4.65
1.00-1.99	1.47	1.44	2.91
2.00-4.99	0.74	0.70	1.44
5.00-9.99	0.44	0.34	0.78
10 acres & above	0.20	0.23	0.43
All holdings	0.74	0.68	1.42

While taking into account labour demand, a factor that needs critical consideration is the fragmentation and the consequent multiplication of tasks. In the past, many tasks such as cutting the harvest, carrying the load to the threshing yard, winnowing, drying the hay etc. were part of harvesting for which a single wage rate existed. Now many of these tasks are segregated from harvesting and each task carries a separate time or piece wage rate. So is the case with after-harvesting operations. Making the hay into bundles, carrying the bundles and paddy to the customers or the homes of the cultivators etc. which were part of a single task are independent tasks now. Thus we see that new jobs are additionally created out of the existing ones. All these have further enhanced the demand for farm labour.

Labour Supply

The labour supply function in the rural economy of Kerala has been made extremely complicated by the interaction of a number of inter-connected and varied factors. It is generally argued that the labour supply in a rural economy, to a large extent, is influenced by land holding of labour households. We have seen elsewhere that the size of holdings of even cultivating households is relatively small in the sample villages as in the rest of Kerala. Naturally the size of holdings of rural labour households is still smaller, in almost all cases less than 10 cents. But as high as 95 per cent of all labour households own at least a small homestead with a garden plot (Table 16.5). In the typical Kerala situation, even a small holding produces some output, most often cash crops such as coconut and rubber which generate some income, however, small it may be. This, along with the social and food security measures of the government, obviously increases the reserve price of the labour.

The caste composition of labour households has a direct influence on labour supply. Traditionally, a substantial proportion of rural labour, more particularly agricultural labour, has been forthcoming from the scheduled caste communities. In our sample, 60 per cent of the labour households belong to scheduled caste, scheduled tribe communities and the remaining 40 per cent to other communities. A decline in the proportion of scheduled caste labour households indicates a major supply constraint. The implementation of land reforms in Kerala has bestowed on the *harijan* communities a homestead and a few cents of garden land. As argued above, labour supply has a negative asset effect.

Table 16.5 Distribution of Labour Households by Landholding and Caste

	SC/ST	*Others*	*Total*
No. of landholding households	138 (95.2)	92 (95.7)	230 (95.4)
No. of landless households	7 (4.8)	4 (4.30)	11 (4.6)
All households	145 (100.0)	96 (100.0)	241 (100.0)

Another factor which has decisive influence on labour supply is the size of the labour households. The average size of the labour households is 4.75 which is marginally lower than that of the cultivating households (Table 16.6). Five per cent of the households have only 2 or less than 2 members per household. About 67 per cent of the households have 3 to 5 members. Once allowance is made for the aged and children, the average households size declines to 3.71. Further, even among those who are in the workforce, all are not available for manual work whether it is on farm or off farm. Some of the them are engaged in other activities as well.

Table 16.7 indicates the type of activities engaged by members of the labour households. Only 1.52 members per household are available for manual out of a total of 4.75. The rest of the household members do not enter the market for manual work. Above 5 per cent are engaged in petty business and another 6 per cent in salaried jobs. About 32 per cent consist of children and the aged. Eighteen per cent of the members are educated (in the sense that they have passed at least SSLC examination) and unemployed, but not available for manual work. The percentage of unemployed, who are available for manual work is only 6.5. The dependency ratio i.e., the ratio of non-working members to the working members per household is 1.28. This ratio is higher among landholding labourers (1.37) than among the landless (0.53). This ratio also supports the negative asset effect hypothesis mentioned above. Thus it is clear that only a relatively smaller proportion of the rural workers are available for activities associated with manual work either on or off farm. This further points to the limited labour supply base of the villages.

Table 16.6 Household Size and Dependency Ratio for Labour Households

Household size	*No. of households*	*Dependency ratio for landholding households*	*Dependency ratio for landless households*
0-2	12 (5.0)		
3-5	161 (66.8)		
5 and above	68 (28.2)		
All labour households	4.75 (100.00)	1.37	0.53

As argued earlier, labour market segmentation act as a constraint on labour supply. There are different types of labour market segmentation such as segmentation by village, religion, caste, skill etc. In Kerala, it seems that the mobility of workers from one village to another has come down significantly in recent years. This is generally attributed to land reforms which secured a homestead for the labourer. The spread of schools even to remote villages, near hundred per cent enrolment of children in schools, the free noon meal scheme, free distribution of books, lumpsum grant to scheduled caste children etc. are some other factors which prevent the mobility of the workers from their village to distant places in search of work. In our sample it is seen that nearly 86 per cent of the workers work in their own villages. But more than 60 per cent of the landless labourers go out of the villages for work while only less than 14 per cent of the landholding labourers do so (Table 16.8). Moreover, the average distance travelled by a worker to his work place is only 1.84 km for farm work and 3.45 km for non-farm work. This lends support to the hypothesis that workers generally have a strong preference for work in the vicinity. The village segmentation seems to be more pronounced in the case of farm work than in the case of non-farm work.

Table 16.7 Distribution of Members of Labour Households by Types of Activities

Types of activities	*Number of members per household*
Manual work	1.52
	(31.9)
Petty business	0.25
	(5.3)
Salaried jobs	0.30
	(6.3)
Children & the aged	1.50
	(31.6)
Educated & unemployed	0.87
but not available for	(18.3)
manual work	
Unemployed	0.31
	(6.5)
All	4.75
	(100.00)

The most important determinant of labour supply is the wage rate. Kerala as a whole, and more particularly the study area, is characterised by the prevalence of high wage rates for agricultural and non-agricultural rural labour. Though the fact is that agricultural wages are relatively high in Kerala, 82 per cent of the labourers in our sample believe that the prevailing wage rates are lower and the remaining 18 per cent consider it normal. When further asked, 69 per cent of the labour households said that they were not ready to work for lower wages even when unemployed. Even in the lean season, 49 per cent of them reported their unwillingness to work for lower wages. Among those who are ready to work for lower wages, 50 per cent said they would not do so for fear of their fellow workers.

Table 16.8 Distribution of Labourers by Place of Work

Place of work	No. of workers		
	Landholding	Landless	Total
In the vicinity	198	4	202
	(86.0)	(36.0)	(84.0)
Far-off place	32	7	39
	(14.0)	(64.0)	(16.0)
Total	230	11	241
	(100.0)	(100.0)	(100.0)

Though a higher wage rate may bring forth a greater supply of labour, it is sometimes possible that the supply does not respond to wage rates owing to the operation of the backward sloping supply curve. As the wage rates are reasonably high and more than one member of the households go for work, it is possible that the labour household has a leisure preference and hence it offers less number of days for work. This is evident from the fact that 83 per cent of the workers said that they needed at least one day's rest a week and 11 per cent wanted more than one day's rest. As we shall show later, in actuality, they take more than one day's rest.

Closely related to a high wage rate are the various subsidies—both direct and indirect—given to the vulnerable sections by the central and state governments. These subsidies influence labour supply significantly. The public distribution of foodgrains, free education upto higher secondary level, free access to medical care, exemption of the lowest consumers from electricity tariff, IRDP assistance, housing subsidy, special assistance to scheduled caste, scheduled tribe, job reservation for S.C./ S.T. and backward communities in the government, provision of free drinking water etc. not only enhance the real earning of the workers, but also contribute to their high retention price thereby leading to a reduction in the labour supply.

Dynamics of Labour Market Adjustment

Our analysis has shown that while there is a very high demand for labour, the supply has not been elastic enough to respond to the increasing demand. But when the supply and demand were separately analysed, we came across a situation where the total supply of labour exceeded the total demand in the sample villages. At the same time we find from the demand data that there is excess demand for labour. Therefore, a question that arises is: how do we account for this paradox?

One of the reasons for the excess supply of labour in the face of a felt shortage could be statistical. It is possible that a person is unemployed, but he is not available for manual work. While such a person adds to the data on rural unemployment, he does not actually enter the casual labour market as a contestant. Another reason could be that the mismatch between supply and demand could arise from the fact that that our survey covered only a certain percentage of the cultivating and labour households in the sample villages. Therefore, it is possible that the labour supplying and the labour demanding households do not necessarily correspond to each other in a one to one relationship. There could be other reasons also for the mismatch between supply and demand. Market imperfections, information asymmetries, adverse selection in the labour market, operation of the backward slopping supply curve, market fragmentation, increasing transaction and supervision costs etc. are some of those. Therefore, a study of the dynamics of labour market behaviour should necessarily take into account a host of factors encompassing not only the supply and demand for labour but also the perceptions of both the cultivators and labourers.

Consider the demand condition for labour presented in Table 16.9. It shows that the cultivators do not get as much labour as they need during the peak season. Consequently, there exists a gap between the actual employment and the labour requirement. Only the lowest size class is able to satisfy its labour demand fully. The rest of the classes face a situation of labour shortage. There is an overall excess demand for labour to the extent of 14 per cent of the availability. About 37 per cent of the farmers reported that they would have employed more workers than they did, had they been available in adequate number. The observed shortage was more pronounced in the case of female workers. The excess demand was 15.73 per cent for female workers while it was slightly lower at 13.29 per cent for males.

Table 16.9 Distribution of the Average Number of Workers Employed and Actually Wanted by Households during the Peak Week

	No. of workers employed			*No. of workers actually wanted*			*Excess demand for workers*		
	M	F	T	M	F	T	M	F	T
All Holdings	5.34	2.67	8.01	6.05	3.09	9.14	0.71 (13.3)	0.42 (15.7)	1.13 (14.0)

Data for the previous day of the survey show a much larger excess demand for workers (Table 16.10). The average excess demand is as high as 40 per cent. This, of course, is a peak period phenomenon. During the lean season the actual on farm employment is only 19 per cent of the peak period employment. The corresponding percentages for males and females are 21 and 14 respectively.

Table 16.10 Distribution of Hired Labour Wanted and Actually Employed during the Previous Day of the Survey (peak period)

	Average no. of labour employed per household	*Average no. of labour wanted per household*	*Excess demand*
All holdings	1.06	1.49	0.43 (40.6)

To obtain a comprehensive picture, these data may be compared with the data on employment collected from the labour households. As is seen from Table 16.11, the average number of days worked by a worker during the preceding 7 days in the peak period was 3.04. A further disaggregation shows that the average for non-farm work is much higher (3.70) than that for farm work (2.94). During the lean season the average number of days worked in a week were 1.74, 2.65 and 2.01 respectively for farm work, non-farm work and total. If 6 days' work a week could be considered a norm for full employment, it may be seen that the average employment rate during the peak season is only marginally above 50 per cent. It is 49 per cent for farm work and 69 per cent for non-farm work. During the lean season the corresponding percentages were 33.5, 28.3 and 44.2. But for both the seasons, the employment in the non-farm sector far exceeds that in the farm sector.

Table 16.11 Average Number of Days Worked by Labourers during the Preceding 7 Days of the Surveys in the Peak and Lean Seasons

Seasons	*Average number of days worked per week*		
	Farm work	*Non-farm work*	*Total*
Peak season	2.94	3.70	3.04
	(49.0)	(61.7)	(50.7)
Lean season	1.74	2.65	2.01
	(28.3)	(44.2)	(33.5)

Note: Figures in brackets are percentages to full employment.

Thus the data draw our attention to the excess supply of labour viewed from the supply side and the excess demand for labour viewed from the demand side during the peak period. While the farmers complain that there is a labour shortage even during the lean season, the data show that there is considerable unemployment even during the peak period. This paradox necessitates a detailed enquiry into the factors governing supply and demand for labour. In order to have full information about the situation, it is useful to see how the cultivators and the workers perceive the issue. This is important because there can be a gap between what a worker thinks about himself and what the employer thinks about the worker.

A little more than 40 per cent of the cultivators expressed the view that they wanted to employ more workers than they actually did, but could not do so for non-availability of workers. While 26 per cent of the cultivators very specifically said that there was a seasonal labour shortage for agricultural labourers, 16 per cent of them were of the view that the labour shortage was not merely seasonal, it was there for all seasons.

The fact as reported by cultivators that workers do not keep their promise to turn up for work on the appointed date lends sufficient credence to the labour shortage hypothesis. It has been observed that workers very often, under pressure, promise to go to different employers on the same day and obviously they are not able to keep the promise. Nearly 80 per cent of the farmers reported that they usually had such experiences, while 17 per cent of them categorically said that a majority of workers did not keep promise and hence often they were put to very great difficulty. It was found that during the preceding 7 days of the survey, 93 per cent of the cultivators had to suspend operations for at least two days on account of the non-availability of workers. About 6 per cent of the cultivators had to face such a situation for 2-3 days a week. Similarly, 18 per cent of the cultivators said that they could not get female workers in adequate number for specific tasks.

An issue often raised by the cultivators is that workers, while on a task with a particular employer, do not complete the task on a continuous basis. They leave the task in the middle and go and work with other employers at times. In order to bring them back to complete the task, the employers often have to coax and cajole them. As much as 10 per cent of the cultivators had such experience during the reference week. Further, 48 per cent of them told that workers did not work with one farmer alone even when work was available with him on a continuous basis. It is because they do not like to displease other farmers who also call them for work. In the perception of the farmers, what the workers do is that they ration out their limited time to different employers.

As a matter of fact, 19 per cent of the farmers said that they did not get workers in adequate number because they supervised and monitored the work which was not liked by workers generally. Another factor which led, in the opinion of the farmers, to such a situation was the withdrawal of the workers from the labour market for some reason or the other. The withdrawals were attributed by 20 per cent of the farmers to the fact that children of workers started earning and hence the mothers need not work any more. Data show that 14 per cent of them believe that those who have children going to school or college also withdraw from the labour market because parents' involvement in the casual labour market would affect the social status of their children. There is a host of other reasons also that account for female withdrawal from the labour market.

The data obtained from the workers also corroborate this. About 16 per cent of the workers said that their family members had withdrawn from farm work during the preceding five years of the survey. The chief reason for the male withdrawal was ill-health. While 20 per cent of the female workers switched to non-farm work, 10 per cent said that since their husbands earned enough they did not prefer to go for work. For another 10 per cent, they need not work as their children had started earning.

Labour shortage has made recruitment and transaction cost very heavy. Labour recruitment is the most difficult task faced by the farmer. As the survey data show while 40 per cent of the farmers got workers with enormous difficulty, 42 per cent experienced some difficulty. Only 18 per cent reported that they did not experience such difficulties.

Usually the recruitment of workers in a labour market characterised by a high rate of unemployment is quite easy. The farmers would go to the colony of workers and recruit them on the spot for the day's work and the contract continues for the rest of the days in the season. In the sample villages, such a simple recruitment mechanism does not simply exist. The employer has to inform the workers 2-3 days in advance and at the peak of the season, may be a week in advance. Workers do not usually come and offer themselves for work and therefore, 49 per cent of the farmers generally go either to the house of the worker or meet him on the road or the market place to call him for work. The experience of 37 per cent of the farmers is that they have to reserve the workers 2-3 days in advance. While 14 per cent of them say that not only that the workers are to be informed in advance, but they are to be reminded in the morning of the day they are expected to come for work. Unless he pursues this, some other employer who also had contacted them would 'hijack' them away. This part of the transaction cost is reported to be very high. Labour recruitment is felt cumbersome particularly by those who are old and having no young members in the family to run around for the purpose.

All the same, a peculiar tendency observed among workers is that they generally do not go to the farmer's house to seek work. They consider it below their dignity to ask for work. Moreover, a vast majority of the workers said that they need to be given notice for a day or two by the farmers. While 78 per cent wanted one day's notice, 15 per cent wanted two day's. Only 6 per cent of the workers were ready to work for anyone who called them without any notice. What is more, 15 per cent of workers are not able to respond to everyone who calls them. They are regular workers of certain farmers. They go for work on others farms only if they do not have any work with their regular employers. Other workers have such a tight schedule that they are not in a position to keep up the promise always. While discussing the work schedule, 84 per cent of the workers expressed the opinion that they needed at least one day's rest and 6 per cent wanted two days' rest. This supports the recruitment cost argument we have advanced.

The factors discussed above have acted as compelling forces for the farmers to enter into various labour tying arrangements. But it may be noted that such arrangements are clearly different from the type usually discussed in literature relating to agriculture in the eastern part of India. In Kerala, the tying is to ensure the participation of workers in the operations unlike in East India where the workers are bonded through the collusion of land, labour and credit markets. The farmers seem to be offering the labourers different types of incentives. Some of them (42%) offer a few days' wages in advance which will be deducted in easy installments with a view to ensuring continuous availability of workers. Some others (17.8%) give the workers loans with fairly long repayment period and without charging any interest. Almost all cultivators give perquisites to the workers even though these are not part of the wage contract. Casual workers who are employed for a fixed wage rate are often offered the additional incentive of mid-morning and evening tea and sometimes also breakfast. It saves the working time of the labourers.

A significant factor that partly explains the apparent labour shortage is the cultivators' preference for certain workers. Cultivators generally prefer workers whose capabilities are known to them. In the absence of such information, it may not be possible for a farmer to allocate a worker to a task in which he or she has comparative advantage. This is a case of market segmentation and information asymmetries. If the farmer does not have adequate information about the capabilities and the integrity of a worker, he would rather go without employing anyone. This limits the size of the labour market. As much as 61 per cent of the farmers said that they would rather leave their work unfinished, than employing just anyone.

In this context, mention may be made of the fact that workers also have preferences for certain employers and type of work. A first consideration of the workers is that the farmers should not be task masters and should be "well—behaved". Nearly 47 per cent of the workers subscribe to this view. Another 31 per cent prefer to work for those who give them something extra. A stubborn 5 per cent do not work for those who supervise their work. Nearly 45 per cent of the workers do not like to be supervised. Because of this reason, 79 per cent of the workers do not like to work for pure cultivators as they always hang around the farm and are hard task masters. Non-farm work is shown special preference by 34 per cent of the workers because of higher wages, greater flexibility and practically no supervision.

The work ethics possessed by the workers and the perception of the farmers about them are important factors in this context. A good proportion of the farmers (33%) reported that they preferred to employ certain workers because of the regularity they maintained in making themselves available for work. Further, once they are contacted for a work, they stay on till the work is completed and do not leave in the middle. Presumably for this reason, about 22 per cent of the farmers prefer to call as far as possible those workers who live in their immediate neighbourhood. This ensures the regular availability of workers and reduces the transaction cost. While 27 per cent of the farmers said that they preferred workers who are known for their hard work, 13 per cent indicated preference for workers who are decent in their behaviour. All these are based on the information the farmers have about their workers. Such preferences often lead to the non-selection of other workers resulting in what is called adverse selection. In such cases, recruitment does not become costless. Efficient workers need to be paid a premium to attract them to the job. Once the efficient ones obtain a higher wage rate, the tight labour market situation prompts the less efficient also to bargain for the same. The powerful trade union movement plays a catalytic role in this matter.

An issue closely related to transaction cost is supervision cost. As high as 74 per cent of the farmers said that supervision was necessary. If there is no supervision, workers have a tendency to shirk work. The cost of supervising workers is a barrier to the efficient allocation of workers by task and a source of inefficiency. However, workers do not like to be supervised. As far as possible they avoid the employers who closely supervise their work. The workers also prefer to work in their own villages with a view to reducing search and set-up costs. Our data show that 84 per cent of the workers prefer to work in the vicinity of their houses. Those who do not mind working in far off places are either landless or having no family.

On the whole, 40 per cent of the farmers said that there was a clear shortage for workers. They do not conduct certain operation at the optimal time because an adequate number of workers is genuinely unavailable. An important task which often suffers due to labour shortage is harvesting. During the preceding year of the survey, 13 per cent of the farmers had to suffer due to non-harvesting of their crop in time for labour shortage. Harvesting is an operation which cannot wait. Also important is that harvesting is not an individual activity, but a group activity. Therefore, labour shortage is always felt for such operations.

Thus seen from the perception of the workers there is sufficient indirect evidence to show that there is a relative labour shortage in the rural areas for farm work. But only 10 per cent of the workers openly accept this. It is well known that agricultural wage rates are relatively the highest in Kerala. But more than 80 per cent of the workers feel that wage rates are low. Still some workers prefer to work for lower wage rates. The percentages of such workers are 30 during the peak season and 45 during the lean season. But they are not able to offer themselves for lower wages due to trade union and peer group pressure. Nearly 60 per cent of the workers are union members. Thus as the majority does not go for lower wages, the non-members also feel constrained to do so because of peer group pressure. Further, some degree of control over land and squeezing family consumption levels account for the non-supply of labour below the ruling wage rate.

Conclusion

We have noted above an excess demand for labour in the rural sector in Kerala. But this is not fully borne out by the data on labour supply. An analysis, however, of the motives and expectation of both farmers and workers has clearly shown that there is a relative labour shortage in the rural areas, particularly for farm work. We have considered several indicators of increasing tightness of the labour market. Money wages and real wages have risen rapidly. Workers are not generally available at the going wage rate. In other words, workers are simply unwilling to do agricultural work and more particularly paddy cultivation. This is precisely why nearly 19 per cent of the paddy land is kept fallow in the sample villages. The observed shortage is accentuated by labour market segmentation, information asymmetries, unenforceable contracts, and high transaction and supervision costs. A further point that is of contextual significance is that most of the cultivators in the State, while being small holders, are not farmers *per se*. A good number of them has non-agriculture as their main source of income. The fact seems to be that there is no peasant class in Kerala any longer. This has serious implications for Kerala, as capitalist agriculture—the most dynamic element of the Indian agrarian structure—can thrive only under profits and relatively low wages.

[*Financial support provided by the ICSSR for this study is gratefully acknowledged*].

SEVENTEEN

RESOURCE MANAGEMENT FOR SUSTAINABLE DEVELOPMENT OF KERALAM'S* AGRICULTURE

K. N. SHYAMASUNDARAN NAIR

Performance of the Agriculture Sector

After four decades of development effort Keralam's performance on the agriculture front is described in unenviable terms variously as `stagnant', `moribund' etc. Critics are eager to attribute it to yet another failure of Kerala Model of development. The fact remains that the performance is unenviable though not for the reasons attributed.

The contribution of the agriculture sector to the State GDP declined from 35 per cent in the early eighties to 30 per cent in the mid nineties. Surveying the agricultural scenario of this period, we may say that production of foodgrains (primarily rice) declined from 1.3 million to 1.1 million tons bringing down the share of the State from 1.01 to 0.60 per cent of the country and per capita grain production from 52 kg to 35 kg. The self sufficiency in rice declined from 45 to 25 per cent. Similarly, production of tapioca declined from 4.1 to 2.6 million tons. The production of coconut and pepper increased, but largely due to the expansion of area and less due to increase in productivity. The production of coconut increased from 3010 to 5300 million nuts, largely from expansion in area from 0.65 to 0.90 million hectares and to a lesser extent from increase in productivity which rose from 4600 to 5900 nuts per hectare. Similarly, the production of black pepper increased from 30000 to 50000 largely arising from

* Some authors prefer the Malayalam term `Keralam' to the Anglicised word `Kerala', which historically has a wider currency outside the State. —*Editor*

the expansion in area from 1100 to 1900 thousand hectares and to some extent from productivity which increased from 264 to 276 kg. The productivity of rice, tapioca and cashewnut increased mainly due to shrinkage in extent to more productive areas rather than increase in the productivity per unit area. Productivity of rice per hectare increased from 1.6 to 1.9 tons, tapioca from 16.5 to 19.8 tons, cashewnut from 580 to 823 kg. It is only in the case of rubber that the increase in production from 1400 to 4400 thousand tons came from substantial increase in productivity from 590 to 1000 kg and to a lesser extent from area which increased from 2400 to 4400 thousand hectares. Milk production increased from 0.74 to 2.22 million tons as a consequence of a significant increase in productivity from 2.6 to 5.6 kg per of milk per day per animal. Cattle population declined from 3.1 to 2.9 millions heads of cattle. Fish production increased from 0.35 to 0.56 million tons.

The average size of the operational holdings has been steadily declining from 0.57 in early seventies to 0.33 hectares in the early nineties. During the same period the number of holdings increased from 2.8 to 5.4 million, extent of area operated from 1.6 to 1.8 million hectares. Area under cultivation increased from 2.3 to 2.4 million hectares raising the proportion of cultivated area to total area from 59 to 63 per cent. Area under food crops declined from 0.93 to 0.57 while those under non-food crops increased from 1.37 to 1.58 million hectares. Gross cropped area increased marginally only from 2.96 to 3.05 million hectares. Expansion of land for cultivation has reached its limit with the net cultivated area accounting for as much as 63 per cent while forest land is nearly 28 per cent. Fallow land and culturable waste account for 4 per cent, and barren and uncultivated a little over 1 per cent. Non-agricultural use is significant, accounting for nearly 8 per cent of the land.

Agricultural Resources of Keralam

Keralam is relatively rich in resources which are needed for agricultural production. By virtue of the relatively high incidence of solar radiation and precipitation, being located in the tropical region (between 4 and 12 degree north latitude), Keralam falls in one of the regions in the world with high biomass production potential. Endowed with solar radiation for 365 days despite cloudy days during the rainy months, average annual precipitation of 300 cm, 5-6 types of soil, undulating topography alternating with hills and valleys, altitude ranging from below sea level to soaring 2500 m, Keralam produces a variety of crops grown in high rainfall humid tropics and cool subtropics. The relatively high gross income (nearly double the national average) per unit of the land is a partial reflection of the better natural resource endowment of Keralam. Like the diversity and richness in land resources, Keralam is better endowed with water resources also. The State accounts for one twentieth of the water resources against one eightieth of the land surface of India.

In spite of the relative richness in resource endowments and high gross income per unit of the land, the productivity of most of the crops grown in Keralam is lower than many comparably located regions in the world, and even lower than the Indian average. Notwithstanding the substantial direct investment in agricultural development activities which took place during the past four decades (Rs. 800 crores in crop production and Rs. 2200 crores in irrigation in the State sector alone during the past 8 Five Year Plans), the productivity of many crops important to Keralam's economy has not increased substantially. However the gross income from unit net area has been rising. The gross income from land increased by one half from Rs. 13.05 to 19.35 billion, while the net cropped area increased only marginally from 2.18 to 2.25 million hectares, resulting in a rise in gross income from Rs. 6000 to Rs. 8600 per hectare since eighties. This remarkable increase in gross income is likely to have been achieved by bringing about changes in cropping pattern and increasing the plant density per unit area. However such possibilities in all likelihood seem to have reached the limits.

Proven Resource use Potentials

The technological innovations evolved in the research stations located in the State (both of the Kerala Agricultural University and of the ICAR) have demonstrated that the productivity of uplands constituting three quarters of the cultivated land could be increased to two or three folds, and the use of human labour could be doubled. Similarly research has indicated that by adopting new cropping patterns and cultivating the summer fallow with appropriate crops, it should be possible to increase substantially the income and production from paddy lands. These findings have opened up new vistas in maximising the use of basic resources viz. solar radiation, moisture, plant nutrients and human labour by selecting appropriate crops and practices such as multi-storey cropping, and by recycling resources through integrating crops with livestock rearing and fish culture. Current biomass production is estimated at around 5-6 tons per hectare. Raising biomass output to 20-25 tons per hectare is reported to be within the realm of reach by applying new technologies. (Theoretically the dry matter production potential for the tropics is estimated at around 120 tons per hectare). One of the main reasons for the low productivity in many crops is attributed to our inability to profit from the technological opportunities. By saying so the imperative need for a congenial socio-economic context for the application of science and technology to biophysical resources is not lost sight of or belittled. As the context demands naturally the emphasis in this discussion is on the former.

The Strategy in Resource Use

Generally speaking Keralam has surplus human power while land resource is limited. Hence priority has to be given to the evolution of technologies which maximise production and employment from the scarce land resource. Four possibilities can be identified. First, minimise fallow period on lands which are generally put to annual and seasonal crops (the summer fallow on paddy lands for instance). The aim should be to increase the number of cropping days and thereby increase the per day production. Second, increase production through intercropping on lands put to perennial crops (tree crops). (Through multi-storey cropping the utilization of soil, moisture and solar energy could be maximised). Third, promote on farm value addition by utilising the under-utilised human resource by introducing animals and fish in the production process through recycling of resources and thereby augment farm incomes. In order to augment the synergy in resource use and thereby maximise income and employment, the land-plant-human production chain has to be expanded to land-plant-animal-fish-human. Fourth, increase production and employment through the adoption of intensive management practices such as organic manuring, manual weeding, integrated pest control etc.

New Approach to Resource Use and Management

Except for the coastal belt which accounts for not more than one tenth of the land surface, the landscape of Keralam is dissected and undulating with hills and valleys alternating with each other. The degree of undulation of the landscape varies which is reflected in the three generally recognised broad physiographic formations viz. the highlands, the midlands and the coastal plains running south-north parallel to each other. Within each of the physiographic formations, the land form comprises of more than one facet laid out in topo-sequence commencing from the ridge crest, moving downwards through slope of varying degrees, and dropping into valley of differing size which in turn terminate in a drain of small or big dimension. Typically four types of facets viz. the hill top, the upper slope, the lower slope and the valley could be distinguished on a slope continuum. The type of facets distinguished may not always be identified, for instance it may not be possible to distinguish hill tops from the upper slopes on highlands as the land formation is highly dissected and in turn the slopes are steeper and valleys are narrower. Again on the midlands, the hill tops are distinguishable into flat plateaus or gently sloping humps, the slopes are gentle and the valleys are broad.

The micro environments obtaining on each of the land facets vary, sometimes very considerably, as the soil type, the fertility status, the moisture availability and the drainage capability differ. Consequently, the production possibilities in terms of crops and animals which could be raised are dissimilar even on adjoining facets such as a valley and a lower slope. The land use and crop combinations vary largely on account of the variability in moisture availability on each of the land facets at any given point of time. In general, on the valleys (often recognised as paddy lands) where moisture is retained over a longer period of the year and often the drainage status is poor (especially during the rainy months on account of the water accumulation through infiltration and seepage from the adjoining upper facets, over and above the in-situ precipitation), crops such as rice whose water requirements and tolerance towards poorly drained conditions are relatively high, are grown. On the lower slopes (characterised as uplands) where the availability of moisture extends to a shorter period than the valleys (but longer than the upper slopes) and the land is well-drained, crops like coconut and arecanut which require moisture during the dry summer months are grown. On the upper slopes and hill tops where moisture availability is least during the long summer period, crops like rubber and cashewnut which tolerate relatively longer periods of moisture stress are grown. On the highlands the valleys are narrow and hence water accumulation is greater and drainage is poor. Rice is grown on the valleys. On the slopes where the land is well-drained, depending upon the altitude, coffee, cardamom and tea are grown. Therefore the production possibilities are to be assessed on the basis of the moisture availability (length of growing period), soil fertility, drainage capability and other agronomic factors prevailing on the different facets of the slope continuum under each of the agroclimatic configurations.

Despite the fact that each of the facets in a topo-sequence is endowed with distinctive micro environments, they are mutually dependent, complimentary and supplementary, and not competitive being an integral part of the slope continuum. Together with water, the land base constitutes a resource system. Therefore in developing the land resources, the entire slope continuum has to be seen as an integrated system. Consequent to the undulating topography, the moisture availability on different facets at any given point of time varies even within small farmsteads which in turn creates different micro environments enabling to grow a variety of crops. Basically farmers in Keralam have evolved integrated systems of resource management. It is common to find farmers in Keralam raising 7-8 crops (rice from the valleys; coconut, arecanut, banana etc. from the uplands of the lower slopes; and black pepper, rubber, cashewnut, etc. from the upper slopes) on their farms though small in the size range of 0.5-1.0 hectare. In addition, farmers rear different types of animals (cattle to meet the needs for drought power and manure, goats for meat and cash etc.). They choose production activities which are mutually supportive, and foster synergy in resource use. The inherent heterogeneity of the resource base of the farms, and the multiple uses to which they are put, in order to meet the multiple needs (seasonal, annual and perennial crops for food and cash; trees for fodder, fuel and timber; animals for food, drought power and cash; and fish for food and cash) of the family, demonstrate the symbiotic relationship that exist between the various activities and the linkages, backward as well as forward, in resource use. A holistic perception on the resource base spatially identified as watersheds, and an integrated system approach to its management, instead of the currently pursued truncated activity approach, are imperative for the utilisation of the full production potentials and ensuring returns on a sustained basis. That is what precisely the farmers of Keralam have been doing traditionally. What is necessary is to reinforce that system by applying modern technology. Technology packages are to be evolved for the resource system as such and not limited only for utilising the individual facets within the slope continuum as is being practised currently. Technologies evolved on crop basis confine the application to the facets only and not to the system.

The opportunities and possibilities for increasing the productivity of resources vary depending upon the resources endowments or resource configurations characterised as agroclimatic zones. In Keralam 12 distinct agroclimatic zones have been identified. Several more resource configurations could be recognised. Though possible, it has not been attempted in this discussion to catalogue the production possibilities specific to each of the agroclimatic conditions obtaining in the State. But what is argued is the integrated use of land, water and human power for increasing production and income from a systems perspective instead of the currently pursued truncated, disjointed single-pronged activities like cropping, animal production or fish production. Such an approach to resource management is imperative for generating maximum employment opportunities and increasing income from limited land resource. The first step towards identifying the production possibilities in the various agroclimatic conditions is to evaluate the resource base, land, water and human power. Second, taking a holistic view of the resource endowments packages of technology which are feasible, economically viable, socially acceptable and environmentally friendly, would have to be evolved for each of the resource configurations. In order to attain the objective of sustainable resource management, the present approach towards technology generation with focus on the maximisation of output or productivity through a specific or single use of the resource base or activity, has to be reoriented to the evolution of packages suited for the resource system as whole.

The realisation of holistic and integrated development of resources depends upon the synchronisation of four mutually supporting components viz. technology package, technology delivery, access to inputs and services, and community action.

Constraints in Optimising Resources Use

Notwithstanding the conducive biophysical resource endowments (high rainfall, year round sunshine, responsive soil), inheritance of a basically sustainable land use and cropping system, a good headstart (in mid 1950s, the State had the highest land and crop productivity in the country), apparently favourable institutional changes (land reforms, strong grass-root level rural co-operative movement) and high literacy, as agrued in the early part of this discussion Keralam's agricultural development faltered during the quarter century of green revolution when the nation made significant strides in this sector of economic development. Lack of appreciation of some biophysical and socio-economic features unique to Keralam and their implications in the formulation of policies and interventions in technology development, economic support and political initiatives that foster agriculture, has been primarily responsible for the situation to which the State's agriculture has come to pass. Given the mindset, the State relied on many national mainstream policies, strategies and programmes, most of which turned out to be irrelevant in Keralam's context and hence ineffective, and at times even counter-productive to sustain its agriculture.

Heterogeneity of resource base multiply into micro environments which foster crops requiring contrasting agronomic conditions within a small spatial entity. In turn they demand complex management skills. Though small scale in operation, the complex system results in relatively higher returns per unit of land which is not only due to relatively high value crops but also to intensification of land use primarily through intercropping. Even though productivity of crops per unit of land individually is lower, cumulatively the returns per unit of land (net cropped area) are still higher. Also the system helps to even out both production and price risks.

The high rainfall and the undulating topography bring in rigidity in the cropping patterns through limiting the choice within groups and not across the groups which restricts the maneuverability required to tide over the adverse impacts of fluctuations in price or biotic factors like the incidence of diseases and pests. Predominance of perennial crops also renders Keralam's agriculture less amenable to adjustments consistent with the dynamics of the market conditions and vagaries of economic policies, though generates relatively high value per unit of land (whether as monocrops or intercrops). Further, these crops have low labour absorbing potential and less amenable to mechanisation (to increase efficiency and reduce human drudgery).

Given the small size of landholdings, sustainable productivity increases in Keralam's agriculture depend upon the increasing use of labour-intensive technologies (for land scarce countries modernisation of agriculture means increasing income per unit of land which is obtained through the application of labour-intensive technologies, and not through mechanisation). The persisting inequities in land ownership despite 'radical' land reforms which has not succeeded in vesting land with actual tillers as reflected in the skewed distribution of operational holdings, and the work ethics being evolved imbibing the social values of the upper socio-economic groups are inhibiting the absorption of labour in agriculture. The upper socio-economic groups of the community including the upper castes who own bulk of the land, seldom work on the land as is seen in the low participation of the family labour in Keralam's farming compared to that of other States, and the predominance of agricultural labour over cultivators (2:1) in Keralam's labour force. The reluctance generally found among the schooled youth to work on the farm, work physiological reasons rather than psychological and social, even among the lower socio-economic strata is yet another manifestation of the evolving work ethics. Coupled with the growing inflexibility in the labour market due to enfeudatorisation, the adoption of labour-intensive technologies which are at once employment generating and productivity increasing, is restrained. The trend is manifested in the rapid decline in the area under seasonal annual crops (paddy) in contrast to the increase in perennial crops (the much maligned `conversion' of paddy lands).

The obsession of food self-sufficiency, a legacy of the siege syndrome of the Second World War food shortages, despite the dramatic changes in food availability within the country after the green revolution, leads to sinking massive income in low return investments such as irrigation and to sub-optimal use of scarce land and water resources which together result in starving other crops of resources, material, financial and technical, which the State has to find on its own. The phobia of `conversion of paddy lands' which prevents putting the scarce land to more income generating and employment generating activities such as the production of vegetables, banana, etc., is an extension of this obsession. Irrigation as a panacea for increased rice production in a State which receives over 300 cm rainfall annually on the average, is another manifestation of this obsession.

The outcome of all this is that land is valued as an asset and safe investment, rather than as a productive resource for income and employment generation. No wonder this scarce resource will remain under-used in relation to its potentials, a realistic but uncomfortable prognosis.

EIGHTEEN

KERALA'S COASTAL AREA

The Case for a Coastal Zone Management Plan Covering Coastal Land and Water

C. P. GEEVAN

Introduction

The beautiful coast of Kerala is as much a part of the unique dynamics of Kerala's social history as its natural history. The several ports on the coast facilitated commercial and cultural links of a population confined between the idyllic Western Ghats ranges and the Arabian sea. These links extended to almost all the major ancient civilisations in the world. The fortuitous winds blowing over the oceans, in predictable patterns or what came to be known as the 'monsoon', made these maritime links possible. The seasonable change in winds combined with the existence of the Western Ghats determined the macro and micro climate and ecology or the biogeography of a region nestled between geologically young shoreline and a very old land formation.

The coastal plain of Kerala also constitutes a special ecological mosaic. Along most of its considerable length, except in a few southern parts, water for cultivation has been ample and almost exclusively monsoonal. Two crops have been taken from most of the cultivated tracks behind the coastal backwaters. The substantive influence of these ecological conditions on modes of resource use and thereby the social organisation is only to be expected.

It is important not to forget the role of the various ecotypes in shaping the society, while we examine the various aspects of the development on the Kerala Coast. The physiographic setting of Kerala presents a variety of gradients along the narrow strip of land 32 to 133 km wide, between the Western Ghats and nearly 600 km of shoreline. About 320 km of the coast is subjected to a dynamic process of land erosion and accretion. The coastal waters are not only rich in biodiversity but also support the livelihood of the large number of people dependent on the coastal ecosystem, particularly the fishing communities.

Coastal Environmental Concerns

The environmental concerns of the coastal zone in most parts of the world have tended to take a back seat in governmental policy. However, the spate of development activities specific to the coast have highlighted the question of protecting coastal environment. The gamut of development activities on the coast—aquaculture, mechanised fishing, tourism, nuclear power plants, thermal stations, port expansion, etc.—pose varying degrees of threats to the coastal environment. Apart from the immediate question of adverse environmental impacts is the larger issue of operationalising the paradigm of sustainable development[1] in coastal areas. Due to the peculiar features of Kerala, this is a stupendous task, calling creative cooperation of the State, the local bodies, scientific institutions, political parties and non-governmental organisations.

The interaction between different elements like structural processes, denudation, fluvial processes and marine processes plays a vital role in the geomorphic evolution of the coast. The littoral zone is defined as the zone extending from the shoreline to the tidal (usually upto a depth of 100 fathoms). The transport of sediments in this zone is of importance in coastal engineering and estimation of erosion and accretion rates along the shore. Compared to the opened ocean, coastal and estuarine waters undergo rapid changes due to tidal effects and the close interaction with the land. Therefore, the coastal environment presents an extremely dynamic system, demanding significantly different requirements for monitoring the physio-chemical and biotic changes, as well as environmental impacts.

Though the discussion on the CRZ has tended to reduce the coastal ecosystems to a narrow strip of the shore, it is necessary to discard such an administratively delimited view of the coast and define a scientifically more meaningful idea of the coast. As we travel through the marine environment along a depth gradient starting from the deep ocean into oceanic-self-estuarine systems, we find along with that gradient a number of other gradients that determine the functioning of the system.

From a biological perspective, with decreasing depth, the primary producers tend to come closer to benthic consumers. In deeper water the benthic system is dependent on the fallout from the pelagic. In systems where the tides keep water column more or less mixed, the benthos are able to feed on the pelagic production directly. Conversely, in such conditions the pelagic are also able to take advantage of the nutrient regeneration from the sediments.

Bays, estuaries, different types of coastal wetlands such as backwaters and lagoons, river deltas, mudflats, swamps and salt-marshes, and mangrove forests are closely associated with the near-shore coastal waters. These ecosystems are also very rich in biodiversity. The human activities on both landward and seaward regions have direct bearing on the survival of these biota and their fragile habitats. Besides fish, this complex lifescape consists of a large number of associated animal life such as migratory birds, several aquatic fauna, reptiles, amphibians and an astonishing variety of plant life or flora as well. The coastal ecosystem comprising of all these various elements is highly productive.

Several studies indicate that the coastal waters are much more productive than inland marshes or open seas. Standing crops and productivity of aquatic grasses and abundance of macro-and meiobenthic organisms, fish and crustaceans are higher in estuarine waters. In addition, the rich, shallow shore areas and tidal channels are important as nurseries for fish, shrimp and crabs. The young of many species spend their rapid-growth juvenile stage in these areas. A large proportion of estuarine organisms are migratory species, allowing much higher standing crops during periods of seasonally high food availability than could exist with an entirely endemic population.

Man has been part of the coastal system for thousands of years. However, man has become a significant force modifying the coastal region—seaward and landward regions—only recently and is now tampering with both short and long-term natural processes on the coast. The anthropogenic activities now interfere with natural processes at several scales : the geological processes relating to flow of rivers, land-sea interaction, rates of delta formation; sediment transport, alteration of biotic cycle whose periods range from hours and days to years. This is also accompanied by severe over-exploitation of biotic resources. In several cases, the harvests of biotic resources have not only been unsustainable, but have led to catastrophic situations, resulting in total or near total extinction of several fish species that were abundant less than ten years ago.

Coastal Regulation Zone Act

As population in coastal areas increase and the economic activity diversifies, all the impacts on coastal environment are bound to worsen threatening the survival of several species, productivity of the biota, and render fishing an unsustainable proposition. It is, therefore, clear that unless governments and resource users take appropriate action, the degradation of the coastal and marine environment will become uncontrollable and there will be no possibilities for sustainable use of resources from these waters.

These concerns are expressed in the linkage between development in Chapter 17 of UNCED Agenda 21: "Protection of the oceans, all kinds of seas including enclosed and semi-closed seas, coastal areas and the protection, rational use and development of their living resources." It includes a commitment of nations to sustainable development of coastal areas and the marine environment under their jurisdiction. It also enjoins States to 'identify marine ecosystems exhibiting high levels of biodiversity and productivity and other critical habitat areas' and 'provide necessary limitations on use in these areas through, *inter alia,* designation of protected areas'. In particulars, it states that the priority should be accorded, as appropriate, to :

(a) Coral reef ecosystems,
(b) Estuaries,
(c) Temperate and tropical wetlands, including mangroves,
(d) Seagrass beds, and
(e) Other spawning and nursery areas.

The CRZ Act[3] notified by the Ministry of Environment and Forests in 1991 needs to be seen against this background. It declares coastal stretches as CRZ and regulates certain activities within the zone. The provisions of the Act are to be implemented by the coastal States and Union Territories. It also envisages the creation of an appropriate authority at the State/UT level to be responsible for enforcement and enactment of these provisions.

The Act defines the coastal stretches as seas, bays, estuaries, creeks, rivers and backwaters which are influenced by tidal action, in the *landward* side, upto 500m from the high tide line[4] (HTL) and the land between the Low Tide Line (LTL) and HTL or intertidal zone, as the CRZ. It classifies the CRZ into four categories for regulating the development activities. A short description of these categories is given in Table 18.1.

Table 18.1 Categories for Regulating the Development Activities

Category	*Description*
CRZ-I	(a) Ecologically sensitive areas (national/marine parks, sanctuaries, reserve forests, wildlife habitats, mangroves, coral reefs, areas close to breeding and spawning grounds of fish and other marine life, areas of outstanding natural beauty/historical/heritage, areas rich in genetic diversity.) (b) Those falling between HTL and LTL (c) Those areas likely to be inundated due to sea level rise, due to global warming and such other areas as may be declared by the concerned authority (Central/State/UT).
CRZ-II	Areas that are already developed upto and close to the shoreline. For this purpose, "developed area" is that which falls within the municipal limits or in other legally designated urban areas which are already substantially built up and which have been provided with drainage and approach roads and other infrastructure.
CRZ-III	Relatively undisturbed areas, that do not belong to either I or II. This will include coastal zone in rural areas (developed and undeveloped) and also areas within municipal limits or in other legally designated urban areas which are not substantially built up.
CRZ-IV	Coastal stretches in Andaman & Nicobar, Lakshadweep and islands, except those designated as CRZ-I, II, III.

Note: The CRZ Act is with effect from 19/2/91. Therefore all the prohibitions and regulations apply from that date. Any change in land use after 19/2/91 within the CRZ must be in accordance with the provisions of the Act. For example, an area is considered to be "developed" or "substantially built up" or the status of the existence of a road or other infrastructure must be based on the status as on 19/2/91.

The notification specifies activities that are prohibited or regulated in these categories, with the most stringent regulations applying to CRZ-1. The norms for regulation of activities in different categories of the CRZ are given in Appendix. Certain activities are prohibited in it, such as the establishment and expansion of existing industries, manufacture/handling/disposal or hazardous substances, dumping of wastes, land reclamation and embankment building, dumping of industrial wastes, mining of rocks, sand and substrata. Harvesting of ground water within 200 m is also disallowed. Between 200 m and 500 m, only manual withdrawal of ground water for the purposes of drinking, horticulture, agriculture and fisheries is permitted. It is to be noted that, tourist sector, however, has been allowed to tap ground water in the zone with the concurrence of the Central/Sate Ground Water Boards.

The notification permits a large set of activities subject to environmental clearance from the Ministry of Environment and Forests. Water front and foreshore activities, development work relating to needs of expanding defence facilities etc., are possible. The notification is an attempt to *prevent* uncontrolled and environmentally unsound development on the coast. It is an attempt to provide a legal framework for the protection of the coastal environment, in the background of the concerns expressed in the convention of biodiversity.

It is quite evident that the notification is only a preliminary step in this direction and *not* a comprehensive legislation. Its aims are rather limited, confined to regulating certain acts in a narrow, geographically defined, strip of the coast. In particular, it does not recognise the intimate links between aquatic and landward sides of the shoreline.

Its most glaring drawback is the complete absence of a seaward component in the definition of the CRZ. A major drawback of the CRZ Notification is that while its provisions are supposed to apply to 'coastal stretches of seas, bays, estuaries, creeks, rivers and backwaters which are influenced by tidal action' and several other ecologically sensitive area along the coast, the actual protection zone defined by it covers only an extremely narrow strip of the shoreline.

As evident from several discussions on the issue, the regulatory authority proposed to be set up does not make any provision for representation of the stakeholder and the public. There are no provisions for either public hearings or information disclosures. It is thus a continuation of existing environmental protection Acts and does not contain any new progressive elements. This is despite the Panchayati Raj Act and the concept of joint ecological management that is replacing the approach of managing from above.

A careful reading of the Act shows that the communities traditionally dependent on the coast for their livelihood, who in most cases have lived in harmony with the coastal environment, have little to lose by the stringent implementation of the Act. In fact, they stand to gain a lot. The development pressures which threaten their livelihood would be inhibited by the Act. The Act will help to rejuvenate the coastal ecology in several ways. It can lead to substantial improvement in the quality of coastal habitats.

Further, if the State and local authorities are committed to the protection of environment and are not misled by the environmentally and socially irresponsible noises made primarily from the industry (in its broadest sense), there are possibilities of embarking on new forms of development with community participation. Restoration of coastal ecology, such as restoring mangrove vegetation, safeguarding habitats for migratory birds and other animals, could form part of such initiatives. The State governments (Kerala is no exception), unfortunately, have tended to neglect the responsibility to safeguard environment and have been far too responsive to the arguments against enforcing environmental protection Acts.

The CRZ and CZM is not just a matter of zoning and regulating development on the shore, but is one part of a strategy for coastal biodiversity conservation and ecologically balanced sustainable development of the coastal areas. The threat to ecology of coastal waters, affecting not merely the marine biota, but also that of sustaining an important food source for human communities is at the heart of CRZ and CZM.

Kerala Coast: Ominous Developments

Under the physiographic conditions of Kerala, the population density has tended to increase towards the coastal region. Even the unstable coastline has not deterred large human settlements in close proximity to the sea. Out of a total area of 38,863 sq km of Kerala, 3,355 sq km falls in the coastal area supporting a population of 72.72 lakhs. The density of coastal urban population is 4228 per sq km, as compared to the average urban density of 2,097 in the State. The coastal rural population density is 1700, far above the State average rural population density of 603. Considering the large number of people, the high concentration of industries, the existence of small and large ports, and the enormous fishing potential, the question of limiting development or putting in place a regime of regulatory measures for human activities on the coast is bound to be highly contentious. The complexity of these problems is spelt out in the coastal zone management plan prepared by Centre for Earth Science Studies, Trivandrum[5].

The development efforts in Kerala on the coast have repeatedly ignored the ecological importance of the coastal waters and the backwater system. The development activity in and around the Cochin Backwater System (CBS) or the Vembanad Kayal has in it, all the complexities and environmental dilemmas of coastal area development. The construction of the Cochin harbour between 1930-40 and the creation of the Wellington Island signifies the beginning of dramatic changes in CBS. This led to the ascendance of Cochin region as the major industrial and commercial centre of the State. The rapid growth in the region accompanied by very high population growth, housing shortages, haphazard industrial and commercial development along transportation corridor greatly increased the problems of urban development[6]. The severe environmental impacts on the CBS and its aquatic resources due to the pressures of material, infrastructural and spatial needs of industrial development have been noted even in the late 60s and early 70s.[7,8]

The hydraulic changes in the CBS were mainly on account of port extension, large scale land reclamation, construction of dams on the rivers that discharge into the backwaters, diversion of water flows by the construction of spillways such as the one at Thottapally and barriers to estuarine circulated by the construction of salt water barrier at Thannermukkam. The concentration of chemical industry and the intensification of agriculture in Kuttanad region, closely linked to the CBS, have increased the pollution loads in the backwaters (from point and non-point sources). It is to be noted that for a long period there were no pollution control regulations and the untreated effluents including those from heavily polluting industries were being discharged into the backwaters. Even with pollution control regulations, the enforcement and monitoring are far from adequate.

The ecological changes brought about by the construction of the Thaneermukkam Salinity Barrier across the Vembanad Kayal (or the Cochin Backwaters) in Kerala are a constant reminder of the close links between coastal waters and the ecosystem of coastal area. The reclamation of backwater carried out by the Greater Cochin Development Authority further altered the geometry and bathymetry of the backwaters, changing the flow regimes and circulation. Recently ecologists have expressed serious concern regarding the soundness of the grand development plan for islands adjoining the Ernakulam mainland consisting of large scale land reclamation work and construction of several bridges in the backwaters.

The massive project under the Goshree Island Development Authority which entails further alterations, particularly severe changes in the geometry of the backwaters in complete violation of the CRZ, has been criticised on both socio-economic and environmental grounds[9]. The project is to be carried out in three phases for the development of Vypeen and other islands. The first phase will consist of major works such as reclaiming a total of 154 hectares of land from the Cochin backwaters, the construction of four bridges linking the different islands over 13 km by way of roads and the execution of a master plan for tourism development for creating facilities such as parks, golf courses, and the development of Cherai beach as a resort. The second phase envisages reclamation of another 90 hectares from the backwaters. And in the third phase it is proposed to develop 128 hectares around Vallarpadom. Environmentalists have also questioned the validity of the environmental clearance given by the Ministry of Environment and Forests.

The Bakel Project is another grandiose project promoted by the State government as an exclusive beach resort for tourists in North Kerala (Kasargode). The project has not been subjected to any serious environmental review. The project in its present form can be executed only by violating the stipulations of the CRZ. Besides, the developments planned under the project will entail considerable urbanisation close to the coast with serious impacts on the coastal waters. In addition, it will adversely affect the daily lives of the traditional coastal communities significantly. Moreover, the long term economic benefits of the projects are not clear in the absence of any meaningful cost/benefits analysis. EQUATIONS—a Bangalore based NGO—has examined the ramification of the tourism policies of the state and central governments. They have raised several pertinent questions regarding the tourism projects, such as Bakel Project[10] and raised several questions regarding the approach to tourism development.

CRZ, Kerala Government and Community Participation

Given the fact that the Kerala's development experience has thrown up a large environmental constituency, and has resulted in large mobilisation of people under the aegis of 'people's science movements', the elected representatives of the people can be expected to voice some of these concerns. Moreover, a State government with avowed social concerns can be expected to take somewhat balanced view of the environment/development dichtomy and not to take sides in haste on a sensitive issue. That this has not happened may, perhaps, be one of the many ironies of Kerala's development experience, which need further examination by social scientists. Besides this curious quirk of 'real politick', there is also another irony to the CRZ controversy. This has to do with the fact that much of the scenic beauty of Kerala is inseparable from its complex coastal landscape. While the CRZ, in fact, will go a long way in preventing the wanton destruction of this landscape in the name of development, those who oppose it, including the tourism industry,* appear to ignore this link.

The responsibility for enforcement and monitoring of the Environmental Protection Acts is vested with the State government and its declared opposition to the law should be of serious concern to the citizens. It also brings to the fore the need for the independent regulatory authority in enforcing environmental protection laws. It is one thing for the State government to differ with the provisions at the appropriate time and quite another to side with those who want to violate the law! Moreover, the desirable approach in the matter would have been to strictly implement the Act pending a larger debate or public hearings on the issue, allowing for a highly informed debate. In a highly literate State such as Kerala, where these issues are being debated even in small community meetings, such a course would have been very rewarding in improving the proposed legislation.

The approach of Government of Kerala on the CRZ has neither facilitated an informed debate on the issue nor revealed any serious thinking on the part of the State. Most of the objections that are articulated against the Act were well known at the time the Act was being formulated. All States including the Government of Kerala also had ample time to record its views on the matter. The attitude also reveals a closed mind of the State administration to the delicate task of evolving a sound environmental policy framework for the development of the State. The State which is expected to enforce the environmental protection Acts appears to be aggressively opposed to strict enforcement and monitoring of such laws. This attitude also brings home the sad

---

* The successive State govenments in Kerala have tended to accord high priority to tourism industry. However, the kind of tourism promoted on the coast not only ignores the ecology, but also threatens the livelihood of traditional communities living on the coast. Despite political and ideological postures, the approach to tourism of different State governments is marked by a convergence with the views of the tourism industry which is set on a path of cultural and ecological destruction of the coast.

truth that the political parties are yet to take environmental issues seriously and are far from recognising the need to elevate sustainable development paradigm into the realm of political practice.

The demand for dilution of the CRZ and making 'exception' to Kerala or for that matter any State, is not marked by a sound consideration of either economics or ecology of the coastal region. Unfortunately, the CRZ Act, which is a step in the right direction, despite all its shortcomings, and which is in the interest of fishing communities as well as the majority of people living in the coastal areas, is portrayed as 'anti-people'. However, the concerns attributed to 'people' find strange convergence with that of certain industries whose record of socially and environmentally irresponsible conduct is only too well known. In fact, it is precisely the (mis) conduct of certain industries that has given a sense of urgency for the implementation of CRZ.

Joint management of resources is the new approach to ecological management. The concept itself is being refined and operationalised. However, there are many successful cases of joint forest management. The approach could also be applied to the implementation of the CRZ as well as for drawing up sustainable development strategies for the coast. There are 200 coastal panchayats affected by the No-Development Zone (NDZ) under the State Coastal Zone Management Plan. The plan categorises about 68.58 per cent (341.83 sq km) of the total CRZ area of 498.58 sq km under CRZ-III. As has been pointed out in the recent debates widely reported in the press[11], a rehabilitation programme can be effected though the Coastal Zone Development Authority. It is also to be noted that the informed sections of the fishing community have by and large favoured the implementation of the CRZ, even as they recognise its limitations.

The Panchayati Raj institutions in Kerala can seize the opportunity and enlist the participation of communities living on the shore in the sincere implementation of the CRZ and monitoring the compliance. The regulations can be turned into an advantage to improve the quality of both life and environment. The possibilities opened up by the lively decentralised democracy in Kerala provide a rare opportunity for both a participatory regime of CRZ implementation and people's involvement in developing a CZM Action Plan. The memorandum submitted by the KSSP to the Legislative Committee on Environment contains such suggestions.

It may be of some interest to look at the State of California in USA, which has the most stringent environment protection Acts among the different states in the US. The development experience of Kerala has many ingredients in it to permit such a comparison. The community participation in environmental regulation is also rather high in California. In fact there are instances where the local communities in California have enforced rather strict regulations on use of resources such as water. Even in a sector such as energy, rather strict regulations covering both demand and supply side management have been enforced to ensure the compliance with energy conservation policies. The environmental protection laws in India have followed the US model and has several features of the US law, wherein the federal legislation provides the model Act, laying down the bottom line, beyond which regulations cannot be relaxed by the States. The States, however, are, indeed, free to enact stricter laws if they chose to, Kerala with its high densities of population confined in a small geographically well-delimited areas need to look at sustainable development more seriously. Diluting the regulatory regime of CRZ and accelerating the urbanization will lead to rapid increase in the population density in the coastal area besides promoting a highly unsustainable use of the resource base.

Case for a Larger Coastal Management Zone

The CRZ Act has several important shortcomings. As noted earlier, it is primarily regulatory and does not have a proactive focus.[12] It fails to address the concerns of protecting biodiversity of the shoreline and coastal waters. The complex issues arising from the linkages between coastal marine life and the activities in the coastal region are not reflected in the approach to the CRZ and CZM.

Several provisions are nothing more than a declaration of good intentions. The enforcement and regulatory regimes are not spelt out clearly. Just like many other regulations, it lacks teeth and is not equipped enough to chew what it can bite. It is possible in Kerala, than elsewhere, to rectify these lacunae. It is important that public opinion be mobilised for preventing the certain destruction of the coastal ecology in pursuit of short term economic gains. It is also important to note that the CRZ and a well thought out CZM will not seriously impede economic development; it will only ensure that the industry is forced to take its environmental responsiblities seriously as is being increasingly insisted upon by more and more communities.

It can be seen that development activities have an important bearing on coastal waters and aquatic life. There is strong relationship between quality of waters in backwaters and the coastal waters. Changes such as that of flow regimes, salinity mixing patterns and circulation, flushing action, tidal mixing affect biotic elements in the coastal waters. All these are also linked to the question of sustainable yields in the case of fishing. Similarly the barriers to saline circulation in estuarine waters and backwaters will not only affect the natural biota in these waters, but create undesirable ecological conditions upstream of the barrier as is evident in the case of the effects of Thanneermukkam Salt Water Barrier in Vembanad Estuary.

Considering the close relationship between coastal area (landward side) and the coastal marine waters (the seaward side), the Subsidiary Body on Scientific, Technical and Technological Advice, to Convention on Biological Diversity (SBSTTA/CBD) has favoured an approach that integrates marine and coastal area management.[13] The SBSTTA considers such an approach as the framework for addressing impacts of land-based activities on coastal biological diversity. This is possible by minimising or eliminating inputs of pollutants (including persistent organic and radioactive substances, excessive nutrients and sediments), in particular those arising from municipal waste, industrial effluent, deforestation, watershed degradation, mining unsustainable agricultural practices.

Some of the basic principles[14] of Integrated Marine and Coastal Area Management (IMCAM) are given below:

1. The coastal area is a unique resource system which requires special management and planning approaches.

The coastal ecosystem and key coastal habitats, for instance, coral reefs or mangrove forests, are distinctive and extremely productive. The traditional land-based or marine-based forms of management and planning need to be modified to be effective for the coast, at the transition between land and sea.

2. The land and sea uses need to be managed in combination.

The coastal zone needs to account for lowlands, intertidal areas, lagoons and open waters as a single interacting unit that lies between the upland and the open sea. Ecologically, development activity located anywhere near coastal areas has the potential for damage to the coastal water ecosystem. Because of these reasons, the land and sea uses need to be planned in combination. The relationship between the 'dryside' and 'wetside' of the coast or between the terrestrial and marine ecosystems precludes the effective management of a marine or estuarine resource system without concurrent management of adjacent land.

3. Coping with the natural hazards and conservation of natural resources needs to be combined in IMCAM programmes.

The coast is prone to numerous threats, and development on the coast has to account for the existence of such threats. It is now well-recognised by planners that the measures best suited to conserving ecological resources are often not different from those required for conserving economic resources. Maintenance of natural landform is an important component of this approach.

4. An Environment Impact Assessment (EIA) approach must be preferred to other approaches.

The EIA approach implies that likely impacts of activities/projects on the coastal zone need to be taken into account rather than the location of the activity. The SBSTTA, for instance, emphasises the need to carry out EIA of all major coastal and marine development activities with special attention to the conservation of marine and coastal biodiversity, taking into account the *cumulative* impacts.

5. The SBSTTA also emphasises participation of communities in resource management as another important component of the IMCAM.

Combined marine and coastal area management need to be promoted as a participatory process for decision making to prevent, control or mitigate adverse impacts from human activities on the marine and coastal environment and to contribute to the restoration of degraded coastal areas.

Conclusion

There are large knowledge gaps in our understanding of the coastal ecosystems. There is need to fix fishing limits based on a detailed knowledge of the fishery resources and stability of the habitat. The quotas need to be defined for the different kinds of fishing. A detailed inventory of coastal biodiversity is also lacking and the implementation of coastal zone management plans must be complemented by a rapid survey of the biological diversity. Based on these surveys, guidelines need be worked out for the protection of threatened species. This also means that it is necessary to establish habitat requirements, relationships between different communities and understand the migratory patterns in coastal area, estuarine environment and marine waters.

The aim of this chapter has been two-fold: (a) to emphasise the urgent implementation of Coastal Regulation Zone (CRZ) and (b) to articulate a case for a more stringent and comprehensive approach to coastal zone management covering both the coastal land and water. The CZM needs to cover both landward and seaward sides. It is argued that regulating the activities on a narrow strip along the shore is inadequate to protect the coastal and associated ecosystems. The CZM needs to be based more on periodic assessment of environmental impacts than on mere static zoning to regulate development. It must form part of a larger strategy for conservation of biologically and ecologically balanced sustainable development on the coast.

With respect to the Kerala coast, it is argued that:

(a) CRZ, Acts needs to be not only implemented in full but also its scope needs to be extended.
(b) The people of Kerala have more to gain by strengthening the CRZ Act than diluting it.
(c) The possibilities opened up by the lively decentralised democracy in Kerala provide a rare opportunity for both a participatory regime of CRZ implementation and people's involvement, particularly of the coastal communities, in developing a CZM Action Plan.

Kerala's development experience has amply demonstrated that economic gains based on ecological degradation have proved to be unsustainable even in a narrow economic sense. The coastal area and waters are no exception. Ecologically balanced sustainable development on the coast needs to view the coast as little more than just the shore.

APPENDIX

Extracts from the notification S.O. 114 (E) dated 19 February 1991, issued by the Government of India, MEF issued under sections 3(1) and 3(2) of the Environment (Protection) Act, 1986 and rule 5(3)(d) of Environment (Protection) Rules, 1986.

Norms for Regulation of Activities

The development or construction activities in different categories of CRZ areas shall be regulated by the concerned authorities at the State/Union Territory level, in accordance with the following norms.

CRZ-I

No new construction shall be permitted within 500 meters of the High Tide Line. No construction activity, except as listed under 2(xii), will be permitted between the Low Tide Line and High Tide Line.

CRZ-II

(i) Building shall be permitted neither on the seaward side of the existing road (or roads proposed in the approved Coastal Zone Management Plan of the area) nor on seaward side of existing authorised structures. Buildings permitted on the estuaries side of the existing and proposed roads/existing authorised structures shall be subject to the existing local Town and Country Planning Regulations including the existing norms of FSI/FAR.

(ii) The design and construction of buildings shall be consistent with the surrounding landscape and local architectural style.

CRZ-III

(i) The area upto 200 metres forming the High Tide Line is to be earmarked as 'No Development Zone'. No construction shall be permitted within this zone except for repairs of existing density. However, the following uses may be possible in the zone—agriculture, horticulture, gardens, pastures, parks, playfields, forestry and salt manufacture from sea water.

(ii) Development of vacant plots between 200 and 500 meters of High Tide Line in designated areas of CRZ-III with prior approval of Ministry of Environment and Forests (MEF) permitted for construction of hotels/beach resorts for temporary occupation of tourists/visitors subject to the condition as stipulated in the guidelines at Annexure-II (*of the notification*).

(iii) Construction/reconstruction of dwelling units between 200 and 500 meters of the High Tide Line permitted so long it is within the ambit of traditional rights and customary users such as existing fishing villages and goathans. Building permission for such construction/reconstruction will be subject to the conditions that the total number of dwelling units shall not be more than twice the number of existing units; total covered area on all floors shall not exceed 33 per cent of the plot size; the overall height of the construction shall not exceed 9 metres and construction shall not be more than 2 floors (ground floor plus 1st floor).

(iv) Reconstruction/alterations of an existing authorised building permitted subject to (i) to (iii) above.

CRZ - IV

Andaman & Nicobar Islands

(i) No new construction of buildings shall be permitted within 200 meters of the HTL;

(ii) The buildings between 200 and 500 meters from the High Tide Line shall not have more than 2 floors (ground floor and 1st floor), the total covered area on all floors shall not be more than 50 per cent of the plot size and the total height of construction shall not exceed 9 meters;

(iii) The design and construction of buildings shall be consistent with the surrounding landscape and local architectural style;

(iv) Corals and sand from the beaches and coastal water shall not be used for construction and other purpose;

(v) Dredging and underwater blasting in and around coral formations shall not be permitted; and

(vi) However, in some of the islands, coastal stretches may also be classified into categories CRZ-I or III, with the prior approval of Ministry of Environment and Forests and in such designated stretches, the appropriate regulations given for respective categories shall apply.

Lakshadweep and small Islands

(i) For permitting construction of buildings, the distance from the High Tide Line shall be decided depending on the size of the islands. This shall be laid down for each island, in consultation with the experts and with approval of the Ministry of Environment & Forests, keeping in view the land use requirements for specific purposes vis-a-vis local conditions including hydrological aspects, erosion and ecological sensitivity;

(ii) The buildings within 500 metres from the HTL shall not have more than 2 floors (ground floor and 1st floor), the total covered area on all floors shall not be more than 50 per cent of the plot size and the total height of construction shall not exceed 9 meters;

(iii) The design and construction of buildings shall be consistent with the surrounding landscape and local architectural style;

(iv) Corals and sand from the beaches and coastal waters shall not be used for construction and other purpose;

(v) Dredging and underwater blasting in and around coral formations shall not be permitted; and

(vi) However, in some of the islands, coastal stretches may also be classified into categories CRZ-I or II or III, with the prior approval of Ministry of Environment & Forests and in such designated stretches, the appropriate regulations given for respective categories shall apply.

NOTES AND REFERENCES

1. The broad definition for sustainable agricultural and rural development used by FAO goes as : . . . the management and conservation of the natural resource base, and the orientation of technological and institutional change in such a manner as to ensure the attainment and continued satisfaction of human needs for present and future generations. Such sustainable development (in the agricultural, forestry and fishery sectors) concerns land, water, plant and animal genetic resources, is environmentally non-degrading, technically appropriate, economically viable and socially acceptable . . ."
2. Baretta, J. and P. Rurardij (ed.), *Tidal Flat Estuaries: Simultation and Analysis of the Ems Estuary*, Springer-Verlag, Berling, 1988.
3. Notification S.O. 114 (E) dated 19 February 1991, issued by the Government of India, MEF issued under sections 3(1) and 3(2) of the Environment (Protection) Act, 1986 and rule 5(3)(d) of Environment (Protection) Rules, 1986.
4. High Tide Line is the line connecting the highest point to which water has reached during tidal action over several years. The HTL must account for long cycles in tidal pattern which occur with periodicity as large as 19 years. According to the notification, the HTL is the line on the land upto which the highest water line reaches during the spring tide and shall be demarcated uniformly in all parts of the country by the demarcating authority so authorised by the Central Government in Consultation with the Surveyor General of India.

5. *Integrated Environment Study for Coastal Zone Management of Kerala State* (1980), Centre for Earth Science Studies, Trivandrum.
6. Development Plan for Cochin Region, Part I, Basic Plan (1977). Prepared by the Department of Town Planning, Government of Kerala.
7. Shetty, H.P.C. (1965), Observation on the fish and fisheries of the Vembanad backwaters, Kerala in: *Proceedings of National Academy of Science*, India. Section B, vol. XXXV, Part I.
8 Jingran, V.G. Gopalkrishnan (1972), "Multifarious Uses of the Coastal Areas Suitable for Aquaculture Development." Indo-Pacific Fisheries Commission, 15th Session, Wellington, New Zealand, 10-27 October.
9. Seethi, K.M., Destruction of Unique Ecosystem of Kochi Backwaters. *Economic and Political Weekly*, July 22, 1995.
10. Coastal Zones: An Overview (1995), EQUATIONS (Equitable Tourism Options), Bangalore.
11. Curbs on Coastal Dwellers (1996), *The Hindu* (Cochin), November 15.
12. Chandrika Sharma (1996), Coastal Area Management in South Asia (Background paper), The South Asian Workshop and Symposium on Fisheries and Coastal Area Management: Institutional, Legal and Policy Dimensions, Chennai, September 26-October 1.
13. SBSTTA/2/14, Report to the Conference of Parties (1996), United Nations Environment Programme, Convention on Biological Diversity, Second Meeting, Montreal, September 2-6.
14. Integrated Management of Coastal Zones, FAO Fisheries Technical Paper 327; pp. 48-66, Clark J.R., *Fifteen Principles of Integrated Management of Coastal Zones.*

NINETEEN

CHANGING AGRARIAN RELATIONS AND PRACTICES

A Study with Special Reference to Kuttanad

T. A. THOMAS & JOSEPH A. THOMAS

The agrarian scenario in Kuttanad/Kerala is in a flux. In the last agricultural season, Mr. Antony, a small farmer of Kuttanad, has to wait for twenty nine days to get his paddy sheaves threshed. All through the days and nights, he was seen lying on a make-shift coat on the outer bunds of the *Padashekhram* (Paddy block). Prior to that he was seen frantically searching for labourers for harvesting. But he could secure the service of only eight persons for harvesting his eight acres of paddy field, on the first day.

In the beginning of the season, preparation of the paddy field was delayed for more than a fortnight even when he offered Rs. 75 per day for male agricultural labourers. He is thinking of leasing out his land and take some other occupation or migrate to hilly regions or even to leave his paddy field fallow, as some others have done.

Chinna, a female agricultural labourer, exhibited quite a different scenario. She came back a number of days after working in the field at about 10 O'clock in the morning. She could get work only for two hours on those days.

These episodes are symptomatic of the changes taking place in the agricultural sector of Kerala. The rural labour market there has been exhibiting a 'curious phenomenon' of shortage of labour for agricultural operations amidst persistent rise in wages and rising levels of unemployment. This has taken place in the absence of an increase in productivity and declining area under cultivation, especially of food crops. This has induced a gradual withdrawal of farm labourers and farmers and some changes in agricultural practices. This decline in farm activities, however, has been accompanied by some increase in non-farm employment accelerating the withdrawal of farm labourers and farmers.

This curious phenomenon has implications for labour market behaviour, mobilisation of labour for economic and political ends and for the food security of the State in the background of globalisation and liberalisation.

This overall scenerio is examined in the background of paddy cultivation in Kuttanad, one of the two major rice bowls of Kerala, where the above-mentioned changes have been most conspicuous. More specifically this chapter endeavours to examine:

1. The dynamics of rural labour market in Kuttanad;
2. Reactions of the cultivators to various market signals like shortage of labour, higher wages unrelated to farm income, declining profitability etc.; and
3. The socio-economic implications of such changes.

The Region

Kuttanad region, spread over 76 low land villages in Alappuzha, Kottayam and Pathanamthitta districts, has a total area of 1438 sq km, of which 627.9 sq km was raised from 1 to 2 metres above water level for human habitation and cultivation. It is one of the most densely populated areas in the State. Literacy rate was one of the highest in the State: 97.23 per cent compared to 93.8 per cent for the Alappuzha district in 1991 (Census, 1991). The topographical and agronomic features of Kuttanad are unique. Known as the Holland of Kerala, this is mainly a water-logged region. The paddy fields lie between 0.6 to 2.2 metres below mean sea level and are submerged under water during the greater part of the year (Kuttanad Enquiry Commission (1971)). It is widely believed that the whole of Kuttanad region was reclaimed over a long period of time from Vembanad lake (Pillai and Paniker (1965)). The total area reclaimed was about 3.5 lakh acres consisting of about 300 blocks of *Padashekharams'* (Alexander (1973)).

The reclamation process involved two operations, bunding and draining. Since the depth of the water ranges from 10 to 20 feet, it was a highly labour-intensive venture. Further, breaches of bunds were frequent; nevertheless farming was profitable since the yield was high and the labour cost remained at a low level because of the institutional arrangement prevailing at that time, namely, the existence of attached labour system (Pillai, *et al* (1965)).

Agricultural Operations

Agricultural activity, principally work in paddy field, formed 70 per cent of all economic activities: 57.18 per cent as labourers and 11.13 per cent as cultivators in 1991. Agricultural operation generally starts from October-November to March-April (Punja Cultivation). A second crop is rarely attempted because of the monsoon flood during July-August.

In view of the trends in wages, production, agrarian relations and practices, the analysis is done for two periods: first from 1960-61 to 1972-73 and second from the mid-seventies onwards.

Agricultural Practices, Trade Union Movements and Trends in Wages, Productivity and Farm Prices during the First Period

Agricultural Practices

After the harvest, paddy fields are ploughed and lime strewn. Then the fields are allowed to be flooded. It remains so for about five to six months. During September-October, next agricultural season starts. Outer bunds are strengthened and the fields are dewatered. This is followed by a second round of ploughing. Fields are prepared and sprouted seeds sown. In certain areas transplanting is done. It is a labour-intensive operation and considered to be more productive.

In between sowing and harvesting, a number of operations are undertaken. These include further transplanting in sparse areas, removal of weeds and application of fertilisers each for 3 to 4 times and spraying of pesticides and insecticides, the frequency of which depends on the incidence of various plant diseases. Of all the activities, harvesting and related activities are the most labour-intensive. This involves harvesting of sheaves to transporting them to threshing place, threshing, product sharing, winnowing, drying of paddy and hay and finally transporting them to storehouse.

Wages for harvesting and related activities are paid in kind —a system of product sharing. Harvesting attracted a large number of migrant workers from various places around Kuttanad.

Determination of Wage Rate and Workers Movements

Among the various factors, operations of trade unions are considered to be the most important in the determination of wage rate of agricultural labourers in Kuttanad (Alexender (1973); Jose (1979); Krishnan (1991) and Pushpangadan (1992)).

The growth and expansion of the movement is closely linked to the growth of the Communist Party in Kerala. The capitalist nature of the paddy cultivation involving large scale dependence on labour and climatic conditions was taken advantage of by trade unions right from the beginning of the movement (Alexander (1973)).

'Agricultural workers' movement in Kuttanad began functioning against the background of spiralling prices of foodgrains during 1940s. The early phase of it saw the building up of trade unions against official reprisals and stiff resistance from the farmers. The second phase witnessed a remarkable growth of the unions. By 1974, there were 14 registered trade unions in Kuttanad which together formed 40 per cent of the total number of agricultural labourers' organisations in the State. In Alappuzha district alone, the membership in the Marxists party-led union of agricultural labourers increased from 17,900 in 1971 to 35,000 in 1973 (Jose (1977)).

Trade Union activities brought higher wages and better working conditions for agricultural workers of Kuttanad than prevailing elsewhere. They managed to retain the system of 'kind payment' and succeeded in prohibiting the mechanisation of agricultural operations and in the setting up of the Industrial Relations Committee (IRC).

The wage payments in kind for harvesting operations were raised from less than 10 per cent of the produce to nearly 13.9 per cent in 1951 and after 1970, it was again enhanced to 15.6 per cent through organised bargaining. Further, the duration of the ordinary operations which was 8 to 10 hours a day in the fifties was brought down to 5 hours in *kayal* and 6 hours in other areas (Jose (1979)). Unionisation brought other benefits also. By the Land Reform (Amendment) Act, 1969 all hutment dwellers have become owners of their homesteads. As a consequence the fear of eviction was no longer a nightmare and the attached labour system (Paniyals) disappeared.

Wage, Productivity and Paddy Price Movements from 1960 to 1973-74

It was observed that trade union movements and labour militancy resulted in higher wage rate in Kuttanad than the wage rate prevailing elsewhere. When money wage for males in other areas increased from Rs. 1.69 in 1960-61 to Rs. 4.90 in 1971-72, the corresponding increase in Kuttanad was from Rs. 1.95 to Rs. 6.00 (Jose (1979)).

During the same period, the product sharing rate as noted earlier increased from 13.9 per cent to 15.6 per cent of the produce. Along with this, productivity and farm price of paddy, the other two determinants of product wage, were also increasing. Productivity per hectare since 1960-61 had been increasing consistently. It increased by 72 per cent from 2610 kg per hectare in 1960-61 to 4994 in 1971-72. Along with this, farm price of paddy also increased by 150 per cent from Rs. 3.01 per standard *para* in 1960-61 to Rs. 7.54 in 1971-72 (Jose (1979)). For the farmers, paddy cultivation was profitable despite higher wages.

Higher wage rates and better working conditions attracted migrant labourers in large numbers from the neighbouring areas, to the paddy field. The prevalence of high rates of unemployment among the traditional non-agricultural labourers, who considered agricultural labour *infra-dig*, once upon a time compelled them to join the ranks of agricultural labourers. This has been described as a sort of proletarianisation.

In the sixties there had been a phenomenal increase in the size of the labour force. In Kuttanad taluk alone the increase in agricultural labourers was more than three times the increase in population. During the decade 1960-61 to 1970-71 in the Alappuzha district when population increased by 17 per cent, the agricultural labour force increased by 57 per cent during the same decade, between 1960-61 to 1970-71. The agricultural labour market was thus getting saturated and overcrowded (Jose (1979)). This tendency engendered competition among the workers themselves, on the one hand and struggle between the labourers and cultivators for employing the labourers, on the other. There were many instances of violence erupting in different parts of the region. Strikes, hartals, police interferences and even lathi charges were not unusual in those days.

In those days farmers used to go to the local labour union officers to inform them of the date of harvesting and also request them to limit the number of workers for the operation (Kannan (1988)). Between 1965-71 few agricultural operations in Kuttanad especially harvesting took place without the massive presence of police (Tharamanglam (1981)). In spite of that, overcrowding of labourers was such that they could harvest only for 45 minutes or one and half hours rather than for days elsewhere (Mencher (1980)). There were many instances of harvesting done in moonlit dawns, in collusion with the loyal local workers for minimising the loss due to overcrowding and for showing patronage to their loyal workers.

Wage, Productivity and Farm Price of Paddy since the Mid-seventies

It was observed that the agrarian scenario of Kuttanad exhibited signs of all-round prosperity in the sixties. However, since the mid-seventies, a reversal of this trend has been observed. There has been stagnation or even decline in productivity and price of paddy. In sum, the terms of trade had gone against the paddy cultivators. This is well exemplified in Table 19.1.

Table 19.1 Trends in Wage Rate (Male), Farm Price, Yield and Farm Income in Kuttanad from 1960-61 to 1986-87

Year	*Male Wage Rate*	*Index of Money Wage*	*Farm Price of Paddy per Quintal*	*Index of Farm Price*	*Yield Per Hectare in kg*	*Index of Yield*	*Farm Income (in Rs.)*	*Index of Farm Income*
(1)	*(2)*	*(3)*	*(4)*	*(5)*	*(6)*	*(7)*	*(8)*	*(9)*
1960-61	1.75	100	41.80	100	2610	100	1090.98	100
1960-65	2.75	157	94.44	226	1796	69	1696.14	155.46
1967-68	5.00	286	156.00	373	2861	110	4463.16	409.09
1968-69	5.00	286	114.72	418	2470	94.6	2833.58	259.72
1970-71	6.00	343	97.00	232	4494	153	4359.18	399.56
1971-72	6.00	343	104.00	249	4494	172	4673.76	428.40
1972-73	6.40	366	124.00	297	3034	172	3762.16	344.84
1973-74	7.20	411	—	—	—	—	—	—
1975-76	9.00	514	158.00	378	3049	117	4817.42	441.56
1980-81	11.13	636	179.78	430	3268	125	5849.72	536.18
1985-86	26.08	1490	242.25	576	4211	161	10190.62	934.07
1986-87	28.36	1620	248.24	593	4227	162	10443.10	961.00

Source: Jose, A.V. (1979)
Government of Kerala (1988), *Statistics for planning* and Goverment of Kerala, *Economic Review*, various issues.
Note: The farm price of paddy upto 1972-73 is available in terms of standard para and thereafter available in terms of Quintals. The price in terms of para has been converted into Quintal using the conversion rate, 1 para of paddy = 7.2 kg.

Trends in money wage rate, (male agricultural labour), farm price, farm productivity, farm income and their indices are given in Table 19.1. It shows that during the period from 1975-76 to 1986-87 money wage rate for males increased by 215 per cent, farm price of paddy and farm productivity increased only by about 57 per cent and 38 per cent respectively. The combined effect of the latter two factors was reflected in an increase in farm income by 116.7 per cent. Thus, during this period when money wage rate increased by 215 per cent, farm income increased only by about 116.7 per cent, against an increase in wage rate by 243 per cent and the increase in farm income by 328 per cent, during the period between 1960-61 to 1971-72.

During this period, the ratio of product share also remained unchanged. It meant that the money equivalent of product share did not increase at the same pace as the increase in the wage rate for other operations. This seems to have induced, *inter alia*, a withdrawal of male labourers from harvesting operations which formed the major part of their employment.

Thus, since the mid-seventies, two major developments have taken place in the agricultural sector in Kuttanad. First, money wage rate increased persistently. The increase in money wage was unrelated to farm income and was mainly due to trade unions, demand for higher wages to compensate for the increase in the cost of living and to maintain parity with the wage rate of unskilled construction workers. The wage rate of the latter, it has been argued, became the 'prime mover' of wages elsewhere (Krishnan (1991)). The position of trend setting in wages which was once enjoyed by the agricultural wages in Kuttanad, is now taken by others.

Second, paddy cultivation turned unprofitable due to the factors mentioned earlier. Besides, the farm price of paddy became rather stable at lower levels consequent upon the universalisation of the public distribution system in 1977. This made a large number of farmer-households migrate to less labour-intensive and more profitable investments in plantation and other commercial crops. Those who did not, reacted to high wage rate by employing labour-saving devices in cultivation. We have tried to capture the reactions and responses of farmers and labourers to this situation on the basis of a village level study of 318 households of the region conducted during 1993-94. They are reported below.

Farmer's Reactions

(i) In early times, transplanting was a common practice in the region. It consists of growing the seeds in dry land for 25-35 days and then transplanting them to the paddy field. Farmers have dispensed with transplanting. Dispensing with transplanting saves the use of 18-25 units of labour per acre.

(ii) Reflooding is resorted to as a substitute for weeding out operations which were earlier done either manually or by using weedicides. Reflooding is more ecology-friendly. In this operation water is pumped out and the field is allowed to dry for some days to let the weeds grow. Then field is reflooded to such a level for a duration of about two weeks that weeds are made to decay. This practice has considerably reduced the input of the female labour by about 25-30 days per acre. It may be noted that the cost of dewatering is fully borne by the government.

(iii) Very few farmers store paddy to take advantage of the likely price increase in the future. They sell the produce immediately after harvest for two reasons: first, the cost of drying, transporting and storing is greater than the likely gain and second, the holding capacity of the farmers is weak. Often, they sell in distress.

(iv) Further, the extensive use of tractors, tillers and winnowing machines reduced the use of labour. Construction of permanent granite walls around and on the canals inside the '*padashekharam*' has obviated the annual maintenance and renovation, also considerably reduced the demand for farm labour.

Besides the changing factors, decline in the area under paddy has contributed to a decrease in the number of days of employment. In Kuttanad taluk alone the area under paddy declined from 33,579 hectares in 1975-76 to 30,977 in 1986-87, and the corresponding figures for the State were 8,81,460 and 6,63,800 hectare respectively. (Government of Kerala (1988)). In terms of percentage, for the State the decline was from 29.11 per cent of the total cropped area to 23.65 per cent during the period. This decline would have been sharper but for the physical difficulty to convert paddy field in Kuttanad to alternate crops due to its unique features.

We may now examine how the labourers respond to this situation.

Reactions of Labourers

Many factors contributed to the occupational diversification of the paddy field workers of the region. They may be considered as 'push' and 'pull' factors (Mridul Eapen (1994)). These factors need special investigation since their effects determine the availability of labour in the paddy field.

In earlier days paddy obtained from harvesting served as an insurance against the rainy days. However, since 1977, the availability of rice and wheat through public distribution system as well as in the open market has improved.

The period also witnessed the emergence of a new peasantry from among the agricultural labourers. Large farmers who were not able to withstand the unfavourable terms of trade, militancy of the labourers, the general antipathy of the times against large holders, frequent incidence of various plant diseases and crop failures, began to dispose of or lease out their paddy field. The low price of paddy field in relation to garden lands and the erstwhile stigma attached to agricultural labour encouraged them to withdraw from the casual labour status and to become 'proud owners' of paddy land.

Table 19.2 shows that about 44 per cent of the agricultural labour households had marginal holdings of paddy fields. Of which 56 per cent became holders during 1980s. It is seen that there were 13 households (about 4% of the sample households) had leased in paddy fields. This phenomenon is referred to as new tenancy system in Kuttanad (Harikumar (1991)). Obviously, they were not profit motivated. Unlike the 'gentlemen farmers' of the erstwhile days, the new peasants work in their family farm, but seldom work as casual labourers outside. To that extent, the supply of the labour is reduced.

Improvement in the educational level of agricultural labourers, especially the youth, seems to have bred an aversion towards the work in muddy paddy field which was a low caste occupation in the past. Table 19.3 shows that of the total agricultural labourers only about 3.6 per cent had educational qualification of matriculation.

Meanwhile, many agricultural labourers turned to non-agricultural sector attracted by the higher wage and larger employment opportunities emanating from construction boom, casued by the large inflow of foreign remittances, filling of paddy field, raising of dry land for roads and house plots and the public programmes undertaken through various schemes since the mid-seventies.

Further the development of transport and communication facilities and improved educational status facilitated the mobility of agricultural labour from Kuttanad to other occupations and regions. It is seen that about 10 per cent of the sample population had migrated to other regions (3% to other countries and 7% within the country). Of the migrants, 49 per cent belonged to the erstwhile agricultural households. Correspondingly, there has been a reduction in the supply of agricultural labourers.

Table 19.2 Classification of the Agricultural Labour Households according to the Size of the Paddy Field Owned (in Acres)

Size of Paddy Field	*No. of Households*	*Percentage of Total*
00	49	55.68
0-0.5	16	18.18
0.5-1.00	12	13.63
1.00-1.50	8	9.01
1.5+	3	3.50
Total	88	100.00

Source: Survey Data.

Table 19.3 Educational Status of the Agricultural Labourers

Educational Status	*Male*	*Female*	*Total*	*Percentage of Total*
Below Standard V	36	38	74	41.32
Standard V-VII	31	30	61	34.08
Standard VII-IX	24	14	38	21.23
S.S.L.C. and above	5	1	6	3.36
Total	96	83	179	100

Source: Survey Data.

In a span of about two decades, the number of agricultural labourers in Kuttanad declined from about 1.5 lacs in the mid-seventies to about 90,000 in 1993. Consequently in the place of 10 persons required to harvest an acre, only two or three workers are available (Malayala Manorama (1994)).

Farmers' response to labour shortage and the changing socio-economic realities was discussed earlier. However, harvesting is a unique operation. Labour required for it could not be reduced, since it continues to be labour-intensive and non-mechanised (except winnowing). 76.4 per cent of the sample cultivators reported shortage of labour in harvesting operations. The real life situation of Antony reported in the beginning unfolds the dramatic change.

While farmers in olden days had to report to the police station and party offices for limiting the number of harvesters, these days they go to the hutments of agricultural labourers to invite them for harvesting. Many of them have to wait for 20-25 days in *kalam* (threshing place) to get their paddy sheaves threshed out. Such delay results in considerable loss of grain.

The institution of hoisting red flag and sirens announcing the beginning and the end of the work is no longer seen and heard in the paddy field of Kuttanad region. Eruption of violence, jathas and bandhs leading to the interventions of police are things of the past.

Farmers still stick to this avocation because of the non-diversifiable and non-reclaimable character of the paddy field. For many, cultivation is done in distress. Reduced profitability and decline in the area under cultivation has resulted in a considerable decline in the production of rice, the staple food of Keralites. The growing requirement of rice is mainly met by import from other States. This poses a serious threat to the food security of the State specially in the background of liberalisation and globalisation (Krishnaji (1994)). It may be noted that rice production in the State has declined from about 14 lakh tonnes in the 70s to about 10 lakhs tonnes in 1994-95 (Government of Kerala (1995) *Economic Review*).

This changed agrarian scenario has engendered the casualisation and marketisation of labour. The multiple occupational status has considerably eroded the militancy of labour and labour organisations. In consequence the possibility of political mobilisation of labour is also at stake.

REFERENCES

Alexander, K.C. (1973), 'Emerging Farmer Labour Relations in Kuttanad', *Economic and Political Weekly*, August 25.

Census of India (1961), vol. 7, Kerala II - B(1) 1971, 1981 and 1991.

Government of Kerala (1971), Report of Kuttanad Enquiry Commission.

—— (1988), *Statistics for Planning*, Department of Economics and Statics, Thiruvananthapuram.

—— *Economic Review*, Various Issues, State Planning Board Thiruvananthapuram.

Harikumar, S. (1991), "Informal Leasing in Kerala: A Study of Kuttanad"; *Indian Journal for Agricultural Economics*, vol. XLVI, no. 3, July-September.

Jose, A.V. (1977), "Origin of Trade Unionism Among Agricultural Labourers in Kerala," *Social Scientist*, vol., no. 12, July.

Jose, A.V. (1979), *"Trade Union Movements Among Agricultural Labourers in Kerala : The Case of Kuttanad Region"*, Working paper No. 93, Centre for Development Studies, Thiruvananthapuram.

Kannan, K.P. (1988), *Of Rural Proletarian Struggles: Mobilisation and Organisation of Rural Workers in South West India*, Oxford University Press, New Delhi.

Krishnaji, N. (1994), "Food Security", *Invited Paper for International Congress on Kerala Studies*, Abstracts vol. 1, August 27-29.

Krishnan, T.N. (1991), "Wages, Employment and Output in Interrelated Labour Markets, in an Agrarian Economy : A Study of Kerala", *Economic and Political Weekly*, vol. XXVI, no. 26, June 29.

Malayala Manorma Daily, April 13, 1994, Kottayma.

Mencher, J.P. (1980), "The Lessons and Non-Lessons of Kerala : Agricultural Labourers and Poverty", *Economical Political Weekly*, vol 15, no. 41, Special Number, October.

Mridul Eapen (1994), "Rural Non-Agricultural Employment in Kerala: Some Emerging Tendencies", *Economic and Political Weekly*, May 21.

Paniker, P.G.K. T.N. Krishnan and N. Krishnaji (1977), *Population Growth and Agricultural Development: A Case Study of Kerala,* Centre for Development Studies, Thiruvananthapuram.

Pillai, V.R. and P.G.K. Panikar (1965), *Land Reclamation in Kerala*; Asia Publishing House, Bombay.

Pushpangadan, K. (1992), "Wage Determination in a Casual Labour Market: The Case of Paddy Field Labour in Kerala," Centre for Development Studies, Thiruvananthapuram, Working Paper no. 241.

Tharamangalam, Joseph (1981), *Agarian Class Conflict: The Political Mobilisation of Agricultural Labourers in Kuttanad*, University of Britain, Columbia, Press, Vancouver and London.

TWENTY

KERALA'S AGRICULTURE

Trends and Prospects

V. SANTHAKUMAR & K. NARAYANAN NAIR

Introduction

The purpose of this chapter is to highlight the recent trends in Kerala's agriculture, the factors shaping its performance and in the light of that, to comment on the prospects of growth in the near future.[1] We will begin with a brief analysis of the trends in agriculture. This will be followed by a discussion of the factors shaping agricultural performance, the logic of State intervention and the prospects for growth.

Trends in Agriculture

The debate in the late eighties and the early nineties was centred around the issue whether agricultural production is declining or going through cyclical changes (Narayana (1990); Kannan and Pushpangadan (1990)). Recent indications (Lelithabhai; (1993)) and strengthened by a recent updating show that the agricultural income of the State has been growing since the mid-eighties. Agricultural income of the State (at 1980-81 prices) has grown at a rate of 4.3 per cent per annum from 1983-84 to 1994-95[2]. Compared to this, in the period between mid-seventies to mid-eighties it showed a near stagnation. This revival of growth in agriculture was mainly due to the increase in yield and the shift in cropping pattern to higher-valued crops.

However, there exist wide disparities among different crops. The production of food crops (paddy and tapioca) has declined, mainly due to the decrease in area of cultivation. Area under, and production of, rice has continued to decline at an annual rate of 3.79 per cent and 4.3 per cent respectively, from 1983 to 1995. Area under tapioca cultivation has declined at the rate of 5.55 per cent while its production has declined at the rate of 3.8 per cent. There has been a steady increase in the area (@ 2.84%) and production (@ 5.58%) of coconut. Area under rubber has increased at the rate of 4.2 per cent, yield at 5.5 per cent , and the output at 10.62 per cent. Pepper production has increased at 8.28 per cent due to the increase in the area of cultivation (@ 5.73%) and yield (@ 2.28%). The area, production and the yield rate of banana and other plantains have grown notably during the period. Area under arecanut has increased in north Kerala and it has declined in southern parts of the State. In spite of the reduction in area under cashew, its production has increased due to an increase in the yield rate. Crops grown mostly in highlands (like cardamom, tea, coffee) have undergone a more or less decline (or stangnation) in area and an increase in yield rates. The production of milk, meat and eggs has undergone sustained growth. Milk production has increased at the compound rate of 5.7 per cent from 1983-1993 while egg production has increased by 2.8 per cent. A similar trend is visible in the case of meat production.

Though this would give a picture of an upswing in agricultural production, micro-level studies indicate that the use of inputs and productivity are much below the potentials for a number of crops.[3] This is especially so in the case of paddy, coconut and associated homestead crops. Though there has been an expansion of coconut cultivation, the level of input use (as reflected in the use of irrigation and fertilizers) is far below the recommended one. Similar tendencies are visible for a number of other crops except rubber.

Underlying Factors

Relative prices of crops and profitability have been considered as the main factors that induced changes in the cropping pattern (George and Mukherjee (1986)); Kannan and Pushpangadan (1990)). This was found to be the reason behind the conversion of paddy fields into coconut and tapioca area into rubber cultivation. Low level of income instability has also induced shift towards rubber. The changes in area under different crops are generally in conformity with profitability, except in the case of a few crops like coconut (Kannan and Pushpangadan (1990)). The expansion of domestic demand has contributed to the increase in milk production in the State (George and Nair (1990)).

The increase in the wage rates of agricultural labour has adversely affected the profitability of crops. Whether the increase in the wage rates is due to the opportunity cost or due to the restrictions in labour mobility, is an unanswered question. However, it is a fact that expansion of construction and other activities has driven the wage rates to its present level. The influence of non-agricultural income on agricultural work requiring supervision has not been properly studied in the context of Kerala's agriculture. The expectation of a high income from non-agricultural work (which may not materialize at all) and corresponding investments in human capital discourages people to invest in agriculture. Some evidences show that in areas where rubber can be grown, people opt for this crop irrespective of the sources of their main income.[4] However in the case of coconut, the use of inputs including irrigation seems to be influenced by the dependence of farmers on agriculture. This may have larger implications since part-time farmers dominate coconut cultivation.[5]

Another factor that shaped Kerala's agriculture is the size distribution of the landholdings. The creation of new houses driven by the population increase and the division of joint families led to the emergence of a large number of small homesteads in areas which were previously unused for habitation like hill slope and wet lands. Most of such homesteads sustain coconut. These landholdings cover 30 to 40 per cent of the total agricultural land of mid-land and coastal villages. Such holdings may not make the necessary investment for land improvement or irrigation. This may be the reason for the continuation of low-input cultivation, in spite of the increase in area under coconut. Those who have large holdings have gone for rubber cultivation in areas where such cultivation is possible or prevalent. However such conversion is not prevalent in other areas (mainly in coastal belts and north Kerala). In such areas, even larger holdings continue to sustain coconut and other homestead crops. Whether such large coconut farms have higher productivity or these farms too are at a low level of production like the small ones is not clear.

Since fragmentation of landholdings has depressed agricultural production, attempts have been made for its consolidation. This was initially thought necessary for achieving the economy of scale. However there were perceptional and physical blocks against such consolidation. The group farming—group action in agronomic practices and in the purchase and arrangement of inputs—was effective only for the distribution of subsidies (Jacob (1996)). This may be due to the fact that the group action in paddy cultivation in Kerala does not provide additional benefits compared to the efforts required for such action.

Lease market can be taken as an alternative mechanism for consolidation. However such leasing out is not commonly taking place for paddy cultivation. This may be due to the fact that paddy cultivation does not generate adequate rents to induce absentee farmers to try this opportunity. Because of the particular nature of homesteads (closeness to house, perennial trees, etc.), the homestead plots may not be available for a lease market. Since land prices in Kerala are determined less by the potential agricultural income and more by the demand for housing (or by speculation), a lease market capable of providing 'normal' rents may not be able to attract these lands given the perceptions of uncertainty and risk associated with leasing in the State. However leasing phenomenon is widely observable in the case of highly profitable and short-term crops like pineapple (Vernon (1996)).

On the role of modern technology, its utilization pattern is different for different crops. By and large, the adoption of green revolution package for paddy is fairly slow. In the case of coconut, the technological change in enhancing production has been far from satisfactory. Cultivators prefer traditional varieties of seedlings over the hybrid ones. The level of irrigation has not gone up significantly. The efforts to find out some remedies for the (in) famous wilt disease have not been successful. However in the case of rubber, adoption of high-yielding varieties and use of fertilizers are high. In milk production, there is high level of adoption of technology as evident from the increase in the number of cross-bred cows. In general, the efforts to provide technology, extension and other input services by the government and other agencies and the associated information increased the options available in front of the people in agriculture.

On the impact of irrigation in Kerala, studies suggest that the projects did not succeed in bringing additional area under cultivation or in increasing cropping intensity (Narayana and Nair (1983)). There were also several failures in the provision of irrigation. These include the exclusive orientation to paddy cultivation, failure in the provision of water during summer, the inordinate delay and the cost-escalation of projects and the failures in the implementation of on-farm management programme. Even if these failures were corrected, it is doubtful whether the large surface irrigation projects can create significant impact in raising agricultural productivity in Kerala (Santhakumar *et al.* (1995)).

Increased allocation for irrigation did not influence the cropping pattern in Kerala. However, at the micro-level, the projects implemented in Palakkad and Thrissur districts enhanced the area under double crop. The canal water from the projects in Thrissur district is being used for irrigating banana and coconut to some extent. However canal irrigation is not a reliable source, because of the erratic supply during summer. This made the farmers to seek other sources of irrigation. Coconut farmers, especially those of north Kerala, have increasingly used ground water for irrigating coconut and other homestead crops. Local collective or market-based mechanisms have emerged to 'produce' and distribute water resources in such places where individual systems are unaffordable (Jacob (1996)). The efficient functioning of some of the local collectives, in the background of the general failure of the Government-initiated local action, points to the basic requirements for the collective action. The main factors for the success may be the 'felt need' of the participating beneficiaries. In such regions, farmers are not averse to buying water to meet their water demand. However the improper legal definition of rights over water resources might help such 'water merchants' to increase production to such an extent as to affect the use of water by others.

Another factor which shaped Kerala's agriculture is the agro-climatic features. These features determine the crop-set that can be grown in a zone and in a particular landholding. The rainfall pattern and topography impose severe restrictions on the absorption of modern technology in rice (Santhakumar and Rajagopalan (1996)). Water control in paddy fields is extremely difficult, and the benefit of irrigation is extremely low. On the other hand, the topography is not amenable for converting all the wet lands. The high cost of conversion might have influenced the decision to continue paddy cultivation in some areas, in spite of its falling profitability. The agro-climatic factors are conducive for growing a number of crops like, pepper and cardamom, in Kerala and such advantage is not there in several other states. Thus wherever possible 'ecologically and economically', the cultivation of these crops takes place in the State. Thus the agro-climatic features have determined the crop-set in particular areas, from which farmers have chosen the particular cropping patterns. The presumption that the influence of agro-climatic parameters can be reduced through irrigation and water control was unrealistic. The successful routes in Kerala's agriculture are the ones in which the State has comparative ecological advantages.

To sum up, the discussion of the factors that shaped the present status of Kerala's agriculture, the price factors and profitability (determined by the national and international market), the changes in the landholding pattern and the agro-climatic factors in the State have influenced the cropping pattern and the input levels. Market intervention strategies, provision of irrigation, and the institutional mechanisms promoted for the consolidation of landholdings by the Government have not made any significant impact in orienting the path of Kerala's agriculture to its present state. This warrants an explanation of the logic of Government intervention in Kerala's agriculture.

Logic of State Intervention

The agricultural development strategies of the State have been guided for a long time by the two motives, i.e., food security and ensuring higher employment for agricultural labourers. In fact promoting paddy cultivation was found to serve these two purposes. There was a high emphasis, on paddy production in the investments under the Five-year Plans in the State (Santhakumar and Rajagopalan (1996)). Such an investment strategy was appropriate within the national framework for allocating resources. Within the national allocation, there were more resources and incentives for crops like paddy.

In addition to the emphasis on paddy, all the programmes for agricultural development were crop-specific in the State. These were implemented all over Kerala, without any regard for the location-specificities. Moreover, the promotion effort of one crop might affect the expansion of another production system. For example, the expansion of rubber has implications on the fodder availability and has negatively affected the livestock management. Thus the promotion strategies were not based on an assessment of the capability of the physical resources (i.e., land and water) in each region.

Government initially did not have much information on the limitations that agro-climatic features impose on agriculture, especially on the efforts to increase paddy productivity in Kerala. It also underestimated the market-responsiveness of the farmers or overestimated its own capacity to manipulate market forces/ price factors or to change the attitude of the individual farmers.

Kerala's agriculture has evolved within the overall development process of the State's economy in particular and the national economy in general. For the sake of convenience, one can say that Kerala economy stands on the income from the export of agricultural commodities and manpower to the national and international market, and using this income for purchasing food and consumer items produced outside the State and for financing a large social welfare system in Kerala. The concerns on sustainability and educated unemployment make policy makers to advocate several changes in this unstable equilibrium. One of the popular notions is the following: increase production of those agricultural commodities within the State so as to reduce the consumption bill of Kerala. Several questions remain unanswered in this process. Whether such diversion in production will reduce the agricultural income from exchange in national and international market to the State? Is it not better for the State to concentrate on production of those crops for which the State has comparative advantages though they are not directly consumable? Whether people will be ready to invest in consumption-based agricultural production, given their orientation and acquired human capital, suitable to work in the industrial and service sector at the state, national and international levels? Will the uncertainties in the international and national labour market, encourage the people to plough back their resources to a consumption-based agriculture, given the present status of the globalized production? Does the continued existence of large social welfare state and its employment potential with associated rigidities, itself distort the allocation of land, labour, educational and financial resources by the individuals in Kerala? If it is so, has this (distorted) allocation kept the State's agricultural production far below its potential levels with the present technology and market?

Future Scenario

The same factors which shaped Kerala's agriculture also militate against its future development. Regarding the future of different crops, paddy cultivation may continue without a further drastic reduction in the area of cultivation.[6] In the case of coconut, area increase may decline and the scope for technology-driven increase in yield rate seems to be limited in the near future. Major investments for irrigating coconut may not take place. The market for coconut may continue to face uncertain fluctuations, due to the import of substitutes, competition from other Indian states and the bio-technological revolution in the production of edible oils. Expansion of rubber will also decline and future increases in yield rate may not be drastic. However, the demand for rubber in the national market may continue to increase and the price may not show any falling trend in the near future. However, the gap between international and national price will come down and the restrictions of import may not sustain. Even then, price levels may not go down since the cost of production in other major rubber-growing countries is higher. Rubber may continue to be a major income earner for the State in the near future.

On the general tendencies, the small holders may continue with traditional varieties and low use of external inputs. Those who have an economic size of landholding may orient production to the market and may use input close to the recommended levels. Lease market might emerge for profitable short-term crops. New institutional mechanisms may emerge to produce and distribute water. These may warrant the intervention of Government, mainly for defining the rights over water. However the investment in agriculture depends to a great extent on the non-agricultural opportunities available to the members of the farm family. This is especially so for those crops requiring a substantial supervisory effort.

The ongoing efforts to institute decentralized planning and governance have some potentials. However, the existing institutional framework appears to prevent any radical change in the allocation of resources and power to make decentralized planning and governance effective. This is visible in the mushrooming of State level programmes for supporting the production of different crops, the continuation of the stress on unproductive major projects within irrigation, and in the procedural delays (which are seemingly never-ending) in the devolution of power to the local bodies. Local level assessment of resources and the use of this information by the local government can help the location-specific and resource-based planning of agriculture.

NOTES

1. This paper is part of a project to consolidate research on Kerala's agriculture.
2. Growth rates are calulated as follows:

   Specification: Yt = Yo + (1+r)t:

Linear transformation: Ln (Yt) = Ln (Yo) + t* Ln (1+r)

Linear regression with Ln (Yt) as dependent variable and t as independent variable. The X coefficient is taken as equal to Ln (1+r) and is used for calculating r, the growth rate.

3. For example, see the study of Kalliasseri Panchayat, given in Lelithabhai (1993).
4. Evidences from a survey carried out in three mid-land panchayats of Thiruvanathapuram District by V. Santhakumar.
5. For example, in a coconut dominant area like Kalliasseri, only 14.81 per cent of the population earn their major income from agriculture (Lelithabhai, 1993).
6. This is indicated by the decrease in reduction rate of area under paddy cultivation during the period 1989 to 1995. If area was getting reduced at a rate of 5.12 per cent from 1983 to 1989, the rate has come down to 2.64 per cent during 1989-95.

REFERENCES

George, P.S. and C. Mukerjee (1986), 'Rice Economy in Kerala: A Disaggregate Analysis of Performance', Working Paper No, 213, CDS, Trivandrum.

—— and K.N. Nair (1991), Livestock Economy of Kerala', Trivandrum, Center for Development Studies.

Jacob, J. (1996), 'Group Action in Land Management: A Case Study of Group Farming of Paddy in Kerala', Unpublished project report, CDS, Trivandrum.

—— (1996), 'Institutional Interventions in Water Management: A Micro-level Study of Organisation of Irrigation in Kerala', Unpublished project report, CDS, Trivandrum.

Kannan, K.P. and K. Pushpangadan (1990), 'Dossecting Agricultural Stagnation in Kerala: An Analysis Across Crops, Seasons and Regions', Working Paper No, 238, CDS, Trivandrum.

Lelithabhai, K.N. (1993), 'Constraints to Productivity Growth in Kerala Agriculture: A Micro-Level Study', Unpublished M.Phil. Thesis, Jawaharlal Nehru University, New Delhi.

Narayana, D. and K.N. Nair (1983), 'Linking Irrigation with Development: The Kerala Experience', *Economic and Political Weekly*, vol. 8, nos. 45&46, pp. 1935-39.

—— (1990), 'Agricultural Economy of Kerala in the Post-seventies: Stagnation or Cycles?', Working Paper No. 235, CDS, Trivandrum.

—— *et al.* (1991), 'Coconut Development in Kerala: Ex-post Evaluation', Trivandrum, Centre for Development Studies.

Santhakumar V. and R. Rajagopalan, and S. Ambirajan (1993), 'Planning Kerala's Irrigation Projects: Technological Prejudice and Politics of Hope', *Economic and Political Weekly*, vol. 30, no. 12, pp. A30-A38.

—— (1996), Green Revolution in Kerala: A Discourse on Technology and Nature', *South-Aisa Bulletin.*

Vernon, R. (1996), 'Market-Oriented Pineapple Cultivation, Environment and Development in Kerala', Unpublished project report, CDS, Trivandrum.

TWENTY-ONE

FOOD SECURITY AND PDS IN KERALA

Form and Scope for Reform

M. H. SURYANARAYANA

Introduction

Kerala has received considerable appreciation and acclaim for its achievements in different aspects of human development through deliberate public policy in spite of its low levels of per capita state domestic product.[1] One such policy is that relating to public distribution system (PDS) which has been instrumental in ensuring physical access to foodgrains in Kerala. Access matters because Kerala is a food deficit State with its domestic production meeting less than one third of the foodgrain requirement. During the pre-Independence era, the deficit was met through imports from outside. Food policy of the Government of India (GOI) during the post-Independence years laid emphasis on meeting the foodgrain requirements of the food-deficit regions like Kerala. The first three Five Year Plans, with their strategies oriented towards classical growth models, re-emphasised this approach.[2] PDS was conceived to be major instrument of such a strategy.[3]

Till the early sixties, the PDS was relatively unimportant in Kerala. It accounted for only 13 per cent of the cereals consumed in the State. The PDS evolved in its present form only after 1964 and now covers virtually the entire population. There is a two-tier system of PDS in Kerala today. At the first level, public distribution of foodgrains procured from the Centre through the Food Corporation of Indian (FCI) is handled by the Department of Civil Supplies of the Government of Kerala (GOK). This is supplemented, at the second level, by the Kerala State Civil Supplies

Corporation set up in 1974, which procures rice, wheat products, sugar, pulses, vegetables etc. from the open market and distributes through a network of 'Maveli stores'[4]. As per the GOK assessment, such state-wide coverage of public distribution of essential commodities has benefited the under-privileged sections of society and has reduced the impact of poverty (GOK (1994b)); p.3).

Now, there is a need for an evaluation of the PDS in Kerala in the current reform era which lays emphasis on achieving food security at minimum budgetary cost to the government. Food security refers to both economic and physical access to food, that is, having the necessary purchasing power to buy and physical availability of an adequate amount of foodgrains to ensure an active and healthy life. PDS is one important instrument which has improved food security for a significant section of the population in India. However, the Government of India has been considering reform options for the PDS to contain the mounting food subsidy incurred on it, which exceeds even the budget deficit of the government (Suryanarayana (1995d)). To achieve macro-economic stability, reining government budget deficit by pruning the PDS size and improving its effectiveness by targeting it only to the deserving poor is found imperative. This is because a large part of the food subsidy is not justifiable due to leakages to the non-poor, that is, PDS benefits accruing to the non-poor across income groups and due to urban-bias, that is, PDS favouring the richer urban sector disproportionately more than the rural sector.

The present chapter is concerned with the Center-supported PDS, which has ensured physical access to food to all the households in Kerala, and the scope for its reform during the structural adjustment programme. Kerala is one important State where the question of 'urban bias in PDS' is irrelevant. With one of the highest per capita PDS deliveries in the country, there is a general belief that Kerala provides scope for targeting and redistribution to the poor subject to some nutritional norms, but little scope for reducing government outlay on this account. When it comes to actual reform, it raises many questions, both political and economic. How far would it be possible to target the PDS in Kerala? If possible, how to ensure physical access to foodgrain to the non-poor in a chronically acute food-deficit State? What would be their implications for buffer-stock operations and the Centre-State responsibilities in this respect?

The chapter attempts to address some of these issues with a statistical profile of the PDS in Kerala, examine the scope for reform and its implications for the broader question of food security. The chapter is organised as follows. Section 2 provides a profile of the problem of food insecurity in Kerala. Section 3 examines the trends in the PDS off-take. The cereal consumption, and change in the levels of calorie intake in Kerala between a few select years. Section 4 examines the importance of the PDS in both rural and urban sectors and sectoral bias, if any, in Kerala. Section 6 examines the distribution of PDS benefits across quartile groups of households and looks for evidence of inequity based on the National Sample Survey (NSS) data. Having examined the spread of PDS based on State-wise aggregates, the chapter takes up the crucial issue of scope for reform and its relevance by examining (a) the PDS as it operates in Kerala today in Section 7 and (b) the available data across districts from the Kerala Government statistics in Section 8. The final section is in the nature of a conclusion.

Food Security in Kerala: A Profile

Kerala has a per capita state domestic product less than the national average; at current prices, it was Rs 3843 per annum as against the all-India average of Rs. 5015 in 1990-91 (Government of Kerala (1993)); p. 333). In 1991, 73.61 per cent of the Kerala population was rural (GOK (1993)). Estimates for 1987-88 show that annual average per capita consumer expenditures at current all-Indian prices were higher in rural (Rs. 173.64) and urban Kerala (Rs. 251.49) than the corresponding all-India estimates (Rs. 158.10 and 249.93 respectively). Inequalities, as measured by Lorenz ratios, in consumer expenditure distribution for the same year were also higher in rural (32.2%) and urban Kerala (38.7%) than those in the corresponding national counterparts (29.80 and 35.30% respectively) (Suryanarayana (1996a)). Consistent with this picture, incidence of poverty was either the same or higher in rural (44.02%) and urban Kerala (44.47%) as against the national average of 44.88 and 35.52% respectively (Minhas *et al* (1991)); p. 1976). These parameters capture an important aspect of food security, that is, economic access to food and the message that they convey is not at all optimistic.

Nor is Kerala in a comfortable position with respect to the other most important aspect of food security, that is, physical access to food. Kerala is a food-deficit State. Per capita foodgrain production is one of the lowest in Kerala; it was only 38.38 kg per annum against the national average of 175.20 kg in 1987-88. This is largely because the cropping pattern is weighted in favour of commercial crops with the proportion of cropped area under food crops being only 19.54 per cent and that under rice being 18.53 per cent in 1990-91 (GOK (1993)).[5] Rice is the major staple; but its annual per capita production was only 37.34 kg in 1990-91 (GOK (1993)).[6] This works out to a per capita daily availability of only 102.30 gm which is less than the Indian Council of Medical Research (ICMR) consumption norm of 370 gm per capita per day.

Then how does Kerala manage to deal with food insecurity? How does it ensure economic and physical access to foodgrains? How far has it succeeded in its efforts and policies? What are the relevant issues and their implications for the reform programme? The following sections examine some of these issues relating to the physical access aspect.[7]

PDS and Food Security in Kerala : Trends

One major instrument through which the GOK has ensured physical access of foodgrains is the PDS. In 1991, Kerala lifted 16.71 lakh tonnes of rice and 3.33 lakh tonnes of wheat for the public distribution system from the central pool (GOK (1993)) which together, in per capita terms, worked out to 68.83 kgs per annum, that is, 188.58 gm per capita per day. The PDS evolved in the present form mainly after October 1964 with the imposition of stringent restriction on inter-state movement of foodgrain on private trade account.[8] Today it is governed by the Kerala Rationing Order, 1966 which became effective from July 1, 1966. The present section examines the spread of the PDS in Kerala and its role in ensuring food security in the face of declining foodgrain, particularly rice, production in the State. Tables 21.1 and 21.2 bring out the growing importance of the PDS in Kerala. Over time average per capita cereals delivered under the PDS has increased. It has also got stablised as reflected in the reduced range and variance in annual per capita offtake. Today per capita PDS offtake of cereals in Kerala is the highest in the country.

What strikes one most about food security during the post-Independence period for India as whole is the decline in cereal consumption (Suryanarayana (1996a)). This seems to have been due to a variety of reasons like increased average cost of cereals resulting from declining coarse cereal availability and progressive market dependence of the poor caused by increasing landlessness and changing consumer preferences. This must cause concern since cereals account for more than 85 per cent of the calorie intake of the average Indian diet. In Kerala too, per capita cereal consumption in both rural and urban areas declined between 1961-62 and 1973-74. This decline, however, was compensated to some extent by the increase in tapioca production and consumption. With inadequate cereal supplies, and high prices of rice relative to that of tapioca, people made up for cereal shortfalls by increased tapioca consumption. As a result, between 1961 and 1971 tapioca production increased from 16.8 to 46.2 lakh tonnes (GOK (1995)); p. 11). The picture has changed since the mid-1970s particularly in rural Kerala. With the larger availability of PDS rice, decline in the relative price of rice and increases in income (hence, negative income effect since tapioca is an inferior substitute), consumption and production of tapioca showed a steady decline.[9] Tapioca production declined from 46.2 lakh tonnes in 1971 to 40.6 lakh tonnes in 1981, 28.0 lakh tonnes in 1990-91 and 26.0 lakh tonnes in 1993-94 (GOK (1995)); p. 11). Kerala is the only State in India where rural and urban per capita cereal consumptions have increased since the mid-1970s; this is in contrast to the all-India picture (see Suryanarayana (1995b)). PDS seems to have played a major role in ensuring food, particularly cereals, security to the population of Kerala.[10] Within the rural sector, the

Table 21.1 Per Capita PDS Offtake of Cereals: Kerala

Year	*1973*	*1974*	*1975*	*1976*	*1977*	*1978*	*1979*	*1980*	*1981*	*1982*	*1983*	*1984*	*1985*	*1986*	*1987*	*1988*	*1989*
Per capita cereals per annum (kg)	46	46	46	51	61	39	27	37	46	49	59	58	59	67	66	66	52

Source: Geetha and Suryanarayana (1993).

Table 21.2 Period-wise Average Per Capita PDS Offtake: Kerala (kg, per annum)

	Mean	*Variance*	*Minimum*	*Maximum*
Period 1: 1973-'79	45	113	27	61
Period 11: 1980-'84	50	82	37	59
Period 111: 1985-'89	62	38	52	67
Total: 1973-'89	51	125	27	67

Source: Geetha and Suranarayana (1993).

Table 21.3 PDS per Poor under Hypothetical Perfect Targeting Scenario: Kerala (kg per annum)

1973	*1974*	*1977*	*1978*	*1983*	*1987*	*1988*
71	75	107	68	124	149	149

Source: Geetha and Suryanarayana (1993).

increases in cereal consumption have been progressive; the poorest decile groups have enjoyed higher increases in cereal consumption than the richer decile groups. A similar picture holds for urban Kerala where the bottom three decile groups experienced an increase in cereal consumption (Tables 21.4 and 21.5). This could be due to improvements in (i) economic access with the substantial inward remittances by the Kerala emigrants from the Gulf[11] and (ii) physical access with more or less sustained improvements in the PDS deliveries (Table 21.2).

Consistent with the decline in cereal consumption till the early 70s and a recovery and increase thereafter, available estimates show a decline in calorie intake in rural Kerala between 1961-62 and 1973-74 and an increase between 1973-74 and 1983.[12] A similar picture is not found for urban Kerala. Even though cereal consumption has increased in Kerala, it is less than the ICMR norm. About 80 per cent of both rural and urban population in Kerala have a calorie intake of less than 2,400 units (Table 21.7).[13] This is further confirmed by the National Nutrition Monitoring Bureau's survey in 1988-90 which shows that intake of cereals and millet is less than the recommended level by about 20 per cent, that of pulses is less by 55 per cent, that of green leafy vegetables less by 77.5 per cent and milk by about 42 per cent. The survey results show that intake of calcium and vitamin C are adequate. However, intake is inadequate: of iron (less than the recommended level by 8%), vitamin A (less by 60%), thiamine and riboflavin (GOK (1996)); p. 179). As Frank and Chasin (1989) point out the nutritional outcome based measures like anthropometric indicators, however, convey a much better picture about Kerala than the nutritional intake measures. This could be partly due to better and efficient utilisation of the limited food made possible by the available better health facilities and care (see Vaidyanathan (1985)).[14] There is a need for a detailed verification of these issues. From the perspective of the present chapter, we may examine how far the PDS has been able to improve food and nutrition security in Kerala by verifying its effective spread between sectors and across income groups. These two issues are examined in the following two sections.

Table 21.4 Monthly Per Capita Cereal Consumption (kg) by Decile Groups: Kerala Rural

Decile Group / Year	0-10 Rice	0-10 Wheat	0-10 Others	0-10 Total	10-20 Rice	10-20 Wheat	10-20 Others	10-20 Total	20-30 Rice	20-30 Wheat	20-30 Others	20-30 Total
1961-62	5.15	0.00	0.01	5.16	5.95	0.01	0.01	5.97	7.00	0.00	0.00	7.00
	(99.74)	(0.08)	(0.18)	(100.00)	(99.69)	(0.16)	(0.16)	(100.00)	(99.94)	(0.03)	(0.03)	(100.00)
1972-73	3.62	0.41	0.01	4.05	4.81	0.43	0.01	5.25	5.53	0.50	0.03	6.06
	(89.50)	(10.15)	(0.34)	(100.00)	(91.49)	(8.24)	(0.27)	(100.00)	(91.13)	(8.29)	(0.57)	(100.00)
1973-74	3.53	0.31	0.05	3.89	4.93	0.26	0.04	5.22	5.38	0.28	0.01	5.67
	(90.62)	(8.08)	(1.30)	(100.00)	(94.33)	(4.98)	(0.69)	(100.00)	(94.95)	(4.94)	(0.12)	(100.00)
1977-78	4.66	0.04	0.01	4.70	6.25	0.06	0.01	6.33	7.22	0.09	0.02	7.33
	(99.05)	(0.75)	(0.20)	(100.00)	(98.77)	(1.02)	(0.20)	(100.00)	(98.51)	(1.22)	(0.27)	(100.00)
1983	6.31	2.18	0.02	8.51	7.60	3.09	0.03	10.72	8.04	4.08	0.03	12.16
	(74.12)	(25.63)	(0.25)	(100.00)	(70.92)	(28.81)	(0.28)	(100.00)	(66.17)	(33.56)	(0.27)	(100.00)
1986-87	6.84	0.30	0.02	7.16	8.27	0.43	0.01	8.71	8.66	0.43	0.05	9.14
	(95.52)	(4.14)	(0.34)	(100.00)	(94.93)	(4.93)	(0.14)	(100.00)	(94.75)	(4.70)	(0.55)	(100.00)
1987-88	6.74	0.21	0.02	6.97	8.42	0.23	0.03	8.68	8.79	0.40	0.04	9.23
	(96.67)	(3.01)	(0.32)	(100.00)	(96.99)	(2.69)	(0.32)	(100.00)	(95.22)	(4.39)	(0.40)	(100.00)
1993-94	6.80	0.35	0.00	7.15	8.30	0.58	0.00	8.88	8.62	0.60	0.00	9.22
	(95.10)	(4.90)		(100.00)	(93.47)	(6.53)		(100.00)	(93.49)	(6.51)		(100.00)
Percentage increase in 1993-94 over that in 1961-62	31.98	6.78	(-)0.19	38.57	39.36	9.55	(-)0.17	48.74	23.14	8.57	0.00	31.71

(Contd.)

Table 21.4 (Contd.)

Decile Group Year	Rice	Wheat	30-40 Others	Total	Rice	Wheat	40-50 Others	Total	Rice	Wheat	50-60 Others	Total
1961-62	8.50	0.17	0.02	8.69	9.20	0.05	0.00	9.26	9.83	0.07	0.02	9.92
	(97.84)	(1.97)	(0.19)	(100.00)	(99.39)	(0.58)	(0.02)	(100.00)	(99.06)	(0.75)	(0.19)	(100.00)
1972-73	6.20	0.48	0.07	6.75	6.58	0.48	0.07	7.13	7.39	0.55	0.04	7.98
	(91.91)	(7.09)	(1.00)	(100.00)	(92.26)	(6.70)	(1.05)	(100.00)	(92.61)	(6.89)	(0.50)	(100.00)
1973-74	6.05	0.28	0.02	6.35	6.62	0.24	0.02	6.89	7.33	0.29	0.09	7.71
	(95.28)	(4.41)	(0.31)	(100.00)	(96.19)	(3.52)	(3.52)	(100.00)	(95.07)	(3.76)	(1.17)	(100.00)
1977-78	7.54	0.09	0.02	7.65	8.39	0.12	0.03	8.53	8.92	0.26	0.07	9.25
	(98.50)	(1.24)	(0.26)	(100.00)	(98.28)	(1.37)	(0.35)	(100.00)	(96.43)	(2.81)	(0.76)	(100.00)
1983	8.45	5.33	0.04	13.82	9.04	5.90	0.03	14.97	9.40	6.10	0.05	15.55
	(61.19)	(38.53)	(0.29)	(100.00)	(60.39)	(39.41)	(0.20)	(100.00)	(960.45)	(39.23)	(0.32)	(100.00)
1986-87	9.23	0.48	0.10	9.81	9.76	0.55	0.14	10.45	9.54	0.72	0.11	10.37
	(94.11)	(4.86)	1.04)	(100.00)	(93.36)	(5.39)	(1.34)	(100.00)	(92.00)	(6.94)	(1.06)	(100.00)
1987-88	9.22	0.49	0.03	9.74	9.60	0.49	0.04	10.14	9.74	0.63	0.06	10.43
	(94.68)	(5.01)	(0.31)	(100.00)	(94.71)	(4.86)	(0.42)	(100.00)	(93.48)	(6.04)	(0.58)	(100.00)
1993-94	9.16	0.57	0.00	9.73	9.32	0.65	0.00	9.97	9.29	0.82	0.00	10.11
	(94.14)	(5.86)	(100.00)	(93.48)	(93.48)	(6.52)	—	(100.00)	(91.99)	(8.11)	—	(100.00)
Percentage increase in 1993-94 over that in 1961-62	7.50	4.60	(-)0.23	11.97	1.30	6.48	0.00	7.78	(-)5.44	7.56	(-)0.20	1.92

Note: Figures in parentheses are percentage shares in total cereal consumption.
Source: Various NSS reports.

Table 21.5 Monthly Per Capita Cereal Consumption (kg) by Decile Groups: Kerala Urban

Decile Group	0-10				10-20				20-30			
Year	*Rice*	*Wheat*	*Others*	*Total*	*Rice*	*Wheat*	*Others*	*Total*	*Rice*	*Wheat*	*Others*	*Total*
1961-62	4.48	0.03	0.02	4.53	5.80	0.04	0.03	5.87	7.27	0.01	0.00	7.28
	(98.90)	(0.61)	(0.49)	(100.00)	(98.88)	(0.62)	(0.50)	(100.00)	(99.84)	(0.14)	(0.02)	(100.00)
1972-73	3.64	0.61	0.03	4.27	5.08	0.65	0.03	5.75	5.88	0.67	0.03	6.57
	(85.18)	(14.22)	(0.61)	(100.00)	(88.33)	(11.23)	(0.44)	(100.00)	(89.43)	(10.12)	(0.45)	(100.00)
1973.74	3.84	0.35	0.01	4.20	5.06	0.40	0.01	5.47	5.59	0.52	0.03	6.15
	(91.53)	(8.32)	(0.15)	(100.00)	(92.52)	(7.23)	(0.25)	(100.00)	(90.99)	(8.51)	(0.50)	(100.00)
1977-78	3.83	0.04	0.00	3.87	5.86	0.11	0.02	5.99	6.97	0.17	0.03	7.18
	(98.89)	(1.11)	(0.00)	(100.00)	(97.87)	(1.75)	(0.37)	(100.00)	(97.13)	(2.40)	(0.47)	(100.00)
1983	6.24	0.41	0.03	6.67	7.39	0.68	0.03	8.11	7.96	0.65	0.03	8.64
	(93.52)	(6.09)	(0.39)	(100.00)	(91.18)	(8.43)	(0.38)	(100.00)	(92.09)	(7.57)	(0.35)	(100.00)
1986-87	5.93	0.54	0.02	6.49	6.93	0.56	0.04	7.53	8.04	0.55	0.05	8.64
	(91.37)	(8.31)	(0.32)	(100.00)	(92.03)	(7.38)	(0.60)	(100.00)	(93.06)	(6.33)	(0.60)	(100.00)
1987-88	5.40	0.11	0.03	5.54	7.78	0.34	0.06	8.18	8.44	0.53	0.08	9.04
	(97.47)	(1.99)	(0.54)	(100.00)	(95.17)	(4.13)	(0.70)	(100.00)	(93.34)	(5.82)	(0.85)	(100.00)
1993-94	6.64	0.54	—	7.18	7.68	0.68	—	8.36	8.52	0.70	—	9.22
	(92.48)	(7.52)		(100.00)	(91.87)	(8.13)	—	(100.00)	(92.41)	(7.59)		(100.00)
Percentage increase in 1993-94 over that in 1961-62	47.68	11.26	(-)0.44	58.50	32.03	10.90	(-)0.34	42.42	17.17	9.48	0.00	26.65

(Contd.)

Table 21.5 (Contd.)

Decile Group Year	30-40 Rice	30-40 Wheat	30-40 Others	30-40 Total	40-50 Rice	40-50 Wheat	40-50 Others	40-50 Total	50-60 Rice	50-60 Wheat	50-60 Others	50-60 Total
1961-62	9.16	0.03	0.00	9.20	10.41	0.01	0.00	10.42	9.87	0.17	0.01	10.05
	(99.59)	(0.37)	(0.04)	(100.00)	(99.89)	(0.11)	(0.00)	(100.00)	(98.24)	(1.67)	(0.09)	(100.00)
1972-73	6.38	0.70	0.02	7.09	7.01	0.80	0.01	7.82	7.21	0.90	0.06	8.17
	(89.93)	(9.81)	(0.25)	(100.00)	(89.64)	(10.23)	(0.13)	(100.00)	(88.25)	(11.02)	(0.73)	(100.00)
1973-74	6.15	0.62	0.04	6.81	7.81	0.76	0.05	8.62	7.23	0.70	0.03	7.96
	(90.30)	(9.07)	(0.62)	(100.00)	(90.60)	(8.82)	(0.58)	(100.00)	(90.83)	(8.79)	(0.38)	(100.00)
1977-78	7.36	0.22	0.04	7.62	8.09	0.34	0.07	8.51	8.47	0.43	0.09	8.99
	(96.66)	(2.83)	(0.51)	(100.00)	(95.15)	(4.03)	(0.82)	(100.00)	(94.22)	(4.78)	(1.00)	(100.00)
1983	8.87	0.73	0.05	9.65	9.16	0.81	0.07	10.04	9.11	1.01	0.08	10.20
	(91.85)	(7.60)	(0.55)	(100.00)	(91.28)	(8.05)	(0.68)	(100.00)	(89.31)	(9.90)	(0.78)	(100.00)
1986-87	8.84	0.83	0.09	9.76	9.71	0.87	0.10	10.68	8.57	0.98	0.09	9.64
	(90.57)	(8.50)	(0.92)	(100.00)	(90.90)	(8.18)	(0.92)	(100.00)	(88.90)	(10.17)	(0.93)	(100.00)
1987-88	8.61	0.56	0.08	9.25	9.02	0.49	0.07	9.58	8.63	0.97	0.09	9.69
	(93.08)	(6.07)	(0.85)	(100.00)	(94.13)	(5.14)	(0.73)	(100.00)	(89.06)	(10.01)	(0.93)	(100.00)
1993-94	8.46	0.73	0.01	9.20	8.87	0.83	0.01	9.70	8.45	1.00	0.00	9.46
	(91.96)	(7.93)	(0.11)	(100.00)	(91.44)	(8.55)	(0.10)	(100.00)	(89.32)	(10.57)	(0.00)	(100.00)
Percentage increase in 1993-94 over that in 1961-62	(-)7.61	7.61	0	0.00	(-)14.78	7.87	0.00	(-)6.90	(-)14.12	8.26	(-)0.10	(-)5.87

Note: Figures in parentheses are percentage shares in total central consumption.
Source: Various NSS reports.

Table 21.6 Estimates of Per Capita Calorie Intake Per Diem

Year	*Rural Kerala*	*Urban Kerala*
1961-62	1631	1554
1971-72	1610	1658
1972-73	1559	1723
1973-74	1534	1760
1983	1884	2049

Source: CDS (1977), Sengupta and Joshi (1978 and GOI (1989).

Table 21.7 Per Capita Calorie Intake Per Diem by Decile Group by Sector: Kerala (1983)

Decile group	*Rural*	*Urban*
0-10	1054.07	1085.60
10-20	1330.18	1318.84
20-30	1449.50	1414.72
30-40	1585.65	1672.58
40-50	1754.00	1787.84
50-60	1816.10	1895.00
60-70	1961.00	2201.59
70-80	2242.01	2308.02
80-90	2459.10	2751.69
90-100	3188.39	4054.13
0-100	1884.00	2049.00

Source: GOI (1989)

PDS in Kerala: Sectoral Spread

The rationing system in Kerala had a clear urban bias during the pre-Independence period. Pandit Kunzru, Member, Council of State and Central Food Advisory Committee, in his statement to the press, had explained how badly the poor were hit due to cessation of imports of rice from Burma and poor rice crop in 1942-43. Introduction of rationing in municipal towns only worsened the plight of the rural poor by reducing the physical availability of rice in rural areas (Sivaswamy *et al.* (1946); p.1). Therefore, ration shops were opened in the rural areas to mitigate the plight of the rural population; but it did not really improve their lot as the quality of foodstuffs were inferior to those supplied in the urban areas which led Kunzru to comment, 'There appears to be no reason why the villages should not be looked after as well as the towns are' (Sivaswamy *et al.* (1946); p. 2).

PDS is no longer urban biased in Kerala. As on 31 December 1991, the PDS covered a population of 264.53 lakh which constituted about 91 per cent of the 1991 Census population. Thus, the coverage of the population is nearly complete but for full producers of rice and children below two years. The question and dimension of bias can still be gauged using some important criteria and available latest data, that is, the National Sample Survey on 'Utilisation of Public Distribution System' during July 1986-June 1987. The important criteria are: (i) per capita PDS quantity purchased of a given commodity in rural/urban sector; (ii) relative share of the rural/urban sector in total PDS quantity purchased in total State allocation; (iii) relative dependence of the rural/urban sector on the PDS as measured by the PDS share in total quantity purchased in that sector; and (iv) PDS quantity per market dependent in rural/urban sector.[15]

The statistics relevant for these different criteria are presented in Table 21.8. The PDS is rural biased by the per capita PDS purchase criterion for rice; but it is urban biased for wheat and edible oil and there is no bias with respect to sugar and kerosene. By the second criterion, PDS is rural biased for rice, wheat, sugar, edible oils and kerosene; their respective shares being 82.73, 76.99, 80.96, 70.03 and 79.85 per cent respectively. By the third criterion based on relative shares of PDS in total purchased by sector, PDS is rural biased for rice, wheat, kerosene and sugar only; it is urban biased for edible oils (Table 21.8). By the final and most important criterion of PDS purchases per market dependent population, it is rural biased for all items except sugar, kerosene and edible oils. Thus, the PDS in Kerala does not suffer from any urban bias for foodgrains, in particular. This leads us to the question of the incidence of the benefits of the PDS across income groups within the rural and urban sectors, which is examined in the following section.

PDS across Fractile Groups and Implications for Reform

The NSS data also provides distribution of PDS benefits, as indicated by the relative dependence (that is, proportion of PDS

Table 21.8 Measures of Urban Bias in PDS: Kerala

Commodity	*Per capita PDS purchase (kg)*		*Rural Sector's share in total PDS purchases (per cent)*	*PDs Share in total Market purchases (per cent)*		*PDS purchase per market dependent (kg)*	
	Rural	*Urban*		*Rural*	*Urban*	*Rural*	*Urban*
Rice	4.04	3.60	82.73	51.36	46.19	4.26	3.71
Wheat	0.38	0.48	76.99	92.04	91.48	1.42	1.31
Sugar	0.43	0.43	80.96	55.52	50.41	0.44	0.44
Edible oil	0.02	0.04	70.03	8.86	13.59	0.03	0.05
Kerosene	0.58	0.59	79.85	92.12	82.95	0.57	0.66

Source: GOI (1990).

Table 21.9 Relative Dependence on PDS by Select Fractile Groups of Households: Kerala (Rural & Urban) (Quantity purchased from PDS as per cent of Total Quantity purchased from the Market)

Fracitle Group	*Rice*		*Wheat*		*Sugar*		*Edible oil*		*Kerosene*	
	Rural	*Urban*	*Rural*	*Urban*	*Rural*	*Urban*	*Rural*	*Urban*	*Rural*	*Urban*
0-10	64.91	54.38	94.72	96.08	69.73	60.81	8.86	10.56	95.92	96.61
10-20	58.61	54.10	93.83	100.00	64.92	66.28	9.08	15.77	95.97	84.71
20-40	51.59	51.54	94.84	97.81	63.00	56.89	7.47	18.80	93.43	91.10
90-100	38.84	23.63	76.46	72.18	40-.04	27.44	15.31	21.63	83.56	80.31
All	51.36	46.19	92.04	91.48	55.52	50.41	8.86	13.59	92.12	82.95

Source: GOI (1990).

purchase to total purchase), across quartile groups of households obtained by ranking of households on the basis of their total expenditure. Table 21.9 shows that the relative dependence of the poorest fractile groups of households on the PDS is much higher than that of the population as a whole and that of the richer fractile groups for rice, wheat, sugar, kerosene; edible oils seems to be the only item where the relative dependence of the richer fractile groups seems to be higher (Table 21.9). In gencral, thc benefits of the PDS seem to be equitably spread across fractile groups of households in both rural and urban Kerala. This is further confirmed by the available evidence for 1986-87 which shows that from among those depending exclusively on the PDS, 54.45 per cent for rice and 41.55 per cent for wheat belong to the poorest 40 per cent of the rural households in Kerala; as regards urban Kerala, the corresponding estimates are 56.44 per cent and 53.16 per cent (Government of India (GOI) (1990); pp.S-117 & S-146).

On the basis of these aggregate measures, it appears that there is considerable scope for targeting of the PDS in Kerala and hence, reducing government expenditure on account of food subsidy. If so, what would be its implications for the entitlement of the poor? An earlier inter-state study based on the state-wise aggregate statistics (Geeta and Suryanarayana (1993)) has shown that there is no scope for reducing the government expenditure if targeting is done subject to certain nutrition norms. The study is based on the assumption that it is only physical access and not economic access which is the binding constraint on food security in India. It has shown that if the government achieves perfect targeting of the PDS by reducing the two types of errors (Type 1 and Type II) to nil, then the entitlement of the poor in Kerala would increase sufficiently (Table 21.3).[16] The study has shown that with perfect targeting the entitlement of the poor would be 149 kgs instead of the observed per capita PDS offtake of 66 kgs per annum in 1988. This would have amounted to a daily per capita guarantee of 408 gm of cereals which is more than the ICMR norm. With a prefectly trageted PDS, the poor would have got, on an average during the 1970s and 1980s, a per capita cereal quantity of 106 kgs per annum, amounting to a daily cereal availability of 290 gm. Thus, on the basis of the aggregate measures, it appears that there is some scope for increasing the entitlement of the poor in Kerala without incurring any extra expenditure on additional foodgrains but only with efforts to ensure perfect targeting. How to achieve targeting of the PDS? Scope for targeting by changing the composition of cereals delivered under the PDS is nil since Keralites do not consume any coarse cereals at all (Tables 21.10 and 21.11).

Assuming that the analysis based on aggregate measures for Kerala as a whole is valid, this raises other issues relating to (i) targeting by discretion (which is beyond the scope of the chapter); and (ii) physical access to foodgrains of the non-poor at reasonable and stable prices in an acutely chronic foodgrain deficit State. As regards the latter issue, one option could be setting up bufferstocks of foodgrains in all district headquarters so as to enable the government to regulate physical availability and prices through open market operations in period of crisis or when private trade, as is often feared, holds the public to ransom.[17] This leads us to the political economy of the PDS and the centre-state responsibilities, discussed in the following section.

PDS Form and Its Implications for Open Market Interventions

The Kerala Government obtains foodgrains for delivery through the PDS from the Central Government. The quantity allotted has to be lifted and distributed without any delay since with delay the State will forfeit the allotment. The FCI has to supply foodgrains allotted by the Central Government to the authorised wholesale dealers who are essentially the nominees of the State Government. The allotment secured from the Centre is distributed among the district supply officers who sub-allocate them among their respective taluk supply officers/city rationing officers. It is the responsibility of these taluk/city level officers to arrange for

Table 21.10 Estimates of Engel Elasticities and Ratios for Select Commodities: Kerala Rural

	Engel Elasticity				Engel Ratio (per cent)			
Commodity	1961/62	1972/73	1983	1987/88	1961/62	1972/73	1983	1987/88
Rice	0.581	0.789	0.451	-0.368	30.99	30.67	23.01	16.91
Wheat	1.113	0.379	0.842	1.072	0.24	1.23	0.94	0.96
Jowar	—	—	—	—	—	—	—	—
Bajra	—	—	—	—	—	—	—	—
Maize	—	—	—	—	—	—	—	—
Ragi	—	—	—	—	—	—	—	—
Barley	—	—	—	—	—	—	—	—
Small millets	—	—	—	—	—	—	—	—
Total cereals	0.580	0.769	0.470	0.415	31.23	32.07	24.14	18.11
Edible oil	0.970	1.174	0.822	0.867	2.14	1.94	2.72	3.20
Sugar	1.055	0.925	0.718	0.660	1.76	2.49	2.02	2.17
Total Consumption	1.000	1.000	1.000	1.000	100.00	100.00	100.00	100.00
Calories	NA	0.674	0.524	NA	—	—	—	—

Table 21. 11 Estimates of Engel Elasticities and Ratios for Select Commodities: Kerala Urban

	Engel Elasticity				Engel Ratio (per cent)			
Commodity	1961/62	1972/73	1983	1987/88	1961/62	1972/73	1983	1987/88
Rice	0.395	0.510	0.372	0.312	25.74	22.56	18.17	12.26
Wheat	1.163	0.629	0.804	1.097	0.31	1.72	1.39	1.19
Jowar	—	—	—	—	—	—	—	—
Bajra	—	—	—	—	—	—	—	—
Maize	—	—	—	—	—	—	—	—
Ragi	—	—	—	—	—	—	—	—
Barley	—	—	—	—	—	—	—	—
Small millets	—	—	—	—	—	—	—	—
Total cereals	0.401	0.519	0.407	0.388	26.14	24.35	19.77	13.71
Edible oil	0.699	1.102	0.790	0.836	2.21	2.15	2.80	3.20
Sugar	0.809	0.882	0.633	0.578	2.32	2.82	1.89	1.92
Total Consumption	1.000	1.000	1.000	1.000	100.00	100.00	100.00	100.00
Calories	NA	0.580	0.564	NA	—	—	—	—

Table 21.12 Estimates of Monthly Per Capita Consumer Expenditure: Kerala Rural

Year	Cereals & c. substitutes	Pulses & p. products	Milk &m. products	Edible oils	Meat, fish & egg	Fruits, veg. & nuts	Sugar	Salt & spices	Beverages & refts.	Food total	Pan, tob. & intox	Fuel & light	Clothing & foot wear	Durables & misc. goods & services	Non-food total	Total consumer expenditure
Entire Population																
At current prices																
1970/71	12.32	0.50	1.59	0.84	1.76	2.82	0.88	1.34	3.31	25.36	1.39	1.92	1.76	5.69	10.76	36.12
1972/73	15.83	0.54	1.52	0.82	1.92	2.73	1,05	1,30	4.00	29.71	1.58	2.48	1.83	6.59	12.48	42.19
1973/74	21.71	0.68	1.82	1.12	2.52	4.08	1.23	1.56	4.88	39.60	1.84	2.97	2.69	8.25	15.75	55.35
1977/78	19.84	1.12	3.07	1.58	4.00	5.59	1.51	2.62	6.09	45.42	2.55	4.40	5.64	16.75	29.43	74.67
1983	37.70	2.34	5.97	3.96	8.97	12.25	2.94	6.62	11.71	89.54	4.50	8.45	10.22	32.73	55.91	145.45
1986/87	39.76	3.21	9.57	7.24	15.43	18.78	4.44	5.34	12.67	116.44	6.74	11.79	18.86	42.54	79.93	196.37
1987/88	41.09	3.69	9.76	6.76	15.59	21.86	4.58	6.64	16.75	126.71	6.79	13.53	12.33	52.11	84.76	211.47
At 1970-71 prices																
1970/71	12.32	0.50	1.59	0.84	1.76	2.82	0.88	1.34	3.31	25.36	1.39	1.92	1.76	5.69	10.76	36.12
1972/73	15.03	0.39	1.43	0.82	1.58	2.07	0.83	1.49	3.91	27.55	1.44	2.23	1.54	5.65	10.86	38.41
1973/74	16.37	0.42	1.54	0.67	1.83	2.13	0.98	1.40	4.55	29.91	1.49	2.30	1.77	6.08	11.64	41.55
1977/78	15.23	0.45	1.96	0.98	2.17	2.34	1.11	1.53	3.39	29.14	1.52	2.21	2.89	9.32	15.94	45.08
1983	16.82	0.64	2.51	1.35	2.61	2.97	1.20	3.27	4.53	35.90	1.52	2.36	3.23	9.95	17.06	52.97
1986/87	15.61	0.67	3.31	1.86	2.26	3.17	1.42	2.18	3.96	34.44	1.60	2.38	5.24	9.42	18.63	53.07
1987/88	16.04	0.58	3.08	1.45	2.10	3.21	1.35	1.93	5.02	34.75	1.52	2.63	3.33	10.24	17.72	52.47
Increase (per cent) in 1987/88 over 1970/71	10.29	0.23	4.12	1.68	0.93	1.08	1.30	1.64	4.73	26.01	0.35	1.97	4.34	12.60	19.26	45.27

Note: These estimates at 1970-71 prices are obtained by commodity specific deflation using price indices from Jain and Minhas (1991) and Tendulkar and Jain (1993).

Table 21.13 Consumer Expenditure Proportions (per cent): Kerala Rural

Entire Population																
Year	Cereals & c. substitutes	Pulses & p. products	Milk &m. products	Edible oils	Meat, fish & egg	Fruits, veg. & nuts	Sugar	Salt & spices	Beverages & refts.	Food total	Pan, tob. & intox	Fuel & light	Clothing & foot wear	Durables & misc. goods & services	Non-food total	Total consumer expenditure
At current prices																
1970/71	34.11	1.38	4.40	2.33	4.87	7.81	2.44	3.71	9.16	70.21	3.85	5.32	4.87	15.75	29.79	100.00
1972/73	37.52	1.28	3.60	1.94	4.55	6.47	2.49	3.08	9.48	70.42	3.74	5.88	4.34	15.62	29.58	100.00
1973/74	39.22	1.23	3.29	2.02	4.55	7.37	2.22	2.82	8.82	71.54	3.32	5.37	4.86	14.91	28.46	100.00
1977/78	26.57	1.50	4.11	2.12	5.36	7.49	2.02	3.51	8.16	60.83	3.42	5.89	7.55	22.43	39.41	100.00
1983	25.92	1.61	4.10	2.72	6.17	8.42	2.02	4.55	8.05	61.56	3.09	8.81	7.03	22.50	38.44	100.00
1986/87	20.25	1.63	4.87	3.69	7.86	9.56	2.26	2.72	6.45	59.30	3.43	6.00	9.60	21.66	40.70	100.00
1987/88	19.43	1.74	4.62	3.20	7.37	10.34	2.17	3.14	7.92	59.92	3.21	6.40	5.83	24.64	40.08	100.00
At 1970-71 prices																
1970/71	34.11	1.38	4.40	2.33	4.87	7.81	2.44	3.71	9.16	70.21	3.85	5.32	4.87	15.75	29.79	100.00
1972/73	39.14	1.02	3.73	2.12	4.12	5.40	2.15	3.87	10.18	71.73	3.74	5.81	4.00	14.71	28.26	100.00
1973/74	39.40	1.02	3.72	1.62	4.40	5.13	2.36	3.38	10.95	71.97	3.60	5.54	4,26	14.62	28.01	100.00
1977/78	33.78	0.99	4.34	2.17	4.81	5.19	2.45	3.38	7.52	64.64	3.38	4.90	6.41	20.67	35.36	100.00
1983	31.75	1.21	4.74	2.55	4.93	5.61	2.27	6.18	8.55	67.78	2.88	4.45	6.10	18.79	32.21	100.00
1986/87	29.41	1.26	6.25	3.50	4.25	5.98	2.67	4.11	7.46	64.89	3.02	4.48	9.87	17.74	35.11	100.00
1987/88	30.57	1.11	5.87	2.76	4.00	6.12	2.57	3.68	9.57	66.24	2.89	5.02	6.34	19.52	33.77	100.00

Table 21.14 Estimates of Monthly Per Capita Consumer Expenditure: Kerala Urban

Year	Cereals & c. substitutes	Pulses & p. products	Milk & m. products	Edible oils	Meat, fish & egg	Fruits, veg. & nuts	Salt & spices	Sugar berverages & refts.	Food total	Pan, tob. & intox	Fuel & light	Clothing & foot wear	Durables & misc. goods & services	Non-food total	Total consumer expenditure
Entire Population															
At current prices															
1970/71	11.15	0.76	2.59	1.16	2.14	3.39	1.36	7.62	30.17	1.66	2.42	3.12	10.26	17.46	47.63
1972/73	15.49	1.03	3.06	1.25	2.96	3.74	1.40	8.86	37.79	1.92	3.15	2.98	12.43	20.48	58.27
1973/74	19.84	1.44	3.93	1.72	3.42	5.02	1.51	10.16	46.74	2.15	3.60	2.83	13.61	22.19	69.93
1977/78	17.95	1.50	4.35	2.04	4.77	6.58	2.62	11.16	50.97	2..38	5.20	6.15	19.40	33.13	84.10
1983	35.48	3.02	9.02	5.04	11.62	14.75	3.90	21.83	104.73	4.23	10.23	16.04	44.58	75.09	179.82
1986/87	36.37	3.70	14.04	8.72	15.83	20.96	4.96	35.53	140.11	6.25	12.96	17.36	66.78	103.35	243.46
1987/88	37.34	5.06	16.27	8.53	21.24	26.51	6.73	30.30	151.97	5.48	16.02	15.55	77.19	114.26	266.22
At 1970-71 prices															
1970/71	11.15	0.76	2.59	1.16	2.14	3.39	1.36	7.62	30.17	1.66	2.42	3.12	10.26	17.46	47.63
1972/73	11.14	0.71	2.93	0.82	2.71	4.02	1.45	7.55	31.32	1.70	2.86	2.30	11.56	18.42	49.74
1973/74	11.25	0.92	3.32	0.70	2.34	3.96	1.22	7.73	31.44	1.70	2.74	1.83	11.43	17.69	49.14
1977/78	12.47	0.68	2.96	0.85	2.87	4.42	1.30	6.51	32.05	1.44	2.57	2.77	12.27	19.04	51.09
1983	13.36	0.09	3.91	1.10	3.80	5.27	1.47	8.17	37.97	1.53	2.29	4.76	17.21	25.78	63.75
1986/87	13.50	0.86	4.68	1.00	2.62	5.10	1.30	8.32	37.38	1.66	2.22	4.79	18.79	27.47	64.85
1987/88	13.68	0.98	5.01	0.97	3.41	5.85	1.38	6.64	37.91	1.29	2.68	4.05	20.22	28.24	66.15
Increase (per cent) in 1987/88 over 1970/71	6.03	0.51	4.90	0.34	3.02	4.65	0.03	(-)1.96	16.65	(-)0.74	0.58	1.52	20.72	21.70	38.89

Note: These estimates at 1970-71 prices are obtained by commodity specific deflation using price indices from Jain and Minhas (1991) and Tendulkar and Jain (1993).

Table 21.15 Consumer Expenditure Proportions (per cent): Kerala Urban

Entire Population															
Year	Cereals & c. substitutes	Pulses & p. products	Milk & m. products	Edible oils	Meat, fish & egg	Fruits, veg. & nuts	Salt & spices	Sugar berverages & refts.	Food total	Pan, tob. & intox	Fuel & light	Clothing & foot wear	Durables & misc. goods & services	Non-food total	Total consumer expenditure
At current prices															
1970/71	23.41	1.60	5.44	2.44	4.49	7.12	2.86	16.00	63.34	3.49	5.08	6.55	21.54	36.66	100.00
1972/73	26.58	1.77	5.25	2.15	5.08	6.42	2.40	15.21	64.85	3.30	5.41	5.11	21.33	35.15	100.00
1973/74	28.37	2.06	5.62	2.46	4.89	7.18	2.16	14.53	66.84	3.07	5.15	4.05	19.46	31.73	100.00
1977/78	21.34	1.78	5.17	2.43	5.67	7.82	3.12	13.27	60.61	2.83	6.18	7.31	23.07	39.39	100.00
1983	19.73	1.68	5.02	2.80	6.46	8.20	2.17	12.14	58.24	2.35	5.69	8.92	24.79	41.76	100.00
1986/87	14.94	1.52	5..77	3.58	6.50	8.61	2.04	14.59	57.55	2.57	5.32	7.13	27.43	42.45	100.00
1987/88	14.03	1.90	6.11	3.20	7.98	9.96	2.53	11.38	57.08	2.06	6.02	5.84	28.99	42.92	100.00
At 1970-71 prices															
1970/71	23.41	1.60	5.44	2.44	4.49	7.12	2.86	16.00	63.34	3.49	5.08	6.55	21.54	36.66	100.00
1972/73	22.40	1.43	5.89	1.64	5.44	8.08	2.92	15.17	62.97	3.42	5.75	4.62	23.24	37.02	100.00
1973/74	22.89	1.87	6.76	1.42	4.77	8.06	2.49	15.73	63.99	3.46	5.57	3.72	23.26	36.01	100.00
1977/78	24.40	1.34	5.79	1.66	5.61	8.65	2.54	12.74	62.73	2.81	5.03	5.42	24.01	37.27	100.00
1983	20.96	1.41	6.13	1.73	5.96	8.26	2.30	12.81	59.56	2.40	3.59	7.46	26.99	40.45	100.00
1986/87	20.81	1.33	7.22	1.54	4.04	7.86	2.01	12.83	57.64	2.56	3.42	7.39	28.98	42.36	100.00
1987/88	20.68	1.48	7.57	1.47	5.16	8.84	2.08	10.03	57.32	1.94	4.05	6.12	30.57	42.69	100.00

lifting of allotments through wholesale dealers. The wholesale dealers supply the ration articles to the final retail outlets which directly serve the final beneficiary households.

As on 30 September, 1995, the PDS in Kerala operated through a network of 14,172 authorised retail outlets for distributing the essential articles. On an average, one retail outlet caters for 405 card holders; altogether, the PDS covers a population of 283.4 lakh consisting of 228.1 lakh adults and 55.3 lakh non-adults. The retail shops are served by 316 wholesale shops of which 266 are owned by licensed private agencies and 50 by co-operatives (Table 21.16). These wholesale shops, in turn, receive supplies of ration commodities from twenty sub-depots of the Food Corporation of India (FCI) located across the State.

Table 21.16 Public Distribution System in Kerala: A Macro Profile

	Unit	*As on 30 Sept. 1995*
1. No. of Ration Cards and permits		
(a) Ration cards for families	Lakh	57
(b) Ration permits for institution	No.	13557
2. No. of FCI sub-depots including main depots	No.	39
3. No. of wholesale shops		
(a) Co-operatives	No.	50
(b) Others	No.	266
(c) Total wholesale shops	No.	316
4. No. of retail shops		
(a) Co-operatives	No.	1083
(b) Others	No.	13089
(c) Total retail shops	No.	14172

Source: GOK (1996)

Thus, the job of the State government is concerned with the enforcement part of the PDS operation.[18] The prices are fixed taking into account the Central issue price, taxes, administrative surcharges, wholesale margin, dealer's commission etc. The State government has nothing to do with maintaining buffer-stocks of foodgrains. In this context, if it is to take up the additional responsibility of targeting for the poor and buffer-stocking for open market operations to ensure food security of the non-poor in emergency conditions, it will have to bear extra budgetary costs involving capital expenditures on storage facilities etc., which finally end up in duplication of efforts at the level of both central and state governments and hence, unnecessary government outlays. As a result, subsidy may not subside; instead it may explode.

If so, how far the need for targeting the PDS is imperative? Can not the Kerala Government continue with the existing system itself ensuring food security for all? In other words, how far is the general impression, corroborated by the NSS, that there are considerable leakages to the non-poor (that is, Type II error) really valid?[19] This question is examined in the following section.

Scope for Reform

The discussion so far has not considered the details regarding the PDS like distribution of beneficiaries across income groups, their actual purchases *vis-a-vis* entitlement and their causes and implications. The data on distribution of ration cards across households monthly income classes for the month of December in 1986 and 1993 bring out that this distribution is almost positively skewed with the bulk (more than 75%) of the card holders belonging to the lowest two income classes with incomes less than Rs 300 per months (Table 21.17). Thus, it would appear that the PDS is almost well targeted in Kerala and the debate about targeting the PDS makes little sense. But, this data is subject to the limitation that it is based on the incomes as declared by the ration card holders. As is well known (and informed by the officials in the Directorate of Civil Supplies, Government of Kerala), there is under-reporting of income and this data is not entirely reliable. Further, household ranking by households income could be very different from the one based on per capita income.

The hypothesis about leakages of benefits to the non-poor can be verified further using the Centre for Management Development (CMD) survey data on monthly income group-wise distribution of the PDS beneficiaries (Koshy *et al* (1989)). The data shows that the poorest income groups (those with monthly incomes less than Rs. 100) constitute 7.30 per cent of the beneficiaries; the largest segment of beneficiaries belong to the

Table 21.17 Percentage Distribution of Ration Cards by Monthly Income of Households: Kerala (December 1986 & 1993)

District	*Income Class*							
	Rs. 100 and below	*Rs. 101-300*	*Rs. 310-375*	*Rs. 376-400*	*Rs. 401-500*	*Rs. 501-1000*	*Above Rs. 1000*	*All*
Thiruvananthapuram	51.88	29.37	2.38	1.54	3.40	6.08	5.35	100.00
	(38.03)	(33.14)	(5.44)	3.86	(4.83)	(7.68)	(7.01)	(100.00)
Quilon	55.16	28.58	3.90	2.59	3.23	3.92	2.62	100.00
	(36.55)	(41.91)	(4.74)	(2.31)	(3.12)	(5.28)	(6.09)	(100.00)
Pathanamthitta	37.17	39.94	2.88	3.29	5.32	7.33	4.07	100.00
	(29.39)	(43.06)	(4.59)	(3.05)	(5.79)	(7.73)	(6.39)	(100.00)
Alleppey	40.08	44.61	2.47	1.49	3.04	4.99	3.32	100.00
	(37.17)	(41.25)	(3.61)	(3.29)	(4.36)	(5..95)	(4.36)	(100.00)
Kottayam	21.79	53.40	2.94	2.32	4.82	8.39	6.34	100.00
	(12.46)	(50.54)	(7.56)	(5.87)	(6.58)	(8.65)	(8.34)	(100.00)
Idukki	11.32	63.36	5.39	3.53	4.73	9.18	2.49	100.00
	(6.10)	(61.96)	(8.16)	(4.35)	(6.12)	(8.86)	(4.47)	(100.00)
Ernakulam	25.30	46.87	2.93	2.28	4.47	9.38	8.77	100.00
	(18.32)	(43.68)	(3.76)	(3.42)	(5.74)	(15.45)	(9.62)	(100.00)
Trichur	35.58	44.94	2.96	2.04	3.76	6.26	4.46	100.00
	(26.47)	(45.64)	(4.13)	(3.22)	(4.57)	(7.56)	(8.40)	(100.00)

(Contd.)

Table 21.17 *(Contd.)*

District	*Income Class*							
	Rs. 100 and below	*Rs. 101-300*	*Rs. 310-375*	*Rs. 376-400*	*Rs. 401-500*	*Rs. 501-1000*	*Above Rs. 1000*	*All*
Palakkad	30.74	48.40	3.00	2.41	5.49	6.21	3.75	100.00
	(25.91)	(45.46)	(6.53)	(3.04)	(4.57)	(8.60)	(5.90)	(100.00)
Malappuram	36.58	45.96	4.17	3.57	3.31	4.12	2.29	100.00
	(23.26)	(51.17)	(7.80)	(3.90)	(4.57)	(4.62)	(4.69)	(100.00)
Kozhikode	43.91	38.92	2.77	1.54	3.13	5.22	4.51	100.00
	(36.91)	(40.70)	(2.90)	(2.38)	(3.27)	(5.32)	(8.52)	(100.00)
Wayanad	21.52	64.70	2.76	2.01	2.90	4.12	1.99	100.00
	(16.31)	(64.62)	(4.31)	(3.15)	(4.58)	(4.30)	(2.72)	(100.00)
Cannanore	24.15	56.57	2.89	2.39	3.83	6.29	3.88	100.00
	(20.74)	(51.99)	(5.60)	(3.77)	(5.20)	(7.12)	(5.58)	(100.00)
Kasaragod	18.76	55.27	10.41	5.16	4.93	3.84	1.63	100.00
	(9.65)	(51.60)	(10.28)	(5.58)	(8.62)	(8.26)	(6.00)	(100.00)
State	35.46	44.26	3.34	2.50	3.94	6.15	4.35	100.00
	(26.46)	(45.27)	(5.36)	3.53)	(4.89)	(7.77)	(6.71)	(100.00)

Note: Figures in parentheses refer to December, 1993.
Source: Government of Kerala (1989 & 1994a).

Table 21.18 Distribution of PDS Beneficiaries by Monthly Income Group: Kerala

Monthly Income	*Percentage no. of beneficiaries*	*Monthly per capita Consumption of rice (kg)*	*Share of PDS rice (per cent)*	*Rice purchased as percentage of the quantity entitled*
Below Rs. 100	7.30	10.95	40	71
Rs. 101-300	27.80	14.38	27	59
Rs. 301-500	17.90	9.69	30	47
Rs. 501-1000	24.20	11.14	26	47
Rs. 1001-2000	17.30	10.86	21	37
Rs. 2001-3000	3.80	10.80	14	26
Above Rs. 3001	1.70	10.65	3	6
Total	100.00	10.92	29	49

Source: Koshy *et al* (1998)

income category between Rs. 101 and Rs. 300 (Table 21.18). Those beneficiaries with incomes larger than Rs. 1001 form only 5.5 per cent of the total. This confirms that the distribution of the PDS benefits across income groups is progressive. As can be expected, the poorer income groups rely relatively more on the PDS than the richer ones.[20] Yet the per capita rice consumption of all income groups is less than the normative levels. The CMD survey was based on a random sample but sample size was inadequate. The survey was based on a sample of only 806 card holders and hence, the estimates, though unbiased, may be subject to large standard errors. Therefore, we may look for indirect evidence on PDS targeting and their implications for reform.

One important evidence indicating that there is some amount of self-targeting is that the actual per capita purchases of rice and wheat from the PDS are much less than their per capita entilements. Contrary to the general impression, per capita entitlements of rice and wheat are substantial in Kerala.[21] Even as early as June 1986, the scale of the PDS was that an adult (considered equivalent to two units) was entitled to 130gm of rice and 240 gm of wheat per day in addition to an extra kg of rice per card per week; in December 1986, it was 220gm of rice and 240gm of wheat per day plus five kgs of rice per card per week (Table 21.19). The current entilement is about 285 gm per day of rice and wheat separately. The scale of rice and wheat per adult per day is much more than the ICMR norm of 370 gm of cereals per capita per day and more than the poverty line cereal bundle of 515gm per capita per day.[22] Yet the actual purchase from the PDS has never been more than 150gm per capita per day (Table 21.20).[23] As the CMD study also shows, the average Kerala population buys hardly 50 per cent of entitlement with respect to rice (Table 21.18). Thus, the effective utilisation of the PDS has been less than fifty per cent.[24]

This is puzzling given the low levels of cereal consumption and nutritional intake in Kerala. What could be the reasons for such low levels of purchases of rice and wheat even though the people are entitled to much larger amounts? Could it be due to inadequate economic access? Could it be due to changing consumer

Table 21.19 Scale of Ration (Rice and Wheat) in Kerala

Period	*Scale of ration (gm. per adult per day)*				*Remarks*
From	*To*	*Rice*	*Wheat*	*Total*	
6-6-1976	26-6-1976	130	240	370	Extra rice 1kg./card issued during the week
27-6-1976	24-7-1976	130	240	370	
25-7-1976	31-7-1976	130	240	370	Extra rice 1 kg./card
1-9-1976	28-8-1976	140	240	380	
29-8-1976	11-9-1976	140	240	380	Extra rice 2 kg./card
12-9-1976	25-9-1976	160	240	400	Extra rice 1 kg./card
26-9-1976	23-10-1976	160	240	400	
24-10-1976	30-10-1976	160	240	400	Extra rice 1 kg./card
31-10-1976	27-11-1976	160	240	400	
28-11-1976	15-1-1977	160	240	400	Extra rice 1 kg./card per week
16-1-1977	5-2-1977	200	240	440	Extra rice 2 kg. per card per week
6-2-1977	26-2-1977	320	240	560	
27-2-1977	20-8-1977	320	240	560	
21-8-1977	3-9-1977	320	240	560	Extra rice 2 kg. once during any time during the period.
4-9-1977	11-9-1977	320	240	560	Extra rice 1 kg./card per week for five weeks.
11-9-1977	24-9-1977	320	240	560	Extra rice 1 kg./card per week.
25-9-1977	29-10-1977	320	240	560	Extra rice 2 kg. per card per week.

Table 21.19 *(Contd.)*

Period		Scale of ration (gm. per adult per day)			Remarks
From	To	Rice	Wheat	Total	
30-10-1977	12-11-1977	320	240	560	
12-11-1977	26-11-1977	320	240	560	
26-11-1977	31-12-1977	320	240	560	
1-7-1978	18-8-1979	320	240	560	Extra rice 2 kg. once during any time during the month.
19-8-1979	1-9-1979	320	240	560	Extra 4 kg. rice per card per week/c
2-9-1979	30-6-1980	320	240	560	Extra 2 kg. rice per card per week/c
1-7-1980	16-4-1983	320	240	560	
17-4-1983	30-4-1983	180	240	420	GOI allotment inadequate
1-5-1983	31-1-1985	200	240	440	
1-2-1985	2-11-1985	220	240	460	During August extra 10 kg. of rice per card.
3-11-1985	16-11-1985	200	240	440	
17-11-1985	5-7-1986	220	240	460	
6-7-1986	9-8-1986	220	240	460	Extra 1 kg. rice per card per week from 6-7-86
10-8-1986	16-8-1986	220	240	460	Extra 2 kg. rice per card per week/c
17-8-1986	6-9-1986	220	240	460	Extra 1 kg. rice per card per week.
7-9-1986	20-9-1986	220	240	460	Extra 5 kg. of rice per card per week.
21-9-1986	27-9-1986	220	240	460	One week's rice ration free to families with income < Rs. 4500

Table 21.19 *(Contd.)*

Period	*Scale of ration (gm. per adult per day)*				*Remarks*
From	*To*	*Rice*	*Wheat*	*Total*	
28-9-1986	25-10-1986	220	240	460	Extra 1 kg. rice per card per week until further order.
26-10-1986	1-11-1986	220	240	460	Extra 2 kg. rice per card for one week.
2-11-1986	30-11-1986	220	240	460	
30-11-1986	6-12-1986	220	240	460	Extra 1 kg. per card per week.
7-12.1986	13-12-1986	220	240	460	Extra 5 kg. per card per week.
14-12-1986	20-12-1986	220	240	460	Extra 1 kg. per card per week.
21-12-1986	27-12-1986	220	240	460	Extra 5 kg. per card per week.
28-12-1986	3-1-1987	220	240	460	Extra 5 kg. per card per week.
4-1-1987	4-3-1989	220	240	460	Information in detail is not readily available.
5-3-1989	3-2-1990	180	240	420	
4-2-1990	19-5-1990	200	240	440	
20-5-1990	13-2-1994	200	240	440	
14-2-1994	till date	286	286	571	

Source: GOK (1987) and personal discussion with the officials at the Directorate of Civil Supplies, Thiruvananthapuram.

Table 21.20 Actual Distribution of Rice & Wheat through the PDS

Year	Ration population as on 31st December	Total PDS distribution (M.T. per annum)		PDS distribution (gm per PDS beneficiary per day)		PDS distribution (gm per beneficiary per day)	No. of units as on 31st December	PDS distribution (gm per unit per day)
		Rice	Wheat	Rice	Wheat	Rice & Wheat		Rice & Wheat
1977	22659221	1362724.00	65174.00	164.77	7.88	172.65	40192707.00	97.33
1978	22617801	895727.00	35791.00	108.50	4.34	112.84	40091366.00	63.66
1979	22658130	548603.00	32630.00	66.33	3.95	70.28	40157326.00	39.65
1980	22887510	769510.00	47679.00	92.11	5.71	97.82	40553532.00	55.21
1981	21592727	1063287.00	43862.00	134.91	5.57	140.48	40068058.00	75.70
1982	21598926	1158706.00	58903.00	146.98	7.47	154.45	40184399.00	83.02
1983	21849260	1288114.00	201810.00	161.52	25.31	186.82	40540297.00	100.69
1984	22065786	1325646.00	147379.00	164.59	18.30	182.89	40872369.00	98.74
1985	24296648	1384275.00	110020.00	156.09	12.41	168.50	43894541.00	93.27
1986	25349929	1554984.00	98441.00	168.06	10.64	178.70	45560817.00	99.43
1987	25600908	1597962.00	104208.00	171.01	11.15	182.16	46023000.00	101.33
1988	25784645	1546264.00	150450.00	164.30	15 99	180.28	46311000.00	100.38
1989	25919522	1269985.00	209238.00	134.24	22.12	156.36	46521000.00	87.11
1990	25916936	1649273.00	232332.00	174.35	24.56	198.91	46463180.00	110.95
1991	26751376	1671398.00	332706.00	171.18	34.07	205.25	46089000.00	119.13
1992	28090537	1804212.00	271505.00	175.97	26.48	202.45	50733749.00	112.09
1993	28231609	1646819.00	218630.00	159.81	21.22	181.03	51036301.00	100.14
1994	28390761	1152975.40	219380.00	111.26	21.17	132.43	N.A.	N.A.
1995	28415662	1132096.30	423017.00	109.15	40.79	149.94	N.A.	N.A.

Source: GOK (1987) & officials at the Directorate of Civil Supplies, Thiruvananthapuram.

preferences in Kerala? Could it be due to the Keralite's preference for quality? Could it be that the PDS is unequally spread across districts such that purchases normalised with respect to the State population show a statistically misleading picture of poor PDS utilisation in Kerala?[25]

As regards economic access, there has been a definite improvement as reflected in the increases in per capita consumer expenditure (at 1970-71) of the rural and urban populations (Tables 21.12 and 21.14) and in decline in the estimates of poverty (head-count ratio) for Kerala as a whole from 67.96 per cent in 1970-71 to 44.12 per cent in 1987-88[26] (Minhas *et al* (1991)). Still poverty is high with almost half the population being poor. Thus, inadequate economic access could be a reason for low levels of cereal consumption and PDS purchases.

To verify the question of changing consumer preferences, the only available time-series information on consumption patterns in Kerala is the NSS. But given its data limitations for demand system estimation, capturing changes in consumption patterns using econometrically rigorous procedures is difficult (see, Suryanarayana (1996b)). Therefore, we have estimated Engel elasticities for some important food items using the concentration curve approach. The estimates of Engel ratios and Engel elasticities for four different years presented in Tables 21.10 & 21.11 show some changes in consumer preferences in favour of non-cereal items. These changes could also be due to changing relative prices. However, the commodity-wise per capita expenditures and budget proportions with adjustments for price changes show marginal changes in consumption patterns in rural and urban Kerala (Tables 21.12 to 21.15). Between 1970-71 and 1987-88, total per capita consumer expenditure of the rural population increased by 45.27 per cent; of this increase, cereals accounted for 10.29 per cent, milk and milk products for 4.12 per cent, beverages and refreshments for 4.73 per cent and durables for 12.60 per cent. Similarly, of the total increase of 38.89 per cent in urban consumer expenditure, cereals accounted for 6.03 per cent, milk and milk product for 4.90 per cent, fruits and vegetables for 4.65 per cent, and durables for 21.70 per cent. Thus, durables and cereals dominate the marginal budget allocations; yet cereal consumption is less than the norm implying that inadequate economic access may be a major binding constraint in Kerala.

In addition to inadequate economic access, poor quality of rice delivered through the PDS seems to be a major reason for poor utilisation of the PDS. As per the NSS survey during 1986-87, only 9.96 per cent of the rural Kerala and 3.98 per cent of the urban Kerala market dependent population relied exclusively on the PDS for rice; the corresponding percentages for those who purchased from sources other than PDS were 8.78 for the rural and 12.86 for the urban areas. A substantial proportion of the market dependent population in both rural (81.26%) and urban (83.17%) Kerala relied on both the PDS and other market sources.[27] Thus, the PDS seems to be operating essentially as a buffer in a foodgrain deficit State. Among those who did not depend wholly on the PDS for rice, about ten per cent cited `quality not satisfactory' as the reason for `no purchase/part purchase' (GOI (1990)). Our discussion with the officials of the Civil Supplies Department only confirmed this. According to them, one major reason for such low purchases is the poor quality of rice delivered through the PDS. They pointed out that the purchases from the PDS increased whenever the rice procured from Andhra was sold through the PDS but the consumers refused to lift the rice from Punjab. There is much talk on reducing the PDs size and reforming it through targeting. But in Kerala targeting in some form has already been taking place. Therefore, the question of reforming the Kerala PDS by targeting it seems to be irrelevant today. It will have relevance only if the GOI seeks to ensure food security of the poor by providing qualitatively better varieties of rice when even the rich will have the incentive to avail themselves of the PDS.

Finally, coming to the question of inequitious incidence of the PDS across districts, available data indicate that the PDS in Kerala is spread more or less equitably. By economic access criterion, that is, per capita income, the four most food insecure districts are Malappuram, Alappuzha, Palakkad and Kasaragod (Table 21.22). By the physical access criterion, that is, per capita

Table 21.21 Percentage Distribution of the Market Dependent Population Across Different Sources: Kerala and All-India (1986-87)

	Kerala				*All-India*			
	Rural		*Urban*		*Rural*		*Urban*	
	Rice	*Wheat*	*Rice*	*Wheat*	*Rice*	*Wheat*	*Rice*	*Wheat*
Only from the PDS	9.96	98.80	3.98	91.74	14.17	26.49	11.13	29.48
Only from other sources	8.78	0.84	12.86	5.32	60.26	68.71	60.89	63.30
Both from PDS and other sources	81.26	0.34	83.16	2.94	25.57	4.80	27.98	7.22
Total	100.00	100	100.00	100.00	100.00	100.00	100.00	100.00

Source: GOI (1990)

rice production, the four most food insecure districts are Kasaragod, Kozhikode, Idukki and Thiruvananthapuram. The PDS distribution of rice per beneficiary broadly matches with the severity of food insecurity indicated by these two economic and physical access measures; it is the highest in Wayanad, followed by Kozhikode, Kasaragod and Malappuram. Palakkad is food insecure by the economic access criterion but with a per capita rice production of 136 kgs per annum, it is the most food secure district in Kerala by the physical access criterion. Except for Palakkad, the per beneficiary cereal (rice and wheat) distribution in all other districts falls within a narrow range around the State average. Similarly, the per unit distribution of cereals is more or less the same across districts and is less than half of the entitlement in majority of the districts.

Thus, two major reasons for incomplete utilisation of the PDS seem to be inadequate economic access and poor quality of rice supplied through the PDS. The obvious solutions for these problems can be economic growth and provision of qualitatively better cereals through the PDS. As regards the former, the current State Plan emphasis is essentially on growth through appropriate investments taking into account the State's comparative advantages. As regards the latter, the real reform of the PDS in Kerala should begin with improvement in the quality of cereals, particularly rice sold to the public so as to stimulate rice consumption and promote food security. It is only in such a context that the question of targeting of the PDS in Kerala would arise. If the PDS were properly targeted, it would still leave open the question of food security for the non-poor in a food-deficit State. And, as already noted, it may not be fiscally prudent to set up bufferstocks to undertake open market operations in periods of market malfunctioning or natural calamities obstructing inter-state private trade in foodgrains. Only with Central assistance and cooperation by providing better quality cereals and stocks for emergency open market operations, would it be possible for the State government to enforce, if required, the suggested reform programme of effective targeting.

Table 21.22 Measures of Economic and Physical Access to Food Across Districts: Kerala

District	*Per capita income at current prices (1994-95) (Rs.)*	*Census population (1991) (lakhs)*	*Rice production total (1990-91) (M.T.)*	*Rice production per capita (1990-91) (kg)*	*Population covered under PDS (lakhs)* as on 31 December, 1992	*Share of PDS population (per cent)@* as on 31 December, 1992	*PDS distribution Rice & wheat per PDS beneficiary per day* as on 31 December, 1992 (gm)	*PDs distribution Rice & wheat per PDS unit per day (1992) (gm)*
Thiruvananthapuram	7039.00	29.47	38363	13.02	28.98	95.79	169.85	92.79
Quilon	6879.00	24.08	58385	24.25	23.51	95.08	171.99	94.78
Pathanamthitta	6770.00	11.88	33226	27.97	11.52	94.33	173.50	95.05
Alleppey	6417.00	20.01	131663	65.80	19.32	94.03	178.48	98.05
Kottayam	6612.00	18.28	62719	34.31	17.68	94.08	174.07	95.38
Idukki	7535.00	10.78	10953	10.16	11.37	102.72	171.01	93.34
Ernakulam	10824.00	28.17	102689	36.45	27.16	93.84	173.67	94.99
Trichur	7219.00	27.37	129287	47.24	27.85	99.04	172.37	95.22
Palakkad	6508.00	23.82	324907	136.40	22.59	92.32	141.24	79.24
Malappuram	4315.00	30.96	80830	26.11	29.01	91.23	188.12	107.58
Kozhikode	7179.00	26.20	14834	5.66	24.93	92.66	193.19	107.21
Wayanad	6724.00	6.72	41974	62.46	5.92	88.86	203.65	114.86
Cannanore	6818.00	22.52	32308	14.35	21.60	93.42	185.48	103.14
Kasaragod	6538.00	10.72	2440	2.28	9.45	85.83	190.52	106.07
Total	6983.00	290.98	1086578	37.34	280.91	93.99	175.97	97.43

@ These estimates below are obtained taking PDS beneficiary population as on 31st December 1992 as a proportion of the district-wise projected population as on 1st March 1993.

Source: GOK (various reports).

Conclusion

By both economic and physical access criteria, Kerala is one of the most food insecure states in India. The adverse implications of this for human development have been considerably mitigated by conscious public policy choice and action in Kerala. While poverty, an important indicator of economic access, has declined due to a variety of redistributive and poverty alleviation measures, per capita production of rice (and also tapioca), an important measure of physical access to the staple food item in Kerala, has declined over time. As a result food insecurity should have worsened, but it did not. Per capita cereal consumption in Kerala, though declined in the 1960s, has recovered and increased since the early 1970s consequent to active government intervention in ensuring increase in physical access to food through public distribution. Today almost the entire population of Kerala comes under the umbrella of the PDS.

Yet per capita cereal consumption in both rural and urban Kerala falls short of the ICMR recommended norm of 370 gm per capita per day. This is not due to inadequate physical access. The scale of ration entitlement per adult is much more; it exceeds the ICMR norm by more than 200gm. But it is not fully utilised; the average utilisation rate is about 50 per cent only. This seems to be due to a variety of reasons like inadequate economic access, changing consumer preferences, better health facilities and hence, more efficient utilisation of the limited food consumption and most importantly, poor quality of rice supplied through the PDS. Thus, much before the recent and controversial proposal to restrict the PDS size by means of changes in commodity composition towards inferior cereals, GOI has been doing precisely the same in Kerala.

PDS in Kerala is well-targeted to the poorer sections. Its size is considerably restricted to less than 50 per cent of its potential size. The need for reform is on the quality front, that is, the quality of foodgrains delivered through the PDS so as to increase the cereal consumption, promote nutritional intake and efficiency of labour. This may be done even with a reduction in the scale of the PDS cereals (which is currently more than 570 gm per adult per day) initially to the poverty line bundle (515 gm per capita per day) and finally to the ICMR bundle (370 gm per capita per day which also happened to be the PDS scale in early 1977). This has to be accompanied simultaneously by a growth process so as to improve the economic access of the poor population.

Acknowledgement

The author would like to thank Shri C.V. Viswanathan, I.A.S. Director, Shri G. Babu, Statistical Officer and Shri Hari Hara Kumar, Statistician of the Directorate of Civil Supplies for useful discussions and statistical information on various aspects, without holding them responsible for the views and errors, if any. Thanks are also due to D. Narayana, Tirthanker Roy and A. Vaidyanathan for comments on an earlier draft.

NOTES

1. See Dreze and Sen (1995). Among the important human development indicators, Kerala's position relative to all-India in 1991 is as follows:

Indicator		*Kerala*	*All-India*
Literacy rate (per cent)		89.8	52.2
Infant mortality rate (per thousand live births)		13	74
Life expectancy at birth (years)	Males	66.8	57.7
	Females	72.3	58.1

Source: Government of Kerala (GOK) (1995)

2. See Suryanarayana (1995 C).
3. As Kumar (1979) shows, public food distribution has played an important role in ensuring high quality of life, low infant mortality rate in particular, in Kerala by ensuring access to food and promoting maternal nutrition.
4. The network of Maveli stores was set up in 1981. In 1987, there were 169 Maveli stores spread over the 14 districts of Kerala. The major items supplied by these stores are:

   (i) raw rice; (ii) boiled rice; (iii) midday; (iv) sooji; (v) sugar; (vi) palmolein; (vii) coconut oil; (viii) cement; (ix) green gram; (x) green gram dhal; (xi) toor dhal; (xii) peas dhal; (xiii) bengal gram; (xiv) black gram; (xv) black gram washed and split; (xvi) lobia (xvii) jaggery; (xviii) chillies; (xix) coriander; (xx) cummin seed; (xxi) mustard; (xxii) methy; (xxiii) turmeric; (xxiv) tamarind; (xxv) sabari tea; (xxvi) kerosene oil; (xxvii) LP gas and gas stove; (xxviii) vegetables like banana, cluster beans, ash gourd, snake gourd, pumpkin, brinjal, ladies finger, elephant foot and tomato; and

(xxix) pertomeum products like petrol, diesel and lubricants. These items are sold at prices below the open market prices. Among these items palmolein, edible oil, levey sugar and free sale sugar are the most important accounting for 73.78 per cent of the total sales in 1986-87.

5. Further, the average size of operational holding is quite small; in 1991 it was a mere 0.31 hectare as against the all-India average of 1.57 hectare (GOK (1995)). The size of about 90 per cent of the land holdings is less than half hectare which indicates the acute pressure on land; this also implies that agriculture may not be that attractive (GOK (1994 b)).
6. In fact, per capita production of rice and tapioca, two major staple items in Kerala, has declined since the 1960s; the former from 63.31 kg per capita per annum in 1961 to 37.11 kg in 1990-91 and the latter from 99.91 kg to 89.35 kg between the same years (GOK (1995)). Crop-specific studies show stagnation in the production of rice and tapioca in Kerala (see George and Mukherjee, 1986; Kannan and Pushapangadan, 1988, 1990, and Pushpangadan, 1988).
7. As regards issues relating to economic access, one may refer to Kannan (1995) and GOK (1996).
8. For more on this, see Centre for Development Studies (1977) and Suryanarayana (1995c).
9. For a rigorous verification, see Pushpangadan (1988).
10. Kumar (1979) and George (1979) show the role of the PDS in promoting rice consumption and nutrition in Kerala.
11. As a result of the remittances, Kerala could improve its rank among the states in terms of per capita consumer expenditure. Per capita consumer expenditures in rural and urban Kerala were below the national averages till the 70s and crossed the national averages thereafter (Ramachandran, 1995; p. 16).
12. Available data on calorie intake collected by the National Nutrition Monitoring Bureau (NNMB) for the period 1975-82 also confirms that Kerala has made significant progress in reducing malnutrition (see Kumar and Stewart, 1992).
13. One may have to make suitable allowances for consumption of coconut and tapioca in Kerala. This may, as shown by CDS (1977), show a better profile of calorie intake in Kerala. However, for lack of complete information, we are not in a position to make these corrections in our statistical assessment.
14. Of course, it could also be due to skewed distribution of poverty reduction across districts in Kerala which we are not in a position to verify here due to non-availability of data at the district level.
15. For the rationale of the different criteria, see Dev and Suryanarayana (1991), Suryanarayana (1994, 1995a,c).
16. These errors are due to (i) failure to reach the target (that is, the poor) population (Type I error); and (ii) excessive coverage and hence, benefiting

the non-target (that is, non-poor) population (Type II error). For more on the two types of errors in targeting, see Cornia and Stewart (1993).

17. That the market can misjudge the extent of shortage or provide scope for a few traders to make profits at the cost of the masses is a real possibility as it happened during the Bangladesh famine of 1974 (Dreze and Sen (1995)).
18. For this purpose, the State government has a separate enforcement machinery comprising one Controller of Rationing at zonal level, 14 district supply officers at district level, 69 taluk supply officers/city rationing officers at taluk level/city level and 268 rationing inspectors at the firka level. This machinery has to regularly inspect so as to prevent malpractice by dealers and take effective action against the offenders. In addition, there is a separate monitoring cell, headed by the district collector, for detecting hoarding, malpractice and black marketing.
19. In fact, the conept of leakages of PDS does not make sense at all in a context of an untargeted programme with universal entitlement like the PDS in Kerala.
20. Other studies (George, 1979, 1983, 1988) also provide evidence of an equitable distribution of the PDS benefits in Kerala. The sample evidence provided by George (1979) shows that while the poorest forty per cent of the households obtain more than 65 per cent of their rice consumption from the PDS, it is less than forty per cent for the richest seven per cent.
21. There is a general impression that the scale of cereals under the PDS is not adequate. For instance, Koshy *et al* point out that: "Although Kerala had an elaborate and fairly well established public distribution system, only selected commodities were distributed through the system. Moreover, the quantities of these commodities distributed met only part of the consumer's requirements, the rest being procured from the open market...." (Koshy *et al* (1989); p. 40). In a similar vein, Kumar and Stewart observe that: "The maximum quantities that each consumer can buy from the shops are fixed at a level such that only a portion of total consumption requirements can be met" (Kumar and Stewart (1992); p. 275).
22. The per capital cereal bundle corresponding to the class interval enclosing the all-India rural poverty line (Rs. 49.09) for 1997-74 is 15.46 kg which works out to 515 gm per capita per day (GOI, 1977; 1979).
23. This raises an analytical question about the concept of subsidy used in many studies in India. Scholars have examined the welfare gains of the PDS beneficiaries in terms of implicit gains as measured by the excess of the open market price over the PDS price of a given item (Howes and Jha (1992); Parikh (1994)). Such an approach is based on the explicit assumption that the PDS scheme is infra-marginal, that is, consumption of the rationed item is greater than the PDS entitlement. But Kerala is a case where the PDS scheme is marginal, that is, the entitlement is more than

the consumption. In an ideal setting, this should have resulted in a single price structure but it has not. This is because the same items delivered under the PDS and the open market are not homogeneous and are incomparable in quality. Hence, such estimates of implicit subsidy and welfare comparisons for Kerala do not seem to make economic sense.

24. Strictly speaking PDS per ration population may not convey a correct picture based on needs. This problem may be overcome by considering ration units. An adult is considered equivalent to two units and a non-adult to one unit. The results remain the same even with normalization of PDS purchases with respect to units (Table 21.16).
25. One may also ask whether such low levels of PDS utilisation could actually be due to low allotment from the Centre? This does not seem to be the case. For instance, in 1978, 1979 and 1980, the Centre actually allotted 16.20 lakh tonnes of rice each year; but the quantity lifted was only 8.54 lakh tonnes in 1978, 5.45 lakh tonnes in 1979 and 7.85 lakh tonnes in 1980 (GOK (1987)). As recent as last year, the Centre allotted 1.5 lakh tonnes of rice every month but actual distribution of rice ranged from a minimum of 0.82 lakh tonnes in April, 1995 to a maximum of 1.10 lakh tonnes in August, 1995 (GOK (1996)).
26. The corresponding decline was from 69.03 per cent to 44.02 per cent for rural Kerala and 62.42 per cent to 44.47 per cent for urban Kerala.
27. This is in contrast with the all-India picture where a substantial proportion depend on sources other than the PDS (see Table 21.17). This contrast is marked for rice where quality differentials are substantial and matter a lot for the consumer.

REFERENCES

Center for Development Studies (1977), *Poverty, Unemployment and Development Policy*, Orient Longman, Bombay.

Cornia, Giovanni Andrea and Frances Stewart (1993), "Two Errors of Targeting", *Journal of International Development*, vol. 5, no., pp. 459-496.

Dev, S. M. and M. H. Suryanarayana (1991), Is PDS Urban Biased and Pro-rich? An Evaluation", *Economic and Political Weekly*, vol.XXVI, no. 41, pp. 2357-2366.

Dreze, Jean and Amartya Sen (1995), *India: Economic Development and Social Opportunity*, Oxford University Press, Delhi.

Franke, Richärd W. and Barbara H. Chasis (1989), *Kerala Radical Reform as Development in an Indian State*, Food Research Development Report No.6, The Institute for Food and Development Policy, San Francisco, CA.

Geetha, S. and M. H. Suryanarayana (1993), "Revamping PDS: Some Issues and Implications", *Economic and Political Weekly*, vol. XXVIII, no. 41, pp. 2207-2213.

George, P. S. (1979), *Public Distribution of Foodgrains in Kerala - Income Distribution Implications and Effectiveness*, International Food Policy Research Institute Report No. 7, Washington, D.C.

—— (1983), *Government Intervention in Foodgrain Merkets in India*, Indian Institute of Management, Ahmedabad.

—— (1988), "Costs and Benefits of Consumer Oriented Food Subsidies", in Pinstrup Andersen, P. (ed), *Consumer Oriented Food Subsidies: Costs, Benefits, and Policy Options for Developing Countries*, Johns Hopkings University Press, Baltimore.

—— and Chandan Mukherjee (1986), *Rice Economy of Kerala: A Disaggregate Analysis of Performance*, Working Paper No, 213, Center for Development Studies, Thiruvananthapuram.

Government of India (1977), " Survey Results: Consumer Expenditure, NSS 28th Round: 1973-74", *Sarvekshana*, Journal of the National Sample Survey Organisation, vol. 1, no. 1.

—— (1989), *Report of the Task Force on Projections of Minimum Needs and Effective Consumption Demand*, Perspective Planning Division, Planning Commission, New Delhi.

—— (1989), "Results on Per Capita and Per Consumer Unit Per Diem Intake of Calorie, Protein and Fat and Perception of the People on Adequacy of Food: NSS 38th Round, 1983", *Sarvekshana*, vol, XIII, no. 2.

—— (1990), "Results on Utilisation of Public Distribution System", *Sarvekshana*, Journal of the National Sample Survey Organisation, vol. XIII, no.4.

—— (1993), *Report of the Expert Group on Estimation of Proportion and Number of Poor*, Perspective Planning Division, Planning Commission, New Delhi.

Government of Kerala (1987), *A Statistical Handbook on Rationing in Kerala*, Board of Revenue (Civil Supplies), Thiruvananthapuram.

—— (1989), *A Statistical Handbook on Rationing in Kerala*, Board of Revenue (Civil Supplies), Thiruvananthapuram.

—— (1993), *Statistics for Planning*, Department of Economics and Statistics, Thiruvananthpuram.

—— (1994a), *Civil Supplies Vakuppu 1993*, Board of Revenue (Civil Supplies), Thiruvananthapuram.

—— (1994b), *Eighth Five Year Plan 1992-97: Final Outlay Approved by the Planinng Commision (Summary Feature)*, State Planning Board, Thiruvananthapuram.

—— (1995), *Selected Indicators of Development: Kerala and India*-1961 to 1993, Department of Economics and Statistics, Thriuvananthapuram.

—— (1996), *Economic Review 1995*, State Planning Board, Thiruvananthapuram.

Howes, S and Shikha Jha (1992), "Urban Bias in Indian Public Distrubution System", *Economic and Political Weekly*, vol. XXVII, no. 19, pp. 1020-1030.

Jain, L.R. and B.S. Minhas (1991), "Rural and Urban Consumer Price Indices by Commodity Groups (States and All-India: 1970-71 to 1983)", *Sarvekshana*, vol. XV, no. 1, Issue no. 48, pp. 1-21.

Kannan, K.P. (1995), "Declining Incidenoe of Rural Poverty in Kerala", *Economic and Political Weekly*, Vol. XXX, nos 41 & 42, pp. 2651-2662.

——, and K. Pushpangadan (1988), "Agricultural Stagnation and Economic Growth in Kerala: An Exploratory Analysis", *Economic and Political Weekly*, Review of Agriculture, vol. XXIII, no. 39, pp. A120 - A128.

——, (1990), "Dissecting Agricultural Stagnation in Kerala: An Analysis across Crops, Seasons and Regions", *Economic and Political Weekly*, vol. XXV, nos. 35 & 36, pp, 1991-2004.

Koshy, Abraham, A. A. Gopalakrishna, V. Vijayachandran, and N.K. Jayakumar (1989), *Report of the Study on Evaluation of the Public Distribution System in Kerala*, Centre for Management Development, Triruvananthapuram.

Kumar, Shubha K. (1979), *Impact of Subsidized Rice on Food Consumption and Nutrition in Kerala*, International Food Policy Research Institute Report No. 5, Washington, D. C.

Kumar, Gopalakrishna and Frances Stewart (1992), "Tackling Malnutrition: What can Targeted Nutritional Interventions Achieve?" in Harriss, Barbara, S. Guhan and R.H. Cassen (eds.), *Poverty in India: Research and Policy, Oxford University Press*, Bombay, pp 259-281.

Minhas, B.S., L.R. Jain and S.D. Tendulkar (1991), "Declining Incidence of Poverty in the 1980s: Evidence versus Artefact", *Economic and Political Weekly*, vol. 26, nos. 27 & 28, pp.1673-1682.

Parikh, Kirit S. (1994), 'Who Gets How Much From PDS: How Effectively Does It Reach The Poor?", *Sarvekshana*,vol. XVII, no. 3, pp 1-34.

Pushpangadan, K. (1988), *Agicultural Stagnation in Kerala: An Econometrioc Study of Tapioca*, Working Paper No. 226, Centre for Development Studies, Thiruvananthapuram.

Ramachandran, V. K. (1995), *Kerala's Development Achievements: A Review*, Reprint/Preprint No. 200-1995, Indira Gandhi Institute of Development Research, Mumbai.

Sengupta, S. and P. D. Joshi (1978), "Consumption of Cereals and Energy Content of Food Consumed", *Sarvekshna*, vol. II, no. 1, pp 1-11.

Sivaswamy, K. G., V. R. Nayanar, R.G. Kakade and L.N. Rao (1946), *Food Control and Nutrition Surveys*, Servindia Kerala Relief Centre, Madras.

Suryanarayana, M. H. (1994) "Urban Bias in PDS", *Economic and Political Weekly*, vol. XXIX, no,. 9, pp. 510-512.

—— (1995a), "Public Distribution of Food in India: A Clarification", *Food Policy*, vol. 20, no. 1, pp.59-62.

—— (1995b), "Growth, Poverty and Levels of Living: Hypotheses, Methods and Policies", *Journal of Indian School of Political Economy*, vol. VII, no. 2, pp. 203-255.

—— (1995c), "PDS: Beyond Inplicit Subsidy and Urban Bias: The Indian Experience", *Food Policy*, vol. 20, no. 4, pp. 259-278.

—— (1995d), "Some Experiments with Food Stamps", *Economic and Political Weekly*, vol. XXX, no. 52, pp A-151 - A-159.

—— (1996a), "Food Security and Calorie Adequacy Across States: Implications for Reform", *Journal of Indian School of Political Economy*, vol. VIII, no. 2, pp. 202-265.

—— (1996), "Poverty Estinates and Indicatiors:Importance of Data Base", *Economic and Political Weekly*, Special Number, vol. XXXI, nos 35,36 37, pp 2487-2497.l

Tendulkar, S. D. and L.R. Jain (1993), "An Analysis of Inter-State and Inter-Commodity Group Rural-Urban Consumer Price Indices in India; 1983 to 1988-89", *Journal of Indian School of Political Economy*, vol. v, no. 2, pp 267-299.

Vaidyanathan, A. (1985), "Food Cousumption and Size of People: Some Indian Evidence", *Economic and Political Weekly*, Review of Political Economy, vol. XX, no, 30, pp PE 79-PE 84.

Twenty-two

ACCESS VERSUS ACHIEVEMENT

A Study of Primary Education in Kerala

N.V. Varghese

Introduction

Kerala occupies an enviably unique position in the educational map of India. As per the 1991 Census, the literacy rate in Kerala was 90.6 per cent against the all-India average of 52.2 per cent; the female literacy rate in Kerala was 86.2 per cent against the all-India average of 39.3 per cent. It was the first State to initiate and successfully complete total literacy campaigns in all of its districts. The achievements of Kerala in school education, especially primary education, are remarkable. Nearly 60.5 per cent of the females in Kerala have completed primary education against an all-India average of 28.1 per cent. It is the only State in the country which has seriously attempted to provide primary education for all children through formal schools.

At present enrolments at primary level are almost universal. Almost all enrolled children are retained in the system. The dropout rate among primary school children is only 3 per cent whereas the all-India averages are above 35 per cent. Girls account for nearly 49 per cent of enrolment at primary level, dropout rate among girls is lower than that among boys. The female teachers outnumber male teachers at primary level. In 1991-92 nearly 63 per cent of the primary school teachers were female. Even in terms of school facilities and teacher-pupil ratios, Kerala stands in an advantageous position. The provision of primary schooling facilities is now becoming relatively excess in supply, primarily due to demographic changes. Unlike other parts of the country, primary schools in Kerala have buildings and instructional rooms, separate teachers for each class and grade, all the teachers are transit and all schools and classrooms possess minimum teaching-learning materials.

Have these favourable conditions led Kerala to a higher level student performance? Do children at primary level in Kerala learn more than their counterparts in other States which are very poorly placed in terms of school facilities? This chapter is an effort to closely scrutinise learning outcomes and factors influencing learning outcomes at primary levels of education in Kerala. This chapter argues that while public initiatives and social mobilization have helped in expanding educational opportunities and promoting an equitous sharing of public resources, they have not been sufficient enough to ensure improved learning outcomes. This may be due to the fact that the political and social pressure in Kerala has always been more on 'creating institutions imparting primary education than on improving effectiveness of the institutions thus created. Therefore, this chapter argues that the advances made through public initiatives are to be sufficiently complemented through initiatives at local and institutional levels to improve schooling outcomes in Kerala.

The plan of the chapter is as follows: The next section discusses some features of educational development in Kerala. Section 3 introduces the empirical premise of the study. Section 4 presents the levels of learner achievement at the primary stage of education in Kerala. Section 5 attempts to compare the levels of learner achievement of Kerala with other States. Section 6 analyses the determinants of learner achievement in Kerala and the final section draws some concluding observations.

Educational Development in Kerala

Kerala has a fairly developed network of schools. The progressive State policies in education, community involvement in developing and sustaining village schools and Madrassas, efforts by Missionaries and indigenous Christian organizations and efforts by various associations formed by other communities (like SNDP by Ezhava Community and NSS by Nair Community) to establish schools and enrol children have played a significant role in shaping educational progress of Kerala.

Historically, two types of indigenous educational institutions existed in Kerala. They were the *Matts* organised at the household level meant for the education of Brahmins and *Ezhuthupallis* or *Kudipalligudams* meant for the education of non-Brahmins (Rao (1957)). These *Kudipalligudams* or village schools were organised like formal schools, they were run in separate sheds with a teacher paid by the community. Such village schools were widespread in Kerala even before the State actively intervened in primary education. In fact governmental efforts from the early decades of the 19th century supported these village schools. For example, as per the Royal script of 1817 in Travancore, each of these schools was to have two teachers paid from the treasury.

In the second half of the 19th century, the governmental efforts in Travancore and Cochin were towards integrating the then existing indigenous system into the modern educational system primarily through changes in curriculum, content and teaching methods. The grants-in-aid-policy was effectively utilised to bring about parity and uniformity among various types of schools including the Missionary schools. Such a well-conceived public policy helped transforming traditional schools into institutions imparting modern education (see Nair (1981) and Tharakan (1984) for details on historical developments). The Missionary activities targeted children belonging to lower castes and girls and their efforts were supplementary to the government efforts.

Many community-based organisation of Christians, Nairs and Ezhavas started establishing their own schools and colleges. However, admissions to these educational institutions were open to members of all communities. One of the important policy statements by the government in 1887 prescribing minimum qualifications for jobs had a positive impact on the demand for education. Qualification-based job selection process cut the caste-barriers. Since education was not equitably distributed among communities, such a policy meant competitions among various communities to establish schools and corner jobs which were based on educational qualifications. This has contributed to increased community involvement in establishing educational institutions in Kerala.

Table 22.1 Growth of Institutions in Kerala

	Primary	*Upper Primary*	*High Schools*	*Total*
1961-62	6745	1985	629	9359
	(72.1)	(21.2)	(6.7)	(100.0)
1965-66	6954	2447	1151	10552
	(65.9)	(23.2)	(10.9)	(100.0)
1970-71	6895	2543	1384	10822
	(63.7)	(23.5)	(12.8)	(100.0)
1975-76	6975	2606	1521	11102
	(62.8)	(23.5)	(13.7)	(100.0)
1980-81	6861	2753	1976	11590
	(59.2)	(23.8)	(17.0)	(100.0)
1985-86	6896	2852	2422	12170
	(56.7)	(23.4)	(19.9)	(100.0)
1990-91	6767	2915	2452	12134
	(55.8)	(24.0)	(20.2)	(100.0)
1994-95	6694	2912	2486	12092
	(55.4)	(24.1)	(20.5)	(100.0)
Growth Rates (%)				
1961-62to1970-71	0.2	1.2	9.2	1.6
1970-71to1980-81	-ve	0.80	3.6	0.7
1980-81to1990-91	-ve	0.60	2.2	0.5
1990-91to1994-95	-ve	-ve	negl.	-ve

Note: Figures in brackets are percentage to the total.
Source: Government of Kerala (1996) *Economic Review*-1995, State Planning Board, Thiruvananthapuram.

Now, with the decline in child birth, enrolment in primary schools is declining in many localities and primary school enrolment as a share of total school enrolment is also declining. It can be seen from Table 22.1 that the school education system in Kerala is almost saturating in the nineties. The secondary sector which used to register a high rate of growth in the sixties is the only sector which does not experience a negative rate of growth in the nineties. However, the growth of institutions even in this sector is negligible. In 1961-62 primary schools accounted for

72.1 per cent of the total schools, in 1994-95 this share has declined to 55.4 per cent. This affects the pressure on higher levels of school education to expand due to the expansion taking place in the primary levels during the past decades on the one hand and declining number of children available to seek primary education on the other.

Although there is a virtual saturation in terms of growth of institutions, enrolments continue to expand at all levels except primary level. However, the increase in enrolment in the previous decades was marginal in the case of upper primary education and has slowed down at the secondary level (Table 22.2) and enrolment at the primary level has declined in absolute terms from the 1980s. This is primarily due to the decline in the child population of the relevant age-group.

Table 22.2 Enrolment by Management (%)

	1974-75	*1984-85*	*1994-95*
Primary			
Government	44.5	42.4	39.4
Aided	54.8	56.4	56.8
Unaided	0.7	1.2	3.8
	(100.00)	(100.00)	(100.00)
Total (000's)	2845.7	2501.1	2325.1
Upper Primary			
Government	34.6	36.3	34.9
Aided	64.6	62.4	62.4
Unaided	0.8	1.3	2.7
	(100.00)	(100.00)	(100.00)
Total (100's)	1448.9	1805.4	1866.8
High Schools			
Government	34.7	39.7	39.8
Aided	64.1	58.7	57.7
Unaided	1.2	1.6	2.5
	(100.00)	(100.00)	(100.00)
Total (000's)	831.2	1342.0	1616.2

Source: Government of Kerala (1996) *Economic Review-1995*, State Planning Board, Thiruvananthapuram.

Unlike other States, Kerala has a high share of private-aided sector in education. This is primarily due to the community involvement in education from the very beginning. Majority of schools and larger share of enrolment at all stages of school education are accounted by the private-aided sector. Trends in the previous decade indicate that the share of government sector in student enrolment is declining at primary and upper primary levels and stagnating at secondary levels. The corresponding share of the private-aided sector is also stagnating at all levels of school education. The only sector which has expanded in the recent past is the unaided sector. The share of students enrolled in unaided schools increased by more than five times between 1974-75 to 1994-95, the corresponding increase at upper primary level is almost two and a half times and that at secondary level two times. This becomes more clear if one analyses the trends of enrolment in grade 1. In 1970-71 government schools enrolled 350.7 thousand children, aided sector enrolled 446.3 thousand children and unaided sector enrolled 3.6 thousand children. In 1994-95 enrolments in grade 1 in government schools declined to 208.3 thousands and in aided schools to 309.1 thousands. Enrolment in unaided schools increased from 3.5 to 23.2 thousands during the corresponding period. This represents a changing preference pattern where people are increasingly opting for unaided sector in education. However, it needs to be noted that the relative size of the unaided sector still continue to be small. One of the reasons for such a preference pattern may be a perceived notion of low quality of education imparted in government and aided primary schools. The remaining part of this chapter analyses this aspect of the problem, namely, learning outcomes at the primary level of education.

The Empirical Base

The empirical evidence presented in this chapter is based on a study of 5319 primary school children, 507 primary school teachers and 113 primary school headmasters drawn from 113 primary schools selected from 11 educational sub-districts from the educationally backward districts of Malappuram, Kasaragode and Wayanad. The study adopted a multi-stage random sampling procedure to select educational sub-districts and schools. The sub-districts were selected at random from each of these districts keeping a norm of selecting a minimum of two sub-districts if the total number of educational sub-districts exceeds five in any district. Based on the share of urban population as per 1991 Census, urban locations and number of schools from urban areas were decided (For details on sampling procedure see Varghese (1994)).

The schools were selected at random from the randomly selected educational sub-districts. In total, the study sample consisted of 40 schools, 794 grade 2 children, 1129 grade 4 children and 187 primary schools teachers from Malappuram; 37 schools, 722 grade 2 children, 977 grade 4 children and 151 primary school teachers from Kasaragode; and 36 schools, 714 grade 2 children, 983 grade 4 children and 164 primary school teachers from Wayanad.

Questionnaire-based primary data were collected from the schools on facilities, from headmasters on school's management, from teachers on teaching-learning process, from students on personal and household characteristics. Tests were developed, pilot tested and finalised to measure achievement levels in Malayalam and Mathematics. These tests were administered to students of grade 2 and grade 4. These achievement tests were based on the competencies expected to be achieved by children at the end of grade 1 and grade 3 respectively and were administered in October-November, 1993. Since, these tests were administered to grade 2 and grade 4 children, the results presented may represent an element of over-estimation of achievement levels. It needs to be noted that the study was undertaken in the context of DPEP (Varghese (1996)) and hence the data were collected from the educationally backward districts of Kerala. Therefore, one cannot assume the sample to be representative for the State as a whole. The result and discussion in this chapter may be seen in the light of these limitations.

How much do Children Learn?

The levels of learner achievement in grade 2 are given in Table 22.3. Levels of learner achievement in grade 2 are reasonably high in both the subject areas. Students in grade 2 perform better in Malayalam than in Mathematics. The mean score in Maths is 59.3 per cent whereas the mean score in Malayalam is 67 per cent. Kasaragode district performs better in both the subject areas followed by Wayanad and the lowest scores are in Malappuram. It is important to note that inter-district variations are lower in learning language than in learning mathematics.

Table 22.3 Mean Scores in Grade 2 (%)

District	*Maths*	*Malayalam*
Malappuram	54.3	66.0
Kasaragode	66.4	69.0
Wayanad	58.6	65.5
Total	59.3	67.0

A further disaggregated analysis of achievement levels is shown in Table 22.4. It shows that nearly one-third of the children attain mastery levels (80% and above) in Maths and nearly half of the children score 60 per cent and above; 67 children scored zero and 437 children scored 100 per cent in Maths test. The inter-district variation becomes more pronounced when we look at the share of children attaining mastery levels. The percentage of children scoring 80 per cent or more in Kasaragode is almost twice as that in Malappuram. More than half of the children in all districts attain mastery levels in language.

Table 22.4 Percentage of Students by Score (Grade 2)

Score(%)	*Malappuram*	*Kasaragode*	*Wayand*	*Total*
Maths				
Less than 40	37.4	24.2	31.9	31.4
40-60	21.9	18.3	20.6	20.3
60-80	17.4	14.8	18.6	17.0
80-100	23.3	42.7	28.9	31.3
Total	100.0	100.0	100.0	100.0
Malayalam				
Less than 40	25.7	22.0	25.5	24.4
40-60	9.7	11.2	11.3	10.7
60-80	14.5	11.4	12.6	12.9
80-100	50.1	55.4	50.6	52.0
Total	100.0	100.0	100.0	100.0

These positive trends disappear as we look at achievement levels in grade 4 (Table 22.5). The achievement levels show a sharp decline. The mean achievement level in Maths is only 37.2 per cent and that in Malayalam is only 47 per cent. Surprisingly, the very same schools which contributed to higher scores in grade 2 in Kasaragode were not in a position to maintain the same levels in grade 4. The tribal district of Wayanad shows a higher level of achievement in grade 4 than the other two districts. It may be noted that the inter-district disparities have declined in Maths score in grade 4 when compared to grade 2 and the same in language has increased. This is primarily due to the low levels of scores in Maths in all the three districts.

Table 22.5 Mean Scores in Grade 4 (%)

Districts	*Maths*	*Malayalam*
Malappuram	34.1	44.8
Kasaragode	38.4	45.3
Wayanad	39.6	51.3
Total	27.2	47.0

A further disaggregated analysis of the achievement scores (Table 22.6) shows a dismal performance by the primary school children in Kerala. Majority of children score less than 40 per cent in Maths and they account for two-thirds of the children in Malappuram. More importantly not even one per cent of the children attain mastery levels in Maths; only 7.5 per cent of the children attain scores above 60 per cent. The situation is better in Malayalam, 4.6 per cent of the children attain mastery levels in Malayalam, three children in Malappuram, one in Kasaragode and one in Wayanad got zero marks in Malayalam. However, the levels of learner achievement even in Malayalam are rather low.

Is Low Level of Achievement Specific to Kerala?

How does Kerala compare itself with other States in terms of levels of learning among primary school children? The mean scores (Table 22.7) shown against all the States are from studies conducted under the same project designed at the national level

Table 22.6 Percentage of Students by Score (Grade 4)

Scores(%)	*Malappuram*	*Kasaragode*	*Wayanad*	*Total*
Maths				
less than 40	66.8	53.4	52.4	58.4
40-60	28.9	36.8	37.4	34.1
60-80	4.3	9.2	9.6	7.5
80-100	0.0	0.0	0.0	0.0
Total	100.0	100.0	100.0	100.0
Malayalam				
Less than 40	41.2	41.0	29.3	37.4
40-60	38.1	38.5	39.5	38.7
60-80	16.4	16.1	25.3	19.3
80-100	4.3	4.2	5.9	4.6
Total	100.0	100.0	100.0	100.0

and hence these results are comparable. It can be seen from the Table that the achievement levels, in general, are low in all the States. However, what is surprising is the lower levels of learner achievement in Kerala when compared with other States. In Mathematics, achievement levels in Kerala are less than that of States like Assam, Haryana, Karnataka etc. Even in language, achievement levels in Kerala are comparable with some of the educationally backward States like Assam and Orissa.

Table 22.7 Mean Scores at the End of Primary Level(%)

States	*Maths*	*Language*
Assam*	49.7	48.3
Haryana	38.0	44.2
Karnataka*	38.9	41.6
Kerala*	37.2	47.0
Madhya Pradesh	28.1	37.0
Maharashtra	29.2	37.7
Orissa	36.5	47.7
Tamil Nadu	28.2	36.3

* Grade 4 and Grade 5 in other States.

Source: Varghese (1994) for Kerala; Jangira (1994) for other States.

It can be argued that the low levels of learner achievement at primary level is neither a unique feature specific to Kerala nor a recent phenomenon in India. Almost all studies on quality of primary education in India have come to the conclusion that students are not learning enough at the primary level. One of the first major studies on learner achievement in India was carried out in 1967 (Kulkarni (1970)). Based on the tests in Mathematics administered to 28,000 primary school children drawn from 15 States, the study concluded that achievement levels of primary school children are low in India. Another study (Shukla (1974)) initiated by the International Association for Evaluation of Educational Research focused on measuring the levels of learner achievement in Hindi and Science. This study again came to similar conclusions as that of the earlier study. Another significant All India Study (Dave (1988)) conducted under the project on Primary Education Curriculum Renewal assessed 3,00,000 children drawn from 2480 schools from 22 States, it showed that there was a sudden slump in the achievement levels as children transit from grade 2 to grade 3 and it continues till the end of the primary cycle. Studies on individual States carried out in the nineties also show similar results. For example, studies on Madhya Pradesh (Govinda and Varghese (1993)), Uttar Pradesh (Bashir *et al* (1993)), Tamil Nadu (Bashir (1994)), Haryana, Assam, Maharashtra, Karnataka (Jangira, 1994) also have come to the same conclusion.

Why does Kerala with better schooling facilities perform poor in primary level of education? Unlike other States, primary schools in Kerala have buildings and separate instructional rooms or spaces for all divisions/sections in any grade of primary cycle; the teachers are qualified and trained; multi-grade teaching is non-existent in Kerala; all grades and each section in each grade has a separate teacher. Even in terms of availability of teaching-learning materials, the status of primary schools in Kerala is better placed than primary schools in other parts of the country. Similarly, all the schools in our sample function for a minimum period of 180 working days. Teacher absenteeism is also not a major problem in Kerala. The initial condition are very encouraging; still the level of learning among primary school children in terminal grades does not reflect the improved provisions in schools. How do we explain this phenomenon?

One plausible explanation can be as follows. In other States the dropout rates are high and hence only a few of the children enrolled in grade 1 reach the terminal grades of primary cycle. And those who are retained in the system may be academically better than those who have dropped out. This may be true even in terms of socio-economic background of the children who are retained in the system. Therefore, it is the relatively better off students (better off both academically and economically) who are tested in other States. The contrast is considerable in Kerala where the dropout rate is minimal. Since almost all children enrolled in grade 1 continue in the system, variations among these children in terms of learner achievement may be higher in Kerala. The promotion policy in Kerala helps this process. At the primary level all children are promoted from grade 1 to grade 2 and 90 per cent of the children are promoted to the subsequent grades from grade 2, 3 and 4. Since almost all children reach grade 4, the achievement level varies and this factor depresses the mean achievement scores of primary school children in Kerala. In other words, what is argued is that the mean achievement levels in Kerala represent average achievement of the age-group population whereas in other States they represent the mean scores of the selected children who may be academically better off than the average of the age-group population. The situation in other States increases the chances to have higher mean scores of grade 4 or 5 children and the situation in Kerala brings down the mean scores. This may partly justify the relative position of Kerala in comparison with other States. However, this is not a sufficient explanation for the low levels of achievement of primary school students in Kerala and more importantly a sharp decline in levels of achievement as one moves from grade 2 to grade 4. This may require a more detailed analysis of factors influencing learner achievement in Kerala.

Determinants of Learner Achievement

Factors influencing learner achievement are broadly categorised into two: (i) school factors, and (ii) home background factors. In the following paragraphs an effort is made to identify factors influencing levels of learner achievement by taking into account school level and household level factors. The methodology followed in this chapter is as follows: First a correlation analysis (Varghese (1995a)) and then a multivariate analysis using OLS methods were attempted. The correlation analysis and OLS methods helped identify significant variables. As a next step, a multivariate analysis using Hierarchical Linear Models (HLM) was attempted, (see Bryk and Raudenbush (1992); Willms (1992) for a discussion on HLM). What is presented in the following paragraphs is only a summary of results of the HLM analysis (for details see Varghese (1995a)).

The first step in the analysis is to identify the significant variables. As noted above the correlation and regression analysis helped in identifying variables which are significantly related to achievement levels in Malayalam and Mathematics. Among the selected variables, pupil level variables are separated out and are considered as level 1 predictor variables in HLM. The school level variables were entered as level 2 predictor variables.

In developing the model, first a null model to partition the total variance between schools and within schools is considered; then level 1 predictor variables are entered and finally level 2 predictor variables are considered. The null model for Kerala shows that between school variances are less in Kerala and within school variances are larger. This is in contrast to the results obtained for other States (Table 22.8). For example, the between school variance in Mathematics in Kerala is only 19.67 per cent whereas the same is 60.6 per cent in Karnataka, 48.3 per cent in Assam etc. The corresponding figure in language is 13.7 per cent in Kerala whereas it is 45.7 per cent in Karnataka, 35.0 per cent in Assam etc. Needless to add, the within school variances are very high in Kerala when compared with other States.

The low between school variance may explain a more equitable distribution of educational facilities in Kerala. It implies that the variation in learner achievement is less due to factors outside the school than due to factors which are within school.

Table 22.8 Between and Within School Variances(%)

	Between School		*Within School*	
	Maths	*Language*	*Maths*	*Language*
Assam	48.3	35.0	51.7	65.0
Haryana	31.3	35.6	68.7	64.4
Karnataka	60.6	45.2	39.4	54.8
Kerala	19.6	13.7	80.4	86.3
Madhya Pradesh	45.6	45.5	54.4	54.6
Maharashtra	39.3	37.7	60.7	62.3
Orissa	44.1	29.3	55.9	70.7
Tamil Nadu	36.0	32.8	64.0	67.2

Source: Varghese (1995a) for Kerala and Singh and Saxena (1995) for other States.

This is in line with the general trend seen more often in developed countries than in developing countries. Such a pattern in partitioning the variance also points to the importance of intervening at the institutional level especially in school practices to improve learner achievement.

The next step in HLM analysis was to see the effect of level 1 predictor variables. The predictor variables selected for analysis are the following :

Level 1: Predictor Variable

1. GIRL - Sex of the student : girl = 1, boy = 0
2. SES - Social Background of the child, it is composite variable consisting of father's education, mother's education and father's occupation.
3. REPEAT - Repeated in any class
4. ASPIRSN - Aspiration of the child, it is a composite variable taking into account educational and occupational aspirations of the child.
5. EXRDMAT- Extra reading material other than textbooks.

Level 2: Predictor Variables

1. MEANSES- Mean of social background of children (aggregated from SES).
2. OPBLACK - Operation Blackboard.
3. TWDAYS - Total working days in an academic year.

4. MORG - School organisation, it is a composite variable taking into account organisation of school activities.

The summary results of the achievement analysis in Mathematics are given in Table 22.9.

Table 22.9 Achievement in Mathematics

		Variance	
		Between School	*Within School*
Null Model		0.195	0.805
Level 1 Predictor Variables	*Coefficient*		
1 GIRL	0.037		
2 SES	0.127		
3 ASPIRSN	0.107		
4 EXRDMAT	0.181		
		0.175	0.701
Variance Explained		10.3%	12.8 %
Level 2 Predictor Variables	*Coefficient*		
1.MEANSES	0.114		
2. MORG	0.267		
3. TWDAYS	0.025		
4. OPBLACK	0.185		
		0.140	0.707
Variance Explained	28.2 %	12.1 %	

The results show that girls do not have an advantage over boys since the coefficients are not significant at .05 level. However SES, ASPRISN and EXRDMAT have positive and significant influence on Maths achievement. An improvement in SES contributes to around 12.7 per cent of an SD increase in achievement. However, SES achievement slope does not vary significantly between schools (p> 05). Similarly, for every change in Aspiration levels there is an increase in learner achievement to the effect of 10.7 per cent. Extra reading material has more influence on explaining the variation in learner achievement when compared with other level 1 predictor variables. A unit change in the availability of reading materials improves learner achievement by 18.1 per cent of an SD. As can be seen from Table 22.9, the level 1 predictor variables explain 10.3 per cent of the between school variations and 12.8 per cent of the within school variations.

The coefficients of the level 2 predictor variables show that MORG, OPBLACK and MEANSES contribute considerably to improvement in levels of learner achievement. The achievement level in language also shows similar trends (Table 22.10). The EXRDMAT has significant positive contribution to improving learner achievement; REPEAT has a negative contribution; girls may be performing marginally better than boys (however the coefficient is not statistically significant) Trends in SES and ASPIRN and other level 2 predictor variables are the same as in case of Maths achievement. The variable considered could explain 21 per cent of the between school variance in Maths, 33.3% in Malayalam and 20.6% of the within school variance in Maths and 20.5 per cent in Malaylam.

Table 22.10 Achievement in Language

HLM Analysis		*Variance*	
		Between School	*Within School*
Null Model		0.138	0.863
Level 1 Variables	*Coefficient*		
1 GIRL	-0.015		
2 SES	0.166		
3 REPEAT	-0.352		
4 ASPIRSN	0.148		
5 EXRDMAT	0.236		
		0.109	0.685
Variance Explained		21.0 %	20.6 %
Level 2 Variables			
1 MEANSES	0.067		
2 MORG	0.166		
3 TWDAYS	0.024		
4 OPBLACK	0.080		
		0.092	0.686
Variance Explained		33.3 %	20.5 %

The analysis of both the achievement test results shows features. Firstly, the relationship between MEANSES and SES achievement slope in language is negative, indicating that better SES children perform better in schools where majority of children are from poor families. In Maths, the results show that individual students from higher SES perform better in school where majority of students are from higher SES background. Secondly, extra reading material influences achievement scores both in Maths and Language. Creation of reading facilities and school libraries may be very helpful in the context of Kerala. It also indicates the facilities at home. Our detailed correlation analysis had shown that children of parents who are educated at least upto secondary level and employed in tertiary sector score better than those whose parents are less educated and employed in primary sector. The children who have better learning situation at home perform better in schools.. Thirdly, repeaters perform poor in general and they perform worse in schools which are less equipped and poorly organised. Fourthly, the Operation Blackboard strategy has more important contribution to improve the level of learning in Mathematics than in Language. Fifthly, total number of working days does not seem to influence learner achievement considerably. Lastly, the organisation of school activities is an important variable influencing learner achievement both in Maths and Malayalam.

One of the important school level variable influencing learner achievement is MORG. As pointed out earlier, this is a composite variable reflecting the organisation of school activities. School vary considerably in this regard. In our earlier analysis (Varghese (1995b)), it has been found that the type of management—whether the school belongs to private-aided or government-managed—is not an important variable influencing learner achievement. Therefore, it is not the type of management but the way schools are managed becomes a more important factor influencing learner achievement. The analysis in this chapter shows that the practices followed within the school considerably explain the variations in learner achievement. Therefore more attention needs to be focussed on internal management of primary schools in Kerala.

For example, PTAs are formed in all primary schools in Kerala. However, they are active only in some schools. It is found that wherever PTAs are active, the schools function better.

The teaching-learning practices are very important factors influencing learner achievement. At present a lot of time is wasted because school activities are not organised in a systematic way. The organisation of school activities through proper planning and better management can increase the effective learning time available to children and this will have a positive influence on the levels of learning of the children in primary schools of Kerala. Therefore, intervention at the institutional level can improve student learning at primary levels at least to a considerable extent.

Concluding Observations

The analysis in this chapter shows that although Kerala has made significant advances in creating educational facilities, enrolling and retaining children in primary schools, its record in terms of student performance is not significantly different from other States which do not have these initial favourable endowments. An analysis of factors influencing learner achievement has shown that within school variances are substantially larger than between school variances. School facilities did not emerge as an important variable influencing learner achievement. What has emerged as important variable is the school level practices. Therefore, the focus of intervention strategies in Kerala has to shift from investment to create facilities to investments to improve school level management practices.

Internal management of the school is very important and headmaster plays an important role in this process. Fortunately, all the primary schools in Kerala have a designated headmaster. However, they are neither adequately trained nor given authority and hence school activities are rarely planned and seldom monitored. Primary schools in Kerala are large in size both in terms of number of students and teachers. Therefore, managing such primary schools requires proper planning and management of school activities. In other words, the efforts need to be to professionalize educational management at the institutional level.

This will improve institutional effectiveness and learner achievement. This is equally applicable to government and aided schools. As already indicated, now there is an increasing trend towards seeking admissions in unaided sector. This may be partly due to the parental perception that children may suffer in government and aid public-funded primary schools without improving the internal management of these schools.

The public policy initiative and funding support in Kerala have helped in creating educational facilities in Kerala. In the absence of complementary efforts from the local level, these positive initial conditions are not getting translated into higher learning outcomes. This requires institutional level initiatives which are not readily forthcoming in Kerala. Therefore, intervention strategies to improve primary education in Kerala should focus more on institutional level changes promoting and encouraging school-based initiatives to improve institutional effectiveness. Such a strategy has more to do with changes at institutional level management practices than changes at the public policy level. Perhaps, it may require a public policy support to strengthen the institutional level actors to initiate school improvement programmes.

REFERENCES

Bashir, S. (1994), Public Versus Private in Primary Education: Comparisons of School Effectiveness and Costs in Tamil Nadu, Unpublished Ph D. Thesis Submitted to University of London, London.

——— V. Ramakrishnan and S. Sharma (1993), *Baseline Survey of Three Districts of Uttar Pradesh, India, Vol.* 1, New Delhi, New Concept Consultancy Services.

Bryk, A.S. and S.N. Raudenbush (1992), *Hierarchical Linear Models: Application and Data Analysis Methods*, Newsbury California, Sage.

Dave, P.N. (1988), *Pupil Achievement at the Primary Stage*, Department of Pre-School and Elementary Education, New Delhi, NCERT.

Govinda, R. and N.V. Varghese (1993), *Quality of Primary Schooling in India: A Case Study of Madhya Pradesh*, Paris, HEP.

Jangira, N.K. (1994), "Learning Achievement of Primary School Children in Reading and Mathematics" *Research Based Interventions in Primary Education*, New Delhi, NCERT, pp 59-84.

Kulkarni, S.S. (1970), *All India Survey of Achievement in Mathematics*, New Delhi, NCERT.

Nair, P.R.G. (1981), *Primary Education, Population Growth and Socio-Economic Change, A Comparative Study with Special Reference to Kerala*, New Delhi, Allied.

Rao, M.S.A. (1957), *Social Change in Malabar Bombay*, Popular Depot.

Shukla, S (1974), "Achievement of Indian Children in Mother Tongue (Hindi) and Science", Comparative Education Review, vol 8, no.2.

Singh, S. and R.R. Saxena (1995), "Achievement Difference and School Effects", *Indian Educational Review*, pp. 1-25 (Special Number of DPEP).

Tharakan, M. (1984), "Socio-economic Factors in Educational Development. Case of 19th century Travancore", *Economic and Political Weekly*, November, pp. 10 & 17.

Varghese, N.V. (1994), *School Quality and Student Learning: A Study of Primary Schooling in Kerala*, New Delhi, NIEPA.

——— (1995a), *School Effects: A Multilevel Analysis of Government and Private Aided Schools in Kerala* (A Study funded by the World Bank). NIEPA, New Delhi.

——— (1995b), "School Effects on Achievement: A Study of Government and Private Aided Schools in Kerala", K. Kumar (ed.) *School Effectiveness and Learning Achievement at Primary Stage : International Perspective*, NCERT, New Delhi, pp. 261-290.

——— (1996), "Decentralisation of Educational Planning in India: The Case of the District Primary Education Program", *International Journal of Educational Development*, vol 16, no. 4, pp. 355-365.

Willms, J.D. (1992), *Monitoring School Performance: A Guide for Educators*, London, Falmer Press.

TWENTY-THREE

COST SHARING IN MEDICAL EDUCATION

C. GASPER & T. K. SEBASTIAN

Introduction

Kerala's achievements in the field of education are well known. In terms of the development indicators such as rate of literacy, level of school enrollment and dropout rates, Kerala's performance is commendable and even comparable with that of the developed nations. However, despite the apparently large opportunities for higher education, there is still an excess demand which is evident from the massive migration of students from Kerala to other States. One of the major reasons for this migration is the mismatch between the courses offered and demanded in the sphere of higher education. A cross-comparison with her neighbouring States would reveal the poor status of Kerala, in terms of facilities available for medical and paramedical educational opportunities

The inefficiency and incapability of the existing public educational network in meeting the demand for higher and technical education has to be overcome. This calls for a fundamental restructuring of courses and curriculum, which demands a massive infusion of capital funds. Funds are also required to reorient, retain and redeploy the existing teachers and to augment the intake capacity and quality of the existing higher education centres.

Higher education sector in Kerala is currently in the grip of a severe financial crisis. This crisis is not unique to India but is faced by many countries, both developed and developing. The slow economic growth, rising unemployment and continued fiscal crisis have compelled many countries to curtail their social expenditure including education to contain the fiscal deficits. The crisis has been further compounded by the introduction of structural adjustment programme in many countries which demands reduction in public investment including higher education. In the prevailing global situation of financial squeeze to the educational sector, various alternatives for financing education are suggested. The alternatives include better targeting of subsidies, subsidised student loans, greater tax, pay roll tax and educational cess. Cost reduction by applying modern management principles and techniques also finds a place in the agenda.

The recent financial crisis in the government-owned higher education sector and its incapability to meet the growing demand forced the policy makers to shift the focus in favour of self-financing colleges and thus to privatisation. In the meanwhile, the private sector is also emerging as an important player in this regard. Privatisation of education essentially aims at increasing reliance on private sources for educational finance in the place of ever-increasing government subsidies. Given this, cost recovery becomes a major instrument of privatisation. Alternative methods with different degrees of privatization of education include: (a) establishment of private sector institutions; (b) rendering management powers to private parties with the freedom to start/stop courses according to market signals; and (c) partial or full withdrawal of educational subsidies; and (d) introducing fully or partially self-financed educational institutions.

Though the role of private sector and the principle of cost sharing/recovery is rational and justifiable, this point cannot be stretched too far in India due to social and equity considerations. It is often argued that the aspect of social equity as manifested in the ability of students to pay should assume as much importance as a cost recovery or economic efficiency in higher education. Public financing of medical education is argued on the grounds of efficient distribution of resource and returns to medical education.

In the case of pure social goods, consumption by various individuals is not rivalry, in the sense that one's partaking of the benefits does not reduce the benefits available to others. In the case of private goods, the benefit of consumption is internalised with a consumer and consumption by him excludes the consumption by others. In the case of private goods, efficient distribution of resources is sought to be taken care of by markets. Whereas in the case of pure social goods, public provision is made for adequate supply. Medical education is neither a pure public good nor a pure private good; it is rather a combination of both. Theoretically, medical education services do not go by the marginal cost pricing rule. The following efficiency reasons demand public provision or subsidy in medical education.

First, some of the benefits of the medical education may accrue not only to the individual user, but also to the society. These extra individual benefits are called externalities. In deciding how much to consume, individuals generally weigh only the personal benefit against the personal cost and does not consider the impact of their consumption on others. Therefore, for social benefits, it is necessary that the government should intervene and invest in medical education. The returns to investments in human capital depend on the discounted value of future wage payments. If these wages are offered at a socially inefficient level, then marginal cost pricing in education would probably be inefficient. In the case of medical education, the private practitioners' earning may be more than the government wage rates.

Secondly, potential users may be unaware of all the personal benefits of educational services in general and medical education in particular. In addition even those who are aware of the services may have insufficient income for the minium amount considered socially desirable by public authorities, without unacceptable sacrifices. The educational services are said to have the characteristics of "merit goods". In other words, public authorities may have more information and resources concerning what is best for users than the users themselves. Thirdly, marginal cost pricing may be inefficient due to distortions in related markets, namely, markets for inputs (such as teachers, when their salaries are inefficiently subsidised); markets (such as the labour market) for other services for which the output (graduating student) of the social (education) would be considered as an input; and market for financial services (such as credit for education and insurance for health). There are important implications for efficiency in access to credit and insurance markets. In India, credit facilities are not widely available from the bank for higher education. So public financing is largely required.

The public intervention in higher education sector can also be justified on equity grounds. It is argued that public expenditure on higher education can be used as a method of income redistribution. For instance, in a highly stratified society like India, the lower social class representation in the professional education, like medical education, is very low. Public financing may induce them to invest in medical education, which has high inter-generational externality. Because of the increasing expenditure on medical education, government finance alone may be inadequate. Hence an optimum mix of public and private financing of medical education is needed. There is however no definite view on the mix of both public and private financing. For a further insight into the required mix of public subsidies and private finances for medical education, one has to understand clearly the returns to medical education. However the availability of comparative data on returns to medical education is inadequate.

Medical education yields return not only to the individuals who possess it, but also to the society at large. The returns accruing to the individual owners of medical education are called private returns to medical education. The returns accruing to the society are called social returns to medical education. Solan (1970) and Lindsay (1973, 1976) have estimated the economic benefits of investment in the medical graduation. According to them, the social internal rates of returns (IROR) are 13.5 per cent, 11.3 per cent and 19.9 per cent in 1948, 1958 and 1970 respectively. The private internal rates of returns (IR0R) are 17.6 per cent, 13.6 per cent and 25.5 per cent in 1948, 1958 and 1970 respectively. In all the three years under consideration, the private rates of returns are higher than the social rates of returns to medical education.

This study aims to estimate the total cost of medical education in Kerala. It calculates the contribution of students to the cost of medical education. Further, it analyses how much of the total cost of medical education the students can and possibly willing to bear.

Data and Approach

Data Sources

Both primary and secondary data are used for the study. The former is obtained through an extensive survey of 231 graduate students from Trivandrum Medical college during the academic year 1995-96. The data collected include details on the education expenses of the students, their family expenditure pattern, the socio-economic background of the family and the ability and willingness to pay to the student. The major secondary sources of data are the Kerala State Budget Papers and the Medical College Documents. The study also made use of various governmental and non-governmental secondary materials. Apart from this, detailed discussions were also carried out with parents, medical personnel and other informed persons.

Distribution of the Respondents

Out of the selected 231 students, day scholars account for 70 per cent of the sample while the remaining are hostlers. About 55 per cent are females. The distribution of the students according to their social category and their class of study (year) is given in Table 23.1. Of the sample, 7 per cent is SC/ST, 39 per cent is OBC and 54 per cent is Forward Castes (FC). Of the total sample I MBBS students constitute 25 per cent, II MBBS, 26; III MBBS, 25 and House Surgeons 24 per cent respectively

Table 23.1 Distribution of Sample Students

	FC			*OBC*			*SC/ST*			*Grand Total*		
	HS	*DS*	*Total*	*HS*	*DS*	*Total*	*HS*	*DS*	*Total*	*HS*	*DS*	*Total*
I MBBS	9	24	33	7	14	21	—	5	5	16	43	59
II MBBS	12	21	33	9	13	22	2	3	5	13	47	60
III MBBS	12	18	30	11	13	24	1	2	3	24	33	57
House Surgeons	11	18	29	6	17	23	2	1	3	19	36	55
Total			125 (54)			90 (39)			16 (7)			231 (100)

Note: HS=Hostel Residents; DS=Day Scholars. *Source:* Survey Data.

Regarding the residential background , on an average 56.7 per cent are from the cities and 21.6 per cent are from villages and towns. Among the SC/ST students, 94 per cent are either from cities or towns. In the case of the other categories (OBC & FC) also the percentage share of urban students is quite high indicating clearly the urban bias in the distribution of medical students (see Table 23.2).

Table 23.2 Place of Residence

	FC	*OBC*	*SC/ST*	*Total*
City	74	48	9	131
	(59.2)	(53.3)	(56.3)	(56.7)
Town	25	19	6	50
	(20.00)	(21.1)	(37.5)	(21.6)
Village	26	23	1	50
	(20.8)	(25.5)	(6.25)	(21.6)
Total	125	90	16	231

Source: Same as for Table 23.1

Calculation of Costs

Investment in medical education comes from three main sources. They are the Governments (Centre and States), the institutions, and the beneficiaries (students and their parents). Hence the analysis of the total cost of medical education consists of the cost incurred by the governments, the institution and the students and parents. In the case of government medical college, the governmental costs are synonymous with the institutional cost. Hence the total cost of medical education consists of institutional cost and private cost incurred by the students and parents.

Calculation of Institutional Cost

Institutional cost means the expenditure incurred by the government and the institution for providing the facilities for education. It is of two types: non-recurring costs or capital costs and recurring or current cost. The non-recurring or capital cost is the cost incurred once which does not change along with changes in the input or output of the system, while the recurring cost is the annual institutional spending to run the medical education.

Capital cost: The capital cost consists of the cost of the durable items such as value of land, buildings, furniture and office, laboratory and workshop equipments, books and all other non-recurring items. The expenditure incurred for the acquisition of assets each year is treated differently in different studies. Certain studies include it under capital expenditure; while some others treate it as a recurring category. The former approach seems to be valid since expenditure on acquisition of assets during a year would yield services in the coming years. It is, however, a common practice to consider expenditure during the subsequent years as current expenditure. But this treatment violates the theoretical aspect of capital cost. An alternative approach to the calculation of capital cost would be to estimate the imputed rent which measures the annual value of the amount of capital used up each year by students at each level of education. This study considers only the recurring cost incurred for medical education in Trivandrum Medical College.

Recurring costs: Recurring costs of medical education comprise of salaries and allowances of the teaching staff (teaching costs), non-teaching staff (administrative cost), current expenditure on laboratories and workshops (laboratory costs), scholarships, stipends and other financial assistance (subsidies), maintenance of buildings, repair of furniture and equipment (maintenance cost), books, journals and dailies in the library (library cost), hostel expenses, cost for conducting games and sports, examination cost, cost in general direction and miscellaneous cost.

General administrative cost: The general administrative cost of medical education in the State is also included in the cost calculation of medical education. Directorate of Medical Education (DME) is the administrative body of all medical colleges in Kerala. Since there are five medical colleges coming under the directorate currently, one-fifth of the total administrative cost is considered for inclusion in the cost of medical education.

Cost of College Teaching and Hospital Teaching

Unlike other higher educational studies, Medical graduate education (MBBS course) is conducted at the college (college education) and at the hospital (clinical education). Every student enrolled for MBBS course becomes automatically a junior member of the college hospital. The student is responsible for a group of patients. The individual clinical student is expected to visit his/her patients regularly, during the second period. He/she learns under the supervision of senior doctors. The student learns how to obtain information from the sick people by history-taking and clinical examinations. Thus the teaching takes place at the college as well as at the hospital. Institutional cost without considering hospital teaching expenditure will give only a partial analysis of the cost of medical education. At the same time inclusion of this item itself raises multifarious issues as discussed below.

From the point of view of economic theory, medical colleges engage in joint production; that is, the same resource produces more than one product. When joint production exists, one must take special precautions in specifying the cost of each product. This issue arises due to the difficulties in calculating the pure costs of patient care and education.

Along with this theoretical problem, a practical problem is also faced in this study. Historically, expenditure for medical education is treated as a part of expenditure for health services; therefore, the services of the hospitals are not easily identifiable and no separate data is available regarding the expenditure incurred by the government for medical education. Thus, there is a question, whether hospital expenditure should be considered as a part of medical education or a part of health services.

Medical education would be impossible without the hospital teaching experience of the doctors and thus, the cost of hospital teaching ought to be included in the cost of medical education. The study attempts to identify the cost of teaching and other services provided by the hospitals to the undergraduate medical students. Since there is no clear rule or definition in this regard, it is assumed that the expenditure incurred on all the academic staff of medical college hospital is a part of expenditure on medical education. All other expenses (e.g. materials, medicine, payments for nurses etc.) are considered exclusively for patients.

Private Cost

Private cost is defined as the cost incurred either by the student or parents or both directly or indirectly. The direct private cost refers to the amount of physical resources spent by the students while receiving medical education and the indirect, which may be called as the 'opportunity' cost, refers to the financial burden on a medical student by way of loss of potential during the period of his/her graduate studies and internship.

In the case of Kerala which occupies the first position in the matter of educated unemployment among the Indian States, the size of the opportunity cost may be equal to zero. Most of the students enrolled for higher education in Kerala typically come from those strata of society where it is not usual for the students to participate in economic activity. The survey has also found that majority of the students have been neither employed nor been offered any job at the time of joining or during the degree course. Therefore, in the study opportunity cost is treated as zero.

Medical Education Facilities in Kerala

The first medical college was started at Thiruvananthapuram in 1951, the second at Kozhikode in 1957, the third at Kottayam in 1961, the fourth at Alappuzha in 1963 and the fifth one at Thrissur in 1985. These are Government college. The sixth one started at Kannur in 1995 is in the cooperative sector. Medical education infras-tructure available in public sector for modern medicine in Kerala consists of five medical colleges and three nursing colleges (see Table 23.3). The total intake under different courses is different. Among the different courses, the intake in MBBS is the highest with 700 followed by 150 for Nursing, 4 for M.Sc Nursing, 6 for M.Pharma, 25 for Master in Dental Surgery (MDS) 10 for Dental Hygienist Certificate Course, and 12 for Diploma in Clinical Child Development.

For Ayurvedic medicine, there are 3 Government Ayurveda Colleges in the State with an annual intake of 50 students in

Trivandrum, 30 each in Tripunithura and Kannur for bachelor degree in Ayurvedic Medicine.

The Post Graduate education in Ayurveda is imparted only at Thiruvananthapuram with an annual intake of forty-two. The two private Ayurveda Colleges at Kottackal and Ollur have an annual intake of 30 students in each college for BAMS course.

Table 23.3 Medical and Paramedical Courses Conducted in Kerala with Annual Intake of Students

	Trivandrum	*Calicut*	*Kottayam*	*Alleppey*	*Trichur*	*Total*
MBBS	200	200	100	100	100	700
BDS	40	30				70
BSc Nursing	50	50	50	—	—	150
Total	290	280	150	100	100	920
PG Degree	110	60	34	2	—	206
Super Speciality Courses	17	13	9	—	—	39
Diploma	307	267	120	65	35	794
Total	724	670	313	167	135	1959

Note: B.Sc., Nursing given in the Table includes those provided by the medical colleges in the State. There are 13 other government nursing schools and 18 private nursing schools with a total intake of 1016. For general nursing there are 9 government nursing schools and 70 private nursing schools with a total intake of 2242.

Source: *Economic Review*, 1995

There are five homeopathic medical colleges in the State, two of which in Government sector and the remaining in the private sector. The Bachelor in Homeopathic Medical Science (BHMS) Degree course and BHMS (graded) Degree Course are conducted in the Government Homeopathic Medical Colleges with an annual intake of 100 students in each course. In one of the private Homeopathic colleges, namely, Athurasramam NSS college at Kurichy, both BHMS Degree and Diploma courses are conducted with an annual intake of 125 students (*Economic Review*, 1994).

Public Expenditure on Medical Education

The State government's allocation for medical education is part of government's spending on public health. It is evident from Table 23.4 that the expenditure on medical education as a proportion of total medical and public health has been less than seven per cent during the latter part of 1950s. It has risen to the level of above 10 per cent during the mid 1980s. This means in Kerala more than 10 per cent of the public expenditure on medical and public health is allocated for training medical personnel.

Table 23.4 Expenditure on Medical Education in Kerala 1958-1985

(Rs. in Millions)

Year (1)	*Expenditure (Medical Education)* (2)	*Medical & Public Health Expenditure* (3)	*Medical Education Share* (4) (2) as % of (3)
1958	1.72	25.52	6.74
1959	2.32	32.84	7.06
1960	2.57	40.03	6.42
1961	2.63	44.49	5.91
1965	6.08	74.40	8.17
1970	11.38	148.56	7.66
1971	11.65	150.11	7.76
1975	20.44	240.02	8.52
1979	33.34	385.47	8.65
1980	44.77	439.11	10.20
1981	49.77	516.36	9.64
1985	87.22	832.06	10.48

Source: Duggal, Nandraj, and Shetty (1992)

Medical Education Expenditure Inclusive of Hospital Teaching

An attempt is made to find out the trends in government expenditure on medical education, with government's expenditure on hospital teaching included. The pattern of total expenditure on medical education in Kerala, drawn from its budget papers, is analyzed. It becomes obvious that the share of medical education expenditure in the total expenditure for medical and public health rises when cost of hospital teaching is included. Total expenditure on medical education, henceforth, includes the expenditure on hospital teaching and the expenditure on college teaching. The percentage share of medical education in the total expenditure on medical and public health in Kerala has risen gradually from 12.13 to 15.19 over the years from 1977 to 1993 (Table 23.5).

Table 23.5 Expenditure on Medical Education in Kerala from 1977-78 to 1992-93

(Rs. in Lakhs)

Year	*Expend. (Medical & Public Health (1)*	*Expend. Medical Education (2)*	*Share of Med. Education in Medical and Public Health (3)*
1977-78	3174.79	385.10	12.13
1978-79	3577.14	426.80	11.93
1979-80	4119.70	518.00	12.57
1980-81	4880.65	602.20	12.34
1981-82	5842.85	698.60	11.96
1985-86	9856.87	1365.73	13.86
1986-87	11375.43	1489.64	13.10
1987-88	11739.20	1535.29	13.08
1990-91	18117.30	2541.04	14.03
1991-92	19231.33	3032.56	15.77
1992-93	20106.93	3055.04	15.19

Note: Col.2 includes hospital teaching expenses and DME expenditures. Col. 3 = col.2 / 1 * 100

Source: Economic Review 1994, and Budget Papers.

The point is that more than one-seventh of the public health expenditure is exclusively spent for training medical graduates in Kerala. In other words, spending larger proportion of the medical and public health expenditure on medical education alone means that the money available for distribution of health services would be less. As a consequence, the poor and needy will be affected. This necessitates a further thought for finding alternative methods of financing medical education and thereby expanding the availability without impairing the quality of public health services.

Per Capita Medical Education Expenditure

Clearer idea can be derived from the per capita medical education expenditure in Kerala (see Table 23.6). As evident from Table 23.6, the per capita expenditure was only Rs. 1.6 in the year 1977-78. More than threefold increase has taken place within a period of ten years. During the year 1992-93, it has reached Rs. 10.22, almost doubled within a period of seven years from 1987-88 to 1992-93. This means State government is spending more than Rs. 10 per head to train medical graduates in the State.

Table 23.6 Per capita Medical Education Expenditure in Kerala from 1977-78 to 1992-93

Year (1)	*Population (Lakhs)* (2)	*Expend. Medical Education (Rs. in Lakhs)* (3)	*Per capita Medical Educa. Expenditure (in Rs.)* (4)
1977-78	242.2	385.1	1.59
1978-79	246.3	426.8	1.73
1979-80	250.4	518.0	2.07
1980-81	254.5	602.2	2.37
1981-82	258.1	698.6	2.71
1986-87	275.1	1489.6	5.41
1987-88	288.4	1535.2	5.32
1988-89	293.6	1798.8	6.13
1989-90	298.9	2054.8	6.87
1990-91	290.1	2145.0	7.39
1991-92	294.9	3032.6	10.28
1992-93	298.9	3055.0	10.22

Note and Source: Same as Table 23.5

Distributive Pattern of Public Expenditure on Medical Education

A major part of the medical education expenditure, i.e., 85.69 per cent on an average, is spent on salaries and the remaining 14 per cent on administrative purposes, laboratory, library, machines and materials. The ratio does not remain the same throughout the period under consideration, rather it varies from 79 per cent during 1981-82 to 93 per cent in 1992-93. The pattern is more or less similar in all Medical Colleges in Kerala including Trivandrum Medical College (Tables 23.7 and 23.8). It is evident from Table 23.7 that largest share of the expenditure is incurred on salary. The share of library, machines and equipment and other laboratory materials is coming down with fluctuations. Expenditure for this category is very important for quality improvement. Table 23.8 shows that the share of different categories which we have seen generally for Kerala is in line with the Trivandrum Medical college, also. Here also the share of library, machines and materials is not getting due attention. It should be a subject of serious concern for academicians and policy makers. Medical education is a field where knowledge is dynamic. Significance of library in higher education like medical education is mainly due to this dynamic nature of the subject.

To equip young doctors with awareness and experience of modern developments in medical field, the expenditure for library, laboratory, machines and equipments should be increased. Along with that, the quality of medical education and research in this field to a greater extent depends upon library collections, machines, materials and equipments available for the laboratory. The insignificant and declining share of this category in the total expenditure should, therefore, be changed in order to ensure quality and to encourage research.

Table 23.7 Distributive Pattern of Public Expenditure on Medical Education from 1977 to 1993

Year	*Total Expenditure (in Rs.)*	*Salary (%)*	*Maintenance and Administration (%)*	*Books, Machines & Materials (%)*	*2+3+4*
	(1)	*(2)*	*(3)*	*(4)*	*(5)*
1977-78	38511915.85	87.16	5.13	7.71	100
1978-79	42686514.55	86.93	6.38	6.83	100
1979-80	51803088.00	80.03	6.87	13.19	100
1980-81	60272974.95	80.85	4.42	15.80	100
1981-82	69868332.65	79.41	5.91	14.80	100
1982-83	72706076.45	83.35	6.83	9.97	100
1983-84	96999227.30	78.49	5.13	17.13	100

Table 23.7 *(Contd.)*

	(1)	(2)	(3)	(4)	(5)
1984-85	115406985.45	88.55	6.13	7.62	100
1985-86	134043957.85	—	—	—	—
1986-87	148968078.40	83.43	9.44	10.61	100
1987-88	153529992.05	88.07	7.90	5.94	100
1988-89	179884178.60	87.97	5.72	8.04	100
1989-90	205478040.05	89.50	5.27	6.85	100
1990-91	254105651.65	88.27	4.71	8.65	100
1991-92	303287357.25	89.33	4.11	7.96	100
1992-93	305505311.40	92.97	4.44	3.69	100

Note: Total expenditure includes hospital teaching expenses.
Source: Budget Papers.

Table 23.8 Total Expenditure of Medical College Trivandrum from 1977-78 to 1992-93

Year	*Total Expenditure (in Rs.)*	*Salary (%)*	*Maintenance and Administration (%)*	*Books Machines & Materials (%)*	*2+3+4*
	(1)	(2)	(3)	(4)	(5)
1977-78	13995575	89.25	2.85	7.89	100
1978-79	16585145	90.31	4.34	7.62	100
1979-80	20631111	77.51	3.85	18.64	100
1980-81	21489683	83.88	3.43	12.68	100
1981-82	25968095	78.36	4.44	17.20	100
1982-83	26879185	78.51	10.94	10.55	100
1983-84	33293903	90.74	2.26	7.49	100
1984-85	38367492	84.79	2.87	12.74	100
1985-86	43092291	—	—	—	—
1986-87	47736896	86.81	4.55	9.54	100
1987-88	42811646	87.08	8.36	4.56	100
1988-89	50306033	91.06	2.45	6.49	100
1989-90	64945251	88.49	2.49	8.01	100
1990-91	70487468	88.78	4.41	8.51	100
1991-92	94553881	88.18	3.88	8.39	100
1992-93	98049878	92.69	4.04	4.03	100

Note: Total expenditure includes hospital teaching expenses and one fifth of DME expenses.
Source: Budget Papers

Institutional Unit Cost

The units of measurement of cost may be of three types, namely, students, class, and institution. In this study, one MBBS student is taken as a unit and the average cost for educating him/her as the unit cost, even though it is sometimes argued that only the students who successfully complete the course should be taken as the basis. Institutional unit cost of medical education is worked out by dividing the total expenditure incurred with the number of seats. It is known from the records that there is no change in the number of seats over the period under study, it remained as 200. Institutional unit cost includes three main components, they are: teaching cost, administrative and maintenance cost and laboratory and library cost. Using the data collected from the State budget papers, average cost per student is calculated and presented in Table 23.9. Column 2 of the Table shows that the unit cost for medical education has more than doubled within a period of eight years from 1985-86 to 1992-93. Except the year 1987-88, we can see an increase in per head expenditure over previous years during the period under study. Column 3 of the Table shows that the highest increment in unit cost over the previous years was shown in 1991-92 and the lowest growth in 1987-88. Index of growth of unit cost shows that unit cost has doubled within a period of eight years, from 1985-86 to 1992-93. In constant terms, it has increased from Rs. 169387.93 in the year 1985-86 to Rs. 214363.55 in the year 1992-93.

The unit cost is estimated from the total institutional cost, which includes the costs of both college teaching and hospital training. Unit cost exclusively for college teaching is presented in Table 23.8. Index of growth indicates that during the reference period in all years except 1992-93 the college teaching expenditure has shown an increase. In constant prices too it has risen, from Rs. 96367.06 in 1985-86 to Rs. 103344 in 1992-93.

Compared to the unit cost given in Table 23.9, unit cost for college teaching alone is on an average 56 per cent of the total unit cost of medical education. This means that hospital training is an important component of cost of medical education, and hence cost calculations will be incomplete if it is excluded.

Table 23.9 Unit Cost for Medical Education

Year	*Total Expenditure (in Rs.)*	*Institutional Unit Cost in current prices (Rs.)*	*Percentage increment over previous year*	*Index of Growth*	*Unit Cost in constant price 1981-82 as base*
	(1)	*(2)*	*(3)*	*(4)*	*(5)*
1985-86	43092291	215461.45	—	100.00	169387.93
1986-87	47736896	238684.50	8.68	110.77	178255.79
1987-88	42811664	214058.32	-10.59	099.34	148548.45
1988-89	50306133	251530.66	17.68	116.74	162592.54
1989-90	64945251	324726.32	29.36	150.71	209907.12
1990-91	70487468	352437.34	8.33	163.57	192904.95
1991-92	94553881	472796.40	34.41	219.43	227524.73
1992-93	98049878	490249.40	3.74	227.53	214363.55

Note: Total expenditure includes hospital teaching expenses and one fifth of DME expenses.

Source: Budget Papers

Table 23.10 Unit Cost Exclusively for college Teaching

Year	*Total Expenditure (in Rs.)*	*Institutional Unit Cost in current prices (Rs.)*	*Percentage increment over previous year*	*Index of Growth*	*Unit Cost in constant price 1981-82 as Base*
	(1)	*(2)*	*(3)*	*(4)*	*(5)*
1985-86	22989371	114946.9	—	100.00	90367.06
1986-87	25833411	129167.1	12.37	112.37	96465.35
1987-88	27117126	135585.6	4.96	117.95	94091.35
1988-89	30011298	150056.49	10.67	130.54	96998.38
1989-90	35502311	177511.6	18.27	154.43	107128.30
1990-91	45277764	236388.8	33.16	205.65	129386.32
1991-92	49730261	246347.71	4.2	214.31	118550.30
1992-93	47269541	236347.7	-4.1	205.61	103343.98

Note: Total expenditure excludes hospital teaching expenses and includes one fifth of the DME expenses.

Source: Budget Papers

Private Cost of Medical Education

Private cost is defined as that part of investment in medical education, made either by students or by parents, or by both. Analysis of private cost has been done with the primary data. A major head of private cost is post-admission expenditure. They are incidental in the form of hostel and transportation, admission fees, books, uniforms, study tours etc. The pre-admission expenditure is given in Table 23.11.

Table 23.11 Pre-Admission Household Average Expenditure Per Student (1995-96) (in Rs.)

Item	*FC* *125*	*OBC* *90*	*SC/ST* *16*	*Average*
Tuition/ Coaching	4000	4350	4510	4171.6
Books	3747	1930	1654	2894.1
Transport and Others	1840	1530	2300	1751.1
Total	9587	7810	8464	8816.8

Source: Survey data

As seen in Table 23.11, there is no particular pattern of pre-admission expenditure across groups. As the average pre-admission expenditure works out to be Rs. 8,817, it makes medical admission inaccessible to children from average and less than average income families. Having examined the private cost on pre-admission into medical graduation, attempt has also been made to analyse their post-admission expenditure.

As evident from Table 23.12, the average post-admission annual private expenditure is Rs. 13,703 including hostel expenses. For the entire course, it is Rs. 68,515. When this cost is added to institutional unit cost, the aggregate unit cost for medical education becomes Rs. 558,764, for the entire course. This gives a relative share of 12.3 per cent in the total unit cost for the year 1992/93. Thus, share of institutional cost accounts for 87.7 per cent of total unit cost.

Table 23.12 Average Private Post-Admission Cost Incurred by MBBS Students in the Year 1995-96 (in Rs.)

	FC		*OBC*		*SC/ST*		*Total*	
	HR (44)	*DS (81)*	*HR (33)*	*DS (57)*	*HR (5)*	*DS (11)*	*HR (82)*	*DS (149)*
Hostel	7850	na	7850	na	e	e	7371	na
Academic	5435	6120	5672	6013	5523	5942	5535.7	6065.93
Transport and others	2131	5423	2376	5649	2237	5548	2236.1	5518.68
Fees	1670	1670	1670	1670	e	e	1670	1670
Total	17086	13213	17568	13332	7760	11490	14517.69	13254.61
Average	14576.3		14885.2		10324.38		13702.97	

Notes: Figures in the parentheses indicate the numbers in respective category,
HR = Hostel Residents;
DS = Day Scholars;
na = not applicable;
e = exempted.

Source: Survey data

Cost Recovery in Medical Education

Cost Recovery in India

In India, doctors and nurses have historically been trained at the expense of public exchequer. Until recently, the role of the private sector has been very much limited. A comparison of the expenditure incurred by the government of India on medical education and the revenue collected by the medical colleges in terms of fees and other charges from 1958 to 1985 is shown in Table 23.13. Here, total expenditure represents the expenditure incurred by all the medical education institutions run by state and central government. Receipts means the income earned by these institutions in the form of fees and other charges. Between 1958 and 1985, the percentage of receipts over cost has declined from 13.43 per cent to 1.4 per cent. This means the degree of subsidisation had gone upto 98.6 per cent by the year 1985.

Table 23.13 Recovery from Medical Education in India (Rs. in Millions)

Year	*Expenditure (Medical Education)*	*Receipts (Medical Education)*	*Receipts as % of Expenditure*
(1)	*(2)*	*(3)*	*(4)*
1958	29.71	3.99	13.43
1959	35.62	4.90	13.76
1960	45.46	5.43	11.94
1961	60.31	6.10	10.11
1965	101.8	10.17	9.99
1966	126.19	11.23	8.90
1970	204.79	16.02	7.82
1971	239.60	14.07	5.87
1975	461.56	15.47	3.35
1980	919.82	14.05	1.53
1981	1077.9	15.99	1.48
1984	1695.44	29.97	1.77
1985	2131.09	29.92	1.40

Source: Duggal, Nandraj and Shetty (1992)

Cost Recovery in Kerala

A comparison of the revenue received from medical education and the expenses incurred for the same at the State level is provided in Table 23.14. The rate of recovery from the students has been 10 to 12 per cent during the 1950s. It has risen to 14 per cent in 1961; and then gradually declined to 3.16 per cent in 1985. The trend in the recovery rate in medical education at the all-India level is much different from that of Kerala. For instance, during the later part of the 1950s, the recovery rate in Kerala was slightly higher than that of India as a whole. On the other hand, by the beginning of 1960s, the recovery rate in Kerala was higher than that of all India, and the same trend continued upto 1985. The only similar feature that emerges is that the trend in the recovery rates in Kerala and all India have followed the same pattern. Both remained relatively higher during the late 1950s and early 1960s and have declined during the early 1980s.

Table 23.14 Cost Recovery from Medical Education in Kerala 1958-1985 (Rs. in Millions)

Year	*Expenditure (Medical Education)*	*Receipts (Medical Education)*	*Receipts as % of Expenditure*
(1)	*(2)*	*(3)*	*(4)*
1958	1.72	0.21	12.21
1959	2.32	0.25	10.78
1960	2.57	0.30	11.67
1961	2.63	0.37	14.07
1965	6.08	1.07	17.60
1966	7.07	1.04	14.71
1970	11.38	1.31	11.51
1971	11.65	1.40	12.02
1975	20.44	1.69	8.27
1979	33.34	2.75	8.25
1980	44.77	2.55	5.70
1981	49.77	2.93	5.89
1984	74.04	3.21	4.34
1985	87.22	3.16	3.62

Source: Duggal, Nandraj and Shetty (1992)

Rate of Subsidization

In this analysis an attempt is made to find out the percentage of the total institutional cost of medical education recovered from the students in the form of tuition fees and what percentage of it is being subsidised in recent years. Here, government subsidy may be defined as the difference between the cost of delivering various publicly provided goods or services and the recoveries arising from such deliveries. The result of the analysis based on the data from budget papers for the period 1985-93 are presented in Table 23.15. It reveals that medical education is highly subsidised in Kerala. In 1985-86, 99.53 per cent of the unit institutional cost of medical education was subsidised. The subsidy rate has increased to 99.79 per cent in the year 1992-93.

The Table also reveals that, while the total expenditure on medical education has doubled, the total revenue, that is, the recovery from the students has been very low and has remained almost stagnant during 1985 to 1993. As a result, the rate of public subsidisation of medical education is very high with almost cent per cent being subsidised.

Table 23.15 Average Subsidy on Institutional Cost for Medical Education

Year	*Total Expenditure (1)*	*Total Revenue (2)*	*Subsidy (3)*	*Percentage of subsidy over cost*
1985-86	43092291	202500	42889791	99.53
1986-87	47736896	202500	47534396	99.58
1987-88	42811664	202500	42609164	99.53
1988-89	50306133	202500	50103633	99.59
1989-90	64945251	202500	64742751	99.69
1990-91	70487468	202500	70284964	99.71
1991-92	94553881	202500	94351381	99.79
1992-93	98049878	202500	97847378	99.79

Source: Computed from Budget papers

Note: Total expenditure includes hospital teaching expenses and one fifth of the DME expenditure.

Social Equity in Cost Sharing

The high amount of subsidy given to the medical graduates calls for the examination of the scope for the cost sharing. This is based on the ability and willingness of the students to share their education cost, given their economic background. Equal weightage is assigned to their social status since equity cannot be addressed on economic ground alone. The family resource base has been taken to examine the 'ability to pay' of the students. The 'willingness to pay' of the students is analysed based in their answer to the relevant questions asked. The analysis is mainly done using the data collected through a primary survey of 231 graduate students of Trivandrum Medical College.

The sample students have been classified on the basis of their family income. The distribution of different social groups to which they belong is presented in Table 23.16. Of the total, 67.6 per cent of the students belong to the category of 'average annual income less than or equal to Rs. 1,20.000'. Of the SC/ST students, about 81 per cent and of the OBC students, 72 per cent belong to the above category. Among the FC students, about 40 per cent belong to the families with the average annual income of above Rs. 1,20,000. It is thus evident from Table 23.16 that a major section of the students comes from the upper income strata. As family income is an important determinant of the students' ability to pay, there is a scope for cost recovery from these medical students of high income strata.

Table 23.16 Distribution of Students according to Socio-Economic Categories

Income Category (Income in Rs.'000)	*Average per capita Income(Rs.) (1)*	*Social Groups*			
		FC (2)	*OBC (3)*	*SC/ST (4)*	*Total (5)*
Below 30	7421	10 (8)	6 (6.7)	1 (6.25)	17 (7.4)
30-60	11354	11 (8.8)	22 (24.4)	—	33 (14.3)
60-90	15780	28 (22.4)	18 (20)	3 (18.75)	9 (21.2)
90-120	21643	29 (23.2)	19 (21.1)	9 (56.25)	7 (24.7)
120-150	34657	23 (18.4)	10 (11.1)	1 (6.25)	34 (14.7)
150-180	42721	8 (6.4)	3 (3.3)	1 (6.25)	12 (5.2)
180-210	49763	3 (2.4)	4 (4.4)	—	7 (3.0)
210-240	56247	6 (4.8)	4 (4.4)	1 (6.25)	11 (4.8)
above 240	68453	7 (5.6)	4 (4.4)	—	11 (4.8)
Total		125	90	16	231 (100)
Average PCI for the entire social group		26087.98	24023.95	21247.93	24948.58

Note: (1) Figures in the parentheses indicate percentages to total.
(2) SC/ST= Scheduled Castes/Scheduled Tribes;
OBC = other Backward Castes; and FC=Forward Castes.

Source: Primary Survey Data

An analysis of the per capita income of the families will also be useful in this context. From Table 23.16, it can be observed that even the average per capita income of the lowest income category is higher than the per capita income of the all-India and state level. Thus, there is a 'pro-rich' bias in the distribution of medical students which confirms the scope of cost sharing. This finding also supports the conclusions of some of the earlier studies in this regard.

Table 23.17 Education-wise Distribution of Parents across Social Groups

Education	Father				Mother			
	FC *(1)*	*OBC* *(2)*	*SC/ST* *(3)*	*Total* *(4)*	*FC* *(5)*	*OBC* *(6)*	*SC/ST* *(7)*	*Total* *(8)*
Unschooled	1 (0.8)	1 (1.1)	—	2 (0.9)	1 (0.8)	—	—	1 (1.4)
X standard	5 (4.0)	7 (7.8)	1 (6.25)	13 (5.6)	9 (7.2)	13 (14.4)	1 (6.25)	23 (10)
X11 standard	7 (5.6)	3 (3.3)	—	10 (4.3)	11 (8.8)	10 (11.1)	2 (12.5)	23 (10)
Graduate	24(19.2)	19 (21.1)	2 (12.5)	45 (19.5)	59 (47.2)	38 (42.2)	4 (25)	101 (43.7)
Post-Graduate	34(27.2)	16 (17.8)	5 (31.25)	55 (23.8)	26 (20.8)	18 (20)	6 (37.5)	50 (21.6)
Engineering	25 (20)	19 (21.1)	3 (18.75)	47 (20.3)	2 (1.6)	2 (2.22)	—	4 (1.7)
Medical Degree	18(14.4)	16 (17.8)	4 (25)	38 (16.5)	14 (11.2)	7 (7.78)	2 (12.5)	23 (10)
Technical	4 (3.2)	6 (6.7)	—	10 (4.3)	2 (1.6)	2 (2.2)	1 (6.25)	5 (2.2)
Law/Mgt	7 (5.6)	3 (3.3)	1 (6.25)	11 (4.8)	1 (0.8)	—	—	1 (0.4)
Total	125 (54.1)	90 (39)	16 (7)	231 (100)	125 (54.1)	90 (39)	16 (7)	231 (100)

Note: (1) Col.4 is an addition of col.1 to 3 and col.8 is an addition of col.5 to 7.
(2) Figures in the parentheses indicate percentages.

Source: Same as Table 23.16

Table 23.18 Occupation-wise Distribution of Parents across Social Groups

Occupation	Father				Mother			
	FC *(1)*	*OBC* *(2)*	*SC/ST* *(3)*	*Total* *(4)*	*FC* *(5)*	*OBC* *(6)*	*SC/ST* *(7)*	*Total* *(8)*
Unemployed	3 (2.4)	—	1 (6.2)	4 (1.7)	59 (47.2)	44 (48.9)	2 (12.5)	105 (45.5)
Clerk	31 (24.8)	19 (21.1)	7 (43.75)	57 (24.7)	12 (9.6)	14 (15.6)	8 (50)	34 (14.7)
Self-employed	5 (4.0)	5 (5.6)	—	10 (4.3)	3 (2.4)	2 (2.2)	—	5 (2.2)
Teacher	3 (2.4)	5 (5.6)	2 (12.5)	10 (4.3)	19 (15.2)	13 (14.4)	2 (12.5)	34 (14.7)
Skilled	16 (12.8)	10 (11.1)	—	26 (11.3)	12 (9.6)	5 (5.6)	1 (6.25)	18 (7.8)
Professional	45 (36.0)	40 (44.4)	6 (37.5)	91 (39.4)	18 (14.2)	10 (11.1)	2 (12.5)	30 (13)
Executive	17 (13.6)	6 (6.7)	—	23 (10.0)	2 (1.6)	2 (2.2)	1 (6.25)	5 (2.2)
Business	5 (4.0)	5 (5.6)	—	10 (4.3)	—	—	—	—
Total	125 (54)	90 (39)	16 (7)	231 (100)	125 (54)	90 (39)	16 (7)	231 (100)

Note: (1) Col.4 is an addition of col.1 to 3 and col.8 is an addition of col.5 to 7
(2) Figures in the parenthses indicate percentage.

Source: Same as Table 23.16

The inter-generational externality of education is widely recognised. It is often argued that the benefits of education accrue not merely to the present generation but to the posterity as well. The distribution of students according to education of their parents is given in Table 23.17.

As seen in Table 23.17, more than 85 per cent students' parents have sound educational background. About 60 per cent of the fathers are either professionally qualified or post-graduates. In the case of SC/ST and OBC students, it is 75 and 56 per cent respectively. With regard to mothers' education, 65.3 per cent of the mothers were either graduates or post-graduate and 33 per cent of mothers had a post-graduate or professional degree.

Out of the 16 SC/ST and 90 OBC students, around 62 per cent are from families where the mother is either a graduate or post-graduate. In short, higher education, particularly medical education in Kerala, still continues to be enjoyed by students from households having higher level of education. This inter-generational externality arising from higher education justifies the application of the principle of cost recovery, on equity grounds. The occupation-wise distribution of the parents across the social groups is given in Table 23.18.

More than 50 per cent of the students are from families where their fathers have highly paid occupations. Professional category is prominent with 40 per cent followed by clerical category (24.7%). In the case of SC/ST students, 43 per cent of the fathers have clerical jobs. In the case of mothers half of them fall in the clerical category. It should be noted that the percentage of employed mothers is high in the case of SC/ST with 87.5 per cent with white collar jobs. The occupation-wise analysis also supports the introduction of cost recovery measures, as majority of the parents are in highly paid occupations.

The Share of Family Expenditure on Education

The family expenditure pattern across social groups is given in Table 23.19. Besides, it is noted that all the respondent families set apart a considerable portion of their income (around 20%) towards educational expenses irrespective of their social status.

Table 23.19 Percentage Share of Education in Total Family Expenditure

Range	*FC*	*OBC*	*SC/ST*	*Total*
Below 5	12 (9.6)	7 (7.7)	1 (6.3)	20 (8.6)
6-10	13 (10.4)	11 (12.2)	1 (6.3)	25 (10.9).
11-15	13 (10.4)	13 (14.4)	2 (12.5)	28 (12.12)
16.20	30 (24)	19 (21.1)	6 (37.5)	55 (23.8)
21-25	12 (9.6)	17 (18.8)	3 (18.7)	32 (13.9)
26-30	17 (13.6)	7 (7.7)	2 (12.5)	26 (11.25)
31-40	13 (10.4)	9 (10)	1 (6.25)	23 (9.96)
Above 40	15 (12)	7 (7.7)	— —	22 (9.5)
Total	125	90	16	231
Group Average	21.84	20.41	19.06	21.09

Source: Same as Table 23.16.

The schooling background of the students and the medium of their education at secondary level is given in Table 23.20. It is evident that there is not much difference in the schooling background and medium of education of the respondents. The unaided private schools contribute the largest share of medical students (45%) followed by private aided schools (34%). Government schools contribute only 16 per cent and the remaining come from the central schools. It is further noticed that the majority of the students, 87 per cent, are from English medium schools.

Table 23.20 Distribution of Students according to Schooling Background and Medium of Education

School type	*FC*	*OBC*	*SC/ST*	*Total*
Government	23 (18.4)	10 (11.1)	3 (18.8)	36 (15.6)
Private (aided)	39 (31.2)	33(36.66)	6 (37.5)	78 (33.8)
private (unaided)	56 (44.8)	43 (47.8)	5 (31.2)	104 (45.0)
Central	7 (5.6)	4 (4.4)	2 (12.5)	13 (5.6)
Total	125	90	16	231
Medium of Education at Secondary Level				
English	106 (84.8)	82 (91.1)	13 (81.2)	201 (87.0)
Regional language	19 (15.2)	8 (8.89)	3 (18.7)	30 (13.0)
Total	125	90	16	231

Source: Same as Table 23.16.

It is clear from Table 23.20 that a major portion of the parents had been bearing cent per cent of the cost of their children's school education. Against this fact, it is paradoxical to see that higher education like medical education is given almost free to students, who are able to meet their educational expenses.

Willingness to Cost Sharing

This section analyses the willingness of the students to bear the institutional unit cost of their medical education in the present condition and under student loan schemes (see Table 23.21). The information is collected by asking about the maximum amount the student is willing to contribute for his/her education. As parents are actually paying fees, they are the better persons to answer questions related to willingness to pay. As the graduate students have better understanding of the financial position of their families, it makes little difference as to who is being asked. When asked those students who are willing to contribute a share (less than full cost), they affirmed their willingness to contribute provided student loans are made available.

Household Income and Willingness to Pay

The income classification and the ability to share the cost will give a clear picture of the feasibility of cost recovery measures in higher education. Out of the 5 per cent students who are willing to pay the full cost, 85 per cent are from families with annual income above Rs. 2,10,000. Twenty per cent of the total sample are willing to bear 40 to 100 per cent of their educational cost, 52 per cent of them belong to the category of families with annual income of more than Rs. 1,20,000.

It is quite reasonable that on an average higher income groups are able and willing to contribute greater part of the cost and vice versa. The lowest income groups' average willingness is to pay 9.4 per cent of the unit cost, while it is 55.5 per cent for the upper income groups. The above facts while indicate the existence of untapped sources regarding the cost recovery of higher education.

Table 23.21 Responses on Willingness to Pay by Income Groups

Income Category (Annual Income in Rs.'000)	Willingness to pay in percentages 1-20 (1)	20-40 (2)	40-60 (3)	60-99 (4)	100 (5)	Total (6)	Unwillingness to pay	Grand Total
Below 30	3 (50)	1 (16.6)	2 (33.3)	—	—	6	11 (64)	17 (7.4)
30—60	17 (85)	2 (10)	1 (5)	—	—	20	13 (39)	33 (14.3)
60—90	22 (59.4)	9 (24.3)	3 (8.1)	2 (5.4)	1 (2.7)	37	12 (24)	49 (21.2)
90—120	22 (44)	15 (30)	10 (20)	—	3 (6)	50	7 (12)	57 (24.7)
120—150	17 (51.5)	9 (27.3)	6 (18.2)	1 (3)	—	33	1 (2)	34 (14.7)
150—180	3 (25)	6 (50)	2 (16)	—	1 (8.3)	12	— —	12 (5.2)
180—210	3 (50)	2 (33.3)	—	—	1 (16.6)	6	1 (2)	7 (3)
210—240	3 (27.3)	1 (9)	4 (36.4)	1 (9)	2 (18)	11	— —	11 (4.8)
Above 240	2 (18)	3 (27.3)	2 (18)	—	4 (36.4)	11	— —	11 (4.8)
Total	92	48	30	4	12	182	45	231 (100)
	(39.8)	(20.8)	(13)	(1.7)	(5.20)	(80.5)	(19.5)	(100)

Note: (1) Col .6 is an addition of col.1 to 5.
(2) Figures in the parentheses indicate percentages.

Source: Same as Table 23.16

Social Status and Willingness to Pay

Table 23.22 shows the responses of different social groups on the basis of their willingness to pay. Out of the 231 students from whom the information is collected, 19.5 per cent are not in a position to pay extra amount as a cost recovery measure, while 5.2 per cent students are willing to pay the full cost of education and 40 per cent are willing to share on an average 10 per cent of the cost. Of the SC/ST, 94 per cent are willing to share a part of the cost and of the FC and OBC, 78 per cent and 88 per cent respectively are ready to share the costs. From this we can make a tentative conclusion that social backwardness need not be a criteria while evaluating willingness to pay. A comparative study of the average willingness to pay of different social groups is given in Table 23.22.

Another matter for discussion is the ability to pay of the families which are getting income from abroad (those families which have at least one member working abroad). Table 23.23 gives a comparative view of the willingness and ability to pay of both categories. The students with external source constitute 23.8 per cent, while 76.2 per cent fully depend on internal sources. Of the total 12 who are able to bear the full cost of their education, 8 are from families having external source of income. Of these, 14 per cent are able to bear the full cost while only 2.27 per cent of the other category without external support are able to bear it. A clearer picture is derived from the average willingness to pay of both groups. Students with external sources of income on an average are willing to pay 31.81 per cent of the total cost, which is 8.6 per cent higher than the total average willingness and 11.2 per cent higher than their counterparts. This supports the general notion that non-resident Indians (NRI) can be asked to pay more.

It is clear that most of the students are able and willing to meet the cost of their education either fully or partially. This justifies the introduction of cost recovery principle in higher education.

Table 23.22 Responses on Willingness to Pay by Social Groups

Social Groups	Willingness to pay in percentages 1-20 (1)	20-40 (2)	40-60 (3)	60-99 (4)	100 (5)	Total (6)	Unwillingness to pay	Grand Total
FC	42 (43.3)	30 (30.9)	15 (15.5)	2 (2.1)	8 (8.2)	97	28	125 (54)
OBC	46 (62.2)	14 (18.9)	9 (12.2)	1 (1.4)	4 (5.4)	74	16	90 (39)
SC/ST	4 (26.6)	4 (26.4)	6 (40)	1 (13.3)	— —	15	1	16 (7)
Total	92	48	30	4	12	186	45	231 (100)
	(39.8)	(20.8)	(13)	(1.7)	(5.2)	(80.5)	(19.5)	(100)

Source: Same as for 23.16

Note: (1) Col.6 is an addition of col.1 to 5.
(2) Figures in the parentheses indicate percentages.

Table 23.23 Responses on Ability to Pay and Financial Assistance from Abroad

Categories	*Willingness to pay in percentages*								
	1-20 (1)	*20-40* (2)	*40-60* (3)	*60-99* (4)	*100* (5)	*Total* (6)	*Unwillingness to pay*	*Grand Total*	*Average Willingness*
Without foreign income	74 (52.8)	35 (25)	24 (17.4)	3 (2.1)	4 (2.85)	140	36	176 (76.2)	20.62
With foreign income	18 (39.19)	13(28.26)	6 (13)	1 (2.1)	8 (17.4)	46	9	55 (23.8)	31.85
Total	92	48	30	4	12	186	45	231 (100)	23.3
	(39.8)	(20.8)	(13)	(1.7)	(5.2)	(80.5)	(19.5)	(100)	

Source: Same as for Table 23.16

Note: (1) Col.6 is an addition of col.1 to 5.

(2) Figures in the parentheses indicate percentage.

Parental Occupation and Ability and Willingness to Pay

The distribution of students according to the occupation of parents reveals that above 50 per cent of the medical students are from families of high level occupation (professional or executive or business). Most of the students from this category expressed their willingness to pay the full cost. Among the mothers, 46 per cent were not engaged in income-earning occupation, still, 50 per cent of the students who expressed willingness to pay cent per cent cost belonged to this category (see Table 23.24 and 23.24 (a)). It can be concluded that parental education is an influential factor in determining the willingness to pay of the students.

The Case of Student Loan Schemes

Of the different methods suggested for tapping resources for higher education, student loan is an important one. By enabling the students to finance current studies out of their future income, these loans encourage educational investments. Bearing this in mind, the present section will re-examine the attitude of the respondents on the question of willingness to pay, given the provision of student loans.

The percentage of students who are unwilling to bear the cost in normal conditions came down from 20 to 10 provided student loan schemes are available (Table 23.25). At the same time the percentage of students who are willing to bear the full cost has risen from 5 per cent to 16 per cent under student loan schemes. The response was more positive among the middle income category. On an average, 26.9 per cent increment in cost recovery can be made if student loans are made available. The highest response was from the income category Rs. 1,50,000 to 1,80,000, where the average willingness has risen from 34.2 per cent to 75 per cent, an increment of 40.8. A subdued response came from the lowest income group (below 30,000), where the increment was only 13.5, from 9.4 to 22.94.

Table 23.26 will give an idea of the response of different social groups to the student loan schemes. Of the SC/ST students, 25 per cent are willing to bear the full cost provided loans are given. Without student loan schemes, 22 per cent of the FC students were unwilling to bear the cost but this came down to

Table 9.24 Parental Occupation and Ability and Willingness to Pay

Father's Occupation	*Willingness to pay in percentages* 1-20 (1)	20-40 (2)	40-60 (3)	60-99 (4)	100 (5)	*Total (6)*	*Unwilling to pay*	*Grand Total*	*Average willingness*
Unemployed	2 (2.2)	—	—	—	—	2	2	4 (1.7)	5
Clerk	25(27.2)	11 (22.9)	7(23.3)	1 (25)	—	44	13	57 (24.7)	17.7
Self—employed	2 (2.2)	1 (2.3)	—	—	—	9	7	10 (4.3)	7.4
Teacher	5 (5.2)	2 (4.2)	2 (4.8)	—	—	9	1	10 (4.3)	21.0
Skilled	10(10.9)	4 (8.3)	3 (4.8)	—	2 (16.6)	19	7	26 (11.3)	21.9
Professional	37(40.2)	22 (45.8)	11(36.6)	3 (75)	7 (58.3)	80	11	91 (39.4)	27.7
Executive	9 (9.8)	6 (12.5)	4(13.3)	—	—	19	4	23 (10.0)	20.4
Business	2 (2.2)	2 (4.2)	3 (10)	—	3 (25)	10	—	10 (4.3)	53.0
Total	92	48	30	4	12	186	45	231 (100)	23.3
	(39.8)	(20.8)	(13)	(1.7)	(5.2)	(80.5)	(19.5)	(100)	

Table 23.24 (a) Parental Occupation and Ability and Willingness to Pay

Mother's Occupation									
Unemployed	34 (37)	19 (39.6)	10 (33.3)	1 (25)	6 (50)	70 (37.6)	35 (77.8)	105 (45.5)	19.0
Clerk	17 (18.5)	6 (12.5)	7 (23.3)	—	1 (16.6)	31 (16.6)	3 (6.7)	34 (14.7)	23.5
Seif-employed	—	—	—	—	2 (1.1)	2 (1.1)	3 (6.7)	5 (2.2)	40.0
Teacher	20 (21.8)	7 (14.6)	5 (16.7)	—	—	32 (17.2)	2 (4.4)	34 (14.7)	19.4
Skilled	7 (7.6)	8 (16.7)	2 (6.6)	1 (25)	—	18 (9.7)	—	18 (7.8)	27.2
Profeesional	11 (11.9)	8 (16.7)	6 (20)	1 (25)	2 (15.5)	28 (15.5)	.2 (4.4)	30 (13)	31.0
Executive	3 (3.3)	—	—	1 (25)	1 (8.3)	5 (27)	—	5 (2.2)	42.0
Total	92	48	30	4	12	186	—	231 (100)	23.3
	(39.8)	(20.8)	(13)	(1.7)	(5.2)	(80.5)	(100)	—	—

Note: (1) Col. 6 is an addition of col.1 to 5.
(2) Figures in the parentheses indicate percentages.

Source: Same as Table 23.16

Table 23.25 Response on Ability and Willingness to Pay under Student Loan Schemes

Income Category (Annual Income in Rs.'000)	*Willingness to pay in percentages* 1-20 (1)	20-40 (2)	40-60 (3)	60-80 (4)	80-99 (5)	100 (6)	*Total (7)*	*Unwilling to pay*	*Willing to pay 100% without loans*	*Grand Total*
Below 30	—	3 (25)	6 (50)	1 (8.3)	—	2 (16.6)	12	5	—	17 (7.4)
30-60	9 (32.2)	5 (17.8)	7 (25)	4 (14.2)	—	3 (10.7)	28	5	—	33 (14.3)
60-90	9 (22.5)	14 (34.1)	9 (22.5)	2 (5)	1 (2.4)	5 (12.5)	40	8	1	49 (21.2)
90-120	6 (11.8)	14 (27.5)	15 (29.4)	4 (7.8)	4 (7.8)	8 (15.7)	51	3	3	57 (24.7)
120-150	2 (6.1)	10 (30.3)	8 (24.2)	2 (6.1)	—	11 (33.3)	33	1	—	34 (14.7)
150-180	—	2 (18.2)	2 (18.2)	2 (18.2)	—	5 (45.5)	11	—	1	12 (5.2)
180-210	—	2 (40)	2 (40)	1 (20)	—	—	5	1	1	7 (3.0)
210-240	—	2 (22.2)	3 (33.3)	3 (33.3)	—	1 (11.1)	9	—	—	11 (4.8)
above 240	2 (28.5)	—	1 (28.5)	2 (28.5)	—	2 (28.5)	7	—	4	11 (4.8)
Total	28 (12.1)	52 (22.5)	53 (22.9)	21 (9.1)	5 (2.2)	37 (16)	196 (89.2)	23 (10.8)	12 (5.2)	231 (100) (100)

Source: Same as for Table 23.16

Note: (1) Col.7 is an addition of col.1 to 6.

2) Figures in the parentheses indicate percentages.

Table 23.26 Ability and Willingness to Pay under Student Loan Schemes by Social Groups

Social Groups	*Willngness to pay in percentages* 1-20 (1)	20-40 (2)	40-60 (3)	60-80 (4)	80-99 (5)	100 (6)	Total (7)	Unwilling to pay	Willing to pay 100% without loans	Grand Total
FC	15 (13.27)	30 (26.54)	27 (23.9)	14 (12.4)	3 (14.2)	16 (14.2)	113	12 (9)	8	125 (54.1)
OBC	13 (16.5)	21 (20.6)	19 (24.1)	5 (6.3)	—	17 (21.5)	79	11 (12)	4	90 (38.9)
SC/ST	—	1 (6.25)	7 (43.75)	2 (1.5)	2 (12.5)	4 (25)	16	—	—	16 (6.9)
Total	28 (12)	52 (22)	53 (22.5)	21 (9)	5 (2)	37 (16)	208 (90)	23 (10)	12 (5.2)	231 (100) (100)

Source: Same as for Table 23.16

Note: (1) Col.7 is an addition of col.1 to 6.

(2) Figrues in the parentheses indicate percentages.

9 per cent under student loans. The significant point is that all the SC/ST students are ready to bear a part of the cost and 24 per cent are willing to bear 100 per cent of the cost, if loans are made available. Compared to the FC group, SC/ST and OBC groups responded more positively.

Conclusion

Many studies have emphasised the issue of cost sharing in higher education; however, a scientific analysis of the rationality of charging user fees in higher education has not so far been attempted. There are studies which analyse the cost structure of higher education without considering the medical education as a separate entity. The report of the High Power Committee for Mobilisation of Additional Resources for Technical Education (1994) has made an assessment of the possibility for cost sharing in the case of technical education. Similar attempts have yet to come in the case of medical education in India. It calls for studying the possibilities of cost sharing in medical education. This study is an endeavour in this direction.

Governmental resources for higher educational institutions are getting reduced. It necessities a need to raise enough resources by higher educational institutions themselves. A strong case may be made in this context for the recovery of cost in higher education. Given the social as well as the economic significance of higher education, and considering our diversely stratified societies, this point cannot be stretched too far in India. The aspects of social equity as manifested in the ability of students to pay should assume as much importance as the cost recovery or economic efficiency criterion in higher education.

The best way of raising resources would be such that it does not hinder, but facilitates the promotion of socio-economic equality in the society. The approach to raise resources, hence, has to be not only rational but also equitable. This would mean that the enquiry has to go beyond the analysis of cost structure of higher education, and into the aspects of willingness and ability to pay as well. With this perspective, the study had the following underlying objectives: (i) to analyse the institutional cost of medical education in the past fifteen years; (ii) to estimate the per student institutional cost and private cost of medical education;

(iii) to assess the contribution of students to the cost of medical education; and (iv) to evaluate the student's ability and willingness to pay for medical education. The public expenditure for medical education as a percentage of total medical and public health expenditure of the country has grown from 4.62 per cent in 1958 to 10.66 per cent in 1985. This has increased from 6.74 to 10.48 per cent in Kerala during the same period. The current figures available suggest that it has significantly risen to 15 per cent in Kerala in 1992-93.

Kerala government spent, on an average, Rs. 10.22 per head for medical education during the year 1992-93. Of the total expenditure on medical education, 86 per cent has been on salary to teaching and non-teaching staff. The expenditure per medical student was Rs. 490,249 in 1992-93. The unit cost had been increasing over the years during the period from 1985-86 to 1992-93, excepting 1987-88. The unit cost has doubled during this period at current prices. This has increased at constant prices too, from Rs. 169,387.93 to Rs. 214,363.55 during the same period. Students spend Rs. 8,817 as pre-admission expenditure for preparing for medical entrance. The private expenditure of an MBBS student amounts to Rs. 13,703 per year. Private expenditure during the entire course amounts to Rs. 68,515. Thus, the unit cost, including private and public expenditure, for medical education works out to be Rs. 558,764.

Secondary evidences suggest that the investment in higher education is productive. A comparison of private and social returns to higher education reveals that the private returns are higher than the social returns. Though the private returns are more, it does not undermine the need for public funding of higher education. The analysis shows that the rate of cost recovery has been continuously declining in the case of all India and Kerala. The receipt as a percentage of expenditure had fallen from 13.43 per cent in 1958 to 1.4 per cent in 1985 at the all-India level. This has declined from 12.21 per cent to 3.62 per cent in Kerala during the same period. From 1985-86 to 1992-93, the element of subsidy has been greater than 99.5 per cent in Kerala. The average subsidy in Kerala shows that medical graduates are educated at a greater degree of subsidy. Of the total unit cost for medical education, 87 per cent is borne by the government.

An analysis of economic background of medical students shows that they belong to relatively higher income groups and to the households of high level occupation. Their social background cut across the communities. Since economic background is an important determinant of the ability to pay, it offers ample scope for cost recovery from these students. As it is, the benefits of liberal government subsidy goes mainly to these privileged sections of the society. Government provides the subsidy out of receipts from the indirect taxes which is its staple tax resource, and hence the incidence of the burden of higher education mainly falls on lower income groups. Medical education of the privileged section is, thus, being liberally financed out of the revenue extracted from the poor. The students' responses show that medical students are willing to pay 23 per cent of the unit cost of medical education. The existence of credit market for medical students would boost up their willingness to accept cost recovery principle. It has also been substantiated by the findings that the student loan schemes had increased the cost recovery rates. Students with external sources of income are willing to contribute more than 23 per cent of the unit cost which, in turn, suggests that Non-Resident Indians (NRI) can be asked to pay more. Major portion of the parents had been bearing cent per cent of the cost of school education of their children. Against these facts, it is unreasonable to provide higher education like medical education free of cost to students who are able to meet their educational expenses.

REFERENCES

Albrecht, Douglas and Adrain Ziderman, (1993) "Student Loan : An Effective Instrument for Cost Recovery in Higher Education". *The World Bank Research Observer 8 (1).*

Bhatt, G.K. (19822). "Profitability of Private Investment in Higher Education in Rajasthan". *Journal of High Education.* Sepetember.

Blaug, M. and Maureen Woodhall. (1979). "Patterns of subsidies to Higher Education in Europe." *Higher Education.* September.

Carl, J.M. and R.J. Knaus. (1993) "A Primer on Graduate Medical Education Financing." *Jounal of the American Osteopathic Association.* 93 (10), October.

World Bank (1986). Financing Education in Developing Countries, An Exploration of Policy Options. Washington D.C.: IBRD

William G. Rothstein. (1987). American Medical Schools, and the Practices of Medicine. New York:Oxford University Press.

TWENTY-FOUR

DEVELOPMENT OF KERALA'S HEALTH SERVICES

The Need for Broadening the Base of Policy-making

V. RAMAN KUTTY

Introduction

Kerala has a long history of organized health care. Before the advent of European medicine, there were families of practitioners of indigenous systems like Ayurveda who continued their tradition through generations. People were used to approaching care givers when they were sick, instead of taking to self-care. When the colonial powers established their presence in the region, they brought their medical system with them. Initially people did not perceive any advantage for this over the indigenous tradition, and it was restricted to the European and military establishment. But in the nineteenth century, the princely rulers of the erstwhile States of Travancore and Kochi took the initiative in making available the Western system of care to their subjects. It would not have taken deep roots had it not been for the royal families who also took to accepting the Western practices of preventive and curative medicine, which had a demonstration effect on the people. The practice of vaccination against small pox was firmly established early in the State of Travancore through the initiatives of the rulers themselves. A royal proclamation of 1879 made vaccination compulsory for public servants, inmates of jails, and students. All heads of departments were instructed to see that those under their care and control are vaccinated. Administrative reports indicate that public health authorities were also concerned about the spread of cholera during fairs and festivals and initiated measures of containment.[1] In 1928, under the auspices of the Travancore government and with the help of the Rockefeller Foundation experts, parasite surveys were conducted in Travancore which led to measures to control hook worm and filariasis. A health unit which incorporated many of the concepts of primary health care was also started in a rural area.

Development of health services was not confined to the provision of preventive measures alone. The general hospitals in Thiruvananthapuram and Kochi (Cochin) are about a hundred and fifty years old. Initiatives were also taken to get the subjects of the respective states who were trained in Western medicine into key posts in the service of the government. The appointment of Dr. Mary Punnen Lukose as the surgeon-general of Travancore in the early years of this century deserves special mention. A doctor trained in England, was the first woman to be appointed surgeon-general in an Indian state, at a time when women doctors were still a rarity in Europe and America.

Development of health services was complemented by other parallel happenings: initiatives to provide safe drinking water, in the capital city of Thiruvananthapuram to begin with, and the universalization of education, including woman's education. Though schooling had not reached the levels of coverage that it has today, the initiatives were taken. Another important factor was the establishment of mission hospitals in remote areas of the State under the auspices of Christian churches. Young girls from the Syrian Christian community in Kerala also took to nursing as a career in a big way.

Health Sector Development in Kerala State

By the time of the formation of the Kerala State on 1 November 1956, the foundation for a medical care system accessible to all citizens was already laid. One indicator of the government's commitment to provision of health services is the proportion of government expenditure set apart for health. If we look at the government allocation for health in the budget after the formation of the State of Kerala, we find that it was a major item of spending from early years. Social sectors, mainly comprising education and health, accounted for a large share of the government development expenditure (Table 24.1). The period from the formation of the State upto the beginning of the eighties was characterized by great growth and expansion of the government health services. Figures show that the annual compound growth rate of the government health care expenditure for the period, at 13.04%, outstripped both the annual compound rate for the growth of total government expenditure at 12.45 per cent and the annual compound rate of growth of state domestic product at 9.81 per cent.[2]

The proportion of government expenditure on health was maintained even during the decade of the eighties, when the revenue deficit in the budget was growing (Table 24.2). The question of the existence and nature of fiscal crisis in this State are put to detailed analysis in an indepth study brought out recently.[3] The main points highlighted in this study are: (1) Though budgetary deficit has become a common feature for all States in India, the magnitude of the deficit in Kerala has been steadily growing and substantively higher than the all-States average. (2) Unlike in other States, the deficit here has its genesis in the revenue account. This means that the recurrent expenditure by the State has been growing at a greater rate than the total spending. The gap between government receipts of money or revenue, and expenditure has been steadily widening.

During the decades from 1961 to 1991, the State expanded its health facilities prodigiously. The number of beds and institutions increased exponentially. Total number of beds in government hospitals in the modern medical sector increased from around 13000 in 1960-61 to 20,000 in 1970-71, 29,000 in 1980-81, and 38,000 in 1996.[4,5] Facilities for medical and nursing education also increased steadily. By the end of the eighties, Kerala had a very favourable ratio of personnel and facilities to the population, even though there were pockets in some districts where access to health facilities was really limited.

A closer look at the items of expenditure reveals that though during the time of growing fiscal difficulty spending on health did not suffer a major cut-back, there were adjustments to the fiscal tightening. Analysis shows that capital spending stagnated by mid eighties and declined fast, whereas revenue spending shows a tendency to decline only after the early nineties (Figure 24.1). This is due to the continuing growth of the salary component in revenue expenditure; this showed no tendency to abate during most of this period (Figure 24.2). But the growing fiscal difficulties led to cut-back on supplies, which shows a definite down-turn by the latter half of the eighties (Figure 24.2). Within sectors, this affected the secondary sector, consisting of the taluk and district hospitals, very sharply. It is no exaggeration to say that middle level hospitals were crippled by the cut-back on supplies (Figure 24.3). Since these accounted for the large number of beds in the health services and these were the hospitals most accessible to the common people, the impact of this resource crunch resulted in a severe fall in the quality of medical care in the government hospitals.

There were many factors in the social milieu of the State which were conducive to the growth of a great demand for health care (Table 24.3). The high level of education, especially female education, ensured that people were easily sensitized to the newer developments on the treatment front. The settlement pattern in the State, with comparatively easy accessibility to the towns and other centres where medical institutions were situated, was another factor contributing to the demand. The rapid proliferation of health facilities in the government sector during the sixties and seventies contributed to a growing sensitization to modern modalities of medical care to which people then became habituated. In this environment, the fall in quality in the government medical facilities provided the impetus for the growth of private medical care. They now outstrip the government facilities in the density of beds and employment of personnel. Number of beds in government institutions grew from around 36,000 to 38,000 in the ten year period from 1986 to 1996, whereas in the same period, beds in the private institutions grew from 49,000 to 67,500.[6] This amounts to nearly 40 per cent growth in the private sector beds in a period of ten years as against merely 5.5 per cent in the government sector. More significantly, they have far outpaced the government facilities in the provision of sophisticated modalities of diagnosis and therapy, such as CT scans, endoscopy units, MRI scans, neonatal care units, coronary units etc. According to one estimate, 22 out of 26 CT (computerized tomography) scan centres in the State were in the private sector in 1995.[7]

Implications for Health Care

The current geographic distribution of total facilities and the public and private mix in these have led to certain imbalances. Government health infrastructure ought to be geared to meet the primary health care needs of the people. With around 74 per cent of the people living in rural areas, in the presence of a proper referral system, the primary health care centres should take care of the majority of preventive, promotive, and curative health care needs of the people. The small proportion of cases that cannot be handled there should be referred to the urban hospitals, and eventually, only the really complicated cases should reach the

Table 24.1 Total Revenue Expenditure, Expenditure under Medical and Public Health Accounts, and Proportions, from 1985-86 to 1992-93

Year	*II Total revenue expenditure (Rupees millions)*	*III Medical and public health (Rupees millions)*	*III AS % & of II*	*III As % of development expenditure by the State*
1985-86	14453.4	1205.5	8.34	11.63
1986-87	16547.7	1437.5	8.69	12.89
1987-88	17806.5	1665.3	9.35	14.32
1988-89	20610.0	2142.0	10.39	15.76
1989-90	22930.9	2395.6	10.45	16.40
1990-91	28249.5	2785.0	9.86	15.45
1991-92	32164.6	2920.0	9.08	14.83
1992-93	38512.5	3379.8	8.78	13.76

Source: Government of Kerala, *Kerala Budget in Brief 1993-94*.

Table 24.2 Surplus/ Deficit in the State Budget, and Expenditure on Health, as Percentage of Total Government Expenditure in Kerala, 1977-78 to 1992-93

Year	*Surplus/ Deficit as percentage of revenue receipts*	*Expenditure on health as proportion of total government expenditure*
1980-81	-4.25	6.95
1985-86	-5.41	5.32
1986-87	-10.43	7.08
1988-89	-8.64	4.16
1989-90	-12.23	5.40
1990-91	-16.93	5.14

Source: Government of Kerala, *Kerala Budget in Brief* (various years).

Table 24.3 Factors Affecting the Growth of Health Services in the Government and Private Sectors in Kerala State

Factors Affecting Demand	*Factors Affecting Supply*
1. Growth of education, especially female education and awareness about health-related matters	1. Tradition of government-provided health care services
2. Settlement pattern and growth of roads and communication favouring easy accessibility	2. Government policy that continued to fund health sector even during time of financial stress
3. Government-provided falsities sensitizing the public to the need for sophisticated care	3. Subsidized medical and nursing education supplying a steady stream of personnel
4. Enhancement of income for a good proportion of households from remitances from the Gulf countries.	4. Comparative lack of regulation that made health sector attractive as an investment opportunity, especially in the case of diagnostics and highly capital intensive procedure
	5. Access to funds for investment: foreign charities, repatriation from Gulf countries, and industrial credit.

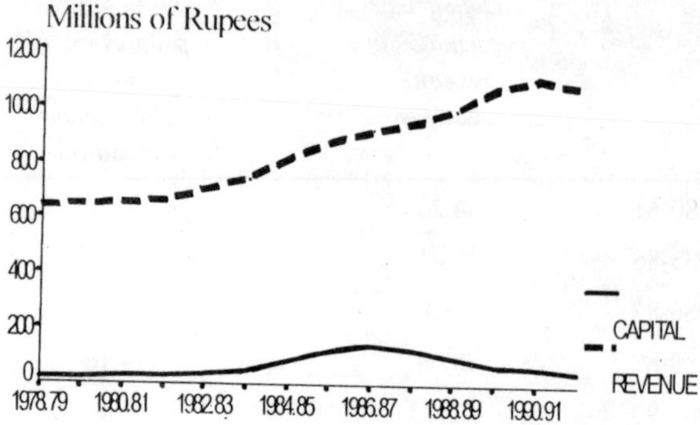

Fig. 24.1 Growth of Revenue and Capital Expenditure in Health in Government, Kerala State, 1977-78 to 1992-93

Source: V. Raman Kutty and PGK Panikar 1995. *Impact of fiscal crisis on the public sector health care system in Kerala, a research report*. Trivandrum. Achutha Menon Centre for Health Science Studies.

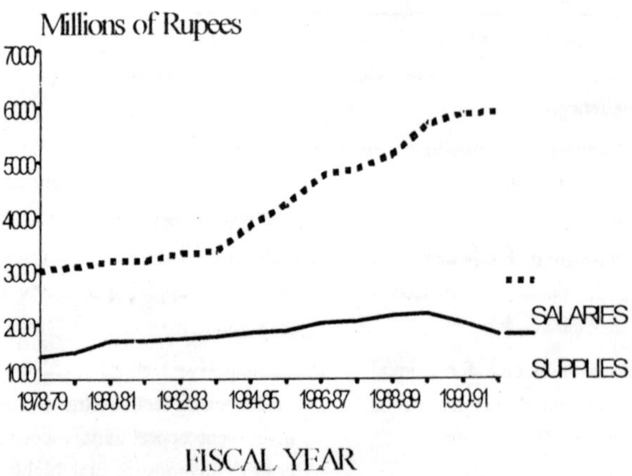

Fig. 24.2 Growth of Salaries and Supplies in the Health Sector in Kerala State, 1977-78 to 1992-93

Source : V. Raman Kutty and PGK Panikar 1995. *Impact of fiscal crisis on the public sector health care system in Kerala, a research report*. Achutha Menon Centre for Health Science Studies.

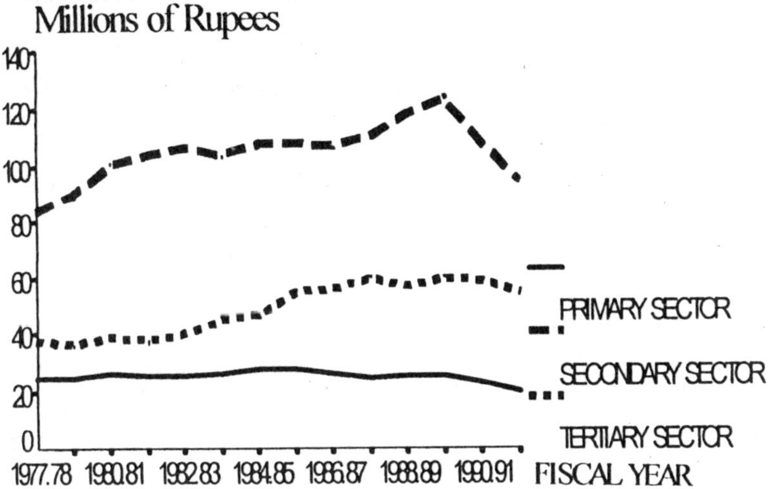

Fig. 24.3 Growth of Expenditure on Supplies in the Primary, Secondary, and Tertiary Sectors in Health in Kerala State (1977-78 to 1992-93).

Source : V. Raman Kutty and PGK Panikar 1995. *Impact of fiscal crisis on the public sector health care system in Kerala, a research report.* Achutha Menon Centre for Health Science Studies.

specialist and tertiary care centres. But the current scenario is that the primary health centres concentrate on maternal and child health, especially immunization, and family welfare activities. This is because these activities are financially supported and closely monitored by the central government, with the aid of international agencies such as the UNICEF. But in the absence of curative care for even minor ailments being available at PHCs, many from even the middle class and poor families in the rural areas do not approach these institutions for routine medical needs. An indication for this is the fact that in many PHCs, the number of deliveries conducted has dwindled to zero.

Most medical needs, apart from immunization and sterilization, are met by private hospitals, private practitioners or the private practice-set-ups of government doctors. This introduces several imbalances in the system:

(i) Most of the private set-ups work on a profit basis. Margins can be quite exorbitant for many procedures, driving up the cost of medical care enormously.

(ii) Since there are no practice guidelines set for any service, there is a tendency to overprescribe, especially the more expensive ones. There is some indication that Caesarian rates are far greater in private hospitals and that there is gross overuse of the various types of scanning procedure in the private sector.

(iii) Private sector tends to ignore those aspects of care that involve more risk, or are less commercially viable. Thus care of the chronically mentally sick, AIDS patients, infectious diseases such as leprosy and tuberculosis, all remain unsatisfactory.

(iv) The system is not geared to intervene in times of medical emergencies. Thus outbreaks of epidemics such as cholera, malaria, encephalitis etc. in the State in recent times are a reflection of the breakdown of the government health care system. This is also reflected in the poor quality of accident and trauma management.

(v) Overall, the system promotes inefficiency. Because of the greater remuneration which specialists command, there is a great desire for specialization among the medical graduates. In the absence of a proper referral system, people with minor complaints approach specialists first, and get shunted from one to the other, shelling out a lot of money in the process for both diagnostic and curative modalities. Most of these ailments could be effectively taken care of by properly trained general practitioners.

Policy Guidelines

Toning up the health care system in the State and making it capable of taking on the burden of provision of equitable, efficient and good quality health care needs concerted action. Some guidelines for policy would be:

A. *Reinstating the primacy of the government health services*, with its emphasis on primary health care. This would necessitate upgrading the facilities in a large number of institutions and ensuring that these are available to the general public.

B. *Strengthening the financial viability of government institutions*. This means greater flow of funds to the peripheral level hospitals, so that quality of care can be adequately maintained. Finding enough funds for the health sector is a challenge that has to be taken up immediately. Apriori, there are several possible ways of improving the health care financing situation in the public hospitals and health centres:

(i) increasing the share of health sector in the budget,
(ii) finding ways of augmenting the State's revenues, so that total expenditure, and as a part of it, health sector's share of it, can be enhanced,
(iii) reorganizing the allocation of resources in the health sector more efficiently, by eliminating redundant posts and cutting down on waste, and
(iv) raising resources within the health sector.

One has to look seriously at option (i), i.e., enhancing health sector's share of total government spending. At present the lion's share for health comes from the State's own revenues. There is a case for further flow of funds from the central government to the State in the health sector. Option (ii), viz., enhancing revenue collection in general, is one which, however justifiable, is socially and politically unpalatable and will meet with wide resistance: nevertheless, its feasibility should be explored. For similar political and social reasons, eliminating redundant posts may also not be an acceptable option at present. Option (iv), i.e., raising finances within the health sector, holds great promise especially in the light of the proposed decentralization of government delegating more administrative power and financial resources to the local bodies.

The interim report of the Resources Commission of the State, a body appointed by the State government to look into ways of improving the financial position of the government, recommended levying user charges for outpatient services, and introduction of differential charges depending upon the income of the patient.[8]

Many developing countries have experimented with the introduction of user charges in the health facilities, even in primary health centres. Not only has this met with great opposition from the public, this has also proved to be disastrous in areas like sub-Saharan Africa.[9,10] User charges, though perhaps simple to operate, have some built-in problems in a developing community.

(i) Sick people are already at a disadvantage economically because of their sickness. To be obliged to pay for hospital services to get well puts an additional burden on them, which is contrary to the principles of equity.
(ii) Charging uniformly for similar services puts differential burden on different classes of people. What may be an insignificant amount to the richer households, may be a heavy encumbrance for a poor household. This introduces an additional element of inequity, the poor are asked to pay a relatively greater price for getting well. If, to tide over this problem, we introduce differential charges, then the additional administrative cost of categorizing people can make the whole exercise counter-productive.

But user charges are not the sole means of improving the finances of the health sector. Other policy options need to be examined with a view to their suitability in the Kerala context.

Community Financing

There can be a community or *panchayat* (village) level tax specifically collected to fund health care. In a well-defined community such as a *panchayat*, a specific amount per household can be collected as decided by the *panchayat*, the poorest households being possibly exempted; this amount can be set apart specifically for running of the local level health institutions such as the primary health centre. There are two pre-conditions which have to be met for the success of this policy. (i) the local level health institution should be brought under the administrative control of the local body such as the *panchayat*, and (ii) the services which will be available at the local level have to be clearly spelt out, anything more complicated being referred to the next higher level. The amount collected locally as health tax can be specifically used for augmenting the facilities of the health centre including its drug supply, since the government is already paying the salaries of the staff. A considerable amount of improvement in the conditions of care can be brought about this way, without collecting charges from the users at the facility. Here the emphasis should be on 'control' and not only on the collection of taxes. Pre-payment is more equitable because the sick are not made to bear the whole burden of financing their own care; since nobody can discount the probability of falling sick, it is not likely to be resented.

Cost Containment

Another option for better performance of the health sector is to see if costs can be contained, without affecting the level of services. The savings thus generated could obviously contribute to expanding services in quality and/or quantity. By streamlining the transfer, postings, recruitment, purchase, and other administrative procedures, a lot of efficiency could be introduced into the functioning of the health services. In this area also, decentralization of administration would be an obvious step towards smoother running of the system.

Effective Decentralization of Health Services and Instituting a Referral System

With legislation empowering the local panchayats to take control of the primary health centres, improving services with local resources should become a reality. Most of the preventive and curative health needs of the people should be met at the primary health centres, and only those who are referred from there for specialist care should go to higher level hospitals. This effectively reduces the load on the secondary and tertiary level hospitals and enables them to provide high quality care. However, this will become a reality only if the primary health centre is adequately equipped and manned to handle the large number of people seeking its help.

Recognizing the Role of the Private Sector

In Kerala, in terms of infrastructure, the private sector has already outgrown the government health services. Policy making in health has to acknowledge their presence. On the one hand, the contribution they make towards taking the load off the government health system needs to be recognized; on the other hand, mechanisms should be in place to check practices which are of dubious value to the patient and only serve to increase the profit margin of the hospital. There should be some independent authority, on the lines of a commission, which should have the onus of looking after the quality of care in both government and private hospitals. Expansion of facilities in both government and private sector should follow a need-based plan.

Conclusion

Growth of health services in Kerala offers many lessons in development. Active role of the government has been a necessary condition for expansion of the health care sector, both in public as well as in private sectors. The sensitization to modern modalities of care which came about through expanding government health services and skilled personnel at different tiers which was a result of policies of the government, has created the demand that is currently sustaining both the public and private sectors in health. However, though government has played a facilitatory role in expansion of health services, their failure to take on the role of a controlling authority has resulted in predatory practices that are probably harmful to both people's health as well as Kerala's development. Transfer of power to the local level or panchayati raj institution can effectively act as a catalyst to a more creative role of government in health service development in future.

The lesson from Kerala's experience in health sector development to other States should be clear. Government taking a leading role in the provision of health services is a facilitatory factor for health development up to a point. Unless the government is also willing to put in place effective supervisory mechanisms, the system may ultimately end up with various imbalances and hazards.

REFERENCES

1. Panikar P. G. K. and C. R. Soman (1984), *Health Status of Kerala, the Paradox of Economic Backwardness and Health Development*, Trivandrum, Centre for Development Studies, p 39.
2. *Ibid.*, p. 91.
3. George K K. (1993), *Limits to the Kerala Model of Development.* Trivandrum, Centre for Development Studies, Thiruvananthapuram.
4. *Ibid.*, p. 93.
5. Government of Kerala (1996), *Government Allopathic Medical Institutions, Kerala*, Health Information Cell, Directorate of Health Services Thiruvananthapuram.
6. Government of Kerala, (1996), *Report on the Survey of Private Medical Institutions in Kerala 1995*, Department of Economics and Statistics Thiruvananthapuram.
7. Sara Abraham (1995), *Diffusion of Medical Technology: The Case of Diagnostic Imaging in Kerala*, M. Phil. dissertation, Centre for Development Studies, Thiruvananthapuram, p. 67.
8. Government of Kerala (1993), *Report of the Resources Commission.*
9. Moses S. F. Manji, J E, Bradley, NJD Negelkerke, M A, Malisa, and FA Plummer (1992), *Impact of User fees on Attendance at a Referral Centre for Sexually Transmitted Diseases in Kenya*, Lancet, pp. 340: 463-6.
10. Loewenson R. (1993), Structural Adjustment and Health Policy in Africa *International Journal of Health Services,* no. 4, pp. 717-730.

TWENTY-FIVE

HOUSING AND HEALTH

Another Kerala Conundrum

K. R. NAYAR

Several explanations have been advanced for the now well-known health transition in Kerala. Female literacy, women's status, accessibility and availability of health services, equity, socio-political factors including social movements, public distribution system etc. have been prominent variables on health improvement. It is also widely maintained that many of the social questions in Kerala have been resolved and the emphasis should be shifted to economic growth as a means to sustain welfare measures.[1]

Health improvement is influenced by three sets of factors: (a) health factors which include medical interventions, (b) health-promoting factors such as housing, water supply, sanitation and hygiene, and (c) non-health factors which include social and economic factors. Historical analyses show that the second and third sets of factors had considerable bearing on health improvement. The European experience of mortality decline in the nineteenth century necessitated such an explanatory paradigm. While the explanations on the pattern of mortality decline hold good for the European countries at a particular stage of their developmental process, trends in the developing countries of the present era indicate the need for a much more complex and wider canvas. Although from a public health perspective, the importance of housing and environmental amenities is well recognised and probably taken for granted, the complexity of relationship (one of which is the linkage between economic status and availability of environmental amenities) needs to be underlined. This chapter adds to the demographic-health conundrum of Kerala by examining the plausibility of an environmental explanation by placing the State in an inter-state framework.

Before attempting such an analysis, let us briefly examine the background with regard to housing and environmental amenities. Studies conducted in many countries show that a medium reduction of 27 per cent in diarrhoea morbidity and 30 per cent in diarrhoea mortality could be achieved by the provision of improved water supply and excreta disposal. Houses with piped water supply had 80 per cent lower diarrhoea mortality rate among infants than those with no access to piped water.[2] Some earlier studies conducted in Kerala also show that although mortality rates among children were associated with availability of latrine, improved water supply was not associated with mortality.[3] However, some recent studies show that morbidity rate has a definite association with environmental status.[4] It was also seen that incidence of sporadic diarrhoea cases is less among population using own wells and piped water supply at home. It was seen to be more among those using public wells and public taps.

Although there are some inconsistencies regarding the type of environmental variables which are associated with mortality and morbidity rates, the earlier studies point out a possible contribution of environmental amenities to health improvement. The studies also indicate the complexity in the relationships.

The complexity of housing-health relationships has also been posed earlier by the Bhore Committee and the Sub-committee on National Housing. Both these historical documents had underlined State's role in the provision of housing. According to the Bhore Committee, the objective to be attained is the creation of hygienic houses in adequate numbers and of adequate size in sanitated areas equipped with all the facilities necessary for community life.[5] The Committee also suggested that the provincial Ministry of Health, apart from the Ministry of Housing, should be concerned with proper execution of housing programmes, and should be responsible for the control and enforcement of minimum standards in the design and construction, not only of the houses but also of environmental amenities such as water supply, sanitation and recreation. The Bhore Committee also recommended that a vigorous policy is essential for the development of a water supply programme which should aim at providing the entire population with safe water for drinking and domestic purposes within a period of about 35 years. Regarding sanitation, the Bhore Committee recommended that improving general sanitation is a matter of urgent importance from the point of view of controlling a large part of preventable ill-health. The Sub-committee on National Housing felt that adequate and suitable housing is such a matter of urgent necessity, that it cannot be left to a private enterprise utterly uncontrolled and wholly innocent of a social conscience.[7] This urgency in housing, water supply and sanitation and the public health perspective was not visible in the programmes undertaken in independent India.

Housing, Water Supply and Sanitation Programmes in India

Housing

The First Five Year Plan (1951-56) admitted that due to financial constraints a satisfactory programme of rural housing could not be envisaged. Therefore, the principle of aided self-help was followed in the case of rural housing. The Second Five Year Plan (1956-61) also continued this approach of aided self-help by mainly earmarking funds for technical advice, demonstration of model houses etc. The Village Housing Scheme was introduced in 1957 for providing assistance to villagers for construction and improvement of houses, for house sites to landless agricultural workers and for streets and drains in selected villages. The Third Five Year Plan (1961-66) also continued the facilitatory approach but identified housing as a part of the larger scheme of rural development. The Fourth Five Year Plan (1969-74) admitted that the Village Housing Scheme introduced during the Second Plan did not make any progress. In 1971, the Rural House Site-cum-House Construction Scheme was launched which for the first time conceived a much more active role of the government in rural housing. However, the role was restricted to providing meagre subsidies for site development and construction. The Fifth Five Year Plan (1974-79) continued this scheme a little more vigorously by including it as a major component of the

Minimum Needs Programme. The Sixth Plan (1980-85) aimed at substantially reducing the number of absolutely shelterless people and providing condition for others to improve their housing environment. The Seventh Plan (1985-90) saw a major shift with respect to the States' involvement in housing activity. It was suggested that the major responsibility for house construction should be left to the private sector, in particular the household sector. It was in the Seventh Plan that the government went back on its commitment as a provider by suggesting promotion of self-help, housing finance and private sector.

The role of the State in urban housing was more active than that of rural housing. However, much of the involvement of the State was limited to construction of housing for government employees and social housing schemes under which departmental housing and house building advance were included. Financial institutions for housing were also actively promoted. On the whole, it is possible to observe the gradual withdrawal of the State from direct participation in the housing sector by encouraging market-based solutions to the housing problem.

While in most States, no innovative solutions to housing the rural poor emerged, Kerala in the seventies evolved a novel scheme called one lakh houses scheme. The Government of Kerala modified a central scheme called House Site-cum-House Construction Scheme and implemented it in 1972 in all the panchayats of the State simultaneously.[8] Along with the site, the programme intended to provide a fully constructed dwelling consisting of kitchen, a bedroom and a larger multi-purpose room. This programme gave a new dimension to the welfare orientation of the State especially in taking care of the housing needs and thereby enhancing the well-being of the poorer sections. The implementation of the programme had also been partly responsible for a fresh thinking on alternate building technology and cost-reduction in construction activities.

Water Supply and Sanitation

The National Water Supply and Sanitation Programme was initiated in 1954 for providing drinking water to scarcity and health problem villages. In the Fourth Plan, the Accelerated Rural Water Programme which was launched in the States was 100 per cent central grant-in-aid. In the Fifth Plan, this programme was included in the Minimum Needs Programme. There was also a quantum jump in the allocation for water supply programme in the same plan with Rs. 3810 crores in all the pervious plans. Another major landmark occurred in the Seventh Plan when the Technology Mission for drinking water in villages and related water management was launched in 1986. Even with such priorities and allocations in the five year plans, total coverage of the population with safe drinking water was still elusive. After the Seventh Plan, it was estimated that a backlog of about 4000 villages would be carried over to the Eighth Plan. These habitation-based estimates and data, however, do not indicate availability, accessibility and quality of drinking water.

Regarding sanitation, the performance was extremely tardy as admitted in the plan documents. The Central Rural Sanitation Programme was launched in 1986 to provide sanitary latrines to rural households. However, due to technical, social and economic reasons, the programme has not made much headway.

Thus, on the whole, the performance in this particular social sector is extremely tardy. In Kerala, an effort was made to address the issue of housing to the rural poor and other weaker sections. It would be, therefore, interesting to examine whether better housing amenities-status has any bearing on health improvement in Kerala in a comparative perspective. The objective is to evolve workable hypotheses in relation to factors related to health improvement and contribute to the already existing analytical framework.

II

The analysis is based on the data on housing conditions collected by the National Sample Survey Organisation in its 44th round. The NSS data, although based on limited samples, have some advantages over the Census data on housing and amenities.[9] The NSS data apart from reporting the availability of amenities also give their physical location. This, we felt, could be important from an epidemiological point of view.

The initial descriptive analysis is based on data restricted to ten States which largely represent the different patterns in terms of quality of life. These are Karnataka, Tamil Nadu and Kerala from the south, Maharashtra and Goa from the west, West Bengal and Orissa from the east and Uttar Pradesh, Haryana and Madhya Pradesh from the north. The housing conditions are assessed in terms of type of house, source of drinking water, distance from the source of drinking water, availability of sanitary facilities and the type of lighting. The demographic and health indicators of these ten States are also assessed in this descriptive exercise in order to explore any possible systematic trends in the housing conditions. In order to find broad associations, inter-correlations among variables related to housing, amenities and certain health indicators were also attempted. This pertains to rural areas of 20 states and Union territories.

III

Demographic and Health Indicators

Table 25.1 Selected Demographic and Health Indicators by States

States	*Literacy rate*			*CBR*[1]	*CDR*[1]	*IMR*[1]	*Life expectancy*[2]		*Sex ratio*
	M	*F*	*T*				*M*	*F*	
Karnataka	67.3	44.3	56.0	25.5	8.0	67	62.1	63.3	963
Tamil Nadu	74.9	52.3	63.7	19.2	8.0	56	60.8	60.8	974
Kerala	94.5	86.9	90.6	17.3	6.0	13	66.2	71.1	1032
Maharashtra	74.8	50.5	63.1	25.0	7.2	50	61.9	62.9	934
Goa	85.5	68.2	77.0	14.6	6.6	20[3]	-	-	967
West Bengal	67.2	47.2	57.7	25.6	7.3	58	60.2	61.2	917
Orissa	62.4	34.4	48.6	27.2	12.2	110	57.1	55.1	971
Uttar Pradesh	55.3	26.0	41.7	36.0	11.4	93	54.1	49.6	879
Harayana	67.8	40.9	55.3	30.6	7.8	65	63.4	62.0	865
Madhya Pradesh	57.4	28.4	43.5	33.4	12.6	106	56.2	54.7	931

Notes 1. 1993 Provisional
2. 1986-91
3. Three year moving average 1991-93 provisional

Source: (a) Sample Registration Bulletin, vol. 29, no. 1, 1995.
(b) Report of the Expert Committee on Population Projection Occasional Paper (1988) No. 4 Registrar General of India.
(c) Census Figures.

Table 25.1 reports some selected demographic and health indicators which are now well-known. Kerala and Goa present the best scenario with respect to all the indicators such as Crude Birth Rate, Crude Death Rate, life expectancy etc. Madhya Pradesh, Orissa and Uttar Pradesh represent the worst scenario. The Crude Death Rate in Madhya Pradesh, Infant Mortality Rate in Orissa and Crude Birth Rate in Uttar Pradesh are the highest in India. All other States present the middle range with minor differences in some indicators.

(b) ***Type of House***

Table 25.2 Percentage Distribution by Type of House (Rural-Urban)

State	*Katcha*		*Semi-Pucca*		*Pucca*	
	R	*U*	*R*	*U*	*R*	*U*
Karnataka	24.45	10.64	51.23	26.70	24.32	62.66
Tamil Nadu	46.12	18.56	22.73	17.38	31.15	64.06
Kerala	26.87	13.79	23.06	17.55	50.07	68.66
Maharashtra	18.17	5.64	49.25	19.66	32.58	74.69
Goa	5.15	3.77	61.74	38.76	33.11	57.47
West Bengal	53.86	6.76	32.76	20.00	13.38	73.27
Orissa	71.43	29.46	19.18	17.39	9.36	53.15
Uttar Pradesh	44.46	9.95	27.38	15.12	28.16	74.93
Harayana	13.82	2.38	10.04	4.15	76.14	93.47
Madhya Pradesh	18.56	9.73	69.37	35.21	12.07	55.06

Source: Results on Housing Conditions, *Sarvekshana*, vol. 15, no. 3, January-March 1992.

Table 25.2 presents data on the type of house—*katcha*, semi-*pucca* and *pucca*—in rural and urban areas. When examined against health indicators, a systematic trend is by and large observable in housing conditions especially in the case of *pucca* houses. The highest percentage of *pucca* houses in rural areas is

Table 25.3 Source of Drinking Water in Rural and Urban Areas by States.

State	*Piped*		*Handpump*		*Well Water*		*Surface and others*	
	R	*U*	*R*	*U*	*R*	*U*	*R*	*U*
Karnataka	21.28	78.57	43.97	9.12	28.33	10.48	3.92	1.84
Tamil Nadu	29.37	74.77	34.74	11.04	30.62	9.15	5.28	5.02
Kerala	11.29	54.26	1.46	0.44	82.83	45.19	4.42	0.00
Maharashtra	33.99	92.97	17.34	2.43	42.93	4.02	4.99	0.57
Goa	23.74	70.56	0.00	0.00	64.25	29.45	12.01	0.00
West Bengal	3.63	58.02	74.72	36.17	19.67	5.76	1.99	0.10
Orissa	0.44	57.85	34.83	12.78	50.92	23.67	13.79	5.69
Uttar Pradesh	6.71	59.84	45.77	32.02	45.71	7.79	1.81	0.35
Harayana	32.90	66.05	35.73	31.68	30.22	3.27	1.14	0.00
Madhya Pradesh	6.77	70.88	35.36	12.56	50.30	15.59	7.56	0.98

Source: National Sample Survey, 44th Round.

reported from Haryana and Kerala. Goa, Maharashtra, Tamil Nadu also present a better picture in the availability of *pucca* housing.

The most significant observation is, however, with regard to Orissa which has the highest percentage of *katcha* houses and lowest percentage of *pucca* houses in India. Lower percentage of *pucca* structures is also found in Madhya Pradesh followed by West Bengal.

Another trend which can be observed from the Tables, especially in the category of *pucca* houses, is the rural-urban disparity. The urban bias is considerably large for States like Orissa, Uttar Pradesh, Madhya Pradesh and West Bengal. Kerala presents a positive picture with regard to rural-urban differentials.

The data on the type of house reflect the indirect and complex relationships between housing and health. The exceptions such as Haryana and West Bengal—both middle order States in health and demographic indicators—which stand at two extremes in housing conditions reveal this complexity.

Sources of Drinking Water

Although, data on sources of drinking water do not indicate any systematic trend, the percentage of households receiving piped water supply is lowest in Orissa followed by West Bengal, Uttar Pradesh and Madhya Pradesh (Table 25.3). However, the picture is not different in Kerala either, except for the fact that the percentage of households depending on well water is highest in this State followed by Goa. The percentage of households using handpump as a source of drinking water is extremely negligible in Kerala while none of the households in Goa belong to this category. Safety of handpumps is an issue which could be raised on the basis of this data.

Table 25.4 gives data on distribution of households by distance from the source of drinking water. The epidemiologically significant observation is that in Kerala, as many as in 60 per cent of the rural households, the source of drinking water is located in the premises itself. This is especially important as large number of households depend on well water for meeting the needs and therefore having an exclusive well would considerably facilitate their maintenance.

Table 25.4 Percentage Distribution of Households by Distance from the Source of Drinking Water

(Distance in kms)

State	*Rural*			*Urban*		
	Within premises	*<0.5*	*>0.5*	*Within premises*	*<0.5*	*>0.5*
Karnataka	13.52	78.15	8.34	50.35	48.35	1.30
Tamil Nadu	8.46	84.35	7.20	40.49	54.48	5.03
Kerala	60.36	37.92	1.71	64.24	35.39	0.36
Maharashtra	17.30	78.58	4.13	58.81	39.94	1.25
Goa	27.56	72.44	0.00	51.84	48.16	0.00
West Bengal	14.72	80.83	4.46	46.99	52.46	0.54
Orissa	11.52	84.03	4.45	42.57	57.06	0.37
Uttar Pradesh	35.41	63.68	0.91	73.00	26.68	0.31
Harayana	15.03	75.89	9.08	72.22	26.75	1.02
Madhya Pradesh	14.26	79.21	6.54	49.06	49.04	1.91

Source: National Sample Survey, 44th round

In all other States, the data indicate that considerable number of households use public drinking water sources. Public handpumps or tube-wells situated away from the premises form the source of drinking water for most of the households in these states.[10]

Sanitary Facilities

Regarding the availability of sanitary facilities, Kerala stands out compared to all other States both in rural and urban areas (Table 25.5). In the case of Goa, sanitary facilities are better only in rural areas. In all other States more than 90 per cent of the households in rural areas do not have any sanitary facilities.

Table 25.5 Availability of Sanitation : Statewise distribution

State	*Rural*			*Urban*		
	No latrine	*Latrine for exclusive use*	*Shared with other households*	*No latrine*	*Latrine for exclusive use*	*Shared with other households*
Karnataka	93.49	4.67	1.84	36.05	35.24	28.70
Tamil Nadu	93.87	4.05	2.08	40.01	28.41	31.58
Kerala	51.54	43.69	4.76	18.67	65.95	15.39
Maharashtra	93.13	3.03	3.84	23.20	27.70	49.10
Goa	66.20	24.66	9.15	30.92	39.55	29.53
West Bengal	89.13	8.28	2.59	17.54	37.51	44.95
Orissa	95.66	2.79	1.55	49.80	34.22	15.98
Uttar Pradesh	92.66	5.04	2.29	28.65	43.98	27.37
Harayana	96.11	2.23	1.67	37.15	38.96	23.88
Madhya Pradesh	96.80	2.12	1.07	45.63	33.84	20.53

Source: National Sample Survey, 44th round.

The data also indicate that among those who have sanitary facilities in Kerala, a large percentage of them have latrines for exclusive use both in rural and urban areas.[11]

Regarding urban areas, it is seen that in both Maharashtra and West Bengal, a high proportion of households have latrines which are shared with other households. Studies show that in urban areas the incidence of shared latrines is extremely high at lower levels of consumption.[12] This means, as seen from the case of Kerala, that although economically determined, having an exclusive sanitary facility is culturally and epidemiologically significant even if the latrine is qualitatively inferior.

Type of Lighting

Data on availability of electricity show that in the case of West Bengal, Orissa and Uttar Pradesh, the availability of electricity in the rural areas is extremely low (Table 25.6).

Table 25.6 Type of Lighting

State	Rural			Urban		
	No lighting	Electricity	Kerosene & others	No lighting	Electricity	Kerosene & others
Karnataka	3.78	35.86	60.37	2.54	74.85	22.61
Tamil Nadu	3.33	43.22	53.45	3.75	73.90	22.36
Kerala	1.63	42.24	56.14	1.49	70.08	28.43
Maharashtra	2.87	45.95	51.17	1.78	83.01	15.21
Goa	6.93	80.37	12.70	1.63	90.73	7.64
West Bengal	2.63	5.86	91.50	2.06	63.07	34.87
Orissa	2.97	10.90	86.13	1.80	61.45	36.74
Uttar Pradesh	1.30	9.27	89.43	2.62	66.73	30.66
Haryana	0.78	57.18	42.04	0.39	91.85	7.75
Madhya Pradesh	6.98	29.85	63.17	4.17	71.91	23.93

Source: National Sample Survey, 44th round.

Goa, however, stands out being the only State where electricity is available in about 80 per cent of rural households and the rural-urban difference is negligible in this case.

Broad Trends

An examination of data from ten States in India indicates a definite contribution of environmental factors in health improvement. Kerala's health transition, apart from the available explanations, needs to be located also in health-promoting factors such as housing and amenities. The large rural-urban differential which is observed in all States except in Kerala and Goa needs further examination.

Although the data show a few inconsistencies, it is possible, to evolve a systematic trend. For instance, mere availability of housing or drinking water may not generate good health. There may be underlying epidemiological causal mechanisms connected to these conditions which need to be highlighted. Availability of drinking water is a variable at a broader level; the data do not indicate any systematic trend. It could be that having an exclusive drinking water source, even well water, may facilitate the quality

Table 25.7 Inter-Correlation among House Amenities and Health Indicators

Correlations	*1*	*2*	*3*	*4*	*5*	*6*	*7*	*8*	*9*	*10*	*11*
1. IMR	1.00										
2. CDR	0.93	1.00									
3. CBR	0.68	0.56	1.00								
4. Pucca House	-0.23	-0.25	-0.03	1.00							
5. Katcha House	0.19	0.11	0.09	-0.67	1.00						
6. Piped water	-0.32	-0.42	-0.12	0.31	-0.51	1.00					
7. Water community	0.30	0.22	0.21	-0.32	0.20	-0.01	1.00				
8. Water premises	-0.38	-0.29	-0.24	0.40	-0.18	-0.04	-0.94	1.00			
9. No latrine	0.63	0.63	0.45	0.31	-0.36	-0.05	0.34	-0.33	1.00		
10. Latrine premises	-0.61	-0.62	-0.41	-0.31	0.37	0.06	-0.35	0.34	-0.99	1.00	
11. Electricity	-0.48	-0.44	-0.38	0.62	-0.78	0.71	-0.25	0.25	0.01	-0.03	1.00

of water. This may be an epidemiologically important hypothesis for future examination. The same hypothesis is applicable for sanitation as well.

In order to further examine these broad hypotheses, correlations among housing, amenities and some health indicators are attempted (Table 25.7). Moderate to strong negative correlations are observed between (a) availability of piped water supply and crude death rates, (b) households with water source in premises and infant mortality rate, (c) households with exclusive latrine and infant mortality rate, crude death rate and crude birth rate, (d) availability of electricity and infant mortality rate, crude death rate and crude birth rate. Similarly, positive correlations exist between proportion of households without latrine and infant mortality rate, crude death rate and crude birth rate. Low correlations exist between (a) pucca housing and infant mortality rate, (b) pucca housing and crude death rate, (c) community source of water and infant mortality rate, crude birth rate and crude death rate, (d) households with water source in premises and crude death rate, crude birth rate etc. thereby indicating slight associations.

The inter-correlations largely support the hypothesis that although availability of housing or safe source of drinking water could be important for health promotion, it would not alone explain health improvement in Kerala. Even an open source of drinking water may be safe, if it is an exclusive source. As expected, based on many other studies as well, the linkage between sanitation and health is prominent. The association is stronger than many other linkages. As discussed earlier, Kerala again stands out in terms of availability of latrines as well as availability of exclusive latrines.

This preliminary exercise substantiates the position that health improvement in Kerala is largely located in health promoting factors and non-health factors. The contribution of environmental factors appears to be significant in this transition. This also shows that any action on health improvement cannot be based on notions of unilinearity and ready-made models as it is being done at present. The complexity in housing-amenities-health relationships shows that the framework has to take into cognizance the epidemiological undercurrent below the visible layers of economic and human development.

REFERENCES

1. Thomas Isaac, T.M. and P.K. Michael Tharakan (1995), "Kerala: Towards a New Agenda", *Economic and Political Weekly,* vol. 30, nos. 31 & 32, pp. 1993-2004.
2. Dean T. Jameson, *et al* (eds.) (1993), *Disease Control Priorities in Developing Countries*, OUP, pp. 100-101.
3. Quoted in K.P. Kannan, K.R. Thankappan, V.Ramankutty and K.P. Aravindan (1991), *Health Status in Rural Kerala: A Study of Linkages Between Socio-economic Status and Health Status*, IRTC of the Kerala Sastra Sahitya Parishad (KSSP), p. 15.
4. *Ibid.*, pp. 100-102.
5. Government of India (1946), *Report of the Health Survey and Development Committee*, vol. II, pp. 235-236.
6. *Ibid.*, p. 250.
7. National Planning Committee (1948), *Report of the Sub-committee on National Housing*, Vora & Co., p. 21.
8. Centre for Development Studies (1975), *Poverty, Unemployment and Development Policy: A Case Study of Selected Issues with Reference to Kerala* (mimeo), Appendix-D.
9. Government of India (1993), Census 1991, Housing and Amenities, New Delhi.
10. A similar observation in urban areas is made by Amitabh Kundu (1993), *In the Name of the Urban Poor: Access to Basic Amenities*, Sage, p. 247.
11. K. P. Kannan, *et al, op. cit.* The study shows that at least 48 per cent of the households have a private latrine with or without a septic tank or leach pit.
12. Kundu, *op. cit.*, p. 249.

TWENTY-SIX

ENERGY PLANNING

The Need for a Departure from the "Kerala Model"

R. V. G. MENON

Prima facie, there is no connection between what has come to be known as the Kerala Model of Development and any particular approach to Energy Planning. Yet, Energy Planning in Kerala has followed a particular pattern, which is rather unique. So, this pattern also might very well be called a "Kerala Model", even though it has nothing to do with the more familiar and noteworthy socio-economic aspects of the Model.

The Unique Features

Technically, the Kerala approach to electricity development has been one based entirely on hydro-electric projects. No doubt, there were many sound reasons for this preference. Kerala has no coal or oil or gas resources. It is fairly well-endowed in water resources, with 41 west-flowing and 4 east-flowing rivers. The first Master Plan prepared for Kerala's water resources in 1958 estimated its total hydel potential at an impressive 3600 MW. Moreover, the cost of electricity generated through hydel stations was far less than the cost of thermally generated electricity. The concentration on hydel power, to the exclusion of the more expensive thermal variety, enabled Kerala to sell power at a much cheaper rate and use this as a bait for attracting more industries to the State. This was, of course, a mere continuation of the imaginative policy of Sir C.P. Ramaswamy Iyer, the Diwan of Travancore. The Indian Aluminium Company had been thus enticed into starting an Aluminum extraction plant at Alwaye, even though they had to bring the raw materials from far away places, with the promise of bulk electricity at 2p/unit. Even now, Kerala has the distinction of selling electricity at the lowest tariff to industries (Table 26.1).

Table 26.1 Comparison of Electricity Tariff among Southern States

(Paise per unit)

State	*Domestic*	*Commercial*	*Industry*
Andhra Pradesh	190	274	311
Tamil Nadu	113	394	345
Karnataka	180	453	340
Maharashtra	95	329	359
Kerala	70	214	105*

* For new industrial units, the pre-revision rate, i.e., 54.25p/unit, only is being charged.

So What is Wrong?

As pointed out earlier, there is an obvious logic in this policy. But this is not as simple as that. For one thing, States like Tamil Nadu also have significant hydel potential (their installed hydel capacity is higher than Kerala's). Yet, quite early in their development they chose to go for thermal power plants also. There was a sound technical reason for that. All over the world, it is well accepted that there should be a healthy mix of thermal and hydel generating capacity, wherever possible. Thermal stations are ideally suited for base load operation and hydels excel in peak load application. We can use hydel units for both peak as well as base load operation, but then we must have enough water in the reservoir to operate the plants at a fairly high Plant Capacity Factor. This was true of the earlier hydel stations of Kerala. But, after Sabarigiri, Kerala has been designing its hydel plants with Capacity Factors of the order of 50 per cent or less (sometimes, as low as 36 per cent, as at Idukki-see Table 26.2). These can, obviously, operate only as peak load stations. Then what about base load? This has been the big lacuna in our planning and so far we have been managing to avoid a major breakdown only, thanks to the industrial underdevelopment of Kerala. It is well known that base load demand increases directly in proportion to industrial development. Kerala's consumption pattern, with its unusual emphasis on domestic and commercial sector, has a predominant peak and poor base load (see Table 26.3).

Table 26.2 Kerala's Hydel Stations: Installed Capacity, Energy Potential and Plant Capacity Factor

Sl. No.	*Station*	*Installed Capacity (MW)*	*Energy Potential (MU)*	*Plant Capacity Factor*
1.	Pallivasal	37.5	284	87%
2.	Sengulam	48	182	43%
3.	Poringalkuthu	32	170	60%
4.	Neriamangalam	45	237	60%
5.	Panniar	30	158	60%
6.	Sabarigiri	300	1338	51%
7.	Sholayar	54	233	49%
8.	Kuttiadi	75	268	41%
9.	Idukki	780	2398	36%
10.	Idamalayar	75	380	58%
	Silent Valley (for comparison)	240	522	24%
	Pooyamkutty (for comparison)	240	645	31%

Table 26.3 Power Consumption Pattern—Kerala Electricity System

1.	Domestic	—	32.9%
2.	Commercial	—	13.3%
3.	Water works	—	1.9%
4.	Agriculture (Irrigation)	—	4.2%
5.	Public lighting	—	1.8%
6.	Bulk supply	—	2.0%
7.	Industries (LT)	—	7.9%
8.	Industries (HT,EHT)	—	36.1%

The second argument against depending exclusively on hydel plants is that it puts us squarely at the mercy of the monsoons. A glance at the annual variations of rainfall in Kerala will show that there can be very large deviations from the mean (Table 26.4). This is in the very nature of the monsoon and we should not blame the monsoon of "cheating" us or "letting us down".

Table 26.4 Variations in the Annual Rainfall in Kerala

Year	*52-53*	*53-54*	*54-55*	*55-56*	*56-57*	*57-58*	*58-59*	*59-60*	*60-61*	*61-62*	
Average rainfall in mm	1699	2804	2737	2690	2853	2956	2986	3309	3733	3310	
62-63	*63-64*	*64-65*	*65-66*	*66-67*	*67-68*	*68-69*	*69-70*	*70-71*	*71-72*	*72-73*	*73-74*
3125	2465	3169	1209	2628	2746	3250	2695	3046	2600	2704	2183

An Unwise Incentive

Offering electrical energy at very low rates may appear to be a clever strategy to attract industry. But, it has its drawbacks too. Experience has shown that only electricity-intensive industries, for which the energy cost is a major component, consider this to be a decisive factor influencing their locational choices. In order to appreciate the significance of this point, we must remember that different industrics use electricity in different ways and with different results. Two useful indicators are value addition per kWh and employment generation per kWh. While engineering industries and information industries fare very favourably on both counts, chemical industries, especially electro-chemical and electro-metallurgical, fare very badly (Table 26.5).

Table 26.5 Electricity Consumption and Employment Generation in Certain Industries*

Industry	*No. of kwh per worker per day*
1. Transformers & Electricals	12
2. Malabar Spinning	17
3. Hindustan Newsprint	19
4. Western India Plywoods	20
5. Apollo Tyres	30
6. Periyar Chemicals	33
7. Permier Tyres	35
8. HMT	43
9. Gwalior Rayons	45
10. Travancore Rayons	48
11. Steel Complex	200
12. Carborundum Universal	260
13. Cominco Binani	370
14. Travancore Electro Chemicals	580
15. Indian Aluminium	1000

* *Source:* A study conducted by KSSP in 1986.

A sordid sequel to this sad policy is that even in 1996, when the EHT (extra high tension) industries were subjected to an unprecedented 100 per cent power cut, some new industrial units were being supplied energy at concessional rates of 54.25 p/kWh. These were Steel Melting Units and Electro-chemicals with energy

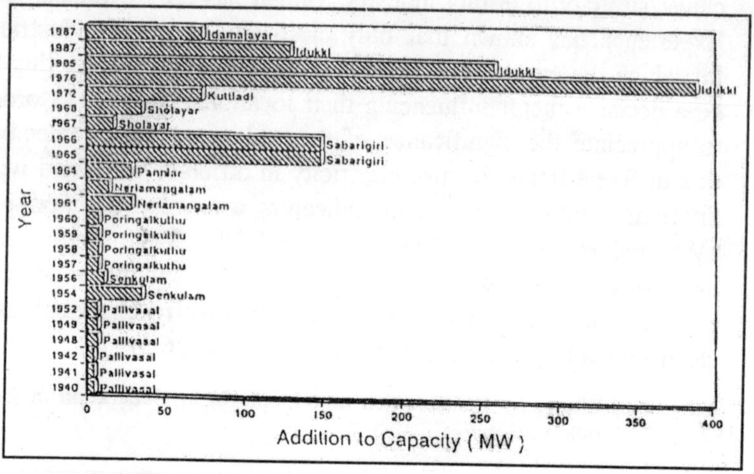

Fig. 26.1 Kerala State Electricity Board : Addition to Installed capacity.

to employment ratios of over 600 to 1000 kWh/person/day. The KSEB had estimated that just two such units were draining away more than 8.7 MU every month at such concessional rates. The tariff difference alone must give them an advantage of about Rs. 30 crores every year ! And the employment generated is hardly 350. In effect, the KSEB is forced to give a subsidy of about Rs. 8 lakh/year for each job thus created !

The Fatal Attraction of Low-cost Power

The fatal fascination with cheap electricity has forced Kerala into a vicious circle. Most of the available funds were spent on the big and medium hydel projects. Very little was spent on strengthening the Transmission and Distribution Systems, with the result that sometimes when the power plants were ready for commissioning the power evacuation lines were not in place. The traditional rivalry between the Civil and Electrical Wings of the Board was also responsible for this lopsided investment policy. As a result, the lines got overloaded and the T&D losses mounted to all time highs of as much as 30 percent. In some parts of the State, the customer's voltage is as low as 30V instead of the regular 230. And when the annual rains were not bountiful, load shedding and power cuts became regular features. As the demand-supply gap widened, and the system could not meet even the energy load, power cuts and load sheddings had to be resorted to as a regular practice, even when the monsoon was in full force.

Enormous amounts are being spent by the consumers on voltage stabilizers, boosters, UPS, emergency lamps, and other electronic equipments to seek individual salvation from this morass.

Who Benefits ?

So we have a peculiar Kerala Model in Energy Planning in which the electricity prices are kept artificially low by an exclusive reliance on hydel power plants, resulting in all-around hardship. But the curious question is, why did the State Electricity Board persist in such a policy, even in the face of such reversals? The official reply has been that there was nothing wrong with the policy. The only problem was the setback suffered by the Silent Valley and later the Pooyamkutty projects, on account of environmental opposition. The Silent Valley Project had a total energy potential of only 522 MU which is roughly 5 per cent of the projected demand for the year 2000 A.D. The capacity of Pooyamkutty is also only around 645 MU. On the other hand, the Kayamkulam Thermal Project alone has a capacity of 2400 MU. But the State Electricity Board has always been lukewarm, if not outright antagonistic, towards thermal power plants. Even as early as the VI Plan, the KSSP had strongly advocated the starting of a Thermal Power Project. But the Board opposed it, arguing that the State should spend all its available energy and resources in developing its cheap hydel resources in full, before diverting any of it into the expensive thermal power projects. Again during the VII Plan formulation the controversy was revived. This time, the proposal was included 'in principle', but hardly any progress was made due to the lack of earnestness. Finally by about 1987, the

Kayamkulam site was identified and in 1989, the NTPC (National Thermal Power Corporation) was requested to take up the project. But the actual work on the project commenced only in 1996.

One question has to be asked. Who was been the real beneficiary of this strange policy ? Not the domestic consumers: they are constantly bothered by interruptions, official and unofficial load sheddings, power cuts, voltage fluctuations, etc. Nor the commercial consumers, who also have the same problems. Many of the above two categories actually incur considerable expenditure to escape these. So, in spite of their ritualistic protestations to the contrary, most of them would willingly pay a higher tariff for assured power supply of good quality.

Charging higher tariffs would not be inconsistent with the socio-economic objectives of the Kerala pattern of development. There can be a slab system, by which the poorest classes (for example, those who consume less than 50 units per month) are given electricity at heavily subsidized rates (not free), those who consume between 50 and 100 units, at cost, and those who consume more than 100 units per month at penal rates, providing some kind of cross subsidy.

The LT/HT industries, which have to bear the brunt of the power cuts, also may welcome the move. Most of the small workshops and production units are denied permission to operate during peak hours. By the very nature of their operation, their value addition is quite high and they also could very well afford to pay a stiffer tariff for better power supply.

Even among the EHT (Extra High Tension) consumers, there are some who can afford costlier power, provided it is of assured quality. In fact, some of them have built captive power plants to ensure this. Obviously, they are not going to object if tariffs are raised to accommodate thermal input.

But there is a group of industries who cannot afford any increase in tariffs. They are the EHT consumers who run energy-intensive enterprises, with comparatively little value addition, comparatively inefficient technologies, and who are just happy with things as they are. They would rather have the present mess of voltage fluctuations (from which they are mostly insulated by virtue of their EHT supply) and power cuts (during which they can have their annual maintenance shutdowns) than suffer any steep rise in tariffs. So, one is forced to conclude that they, and they alone, have been the beneficiaries of the system.

The other group which has benefited from the exclusive reliance on large hydels, even to the exclusion of small/mini hydel projects, has been the big construction contractors. This could perhaps explain why the KSEB has been strangely reluctant to pursue the small hydel option with any seriousness. Even the few projects it did take up were dragging on for years, thereby seemingly disproving the casc that small hydels could be completed far quicker and hence ought to be accorded preference. Finally it took a private firm (M/s. Carborundum Universal) to demonstrate that a small Hydel Plant (Maniyar) could be completed in as short a time as 22 months. Then the Board went overboard, taking the stand that it was getting out of the small hydel field altogether, leaving it completely open to the private enterprises. Anyone can see that this would be a suicidal policy, as the private entrepreneurs would only pick and choose, so that only the most profitable demote projects and tailrace projects would be harnessed, leaving the bulk of the State's potential (estimated to be of the order of 400 MW or more) untapped.

The Need for a New Policy Initiative

It is obvious that Kerala cannot progress without industrialization. But what kind of industries do we want? Certainly not any more of the variety which guzzle our precious electricity and cough up so few job opportunities. We must go for more value-adding, employment-generating, industries. For that we must offer other attractions than cheap power. What these are, needs to be carefully studied with an open mind. It is instructive to remember that while domestic electricity consumption has been growing in Kerala at an annual rate of 15 per cent, the industrial consumption has been growing only at about 3 per cent p.a. even during the post-Idukki phase, when we were exporting power (see Figure 26.2).

Anyway, it must be obvious that a necessary, though not sufficient, condition for industrial development is assured power supply of good quality. It costs money to do that and higher tariffs are inescapable. A deviation from the traditional fixation with

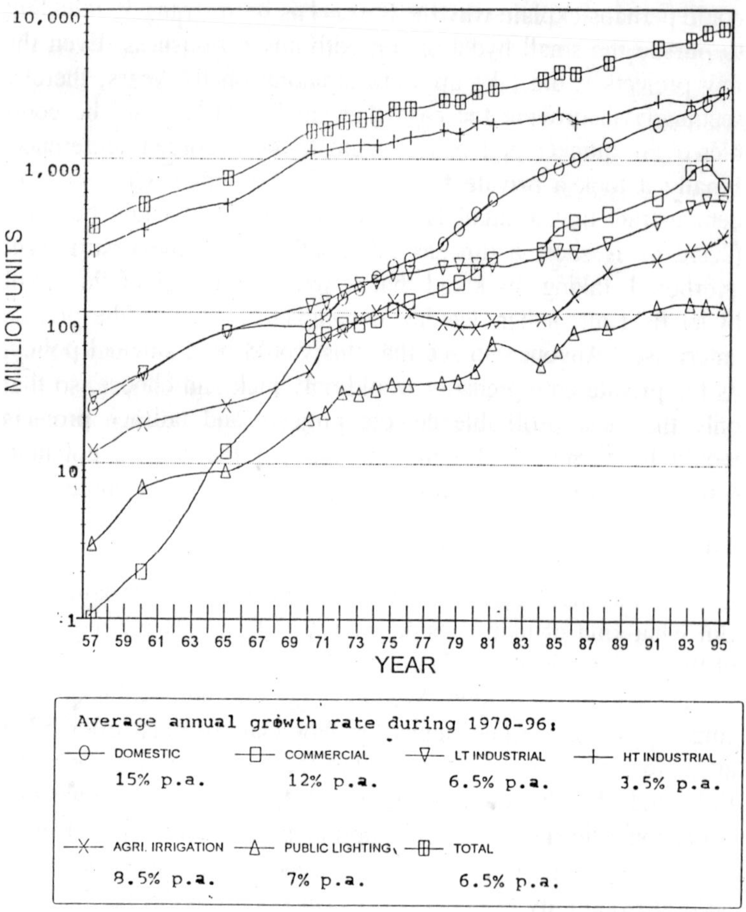

Fig. 26.2 Patterns of Electricity Consumption in Kerala from 1957-1995.

cheap hydel power with emphasis on big projects is urgently called for, if we are to prosper. The official view is gradually coming around to that, but still there is an unwillingness to commit the Board's own resources to the thermal projects or to small hydels. The refrain seems to be: "Let the IPPs take care of the thermal plants and small hydels. We will spend whatever we have on the big hydels. Let us go for Pooyamkutty, and if possible, resurrect Silent Valley."

But, if we are convinced that commissioning a few major thermal plants for base load is top priority for our electricity development, and that the environment-friendly small hydels should get preference, should not those get priority in investment options also?

We hope that the State is able to free itself from the vested interests and hangovers of the past. The earlier it is done, the better it is for the State.

TWENTY-SEVEN

AN OBJECTIVE APPROACH TO TRANSPORT DEVELOPMENT IN KERALA

M. N. PRASAD

Some General Observations

1.1 Transport is a basic necessity for any civilised society, but it seldom receives the due attention, or recognition. More often than not, it is taken for granted.

1.2 For a growing economy, the transport infrastructure needs to be developed ahead of the anticipated growth of traffic. This should be planned, based on an optimum inter-modal mix.

1.3 Objectivity in transport planning and allocation of adequate resources for the purpose were a noteworthy feature of the early years of our Independence. But, over the last three decades, there has been a steep decline in both. Subjectivity in investment decisions to suit narrow political interests has been particularly in evidence on the Railways. The following Table shows how the share of plan allocation for transport in general and railways in particular has been on the decline.

Resource allocation during	*Percentage of Total Plan outlay*	
	Transport Sector.	*Railways' Share*
First 3 Plan periods	23.0	14.0
From IV to VIII Plan	13.8	6.3

1.4 Due to inadequacies in inputs where needed, the country's road and rail infrastructures have been in a state of growing saturation, especially on the major routes where the bulk of traffic moves. Traffic which cannot be moved by rail due to capacity limitations generally spills over to roads.

1.5 Energy efficiency of rail transport is over five times that of road transport. Indian Railways also have the advantage that nearly 50 per cent of the freight traffic is already moving on electric traction, saving petroleum fuel and reducing environmental pollution. Hence, it would be in the national interest to maximise the Railways' share of transport.

1.6 Roads cater for door-to-door services. Road transport at both ends is an essential complement to all other modes of transport, whether rail, air, inland waterways or shipping.

1.7 Railways are capital-intensive, since investment has to cover the total system and its operation, whereas for most other modes of transport public funds are needed only for the infrastructure. Taking also into account the cost of complementary road transport and handling at both ends, a railway will normally be justified only where the anticipated traffic flow is large enough and the bulk of it is long-lead traffic.

1.8 Unfortunately, the people's aspirations for new railway lines are never bound by the above norms. Demands are often voiced on the basis of land area or population, as found convenient. Depending on political patronage, some of these demands lead to sanction of surveys and a few of these may even result in construction of new lines, otherwise not justifiable.

1.9 Inadequacy of public transport, whether road or rail, has led to proliferation of other road vehicles, thereby putting undue pressure on the road network. Increased production of cars, two-wheelers and three-wheelers in recent years has aggravated the problem, thereby affecting road safety as well.

Kerala Scenario

2.1 Kerala is blessed with a variety of transport modes, road, rail, air, inland waterways and shipping. The extensive network of roads, connecting all the villages, had played an important, though invisible, role in shaping the so-called "Kerala Model" of development.

2.2 Unfortunately, due to inadequacy of inputs, both the highways and the rail network of the State are presently in a state of acute saturation. Inland waterways, which could have helped to ease the congestion to some extent, are in a state of neglect and disrepair.

2.3 The total length of the road network, as on 31 March, 1995 was 14,343 km. This gives an average density of 3.67 km of roads per sq km of area, which is over five times the national average. However, surfaced roads (including metalled ones) constitute only about 22 per cent of the total.

2.4 While the phenomenal growth of the road network has helped to disperse the growth of population and economic activities, it has given rise to certain incidental problems like progressive reduction in agricultural lands, deforestation, destabilisation of hill slopes, soil erosion and interference with natural drainage.

2.5 Much-needed improvements to roads, like strengthening, widening, rebuilding of bridges and easing of curves and gradients, have been lagging, mainly for lack of budgetary allocations. Even in the case of National Highways, nearly two-thirds of the total length of 1011 km are yet to be brought up to the prescribed minimum standards for two-lane traffic (i.e., 7.5 m width). Upgradation of M.C. Road into a NH, although well justified, has been ruled out because of physical and financial constraints. Delay in completion of by-passes around the cities and major towns en-route has been adding to the congestion of urban roads, besides slowing down traffic on the National Highways.

2.6 Narrowness of 'right of way', improper maintenance and upkeep of roads and shoulders, lack of discipline of vehicular traffic and pedestrians and of civic sense among the urban population and non-enforcement of traffic rules by the Police have led to a near-chaotic condition of most of the roads in cities and towns, consequent on the steep rise in vehicle population.

2.7 During the 20 year period, 1975 to 1995 the growth in the length of PWD roads was only 1.48 times and that of other roads 1.97 times, whereas the increase in the number of motor vehicles was 8.4 times. Curiously enough, the increase in number of buses was only 4.5 times, which clearly shows the lack of emphasis on public transport. No wonder, therefore, that the incidence of road accidents in Kerala is the highest in India and the figure keeps mounting year by year.

2.8 A major deficiency in the road infrastructure of Kerala is the existence of a large number of old bridges which are of inadequate width or doubtful strength, or in poor condition of upkeep. Apart from forming traffic bottlenecks, such bridges may even cause prolonged disruption of traffic, as a result of their collapsing or showing signs of distress.

2.9 The railway system in Kerala presently has "route kilometrage" of 1040, of which 180 km from Walayar to Ernakulam Jn. and 41 km from Kayamkulam to Kollam are double line, thus yielding a "running track kilometrage" of 1261. Contrary to popular notion, the growth of railways in Kerala since Independence has been very substantial, with an increase of 53 per cent in route-km and 86 per cent in running track km, which are far above the all-India figures of 17 per cent and 34 per cent, respectively. Yet, because of the resultant upsurge in rail-borne traffic, especially passenger traffic, several stretches of railway lines in the State have been in a state of saturation for several years past. Important among these are the sections Ernakulam-Thiruvananthapuram and Shoranur-Kannur. Unfortunately, the schemes for augmenting capacity on these routes have suffered serious delays on account of the overriding priority given by the Railways Ministry to the "Unigauge project" for the past 4 years.

2.10 Long-distance passenger traffic is predominantly with the Railways and so is the daily commuter traffic along the N-S corridor, thanks to the concessional season ticket facility.

2.11 Haulage of freight traffic, even for long leads, is mostly by road, except for a few commodities which are moved in full train-loads. The Railways are presently unable to satisfy the demand of piecemeal traffic (i.e. in loose wagons) because of line capacity constraints and shortage of rolling stock. This problem is likely to continue for a long time because of the priority given to the "unigauge project" in the matter of investments. In the meantime, some new possibilities for bi-modal movement of freight traffic to Kerala, as an alternative to movement by road along the West Coast, are likely to open up with the commissioning of the Konkan Railway.

2.12 The State has a system of canals and backwaters all along the coastline from Thiruvallam (near Kovalam) in the south to Hosdurga in the north, a distance of about 550 km. Of this, 168 km from Kollam to Kottappuram, including navigable stretches of rivers crossed enroute, have already been declared as National Waterway No. 3, but very little progress has been achieved on its improvement. The portion south of Kollam is presently in a state of neglect, with the canal tunnel at Varkala having suffered some blocks due to collapse.

2.13 Inland waterways offer considerable scope for tourism, apart from meeting the local needs for cheap transport. If activated, these can help to relieve, to some extent, the growing pressure on roads in the coastal belt.

2.14 In regard to shipping, apart from the Major Port of Kochi, which is centrally administered, there are three Intermediate ports (Neendakara, Alappuzha and Kozhikode) and ten Minor Ports (Vizhinjam, Thiruvananthapuram, Kollam Munambam, Vadakara, Ponnani, Thalassery, Kannur, Azheekkal and Kasargode) under the administrative control of the State Government.

2.15 While there has been a reasonable yearly growth of cargo handled at Kochi, the traffic handled at the remaining ports has been unsteady and confined largely to the intermediate ports of Neendakara and Kozhikode and the Minor port of Vizhinjam and Azheekkal, with Neendakara contributing the lion's share. However, none of these ports has any appreciable role to play in relieving the pressure on road and rail.

2.16 Kerala, despite its small size, has the distinction of having three airports, with Thiruvananthapuram and Kozhikode already handling international flights and Kochi also poised to have a new international airport of its own at Nedumbassery. However, there is no large potential for traffic growth, unless there is a major spurt in international tourism in future. In any case, the development of airport facilities in Kerala will be of no consequence, as far as the pressing transportation needs of the State and its people are concerned.

Recommendations for an Objective Approach

3.1 In view of the close similarity between Kerala and Greater Bombay in geographical shape and the travel needs of the population, development of the transport infrastructure of the State could well be planned on the Bombay model, i.e., with the North-South arterial roads and railway lines forming the backbone, or main arteries, and the rest of the road network serving as feeders (vide sketch).

3.2 *In the case of roads, priority should be for the following:* Bringing the whole of the National Highways up to the minimum prescribed standard for 2 lanes; four-laning of NH-47 between Thrissur and Thiruvananthapuram carrying out essential improvements to the MC Road; completing the NH By-passes for Thiruvananthapuram, Kollam, Alappuzha, Kozhikode and Thalassery; construction of Varappuzha bridge on NH-17; carrying out long-term and short-term measures to ease the growing congestion of urban roads; increasing public transport. Side by side, a detailed review should also be undertaken on the strength and condition of all road bridges and a permanent machinery set up for their inspection, upkeep and rehabilitation where called for.

3.3 In the case of urban roads, the first priority should be to optimise the use of the available R.O.W. This should be achieved by improving the upkeep of road surface and the road-sides, shifting the upkeep of road surface and the road-sides, shifting of offending posts/poles, educating pedestrians to walk on the right side, enforcing traffic regulations with provision of adequate road signs, curbing road-side stacking of building materials and debris, changing over to centralised asphalt mixing for roads in major towns, and so on. In the short term, pedestrian subways/overbridges and provision of raised pavements (footpaths) ought to be taken up so as to minimise the incidence of pedestrians coming in the way of vehicular traffic (vide sketch).

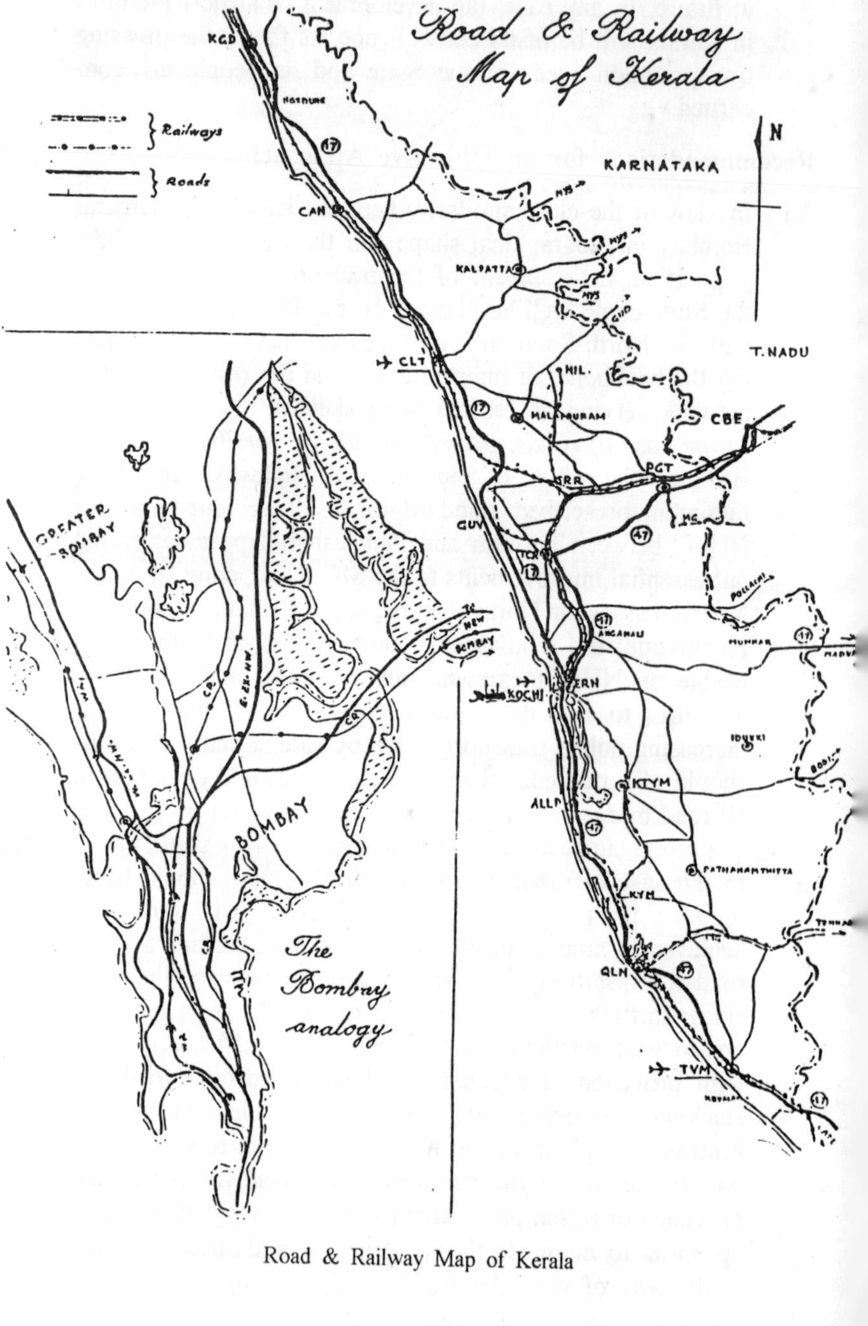

Road & Railway Map of Kerala

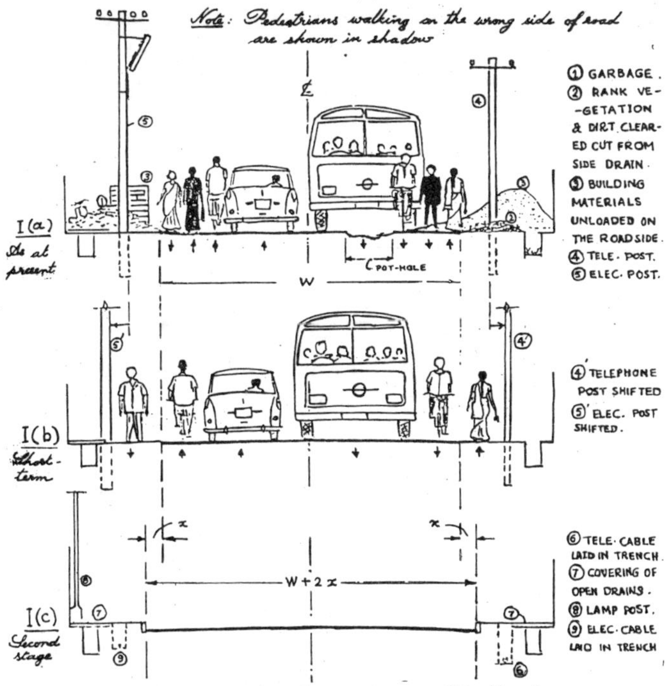

Fig. 27.1 Easing Congestion on City Roads

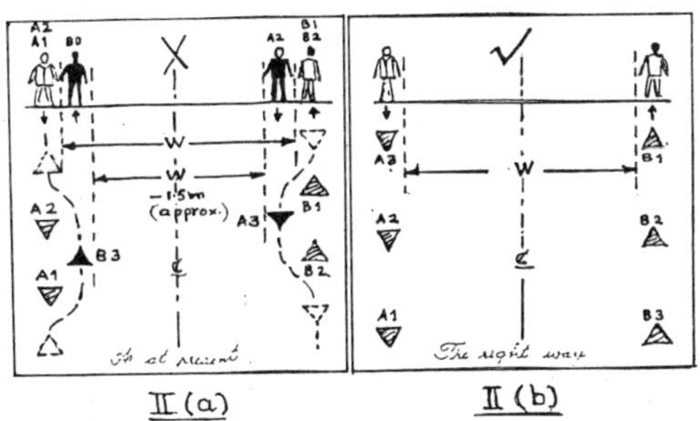

Fig. 27.2 Relief Due to Pedestrians Keeping Right

3.4 *In the case of railways, the following should be the priorities:* Completion of the sanctioned doubling of line between Kollam and Thiruvananthapuram; Line capacity augmentation on Shoranur-Mangalore section (mainly consisting of extension of Thrissur-Guruvayoor line upto Kuttippuram and doubling between Kuttippuram and Kannur) to cope with the anticipated additional traffic on completion of the Konkan Railway, doubling of line between Ernakulam and Kayam- kulam, via Kottayam.

It would be pointless to demand electrification of Ernakulam-Thiruvananthapuram route until the State's power supply position improves sufficiently.

3.5 Long-distance freight movements should be rationalised, based on a 'bi-modal' concept. Domestic container terminals should be set up at a few nodal points so that containerised cargo can be moved by rail over long distances, with short hauls by road at both ends for door-to-door services. This is particularly important because Konkan Railway has become a reality.

3.6 To relieve the congestion of roads in the coastal belt, as well as to promote tourism, the State's inland waterways should be fully restored and developed and made a National Waterway with a total length of 550 km.

3.7 Public awareness should be created about the right priorities and perspectives for transport development in the State, as well as the need for optimal utilisation of the scarce resources. Their aspirations and energies should not get diverted to the pursuit of fanciful and unaffordable schemes being talked about by some politicians, like the laying of a new arterial railway line through the midland region of Kerala, comprising hilly and semi-hilly terrain. Apart from prohibitive cost, such construction would also entail largescale land acquisition, environmental degradation and creation of hundreds of new level crossings, impeding road traffic. As and when resources become available, it would be far more economical and advantageous to build a new National or State Highway along the same route.

TWENTY-EIGHT

GIRLS AND WOMEN IN KERALA

Some Less Acknowledged Facts

AMMU JOSEPH

Traditional development indicators suggest that the status of women in Kerala is extremely good, especially in comparison to the situation of women in most other parts of India. However, there are some less well-known and certainly less acknowledged indications that all is not entirely well with women in the State, despite high rates of female literacy and education, work participation, life expectancy and other such commonly cited evidence of well-being.

Some of the contradictions in the situation of women in Kerala are revealed but, I believe, side-stepped in the Human Development Report 1996 (HDR 96) brought out by the United Nations Development Programme (UNDP). Two sections of this otherwise informative, thought-provoking and useful document, which refer to Kerala, tend to perpetuate the popular mythology about the status of women in the State. This, I think, is a typical example of the way the situation of women in Kerala and, indeed, many other aspects of Kerala's development (for example, its relative successes in the fields of family planning and child labour) are routinely presented, conveniently highlighting certain facts and obscuring others or masking the complexity of the situation with somewhat misleading generalisations.

The HDR 96 has a section which discusses the disaggregated Gender Development Index (GDI) for 16 Indian States. Kerala is expectedly placed at the top of the list in terms of "basic female capabilities." With a GDI value of 0,597, Kerala comes next to the Maldives in the global ranking, at 80 out of 137 countries—

which is far better than India's ranking of 103 and, of course, that of Uttar Pradesh, at 123. As the report says, Kerala's relatively good ranking is due primarily to its high female literacy rate, with the disparity between male and female rates nearly 20 percentage points lower than most other States. However, and I think significantly, it also reports that women's "share of earned income" in Kerala is only 12 per cent, compared to 38 per cent in Himachal Pradesh, 30 per cent in Maharashtra and more than 25 per cent in Andhra Pradesh, Madhya Pradesh, Gujarat and Karnataka.

Commenting on this apparent contradiction, the HDR 96 merely says, "Thus, a higher share in income for women may be a necessary— but not a sufficient— condition for gender equality. Equality in other basic capabilities is also needed." It neglects to mention the corollary, which is particularly relevant in the case of Kerala: that a higher rate of literacy/education among women may also be a necessary—but not a sufficient— condition for gender equality: that equality in other basic capabilities as well as other aspects of life are needed , too.

In another section, which deals with Kerala's success in sustaining human development through public action, the HDR 1996 states, "Women in Kerala have shared the benefits of education and health with men to a far greater extent than elsewhere in India. Women's status in Kerala is reflected in its 1991 sex ratio 104 females to 100 males, higher than Japan's 103 to 100. Matrilineal social structures and lack of organised social opposition to women's education and social and economic advancement contributed to women's progress..." The only negative note is contained in what is almost an aside tagged on to the last sentence: "...although gender discrimination still persists in many areas." Further, while the first two statements are certainly true, the latter is not entirely accurate— for example, not all communities in Kerala are matrilineal.

While Kerala's many commendable achievements in human development have undoubtedly had a beneficial impact on its women in several important respects, a great deal remains to be done in the State in terms of women's empowerment. This is unlikely to happen as long as the status of women in Kerala continues to be viewed through rose-tinted spectacles. In reviewing Kerala's development experience, it may be worthwhile to pay some attention to the question, whether Kerala's "development model" has been adequately sensitive to the gender factor in development.

In terms of conventional development or quality of life indicators, women in Kerala certainly seem privileged, particularly in comparison with their counterparts in other parts of the country. Perhaps this is why even well-known and respected organisations and programmes in the State, which are involved in promoting female literacy, education and/or economic welfare, do not seem to have gender on their agendas. However, my recent conversations with adolescent girls in different parts of Kerala (as well as Tamil Nadu and Andhra Pradesh)[1] suggest that this neglect of gender is not really justified.

Of course, girls in Kerala do not face some of the life-threatening problems their counterparts in many other parts of the country, including neighbouring States, encounter— infanticide, gross discrimination in nutrition, denial of education, child marriage, early childhood labour, lack of access to health care, and so on. This is certainly cause for celebration but, in my opinion, not sufficient reason for complacency.

It is true that some of the most blatant and brutal forms of gender-based discrimination and oppression are not widespread in the State. But that does not mean that the problems, girls in Kerala do face— in common with girls elsewhere in the country—can be dismissed as negligible. While these problems may not always be physically endangering, they are often psychologically debilitating -- so much so that they sometimes end up being life threatening : witness the high rate of mental illness and suicide among women and cases such as the collective suicide of sisters (reported from progressive Kerala as well as backward Uttar Pradesh) in the face of their families inability to raise the mandatory dowries for their marriages, which first hit newspaper headlines in the late 1980s.

It is significant that girls in Kerala (from a variety of communities and socio-economic backgrounds) confessed in conversation that they had often wished they had not been born female. Hardly any of them could think of any advantage attached to being female— except, revealingly (with respect to their sense of self), that as girls they were able to help, love and look after their parents. On the other hand, they could easily point out several disadvantages associated with their gender.

At their age, understandably, the most aggravating aspect of being female seems to be the curtailment of their freedom and mobility, especially from the pre-adolescent stage onwards. The girls said they were unhappy about their lack of "swaathanthriam" (freedom). The detail of freedom is clearly the main and most galling difference they perceive between boys and girls. In addition, said a teenager from an economically weak but urbanised tribal community in Kochi, " Boys have more "adhikaaram" (authority) and more "avakaasham" (rights)." According to her, boys are not only more mobile than girls of their own age but actually more free to come and go than adult women of the community, who generally need permission from male family members— sometimes even their own sons— to move about.

Girls from this community, like most of their counterparts in the State irrespective of socio-economic status, are allowed to go to school and tutorials , usually travelling in groups, but have to come straight home after classes. There is apparently no question of going anywhere else except with adult family members. On the other hand, their brothers are free to roam about where and when they please.

According to high school students in elite, English-medium institutions, who live in a genteel residential area in Kochi, the bane of their lives is gossip, the threat of which makes their otherwise sensible and reasonable parents keep an uncomfortable light rein on them. They chafe at restrictions on their mobility, as well as the strict dress code to which they are expected to conform.

The girls are aware that the restrictions placed on them are meant primarily to safeguard their all-important "reputation." As far as society is concerned, they say, the most valued attribute in a girl is what is known as "good character," best demonstrated by socially acceptable behaviour ("swabhaavam"). Anything that could give the impression that their character and behaviour are not quite up to the socially defined mark is, therefore, frowned upon. According to them, girls are expected to be quiet, sensible, hard-working, well-behaved, obedient and, above all , unassertive. As one of them put it, the same behaviour that would be seen as "smart" in a boy is deemed "over-smart" in a girl.

They suggest that their mobility is inhibited by the fear inculcated in them from childhood— fear of gossip and fear of violence. They admit that reports of atrocities such as rape, wife battering, dowry-related violence, and so on, against women make them nervous and diffident. The recent "Suryanalli case" and other similar cases of what has apparently come to be known as "relay rape" have obviously made girls in Kerala particularly conscious of their vulnerability.

The curtailment of girls' freedom and mobility usually stems from parents anxieties about their safety and security, which are no doubt well-intentioned and grounded in current realities. But it does seem unfair to penalize girls for crimes they could fall victim to and turn them (rather than the criminals) into prisoners, literally and/or figuratively. Clearly this is an issue that has to be tackled if girls are to grow up into confident and independent citizens, capable of not only looking after themselves but making the world a safer place for everyone.

Apart from the possibility of outright violence, there is the ever-present reality of sexual harassment on the streets (euphemistically known as eve-teasing), which also plays a major role in diminishing girls' mobility and self-confidence. Virtually every girl in Kerala and elsewhere has experienced some form of sexual harassment in the public sphere[2]. While some say the boys and men of their own community or neighbourhood do not harass them, others complain that even local boys, including those younger than them, indulge in eve-teasing.

Although they seem to regard sexual harassment as an inescapable irritant, their responses to it vary, some say they talk back to their tormentors in an effort to shock them into silence. Others say they prefer to ignore these roadside romeos because they believe the slightest attention, even when it is negative, only serves to encourage them. Also, they are afraid of further and more severe harassment if they publicly humiliate such aggressors with retorts. Sadly, they are not confident of public support in such an eventuality; in fact, they believe they would risk being branded as too bold and forward for their own good if they react strongly and vocally.

The phenomenon of sexual harassment is clearly a constant source of tension on the streets and other public spaces. The daily dilemma of having to decide how to deal with it is not only stressful but clearly wasteful of valuable time and energy. In addition, the threat and fact of such regular harassment both restricts their freedom and contributes towards making them more timid and inhibited than they might otherwise be. The shyness and self-consciousness generated by this hostile environment is certainly reflected in the body language of Kerala girls and women in the public arena, which often takes visitors to the state by surprise.

It is clear that the curtailment of their freedom and mobility and the reasons underlying the restrictions placed on them are extremely important issues which shackle girls and prevent them from realising their full human potential. Although this is clearly a matter for public concern it has not yet received serious attention in the State.

The fact that a large number of girls and women from Kerala are allowed to travel afield in pursuit of education and employment does not alter the situation significantly. This is just another example of the many contradictions that abound in the profile of women in the State. Growing economic needs and aspirations coupled with widespread unemployment within the State have, indeed, propelled both men and women to different parts of the country and the world in search of job opportunities. But for women financial self-sufficiency does not always mean social independence. And, significantly, one of the prime factors that prompt parents to allow their daughters to seek employment wherever it may be found is the need to raise money for their dowries.

The dowry system, widely accepted as an inevitable and inescapable reality in most communities in Kerala (however educated), is sometimes acknowledged as a source of financial stress for families. But it is not commonly recognized as a source of psychological stress for girls. Yet, girls in Kerala have confessed that the pernicious practice is one of the main reasons why they have often wished they had not been born girls. And girls in Kerala, like the sisters from Palakkad who made news in the late 1980s, have reportedly killed themselves in despair over their parents' inability to drum up their dowries. Obviously the system, which continues unabated and unchallenged on the eve of the 21st century, despite girls access to education and employment, has the potential to damage their self-image and self-esteem to the extent of making them wish they had never been born or actually driving them to suicide.

Even when that is not the case, the practice does have an adverse effect on girls' image of themselves, their sense of self-worth and the attitudes and behaviour of others (including family members) towards them —which, in turn, negatively affect their self-image and self-esteem. The most depressing aspect of this is the overwhelming sense of helplessness that characterizes the responses of most women and girls to the problem.

Take, for instance, women involved in the celebrated Community Based Nutrition Programme in Alappuzha (designed "to empower poor women for poverty eradication through group action and self-help"). While they were clearly confident about taking on poverty alleviation and community development, they confessed their inability to tackle the pernicious dowry system that plagues most girls and ruins many a family in Kerala. What is more, they had obviously never been encouraged within the programme to question the practice of dowry, let alone consider the possibility of organizing against it. It is small wonder that the daughters of these able and newly assertive women say they cannot see a way out of the dowry trap. Since marriage is constantly projected as the ultimate goal of a women's life, dowry is accepted as a necessary evil that can be questioned only at one's own peril. As some girls put it, "If we protest too much, we'll just be left behind."

Another area of discrimination that girls are unhappy about is the gender-based division of labour, with the burden of housework exclusively reserved for the female members of the family. According to one girl, the amount of domestic work she has to do while her brothers get away with none makes her wish she was not a girl. If at all men in Kerala help out with household chores, the phenomenon seems restricted to low income families.

As for education, access to at least elementary school is admittedly not a major problem for most girls in Kerala, except perhaps Muslim girls in the northern parts— although going by the finding of a 1992-93 study by the National Council for Educational Research and Training (NCERT), educational achievement for both boys and girls in primary school is another story, even in Kerala.

However, it seems clear that education does not do much to foster positive feelings in girls about themselves as persons or as members of the female gender. Nor does the curriculum provide them with any clues about women's historical or current participation in society. Going by what they are taught— in history, for example— women may as well not have existed through the ages. In this respect, educational institutions and programmes in Kerala may have something to learn from initiatives in other parts of the country— in both the formal and informal streams—that have consciously attempted to build gender sensitivity into their curricular as well as extra-curricular activities.

Gender relations and sexuality are two related areas in which girls in Kerala do not seem to be better off in any way than girls elsewhere. Indeed, according to some girls, the mores governing girls mobility, behaviour and style of dressing, as well as interaction between the sexes, are probably more restrictive in Kerala than elsewhere. Moreover, girls, assured access to formal education in Kerala does not seem to guarantee their access to sex education of any kind. In fact, the social conservatism that co-exists with political consciousness and progress in human development in this model State ensures continued segregation of the sexes in the public sphere even today.

While Malayalam films have earned a reputation in the rest of India for sexually explicit scenes, expressions of non-celluloid sexuality are generally frowned upon within the State. Despite the many indicators that point to the relatively good status of women in Kerala, the question of female sexuality is kept strictly under wraps here. One of the first attempts by women in the State to break the silence on this issue took place only in the summer of 1996.

In another path-breaking effort, *Abhinethri*, a newly formed feminist theatre group in Kerala, staged an avant-garde play on the streets of Thiruvanthapuram in July 1996, exploring the social construction of gender and sexuality in the context of the reportedly rising trend of sexual atrocities against girls and women in the State. According to its young members, the play— radical in content, form and body movement— evolved out of discussions about their bodies and sexuality as they tried to shift their own thoughts and feelings from the attitudes and perceptions formed through social conditioning.

But these are just fledgling efforts to take the cover off the topic of sexuality in Kerala. It may be a long time before their impact is felt by girls growing up in the state unless deliberate attempts are made to provide them with appropriate information, as well as the opportunity to openly discuss their own experiences and feeling and to question the silence and restrictions placed on them by society.

Even the whole question of gender relations— going beyond sex and sexuality to encompass the equally complex areas of love and romance, understanding and respect, freedom and responsibility, equality and equity— goes largely unaddressed in Kerala, as elsewhere in the country. At the same time, young people are exposed to a variety of messages that urge them to break free of the shackles that bind them without much guidance on how to ensure that their quest for freedom does not land them in an even worse prison. For example, the romantic spell of commercial cinema— coupled, perhaps, with the desperate desire to escape the dowry trap— now seem to propel a number of girls into what they believe is elopement. Unfortunately, too many of them discover too late that they have been conned or worse.

At another level, the paucity of social interaction between the sexes— obvious to an outsider even in creative and otherwise progressive circles— creates a barrier which unnecessarily inhibits natural, relaxed, healthy gender relations. This seems to apply even in the conduct of teachers, with some girls complaining that male teachers are reluctant to come to their side of the class (obviously boys and girls still sit in separate sections of the room even in elite urban schools), even when they need clarifications, obviously out of bashfulness and lack of familiarity with members of the opposite sex.

One other issue which calls for serious soul-searching is the question of discrimination on the basis of caste, which does not seem to have disappeared with education. Dalit girls in Kerala may not be vulnerable to the kind of gross discrimination and oppression that their counterparts in other states often have to face, but their stories of how they are marginalised and belittled even in educational institutions are quite shocking. Not only are they called derogatory names but they are sometimes prevented from taking part in activities that others feel they are not fit for, purely on account of their caste and, possibly, skin colour. Apparently, things are relatively better at the school level, perhaps because there are more dalit girls at that stage of the educational process and there is some strength in numbers, but the situation at the college level, where there are fewer dalit girls, seems quite terrible. This double burden carried by dalit girls is obviously a problem that needs to be urgently tackled.

In conclusion, I believe the situation of women in Kerala— the State which boasts of the highest female literacy, the lowest number of households below the poverty line, the highest level of human development, and so on— provides ample proof that literacy/education, employment and other such indicators of development do not, in and by themselves, guarantee freedom and equality to women.

A pilot study by Sr. Alise Lulose and her WIN team on the experiences of young women from Kerala who had worked as migrant labour in seafood processing industries in various States along the coastline provides an interesting indication of this. Although working and living conditions in the processing factories are often subhuman, most of the girls were surprisingly positive about the impact of their work experience outside the State on their personal growth (decision-making capacity, independence, self-confidence and self-reliance), as well as on their status within their families and in society— and not merely because of their newly acquired financial independence. I think it is telling that, despite the prison-like conditions in their workplaces, the girls said they experienced more freedom and independence away from their families and communities.

I personally found this revelation extremely disturbing. To me it seemed to signify how chronic devaluation can lead to a situation where a person will tolerate high levels of exploitation. Moreover, it suggests that however subtle gender-based discrimination and oppression in Kerala may be, it is palpable enough to make girls feel that the very fact of getting away from family and community— even to what would seem like a much worse situation at work— has a positive effect on their personalities as well as their social status.

I believe the story of women's emancipation and empowerment in Kerala will remain incomplete unless some of these aspects of life in the State are acknowledged and addressed.

NOTES

1. These were reported in a series of eight articles in the Hindu's Sunday Magazine from October to December 1996, as well as in "Spaced Out," my fortnightly column for children in the Hindu's Young World, in the second half of 1996.
2. These are cases in which young girls have been deceived or lured into a situation in which they are subjected to sexual abuse by a series of men, including socially, financially and/or politically powerful individuals.

TWENTY-NINE

DEMOCRATISATION OF THE PLANNING PROCESS

Experience of People's Campaign in Kerala

T.M. THOMAS ISAAC & K.N. HARILAL

The unique democratisation process of Kerala society is yet to receive the attention it deserves. The modern history of the region deserves to be recognised as a saga of collective intervention by the people to shape their common destiny, even though it meant, more often than not, challenging well entrenched customs and traditions of the earlier era, defying the logic of the market, and even struggling to change the State policy. The People's Campaign for Planning well underway in the State unfolds the latest episode in the region's experiments with democracy.

An important feature of the Campaign, which distinguishes it from similar attempts at decentralisation elsewhere, is that it is a people's movement, a movement by the people to establish their rightful role in decision making by empowering themselves and the local self governments as opposed to the usual apologetic propaganda to manufacture popular consent for what the state does from above.

Even the best efforts so far to involve people in development activities of the State were confined to ensuring their participation at the implementation stage. The Campaign in Kerala unmistakably is an attempt at ensuring genuine participatory planning from below, wherein people's involvement is sought to be maximised first in plan formulation and thereafter in implementation.

The People' Campaign was formally inaugurated on 17 August 1996. Even though the Campaign was launched more than a year ago, it is not as yet time to undertake an evaluation of the same. What is being aimed by the Campaign is nothing less than a total overhaul of the system of planning and implementation of development plans. The restructuring of the system itself is a long drawn out process, not to speak of the time lag with which its full effects are going to be realised. To say the least, its impact on the economy and society of the State would continue to be felt for a long time to come. Obviously, therefore, a comprehensive evaluation of the Campaign may have to wait. Instead, our attempt in the present chapter is confined to a brief discussion of the broad phases of the people's planning process in Kerala.

I

A People's Movement for Planning ?

Importance and timeliness of the People's Campaign is best understood in the light of the following :

(a) The prevailing critique of centralised planning and administration in the country;
(b) Failure of hitherto efforts at decentralisation and the intimidatingly long list of obstacles that new attempts at genuine decentralisation face;
(c) And the contemporary development challenges of the State of Kerala which by consensus demand a decentralised approach to planning as also a revival of the participatory spirit to protect the widely acclaimed gains of the past.

Experience of Centralised Planning

Notwithstanding wide differences of opinion among scholars regarding details, they agree that the centralised system of planning had been a failure in addressing fundamental problems of development faced by the country, such as mass poverty and unemployment. Even though, it would be too simplistic to attribute the above failure exclusively to what may be referred to as 'centralisation', there is growing consensus around the view that over-centralisation had been a major debilitating feature of the Indian polity and development process.

The widespread apathy among people and their lack of involvement in nation building activities, indifference to the development needs of the people and channelling of resources for wrongly perceived goals, total disregard of local specificities even where it matters most, lack of efforts at integration of fragmented development interventions which often tend to work at cross purposes, and above all rampant corruption are commonly identified evils of the system that are attributable more to centralisation than to any other feature of the system that was in force.

All the same, it would be unrealistic to assume that planning of everything is best done at the local level. While optimal solutions for many problems are to be found at the local level, there are also several issues which require to be addressed at higher levels. It is also important that develoment interventions are integrated both horizontally and vertically among various tiers of decision making so that complementarities maximised and conflicts reduced to the minimum. What is being advocated in the context of the People's Campaign, therefore, is a system of multilevel planning, where the lowest unit is allowed to plan and implement everything that can be performed most effectively at that level and only the residual is left to the higher levels.

Obstacles to Genuine Decentralisation

Desirability of a decentralised system of planning has never been in doubt. The slogan 'gram raj' is as old as the freedom movement. During the post independence period, the demand for making the country's governance more democratic through a meaningful process of decentralisation of power continued to enjoy pride of place on the national agenda.

In spite of such conviction and support the process of decentralisation could not make much headway in the country. The failure of earlier efforts are usually attributed to a variety of reasons, viz., resistance offered by the vested interests nurtured by the centralised structure, lack of pressure from below due to the absence of representative governments at levels below the States, paucity of expertise and preparedness at the local level, and the like.

There were many efforts in the past to identify factors constraining the process of decentralisation and to suggest concrete measures to overcome the hurdles. Not to be lost sight of are also some important experiments at the field level, including the efforts of States like Rajasthan, Karnataka and West Bengal and many micro-level interventions under the auspices of various agencies, which provided valuable insights for future attempts in the same direction. But the country had to wait till 1993, when the 73rd and 74th constitutional amendments were enacted, to see a comprehensive and determined effort to tackle the various factors that hinder the process of decentralisation.

Nevertheless, the constitutional amendments, at their best, serve only as an enabling framework. As the inter-state variations in the responsibilities, powers, and resources devolved to the newly constituted Panchayat Raj institutions would amply testify, the constitutional amendments leaves many important parameters of the process of decentralization to be determined by the State legislatures even now. The State Governments can either make use of the constitutional provisions to establish true local self governments or misuse the loopholes to maintain the status quo.

It was a favourable development to the cause of decentralisation in the State that a new government fully committed to the objective of establishing a decentralised system of administration and planning assumed office in the meantime. But this alone was not enough. It has been the experience of the State that success of government initiatives and legislations depends a lot on the environment in which such moves are made and the pressure exerted from below. This is more so because what is envisaged in the context of decentralised planning is a total restructuring of the system. Viewed in this sense, the Peoples Campaign was also an effort to consolidate and articulate public opinion in favour of decentralised planning and thereby help the government to translate its commitment to concrete actions. The process of planning from below would not have been possible without the series of measures taken by the State Government to facilitate the same. It should, however, be noted that these measures were not ready in place at the beginning, but were evolved in response to the popular demand from below and requirements of the Campaign as it progressed from one stage to other.

A comprehensive review of the Campaign should ideally make an attempt to study the various measures initiated by the government to facilitate the process of planning from below. Here it suffices to note that the State government has already set a good example for the rest of the country with respect to division of responsibilities; devolution of power and resources, provision of facilitating services, and complementary changes in administrative procedures and practices. A point that needs to be highlighted however, is the path breaking decision to earmark 30 to 40 per cent of the State's Ninth Plan outlay to be distributed among local bodies to finance development projects evolved from below with people's participation. The government has overcome all the resistance, including the pressures of the severe fiscal crisis, to implement this earlier commitment and has already allocated Rs. 6000 crores to the local bodies from its Ninth Plan outlay of Rs. 16,100 crores. During the current annual plan period (1997-98) local bodies would get Rs. 1025 crores from the total State outlay of Rs. 2,825 crores.

Devolution of powers, responsibilities, and resources and the complementary measures taken at the government level are necessary conditions, but not sufficient in themselves to ensure genuine democratisation of the planning process. Hardly any tier of the local self governments can claim to have prior experience in the art of development planning. Nor are they equipped with expertise, infrastructure or the required information base to take up the task of making development plans, all by themselves, for their respective regions. Further, many of them may not even be prepared to come out of the shell of inactivity with which they have been accustomed for long. In fact, many even suspected that the latest episode of decentralisation was another bureaucratic exercise.

Thus, the primary objective of the People's Campaign, has been to motivate and empower the local self governments to take up the new challenge of development planning. It was sought to be achieved by mobilising people regardless of their political affiliations, religion, caste, etc., to help the local governments in all the stages of development planning from plan formulation implementation and maintenance.

Enthusiasm of the masses and their whole hearted partcipation is the key to the success of any effort at decentralisation. But government orders, and directions are no guarantee for informed and enthusiastic participation of the people. This is especially so in the context of the contemporary reality of near total alienation of people from development activities. Therefore, a mass conscientisation and education programme was found to be necessary to mobilise people and motivate them to take up different tasks related to planning from below.

The centralised system of planning was insensitive not only to local specificities but also to local knowledge on development problems with which people of each locality are richly endowed. In this respect, what the Campaign sought to do was to establish a system at the village level in which the villagers themselves harness such scattered information and knowledge to be used in evolving future development activities. But local experience and knowledge constitutes only one of the many pieces of information required for making development plan at the local level. The local knowledge needs to be blended with information on modern technological alternatives, alternative sources of funding, ongoing development programmes of line departments and other agencies etc. In short, the Plan Campaign had to ensure that minimum necessary skills of development planning are imparted to the local people and the representative governments at that level. In other words, what is being sought through the Campaign is not just nominal participation but informed participation of the people.

The Development Challenges of Kerala

The People's Campaign can also be seen as an outcome of the long-drawn out and extensive development dialogue in Kerala, sparked off as it was by the crisis faced by the 'Kerala Model of Development'. Kerala's development experience came to be hailed as a cheap model of development, suitable for copying by other

Third World regions, for the reason that in spite of economic underdevelopment, the State could achieve very high quality of life for its people. But during the last two decades or so, the very same model of development has been encountering a severe crisis on many fronts, viz., stagnation in agricultural and industrial production, widespread reduction in productivity levels, acute power shortages, out-migration of industries and skilled labour, extremely high unemployment rates, rampant reduction in the quality of services, and the deepening fiscal crisis of the State.

Notwithstanding the pains and tensions caused, one saving feature of the crisis has been the process of soul searching it provoked. The development dialogue that followed has been phenomenal in terms of widespread participation, range of issues raised, amount of details and insights generated and, therefore, would merit a separate study. For our purpose, it is important to note the growing consensus in favour of a decentralised process of decision making and revival of the legacy of collective intervention by the people in development activities. If Kerala is to protect and strengthen its past gains, it can hardly afford to lag behind in production and productivity. The decline in the quality of services, especially of those supplied by the public sector needs urgent remedial measures, for it has already started affecting the quality of life of people, especially the vulnerable sections of the society. The over centralised system of development planning and implementation is totally unsuitable to take on these challenges. This is especially so with respect to land and water management, development of agriculture and allied sectors, rural and cottage industries, drinking water, sanitation and many of the social service sectors.

In view of the consensus in favour of a decentralised system, the State also witnessed some important moves to evolve a viable mode of decentralised system of administration and planning. The State Government's move to establish district councils, micro-level experiments taken up by mass organisations like K.S.S.P. etc., are good examples. It was the experience of such earlier experiments that led to the articulation of the idea of a People's Campaign for Planning. The case for the People's Campaign mode was further strengthened by the literacy campaign and the people's resource mapping programme successfully undertaken earlier in the State.

The Objectives

The Campaign was launched with the solemn assurance of the government that 35 to 40 per cent of the State's Ninth Plan would consist of projects formulated and implemented by the local bodies. Thus, the primary objective of the Campaign has been to empower the local self governments so that they formulate their respective Ninth Plan proposals with maximum people's participation. But, the real agenda of the Campaign has been much more challenging than the immediate objective of drawing the plan proposals.

Broadly speaking, the Campaign is an attempt to conceptualise, operationalise and institutionalise a system of multi-level, people-centred planning process suitable to the regional specificities of Kerala. As a corollary of the above objective, the Campaign also aims at bringing about a major transformation in the attitude of various actors in the development process, viz officials, elected representatives, intelligentia, and the people at large. What is needed is a new development culture itself, which requires the creativity of a people's movement. It is also of equal importance to the Campaign that the system of multi-level planning thus put in place help the State to overcome its contemporary development crisis.

Needless to assert that the broad goals of the Campaign identified above could be broken into a series of detailed objectives, viz., reconstructing the received ideas on decentralisation and people's planning; enabling the State government to translate its commitment to concrete actions by conscientising and mobilising people in support; harnessing popular opinion and will to overcome resistance offered by vested interests; correcting popular and wellentrenched but wrong notions of development by initiating developoment dialogues and introducing plausible alternatives; involving mass organisations of the people in development activities; imparting knowledge and skills needed for local level planning, and above all evolving and institutionalising a systematic procedure by which development needs of the people are

CHART 29.1

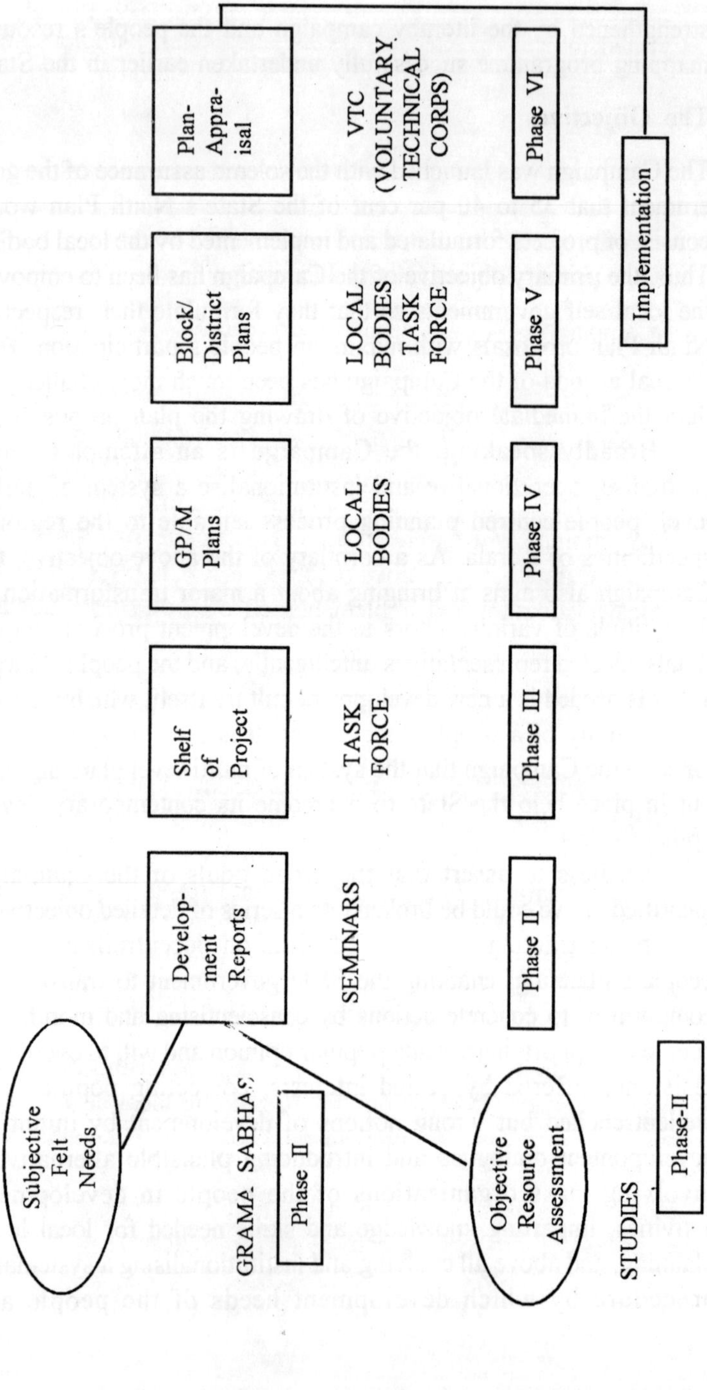
Subjective Felt Needs
Objective Resource Assessment
Develop-ment Reports
Shelf of Project
GP/M Plans
Block/ District Plans
Plan- Appra- isal
GRAMA SABHAS
SEMINARS
TASK FORCE
LOCAL BODIES
LOCAL BODIES TASK FORCE
VTC (VOLUNTARY TECHNICAL CORPS)
STUDIES
Phase II
Phase II
Phase-II
Phase III
Phase IV
Phase V
Phase VI
Implementation

articulated, suitable solutions arrived at, projectised, prioritised, integrated into comprehensive development plans, implemented, and monitored with maximum people's participation at all levels. Last but not the least is the objective of horizontal and vertical integration of planning between various tiers.

II

The Process of Decentralised Planning

The Campaign was built around the process by which the local self governments in the State formulated their Ninth Five Year Plan proposals. The progress of the Campaign, however, has not been along a known or exante design. As a comparison of the original approach paper and what has actually happened would reveal, on many occasions the Campaign had to keep reorienting its programmes to be able to address concrete problems. The people's Campaign has now reached its sixth phase wherein technical evaluation and implementation of projects included in the local plans are progressing simultaneously. Following is a brief outline of different phases of the Campaign.

Chart 29.1 would provide an idea regarding time/functional phasing of the people's planning process. The first step in drawing up a local development plan is identification of the felt needs of the people. But, a plan cannot be drawn based on the subjective needs alone. It is equally important to make an objective assessment of the natural, human, and financial resource potential of the region. The People's Campaign has attempted a judicious blend of the need-based and resource-based planning methodologies.

I Phase (August-October 1996)

The first stage of the Campaign was the convening of Grama Sabhas and Ward Conventions for identifying local development problems. During the Grama Sabha phase, the Campaign was oriented towards;

(1) ensuring maximum participation of people, especially, women and other weaker sections of the society.

(2) guiding the deliberations to identify and prioritise the needs of the people and finding the gaps in local development.

In order to ensure maximum participation, the Grama Sabhas were convened on holidays; squads of volunteers visited households and explained the programme; preparatory meetings of mass organisations were held; and an active propaganda using posters, advertisements and involving all branches of the media was resorted to. It is estimated that around 3 million people participated in these Grama Sabhas/Ward Conventions, of which about 27 per cent were women. Around 1,00,000 resource persons at the local level were given training to take an active part in the conduct of Grama Sabhas and group discussions on development sectors, and facilitate structured discussions. A set of questionnaire was also distributed to regulate the flow of discussion.

The most important outcome of the Grama Sabha was the listing of local development problems. They have also been instrumental in bringing about a welcome change in the attitude of people towards development activities.

II Phase (October-December 1996).

The objective of Local Development Seminars, organised during the second phase, was to make an objective assessment of the resource potential and problems arising out of the way in which they are currently being used. They were also supposed to come out with a list of tentative solutions to the development problems identified. In order to provide necessary background information for sector-wise discussions, a printed report on the socio-economic status of the grama panchayat/municipality had to be made available to the participants. The Development Reports were drafted on the basis of the following;

(1) consolidation of Grama Sabha reports
(2) review of ongoing schemes
(3) collection of secondary data
(4) geographical study of the area, and
(5) a brief survey of local history

A quick assessment of the Development Reports suggests significant variation in their quality. But it is a matter of considerable importance to the cause of decentralisation in the country that majority of these reports prepared by the people easily qualify for the best available bench mark study on development of their respective regions.

A massive programme of training of state to local level resource persons was one of the preparatory tasks undertaken. Further, the line departments were directed to provide available data and information on ongoing projects. The State Planning Board has also published a handbook on the preparation of Development Reports.

Output of the second phase include;

(1) generation of an extensive local data base,

(2) a comprehensive survey of all development sectors for all panchayats and municipalities,

(3) a list of plausible solutions to the development problems, and,

(4) formation of task forces to prepare development projects for each development sector.

It is estimated that around 5 lakh people, consisting of representatives from Grama Sabhas, elected representatives, local leaders of political parties, line department officials, local experts, etc., participated in the Development Seminars.

III Phase (December 1996-January 1997)

Sector-wise task forces constituted at the grass root level were supposed to projectise the recommendations and suggestions which emerged from the Development Seminars. On an average 12 task forces were constituted in each local body to cover various development sectors. As many as 12,000 task forces functioned at the village level alone with a total participation of at least 1.2 lakh persons. The task forces prepared around one lakh projects for the consideration of the Panchayats.

The task of project preparation demanded participation of more officials and technically qualified people than the earlier phases. Accordingly, special efforts were made to ensure participation of officials and local level experts. While the chairperson of the task force was an elected representative, an officer from the concerned line department was supposed to be its convenor.

The training programme, and the handbook published during the third phase, suggested a simple and transparent format for the projects to be prepared by the task forces. In order to ensure uniformity, it was suggested that the project reports should generally have the following components:

1. Introduction; explaining necessity and relevance of the project.
2. Objectives; in well defined (as far as possible in quantitative/measurable) terms.
3. Beneficiaries; criteria proposed to be followed in selecting beneficiaries or benefiting areas.
4. Activities; technical analysis and time-frame of all project activities.
5. Organisation; agencies and their role in implementing the project activities
6. Financial analysis; investment needed for each activity and identification of source of funds.
7. Achievements; preliminary analysis of all direct and indirect benefits and costs.
8. Monitoring details of the proposed monitoring mechanism.

The Planning Board has also issued a set of guidelines for the preparation of Special Component Plan (SCP) and Tribal Sub Plan (TSP) projects specially meant for scheduled castes and tribals. Further, it was recommended that the local bodies earmark 10 per cent of the plan assistance for projects meant for development of women. Special care was also taken to see that the task forces prepare projects with an integrated approach.

IV Phase (February-April 1997)

At the end of the third phase every grama panchayat and municipality had a shelf of projects corresponding to the development problems identified by the people. By then the grant-in-aid allocated to each local body by the State government was also made known. This set the stage for the fourth stage of the Campaign, wherein the projects prepared by the task forces were prioritized and incorporated into the Five Year Plans of the panchayats. For finalising the plan, the panchayat had to:

1. make a clear assessment of their capacity to mobilise resources from various sources to finance the plan
2. evolve a development strategy on the basis of problems identified and resource potential of the locality, prioritise and select projects to be implemented, and
3. decide on a monitoring mechanism for successful implementation of each project selected.

On the basis of the above analysis, each panchayat was supposed to prepare a plan document comprising of eight chapters, viz., introduction, the development strategy, resource mobilisation, sectoral programmes, integrated development, welfare of scheduled castes and scheduled tribes, women's development programmes, and monitoring.

In order to ensure that the local plans were sensitive to the development challenges and priorities at the state level, certain broad guidelines on sectoral allocation of plan funds, especially with respect to SCP and TSP programmes were given. Further a massive training programme covering resource persons, elected representatives and officials was also undertaken.

V Phase (April-September 1997)

During this phase, the Block and District Panchayats were supposed to prepare their plan documents. Block and District plans had to integrate local level plans and design complementary programmes. In order to achieve this the Blocks and District Panchayats had to undertake a detailed analysis of local development reports, local plan documents and recommendations from below. The handbooks and the training programme of the fifth phase focused on the problem of integration of local level plans at higher levels. A simple methodology of integration of plans of the lower tiers at higher levels was devised to avoid duplication, minimise conflicts as also to ensure complementality.

VI Phase (April-1997)

When the Campaign was launched, only the above five phases were visualised. However, it was later found that a significant proportion of the projects prepared at the village level had to be examined for their technical soundness and viability and corrected before they are implemented. But, it was realised that the District Planning Committees did not have the technical manpower or infrastructure to undertake such a thorough scrutiny of the projects. This situation necessitated a major improvisation in the original programme of the Campaign: A new (sixth) phase was added for technical and financial appraisal of the projects and plans. It was how the Voluntary Technical Corps (VTC) came to be constituted at block and district levels. The experts, were drawn mostly from the ranks of retired professionals and certain categories of officers, whose participation was made mandatory by the government. Nearly 10,000 professionals came forward to be members of the Voluntary Technical Corps.

It may be noted that the VTCs were not given the right to question the priorities decided upon by the local bodies. Instead, their responsibility was to help the Panchayats in making the projects technically feasible and financially viable.

The six phased Campaign is drawing to a close. On the basis of the recommendations of the VTCs, the District Planning Committees have approved nearly all the grama panchayat and municipal plans. The process of distribution of plan funds for the annual plan (1997-98) period could also be completed without undue delay. As of now, the elected representatives, the volunteers, and the officials are fully involved in the process of implementing the projects.

As stated earlier elaborate preparations had to be made to ensure that the task of each phase was successfully completed, the most important among them being the three tier training programme that preceded every phase. Around 600 Key Resource

Persons were trained at the State level who in turn trained about 15000 District Resource Persons. At the local level nearly one lakh resource persons were trained. The printed training materials came to around 3000 pages. Similarly video programmes of nealy 15 hour duration were prepared. Despite these efforts, as we have already noted in connection with the sixth phase, there were many lapses and weaknesses. But, what is important to be recognised is the dynamism of the movement to improvise on its own and adapt to the situations as and when they develop.

A Balance Sheet of the First Year

As stated earlier a critical empirical evaluation of the Campaign is beyond the scope of this paper. Nevertheless, by way of conclusion, we shall attempt to outline certain important achievements of the past one year of the People's Campaign. The primary objective of the Campaign has certainly been realised. A plan did emerge from grassroots. The Annual Plans for 1997-98 prepared by the local bodies have been approved and their implementation started in right earnest. It indeed is a giant leap towards the ideal of self governance. Nearly 37 per cent of the annual plan resources has been set aside to finance the local plans. The ratio of expenditure of the panchayats in Kerala to the total expenditure of the State government over the last three decades has been less than 3 per cent. In sharp contrast, in the current year, the plan devolution alone constitutes nearly 10 per cent of the State government expenditure. What it represents is a four to five fold increase in the financial resources of the panchayats!

A cursory look at the Five Year Plans formulated by the Grama Panchayats, in connection with the People's Campaign reveals a number of encouraging trends. Earlier, the major thrust of the panchayats (out of untied funds) was for construction of roads, bridges and buildings. Therefore, it was rightly feared by many that most of the plan assistance would be diverted by the panchayats to the infrastructure sector. But, our initial estimates prove the critics wrong. In fact, there is a total turn around in the pattern of spending with emphasis on productive sectors, mainly agriculture and allied activities, followed by social sectors including education, drinking water and health. Another outstanding feature of the local plans is their efforts to mobilise local resources. According to our estimates, the total outlay of the local plans would be atleast 30 to 40 per cent higher than the State's plan outlay earmarked for the local bodies.

But there are also important limitations to be overcome in the future. The problems that cropped up during implementation suggests that there are many weak spots in the current year's plan proposals. There has been considerable duplication of activities being undertaken by the different tiers of government, including the State government. The vegetable cultivation programme is one glaring example. The programme is being implemented by all the four tiers of government, each with its own norms. But little thought has been given to the problem of marketing or the shortage of planting materials, which the panchayats are now reported to be facing. This is just an example among many such problems that call for greater integration of the programmes drawn up by different tiers of government. Similarly, there are many critical gaps in the plan arising from neglect of backward and forward linkages. Such criticisms can be multiplied.

The Annual Plan for 1997-98 may not rise up to the ideal, but represents a remarkable improvement in terms of the form as well as the content of development planning. People are learning by doing. The incremental knowledge from the experience is the guarantee that the current weaknesses can be overcome.

The decentralised planning exercise involves multi-level planning at the level of three tiers of the local bodies and that of the state and central governments. If an integrated plan is to emerge from the exercise each tier has got to take into consideration the programme of the higher and lower tiers. The process of planning that we discussed in Section II had ensured that the grama panchayat plans were integrated at higher levels before the plans of the latter were prepared. But there was no similar feed back from the higher tiers to the grama panchayat level. As for the block and district plans, they had to be prepared simultaneously. The State level departmental planning was an independent exercise altogether. The cycle of decentralised planning can be considered to be completed only when there is simultaneous feed back between higher and lower tiers.

Currently a review of the local plans is in progress so as to undertake certain mid-term correctives during implementation. The review will also be the basis for the preparation of the Consolidated Plan of the District. The Consolidated District Plan would list all the projects and schemes of all the five tiers of governments in each district for each sector so as to identify complementarities, duplication, gaps and contradictions in the plan programmes. It would also provide guidelines for better organic integration of the local plans keeping in view the resource potential and development needs of the district and provide the necessary feed back from above.

Thus viewed, it is clear that the agenda of the People's Campaign, even with respect to preparation of the plan from below, has not been exhausted by the past one year's exercise. It is even more true of the other indirect objectives of the Campaign. With respect to the objectives of generation of a new development culture and its institutionalisation, the claim is even more modest: A beginning has been made.

The first point to be mentioned in this connection is the broad based people's unity that appears to have emerged cutting across narrow sectarian divisions for solving developmental problems. In a State, characterised by extreme political fragmentation and rivalry, it has been a creditable achievement that around 15,000 Grama Sabhas and Ward Conventions could be successfully convened without any serious political disruption, except in rare cases. Similarly, in the State where the annual budget of the local bodies are ritually voted upon, the Annual Plan of 1997-98 was adopted unanimously in almost all panchayats.

Another instance is the overwhelming response of experts to join the Voluntary Technical Corps. At the start of the People's Campaign a special appeal was issued and an attempt made through the good office of the local body representatives to get the professional experts involved. The response was poor and it was a major factor that adversely affected the progress of the third phase. But the appeal for experts to serve in VTCs during the last phase of the Campaign drew widespread sympathetic response. Something had happened in between that struck a sympathetic chord in the minds of even the professional elite. Many of them too felt that the People's Campaign for decentralised planning was a movement which merited a helping hand. Similarly, during the initial phase of the Campaign there had been very little involvement of the government bureaucracy. The attempts to rectify it in the third phase was also not very successful. But since then there appeared a visible sign of change. For instance, even though the target for the State level implementation training was only around 1000 resource persons, the actual attendance exceeded by nearly 50 per cent, the additional trainees being drawn mostly from the ranks of officials.

Yet another piece of evidence comes from the criticism that the Campaign was generating false hopes and unreal expectations. This criticism apparently has been provoked by the unprecedented participaion of people in the Campaign activities. Incidentally, one of the central objectives of the Campaign has been to sensitise the people towards development problems and thus to inculcate, in the place of the current widespread apathy, a sense of concern and optimism among them. And it is our position that once people are sensitised and allowed to take control over the development activities, they would be in a better position to find the ways and means to meet their aspirations.

The spirit of self help and self reliance that the People's Campaign sought to propagate is evident in the very manner that it has been organised. More than half the expenditure of the People's Campaign at the local level have been raised voluntarily. But for a few dozen persons, all the other resource persons have been working on voluntary basis, sparing their leisure time and holidays for the Campaign. As reported earlier, there has also been a concerted effort by the local self governments to mobilise additional local resources to supplement the grant-in-aid from the government.

Thus signs of change are evident. Whether they will be sustained, strengthened and made irreversible is an issue that can be settled only by future. However, the success that has already been achieved in institutionalising the new styles of public functioning, with its accent on people's participation and transparancy, is a major source of optimism regarding the long run prospects. Take for instance, the new rules for selection of beneficiaries: They have, at one stroke, undermined the system of local political patronage. All beneficiaries now onwards will have to be selected in Grama Sabhas, that too on the basis of objective and transparent criteria. Not that there was no resistance to the new set of rules; in fact, at least a minority of the elected representatives took it as a major irritant. But, the People's Campaign has created a conducive environment for legislative institutionalisation of the transparent and participatory system of beneficiary selection. Similarly, the new work rule promises to be a major challenge to the rein of 'contractor raj' in the State. All shackles that constrain the efficient functioning of genuine beneficiary committees have been removed. Implementation of the remaining recommendations of the Sen Committee[1] would herald a total overhaul of the administraive system, especially at the local level, and thus ensure institutionalisation of the legacy of the People's Campaign.

Equally important are the new laws and rules strengthening new development institutions. Most important among them is the Grama Sabha. The accepted wisdom in the State until the Peoples's Campaign that the Grama Sabha was impractical in the specific conditions of the State has been proved wrong. The Grama Sabha has become a part of the political landscape of the State. It also appears that the State has been moving towards strengthening of Neighbourhood Groups. A survey of the plan documents and project reports would bring out a rich array of new popular institutions for land and water management, marketing, industrial production, monitoring of project implementation and so on.

In view of the unfinished agenda, it may be important that the People's Campaign continues for some more time so that the process initiated by it is made self-sustainable. The future course of action and the tasks to be undertaken could be finalised only after a careful consideration of the experience gathered over the past one year. The review exercises pertaining to plan proposals and implementation being undertaken by the Board are expected to bring out valuable insights in this regard.

NOTE

1. The Government of Kerala has appointed the Committee on Decentralisation under Dr. S.B. Sen in 1996 almost coterminous with the Plan campaign to devolve functional, financial and administrative autonomy to the local bodies. Although Dr. Sen passed away after a few weeks of the Commencement of the work of the Commission, the Committee is popularly known after his name (Editor).

INDEX